Praise for *Islam and Statehood*

Islam and Statehood is a field-defining tour de force. It is deeply reflexive about its own premises and commanding in its long-durée approach to history. The result is a work of extraordinary maturity that is self-aware, theoretically exciting, and punctuated by a reflexivity that is itself a methodological contribution. This is what scholarship should be: courageous enough to reinvent itself, and wise enough to know why.

– **Kamaludeen Nasir,** *Nanyang Technological University, Singapore*

Salvatore's *Islam and Statehood* is a work of impressive ambition and erudition that makes a vital contribution to debates at the intersection of Islamic intellectual history and political theory. Salvatore demonstrates that Islamic statehood was not a failed approximation of Western political modernity but an original modernity in its own right—one whose characteristic emphasis on connectedness, civic solidarity, and the distribution rather than monopolization of authority stands in sharp contrast to the Leviathan-like logic of Westphalian sovereignty. In doing so, the book offers a searching challenge to eurocentric frameworks in the study of political thought and state formation, illuminating dimensions of the Islamic tradition that have too often been obscured by those frameworks.

– **Usaama Al-Azami,** *Hamad Bin Khalifa University, Doha*

In this volume, Salvatore continues to enrich the field of the sociology of Islam through moving the current debate on the "Islamic state" to a more complex terrain of analyzing statehood in Islam. Long awaited and simply brilliant, this book marks the zenith of over three decades of research in the sociology of Islam and its ecumene, civility, and translocal connections. A must-read across the social sciences and humanities.

– **Heba Raouf Ezzat,** *Ibn Haldun University, Istanbul*

Armando Salvatore consistently elevates discussions of Islam to a level of sophistication often missing in current debates. *Islam and Statehood* is analytically rigorous, rethinking key concepts in Islam and situating them within the broader debates of the Islamic ecumene. This book is an outstanding continuation of his earlier works and is essential reading for anyone working on Islam.

– **Raihan Ismail,** *University of Oxford*

ISLAM AND STATEHOOD

INSTITUTING THE ECUMENE

ARMANDO SALVATORE

WILEY

Registered Offices
John Wiley & Sons, Inc., 111 River Street, Hoboken, NJ 07030, USA
John Wiley & Sons Ltd, New Era House, 8 Oldlands Way, Bognor Regis, West Sussex, PO22 9NQ, UK

For details of our global editorial offices, customer services, and more information about Wiley products visit us at www.wiley.com.

The manufacturer's authorized representative according to the EU General Product Safety Regulation is Wiley-VCH GmbH, Boschstr. 12, 69469 Weinheim, Germany, e-mail: Product_Safety@wiley.com.

Wiley also publishes its books in a variety of electronic formats and by print-on-demand. Some content that appears in standard print versions of this book may not be available in other formats.

Library of Congress Cataloging-in-Publication Data applied for:

Paperback ISBN: 9781394180684
EPUB ISBN: 9781394180691
EPDF ISBN: 9781394180707

Cover Design: Wiley
Cover Image: © Cavan Images/Alamy Stock Photo

Set in 10.5/13pt MinionPro by Straive, Pondicherry, India
Printed and bound by CPI Group (UK) Ltd, Croydon, CR0 4YY

C9781394180684_080826

For Kieko

Contents

INTRODUCTION
Beyond the Sociology of Islam?

Toward an "Islamic Frame"

In my book *The Sociology of Islam* (2016), which was planned as Volume I of a trilogy, I expressed my indebtedness to the work of Marshall Hodgson not just as a historian, but also as a champion of what we might call sociopolitical thought. Working within the Western orientalist tradition of scholarship, Hodgson was able to dodge most of the epistemic pitfalls that have plagued Orientalism at large, which has been subjected to continuous—if limitedly effective—criticism since the 1960s. More than any other Western scholar, he was able to capture the long-term vitality of Islam as a self-sustaining, though not self-absorbed, force of history that impacted human and social life in core regions of the Afro-Eurasian landmass. He did so by engaging with and constructively critiquing the champion of Western sociological theory, Max Weber. Inspired by Hodgson, the edited volume titled *The Wiley Blackwell History of Islam* (Salvatore et al. 2018) served as a companion to Volume I of the trilogy by promoting an interdisciplinary collaboration between historians and sociologists.

Volume I and the edited volume were in the making in tandem and—at least from my combined authorial and editorial viewpoint—built a synergy in refining key concepts that served what I defined as an "Islamic perspective" (Salvatore 2016, 240–241). While the single-authored volume advanced a field-building enterprise under the label of the "sociology of Islam," the extended editorial experience and the follow-up discussion of its output (Aishima et al. 2021) clarified the next steps in the trilogy's arc: it brought home the realization that rather than constituting a scholarly field in its own right, the sociology of Islam could make sense only as part and parcel of an increasingly critical interrogation in global academia of how

Islam should be defined, understood, and explained (see, e.g., Peter, Schrode, and Stegmann 2025). This reframing set the stage for the subsequent volumes, which move beyond field-building toward a reorientation of the very epistemic grounds on which Islam is studied.

The continuation of the planned trilogy has required time and uncompromising self-critique to sharpen this realization and to break decisively beyond the narrow limits of both general sociology and any of its specialized subgenres. It depended on elaborating a plausible sociopolitical vision of Islam as an ongoing, dynamic, even mutating force in human history—a force that refuses any confinement to the status of a passive "object" to be observed, classified, or domesticated. For too long an objectified formatting has prevailed, producing the familiar essentialist fantasy in which complex and often contradictory historical constellations are flattened into a single, seamless, and unchanging "Islam." Yet the opposite gesture—celebrated in some quarters as the antidote to essentialism—is no less reductive. One can see an objectifying Western reductionism at work also—if not more acutely—when Islam is disassembled into its alleged components or local practices, as if its truth were recoverable only in the semblance of "real-world Muslims." Here one encounters a Western reductionism that is arguably even more insidious: an identitarian minimalism parading as critical sophistication, now repackaged in formulations such as "Muslimness." Both moves—essentializing the whole and fragmenting it into purportedly authentic parts—participate in the same epistemic foreclosure. They deny Islam its status as a productive and connective force of history. In this sense, the trilogy's conceptual arc moves toward an approach attentive to thresholds, relationalities, and multiple coexisting forms of agency—precisely to escape the binary between an inert "Islam" and its no less reified "Muslim" instantiations. The shift should enhance our capacity to study Islam not as a fixed essence or as a mere aggregate of identities, but as a shifting horizon of intelligibility shaped by, and shaping, diverse, yet connected, historical actors.

This move has been helped by the transdisciplinary debate on *What Is Islam?*—a debate triggered, or at least made more reflexive and visibly accelerated, in the wake of the publication of the widely read, voluminous book by the late Shahab Ahmed (2016), whose blunt and direct title was itself a provocation. Discussions on methods for *Understanding Islam*—the no less straightforward title of an even more recent book by Bryan Turner (2023)—likewise intensified in ways that Volume I of the trilogy could not anticipate. In light of such debates, that volume may now appear as a provisional, and perhaps forgettable, attempt to weave an epistemic horizon within which to assemble and power up an empathic, non-distorting, and non-objectifying lens that, for lack of a better expression, I termed an "Islamic perspective." By this, I nodded to Hodgson's idea of Islam as a venture in human history that mapped itself on the world rather than being a docile object at the mercy of eager, primarily Western, self-appointed "specialists" (whether identified as "orientalists" or otherwise). Of course, the appropriateness of adopting such a perspective entailed numerous, and largely unarticulated, allowances. These cannot be left unmentioned at the beginning of this Volume II if I am to keep faith with the promised trilogy. As a preliminary step, I need to revise my earlier and somewhat naïve assumption that the idea itself of a "perspective" could unproblematically derive from Islam's unfolding in history. As Wendy Shaw has meanwhile taught us eloquently in her *What Is "Islamic Art"?* (2019), the notion itself of "perspective," broadly assumed to be an exclusively Western creation in visual art,[1] turns out to be a quite blunt and self-centered epistemic instrument that suppresses, rather than acknowledges, difference in "viewpoints." Perspective, in this sense, is an apparatus of reduction rather than an opening to relational plurality. Therefore, I shift here to the wording "Islamic frame." By "frame," I intend a product of a synthetic assemblage of viewpoints and positions converging on what Ahmed defined as "the importance of being Islamic." The frame in question, assembled to resist reduction, reification, and fragmentation, should be conceptually and methodologically congruent with the goal of understanding and explaining the very centrality of Islam in human history and society (see Chapter 1).

While participating in the critical debate on conceptualizing Islam, I greatly benefited from a wealth of new—at times theoretically conscious—historical monographs, particularly on the early-modern Muslim empires. Such works were often accompanied by a revaluation of the intellectual generosity and theoretical proclivity of Hodgson's oeuvre (Lawrence 2021). The imperative to keep up with the new findings and discussions slowed down progress on the trilogy, as I felt increasingly challenged both to test the initial presuppositions of the Islamic frame and to spell out its methodological implications. This train of reflections led to a growing disillusionment with the reductive, ambivalent, and readily manipulable label of the "sociology of Islam." No doubt, during those years, the label acquired a degree of popularity in some academic discussion. Yet this sudden popularization often came at the cost of a narrow politicization, if not weaponization, of the term for parochial agendas. At that juncture, it became clear that my project needed to be, also in the public eye, radically dissociated from this impoverished use and situated within a far broader enterprise. This larger undertaking promises to complement historiographic work by offering a historically informed and cross-culturally nourished type of sociopolitical thought that seeks inspiration within an Islamic frame and speaks to a global anglophone public.[2] I came to recognize this evolving, if implicit, cross-disciplinary dialogue—even if constrained by the ongoing hegemony of English-language publishing and the buzzwords it tends to promote—as a potential source of conceptual coherence, even in the absence of a systematic treatment of methodological issues.

This shift from sociology to a historically informed sociopolitical thought was also urged by the fact that while most reviews of the English and Arabic editions of Volume I seemed to endorse the field-building project of the sociology of Islam, the few negative ones alerted me to a fundamental misunderstanding lurking behind the use of "sociology" in labeling the field—and even the risks entailed in naming it a "field." I addressed such issues insofar as they compounded the ambiguities of the label "sociology of Islam," given how easily it could obscure, rather than illuminate, the ongoing conceptual and methodological dialogue on the knowledge of Islam. The shared problem at stake was that the term sociology evoked in a few observers a promise that could not be fulfilled. This promise went back to a 19th-century understanding of the discipline, as it first emerged with August Comte, before the subsequent complexification of the sociological paradigm by the figures usually counted as its founders (Durkheim, Weber, Simmel, and—retroactively—Marx). The lingering of such an obsolete "scientistic" conception of sociology ('Ayyiq 2018) in certain circles is also reflected in the long-term prevalence of quantitative methodologies in several national sociological traditions and in the resilient myth that the social sciences, by default, possess a scientific character allegedly warranted by positivistic postulates of verifiability (and falsifiability: Menchik 2017). Given that my upfront use of "sociology" in labeling the trilogy risked activating precisely these outdated epistemic associations, I am glad to set it aside, without banning it altogether, and without any damage to the enterprise overall. I will also bracket the likewise charged word "theory," as used in the labels of "sociological/social" and "political theory." This term, too, is entangled in an arbitrary, Western and colonial, epistemic frame that sharply separates the field it designates, namely "theory," from "empirical knowledge," before reuniting them in a mutually complementary apparatus designed for management of academic "objects." The resulting division of labor is less a clarification than a mechanism of control—an instance of the self-serving process of objectification characteristic of Eurocentric theoretical frames that Dainotto (2007) incisively diagnosed.

No doubt, the "sociology of Islam" is still occasionally invoked without much trepidation by leading sociologists in the broader field, from whose work I continue to learn (see Bamyeh 2019; Turner 2023). Nevertheless, one should also admit that in the "sociology of Islam" the scientistic promise of "sociology" often seems to be "applied" to what appears to many observers—and with good reasons—as a suspiciously wholesale, essentialist, neo-colonial construal of "Islam" and what is "Islamic."[3] This perception continues to haunt—even when exorcized in various manners, if not dressed in an anti-orientalist garb—today's post-orientalist epistemic landscape. It was elegantly reframed, rather than confuted, by Hodgson when he understood Islam as "religion and civilization." Nevertheless, by imposing on it such a religio-civilizational straitjacket, Islam is subjected to another, if less blunt, objectification based on a narrow-minded, and explicitly Western, classificatory grid. In this guise, Islam is deprived of its power to offer a capacious umbrella category covering an open-ended historical process or venture—precisely the most valuable hermeneutic legacy of Hodgson's empathic work (Arnason, Salvatore, and Stauth 2006). The question is then how to take decisive steps to decolonize the understanding of Islam while recalibrating the use of the term accordingly. This step requires protecting the word-idea of "Islam" from its misuse in identifying a *homo islamicus* as the antithesis of the Western rational *homo economicus* (Haleh Davis 2022), rather than discarding it altogether for fear of essentialism. The iconoclastic fury unleashed against "Islam," wrongly taken as an essence domesticated and manipulated by Western Orientalism, only forecloses the comprehensive path, which has critical methodological implications, that Shahab Ahmed opened up for all of us. By calling Islam a word-idea, I emphasize its historical generativity rather than an essence, one naming a pattern of interconnectedness and, as will be argued, an instituting process, rather than a cultural invariant.

Despite these challenges, and the ensuing reframing of my project, we can view the present book as initially conceived, namely as Volume II of a trilogy on the sociology of Islam. At the same time, we should be reminded that the idea of a trilogy was prevalently a tribute to Hodgson's own majestic three-volume magnum opus through a minor, ancillary one. The specific mission of this supportive trilogy was and is expanding, critically and conceptually, on the dimensions of sociopolitical thought included—more often implied rather than fully spelled out—in the major, Hodgsonian trilogy—while also taking on board insights generated by the increasing wealth of both historiographic and reflexive works produced in the intervening half a century. This period has also witnessed the mainstreaming of the critique of Orientalism, with uncertain and often ambivalent results, given how it has been too often instrumentalized to parochial and polemical aims rather than used for a consistent paradigm shift. And yet this critique acquires added value if placed in a longer-term perspective. It was not single-handedly invented by Edward Said in the 1970s but is as old as the resistance against Western imperialism and colonialism (Aydin 2007; Salvatore and Obuse 2023). In this sense, it was and is integral to the methodological path I seek in the trilogy by developing a decolonial Islamic frame. This undertaking reflects how the academic knowledge of Islam, reflected in the Western orientalist hegemony, started to be contested more than a century ago. The urgency to retrieve this decolonial long durée should trump, or at least absorb, the numerous attempts to, somewhat hubristically, create anew, as it were, a decolonial critique. Our contribution to reframing the study of Islam by rebranding the time-honored, decolonial critique of Orientalism should also provide the red thread to the culmination of the trilogy in Volume III. This final volume is being planned to deepen questions of institutional and intellectual conditions of production of knowledge on Islam in the context of the long-drawn-out process of birthing a post-Western world and, with it, academia, via thus far neglected global refractions of Islam's historical cosmopolitanism (Salvatore and Obuse, forthcoming).

Reframing the "Islamic Ecumene"

To chart a plausible path to defining an Islamic frame capable of reorienting the previous engagement with a sociology of Islam, I adopt a three-step approach. First, I revisit my use of the expression "Islamic ecumene" in Volume I—a move encouraged by the appreciative reception of the term in several reviews of the book, especially of its Arabic edition, where several comments were made on the Arabic match to the concept of an "Islamic ecumene." Second, I am processing several contrastive thoughts on the mutual risks inherent in either sticking to "Islam" and "Islamic" as the noun and adjective covering the elaboration of an Islamic frame or yielding to an approach, originally devised by Marshall Hodgson and currently elaborated upon by Bruce Lawrence (2021), embracing instead the double binary "Islam/Islamic" vs. "Islamdom/Islamicate." These paired distinctions, intended to reflect a "religious" vs. a "civilizational" dimension of Islam's broader venture in history, entail their own conceptual constraints. Third, and perhaps most crucially, I examine how these moves might be folded into an episteme that unsettles the opposition between insider and outsider. The process of overcoming this dichotomy, in turn, would help make the "Islam/Islamic" of an Islamic frame irreducible to an "object" of study, operating instead as the sociohistorical engine of the "venturing" force in history that is Islam. The resulting Islamic frame would then emerge from the composite meanings of the word-idea of Islam (which, as this book shows, rests on a self-feeding process of instituting human life) and "the importance of being Islamic," reflecting a unique legacy of humankind far exceeding the limitations of the still-current expression "the Muslim/Islamic world." This formulation was essentially the creation of Western colonial enterprises and imperial hegemony (Aydin 2017) and relegates the significance of Islam to a peripheral position in the archive of human history. Overcoming this orientalist legacy, the Islamic frame is intended to place "Islam" at the center of a comprehensive, historically mediated, and dialogic type of sociopolitical thought that emphasizes multiple, overlapping webs of connectedness. Most crucially, the Islamic frame pierces through the conventional inside and outside of the ecumene, allowing for (if not even feeding on) productive ambivalence, tensions, and variations in the modes of instituting life. Let us set out the three steps in more detail.

First, in Volume I, I used the notion of an "Islamic ecumene" to refer to the ensemble of both the geopolitical area and the sociocultural patterning in which the Hodgsonian "venture of Islam" unfolded historically. Therefore, I took the liberty of treating "Islamic ecumene" as a Hodgsonian concept, although Hodgson never used it verbatim. He coined instead the neologism "Islamdom," by which he referred to the "complex of social relations" or "the milieu of a whole society," which, according to him, transcended Islam as religion (Hodgson 1974, I, 58; see also Salvatore 2016, 28). Most notably, in Hodgson's largely original terminology the concept of Islamdom opened onto—if not effectively converged with—the realm of the "Islamicate," which exceeded the "Islamic" proper, understood, less originally, as restricted to "faith" and "piety." On the other hand, Hodgson employed the original Greek word for ecumene, namely Oikoumene (which he wrote so, capitalized but not italicized), to refer to the entirety of the Eastern Hemisphere, coinciding with the Afro-Eurasian landmass, to which Islamdom supplied a crucial connective tissue, thriving, so to speak, in its very midst.

Second, my use of "Islamic ecumene" in Volume I may appear at first glance as a broad match to Islamdom, while avoiding the quandaries of Hodgson's even odder neologism, the "Islamicate," which he understood as a kind of civilizational tegument accruing to Islam as "a religion." Be that as it may, my reference to the Islamic ecumene was intended to rephrase the more general—and, in my view, profound—dimension of Hodgson's vision of Islam's venture in history. It did so by foregrounding the centrality of Islamic sociocultural life within the broader Oikoumene, while treating the smaller "ecumene" as reflecting a straightforwardly "Islamic" (rather than, "Islamicate") articulation of life. This is why the expression "Islamic ecumene" has the advantage of dispensing with any direct or indirect reference to, or implication of, the previously mentioned religio-civilizational straitjacket, which Hodgson inherited from colonial scholarship and refined rather than rejected. In other words, "Islamic ecumene" does away with the compulsion to predicate Islam in terms of eurocentrically charged notions like "religion," "civilization," or, indeed, both. What I also wanted to convey with "Islamic ecumene" was that the "venturing" role played by Islam at a crucial intermediate stage of the sociocultural flourishing of the entire Eastern hemisphere enhanced the sustainability of long-distance connectedness with the broader Oikumene. While "Islamic ecumene" is then, after all, no equivalent to Hodgson's Islamdom, it is not identical with the *umma* (the Muslim "community") or *Dar al-Islam* (the Abode of Islam) either, both of which, although distinct from each other, should be seen as prevalently "juridico-theological" concepts. This is because they cover a collectivity determined by the "technically Muslim" credentials of their members and the normative validity and applicability of *shari'a* in it. The expression "Islamic ecumene" thus extends and complements, while it also recalibrates, key elements of both the *umma* and *Dar al-Islam*. When used, as they frequently are, outside of their conventional (that is, juridico-theological) meaning, they risk reifying and circumscribing "Islam," rather than highlighting its open-ended dynamics and porous borders, which is what Islamic ecumene instead emphasizes. Perhaps a good "emic match" to this expression would be *Bilad al-Islam*, which was used in geographical and historical works more than in juridical and theological discourse, and tended toward a more plural and less-than-normative understanding of "the lands" of Islam.[4] Dubbing the ecumene straightforwardly "Islamic" (rather than "Islamicate") is then part of a strategy to reconceptualize Islam—indeed, the same Islam prominently and "emically" emphasized in *Bilad al-Islam*—without any hint or residue of a malignant essentialization. The Islamic ecumene is thus definable as the evolving, interconnected domain shaped by Islamic idioms, not reducible to territory, empire, or law. It is the historically emergent domain of networked practices and institutions shaped by Islamically inflected habitus, without territorial or juridical fixity. As such, it is a key concept in the path to defining a viable Islamic frame of analysis, one that seeks to remain as far as possible insulated from Western categories like religion and civilization, and yet suitable to understand and explain Islam as a comprehensive (or global) force of history. In this light, I found that the "Islamic" in the "Islamic ecumene" also echoes the "importance of being Islamic" famously argued by Shahab Ahmed (2016), when writing as a critical scholar and intellectual with a Muslim background (see also Chapter 1). A further Hodgsonian dimension of "Islamic ecumene" is that it enables to reconceptualize Islam with the tools of historically informed sociopolitical thought, which was the original terrain of Hodgson's scholarly intervention. Islam is therefore not an abstract or essentialized entity, but that which predicates the ecumene and its unfolding.

Third, our expression, and particularly the choice of "ecumene" as predicated by "Islamic," can be further enriched through conceptual dialogue and translation along modalities that were still far from ripe at Hodgson's time. His epoch was still dominated by quite blunt eurocentric, orientalist conventions, against which he engaged in a valiant, yet, at the time, still quite lonely, political-intellectual struggle (Geyer 2018). Given the different levels of scholarly communication and interconnectedness that characterize our present, if compared with Hodgson's time, it should not be too surprising that my Volume I was translated into Arabic right away (Salvatore [2016] 2017) and that it additionally triggered a long overdue translation of Hodgson's trilogy on the initiative of the same publisher (Hodgson [1974] 2021). Against this background, the concept of an "Islamic ecumene" captured the attention of several reviewers of *The Sociology of Islam*, particularly of its Arabic edition. This is probably because the way ecumene was rendered in the Arabic translation of Volume I, namely as *ma'mura* (or, in full, *al-ma'mura al-islamiyya*), helped deepen the implications of the term. As the English counterpart to *al-ma'mura al-islamiyya*, the Islamic ecumene should then be understood as articulated via the multilayered dynamics of *'umran*. In this vocabulary *al-ma'mura*, a term built on the same triliteral root of *'umran*, designates the ecumene as resulting from a powerful, processual—and yet open-ended—sociopolitical crystallization of the dynamics of *'umran*. Unlike the concepts of *umma* and *Dar al-Islam*, which are conventionally ("juridico-theologically") defined, *'umran* designates a historically unfolding force. As such, it was famously theorized by Ibn Khaldun, the most authoritative scholar inspiring an enterprise of bundling historically grounded sociopolitical reflections via an Islamic frame (see Chapters 1 and 5).

To alleviate the rigidity of the Western religio-civilizational lens in approaching Islam, in Volume I "civility" (rather than the most frequently used "civilization") appears as the conceptual match/translation to *'umran*. The Islamic ecumene (*al-ma'mura al-islamiyya*) would then be defined as the outcome of a patterning of civility (or the civilizing process in history) as defined in that volume—a process for which the idea of *'umran* provides a fundamental nucleus of conceptualization. This is also why I now rephrase *'umran* as the source of a connective and potentially cosmopolitan type of civility. I do so precisely because, following Ibn Khaldun, civility as *'umran* cannot be restricted to *hadara*, the realm of sedentary urbanity, but results from close dialectic dynamics with *badawa*, that is, the social forces and movements shaping rural/nomadic living spaces. Seen through this lens centered on *'umran*, Islam appears sociologically relevant to the extent that it "expressed rather than created global social realities" (Bamyeh 2019, 175). The specific ecumene/*ma'mura* examined here—its significance derived from the articulation of "being Islamic," understood as a kind of sociopolitical ontology—stands out in human history for rendering transparent the inherently open-ended character of processes of human becoming. As a result, the "importance of being Islamic" (Ahmad 2016) transpires through an inwardly diversified and outwardly porous Islamic ecumene that unfolds via the work of patterning human life into social connectedness, a work that is, indeed, what *'umran* ultimately consists of. While *'umran* is intended by Ibn Khaldun as a universal process, *al-ma'mura al-islamiyya* would then be the continuously evolving outcome of how the work of *'umran* is affected, inflected, and catalyzed by Islam as a historical—albeit not totalizing—force. The concept of ecumene/*ma'mura* then delineates a space not fixed at any given moment, like the *umma* or *Dar al-Islam*, but that can expand and contract. It does so not just geographically or territorially, but also, if not mainly, via the inner and outer connectedness it facilitates. As will be seen throughout this volume, an essential part of the work of *ʿumran* in the ecumene is constituted by a self-sustaining and integrated instituting process: the ongoing making of sociopolitical institutions.

This approach differs markedly from how, in Western theory, civility was equated with city life and its urbanity, as exemplified by Max Weber. He gave priority to how medieval Europe became organized around rather self-enclosed cities presiding over the surrounding countryside—a process that unfolded through the institutional crystallization of municipalities and, over time, centralized states. Indeed, the very notion of civility remains tethered to an overly favorable view of city life, a legacy traceable to its etymological root in the Latin *cives*, or "citizen." This approach severely limits the suitability of civility as a match to *ʿumran*. However, if reduced to a modicum, a mild pro-urban bias in translating *ʿumran* as civility could still be acceptable, since in the Islamic ecumene cities did play a crucial role as nodes of long-term connectedness and global circuits of peoples, goods and ideas. It remains, however, that *maʿmura*/ecumene as the continuous, albeit open-ended, crystallization of *ʿumran*/civility as a patterning process does not in fact privilege the city—and this is why I think it is fair to retain "Islamic ecumene" in this volume as a pivotal, if moving, target in the process of elaborating a suitable "Islamic frame." Ecumene here denotes a rather an-organic body of overlapping networks that coalesce into discrete cohesive groups (like a school of *fiqh*, a guild, or a Sufi *tariqa*: see Chapters 2–4) in their various deployments at local, translocal, and global levels. Here the *badawa*, namely the rural and nomadic forces and spaces—as we will see in particular in Chapter 5—played an indispensable, rather than ancillary, role. *Badawa* is not a mere space inhabited by subaltern populations and peripheral to the deployment of *ʿumran*, but, as famously argued by Ibn Khaldun, is its essential sociopolitical engine. It is not an antithesis to urbanity but a generative force that injects cohesion, mobilization, and adaptive capacity into the ecumene.

Be that as it may, we need to delve deeper into the granular texture of the civilizing and instituting process that is *ʿumran*. As suggested by Bruce Lawrence (2021, 45n21)—nimbly expanding on Hodgson's ability to capture the nuances of the Khaldunian vision—alongside standard authoritative translations of the term, one can sense in *ʿumran* a vibration of "inhabitedness" fed with "bustling life." This significant nuance helps explain the creative and diversified unfolding of *'umran* by making more evident the process that yields the *ma'mura* or ecumene, that is, the built-up, inhabited, shared human space. Thus seen, *'umran* becomes the closest approximation to the idea of "society" entertained within Western sociology, while removing from it the exceedingly deterministic and organicistic, rather than creative and open-ended, characterization of the social bond and its formation or institution. And yet, we would still need a sustained explanation of why we tag the *ma'mura*/ecumene we are addressing in this volume as, simply, "Islamic." My working hypothesis is that the meaning and importance of being Islamic were clarified in the very process of instituting the ecumene, which peaked in the formation of statehood.

Chapters' Roadmap

This book could be seen as a path that unfolds in stages. Each chapter examines a particular dimension of Islam's instituting force. The cumulative effect is the unfolding of statehood in the ecumene. The following overview shows how the inquiry itself incrementally constitutes what I call an Islamic frame and how the work of *'umran* provides the connective logic of this itinerary.

Chapter 1 explains the trajectory of dialogic repositioning that justifies my articulation of an Islamic frame in the study of the Islamic ecumene. In the context of our shared postcolonial/post-orientalist epistemic predicament, I outline a dialogic path of method that blurs the boundary between insider and outsider in the knowledge of Islam. I rely in particular on the emergent appeal of a trajectory of Southern/Italian sociopolitical thought that pays attention to the combined dynamics of tradition and innovation and is equipped to capture ambivalences, rather than impose binaries, such as those between the universal and the particular, the ideal and the concrete, and the "religious" and the "civil." I show how this type of thought helps displace prevailing analytical hierarchies and circumvents the Western dichotomous conceptualizations that have construed the Islamic ecumene as a bundle of sociological deficits when measured against its alleged Western counterpart. This approach foregrounds the creative interplay of practice and narrative as the generative soil from which formal normativity emerges, rather than viewing norms as the initial or exclusive drivers of the instituting process.

Chapter 2 examines the inception of the instituting process via dynamics of narration and habitualization, rather than, as done by the large majority of interpreters, by directly addressing the formation of norms and the conceptual foundations of an expert (jurists') law (*usul al-fiqh*). It simultaneously addresses the corpus of exemplary prophetic sayings and deeds (*hadith*) and the multi-genre compendia that provide guidance on forming life in the world (*adab*). The production of the two normative bodies is analyzed through the lens of the dynamics between habitus and narration, both singularly and in their mutual relations, as a quasi-continuum. Accordingly, *fiqh* (including the overarching principle of *maslaha* or "common good") crystallizes as a specialized field within the broader instituting process, understood as including, but not as primarily triggered by, the formation of norms.

Chapter 3 explores the dynamic dimension of the institutional matrix of the *tariqa*, which has been conventionally understood (and translated) as Sufi "order" (borrowing a non-Islamic, monastic organizational concept) or "brotherhood" (a notion that overstresses group cohesion by focusing on imagined bonds of consanguinity). It explains how *tariqa* expresses the idea of path or way, entailing mobility and discovery, as well as how the focus of wayfaring is the interconnected body, with the heart at its center. However, the chapter argues that the instituting engine of the confraternal bond is not the individual body, but rather the intercorporeality of the dyad between a master and a disciple, facilitated by the working of *baraka* or divine blessing. The power of *baraka* is seen as culminating in the character of the *wali* (the Sufi "saint") through the attribute of *walaya*, representing the deepest possible embodied habitualization of relationality between the human and the Divine. The chapter shows how, in conjunction with urban *futuwwa* or "youth clubs," the *tariqa* contributed the power of an intercorporeal habitus to instituting civility patterns suiting the Islamic ecumene. By reframing *tariqa-futuwwa* as a mobile, relational matrix rather than a fixed corporate body, the chapter foregrounds its role as a key conduit for transmitting, stabilizing, and renewing the affective dispositions that undergird civility in the ecumene.

Chapter 4 examines the multifunctional shape and evolution of *waqf*, a term routinely—if inadequately—translated as "charitable trust." This translation fails to convey the originality of the *waqf*'s instituting power within the Islamic ecumene—an originality largely overlooked by classical comparative sociology. The chapter illustrates how the *waqf* instituted the social practice of sharing and circulating various goods, many of which sustained basic services and infrastructure essential to the mobility of people and ideas. It offers an intermediate assessment of how, through the instituting channel of *waqf* and the habitualizing dynamics analyzed in the earlier chapters, institutions were formed. The analysis highlights the rationalities that supported the formation of a malleable and relational type of social institution—one that contrasts sharply with the corporate model that emerged in late-medieval Europe. Ultimately, the chapter challenges the assumption that resistance to the European style of incorporation hindered or delayed institutional development in the Islamic ecumene. Instead, it shows how the *waqf* anchored an alternative logic of instituting shared goods, grounded in patterns of gift-giving and circulation rather than exclusive ownership and corporate personality.

Chapter 5 discusses the approach of the leading sociopolitical thinker Ibn Khaldun through the lens of the instituting process triggered by the dynamics covered in the previous chapters. It shows how his theory of the formation and relaxation of group cohesion (*ʿasabiyya*) as an engine of sociopolitical change contributes to elucidating the unceasing instituting process within the Islamic ecumene. The process culminated in forming a *dawla*, whose meaning oscillates between "turn of good fortune" and "state." The chapter further develops a nexus between Ibn Khaldun's approach and the dynamics of political civility subsumed under the compound notion of *adab–siyasa*. These dynamics—which Ibn Khaldun observed in their intermediate forms, acquired during the Middle Periods—would later play a decisive role in the emergence of early-modern statehood. The notion of *siyasa*, commonly translated as "governance" or "politics," is here reinterpreted as an open-ended process and its associated arrangements—ultimately as a spinoff of the broader *adab* discourse. In this sense, the chapter argues, *siyasa* combined a principled autonomy of rulers with the competence to manage complexity and to implement ruling tasks both wisely and strategically, thereby making them simultaneously effective and legitimate.

Chapter 6 traces the profound transformations in institutional development and political legitimacy that marked the Islamic ecumene before and after the Mongol conquests, during the Middle Periods. Drawing on Marshall Hodgson's notion of the *amir-aʿyan* system, the chapter argues that, contrary to narratives of decline, this era marked a culmination of institutional innovation. Building on Ibn Khaldun's analysis, it presents the Almohad movement in the Maghreb of the Earlier Middle Period (ca. 946–1258) as a textbook case in which *ʿasabiyya*, guided by mystically powered *walaya*, furnished both the sociopolitical cohesion and spiritual grounding that sustained political legitimacy beyond the collapse of the High Caliphate (ca. 661–946)[5]—thus bridging tribal solidarity with extant forms of urban civility. The chapter examines how such movements provided a prototype for Sufi masters appearing as doubles or precursors to political rulers. In the Later Middle Period (ca. 1258–1453), however, the Mongol conquests triggered a new synthesis between the Persianate *adab-siyasa* complex and nomadic structures of rule grounded in the *yasa*, the dynastic law of the Mongols. This combined development, the chapter argues, generated the foundations for more centralized and better legitimized forms of statehood in the early-modern Islamic ecumene.

Chapter 7 explores the making of the "saint-philosopher-king," a figure built through original recombinations of ruling prerogatives and titles. Marking the zenith of the instituting process in reconstructing the legitimacy of governance, this character was ultimately folded into the time-honored institution of the Caliphate. The process, however, entailed significant adjustments to the Caliphate itself, decisively influenced by Sufi conceptions of *walaya*. The chapter highlights the retrieval of the Qur'anic trope of the *khalifa*—God's plenipotentiary on earth—as central to this transformation. Notably, though not exclusively, in the Ottoman Empire rulership was reconfigured through this trope and linked to notions of justice articulated within the *adab-siyasa* discourse. The chapter ultimately shows how the Caliphate became a comprehensive umbrella for managing the institutional articulation of the ecumene, including the expansive educational-charitable complex in which the *tariqa* and the *waqf* played a pivotal role. In doing so, it traces how various instituting paths converged to endow rulership with a composite legitimacy grounded in sapiential discernment and political acumen.

Chapter 8 explores how the emerging original conception of sovereignty relied on the contentious nexus between the legitimate ruler, as a holder of *walaya*, and the prerogatives and skills of the bureaucrats-literati. These administrators continuously reshaped tropes of circular and associative governance—such as the Circle of Justice/Equity—by further elaborating the insights of the Khaldunian sociopolitical cycle. The chapter examines how the discourse on life conduct, refined communication, and expert rule embedded in the *adab-siyasa* complex was often condensed into the notion and practice of *tadbir*, or skillful management, grounded in classical analogies between the self, the household, and the city. It demonstrates that the cohesion of the *dawla*—now increasingly understood as an extended set of instituted practices rather than a mere dynastic turn of good fortune—depended not on a Leviathan-like sovereign imposition of uniformity on the social body, but on a texture of measures and relations. These were intended, at least ideally, not to impinge upon, but to complete the instituting process, support its ongoing recalibration, and stabilize the ecumene.

Chapter 9 and the Conclusion offer a contrastive reading of early-modern political cosmologies of statehood in the Islamic ecumene and the political theology of the European Westphalian state as it emerged in the same epoch. The argument is made that European political theology stabilized statehood through the mutual embodiment of the sovereign and his subjects—ultimately grounded in the idea of incorporation as the basis for legitimizing institution-building in the West. This model stands in sharp contrast to the logic of mediation that operated in the Islamic ecumene through the workings of *walaya* and the adaptive management of *adab–siyasa–tadbir*. These elements worked in concert to sustain a circular sovereignty articulated through interrelated stages and components. The chapter contends that, contrary to both classical and contemporary diagnoses of the impossibility of modern statehood in the Islamic ecumene, the evolving *dawla* commanded a high degree of Islamic legitimacy and achieved a significant level of centralization and political effectiveness. It does so by showing that the supposed institutional "impossibility of the state" in the Islamic ecumene did not concern modern statehood per se, but rather a type of state that is fully sacralized in the guise of the collective body akin to Hobbes's *machina machinarum*. Being a token of European exceptionalism, that model did not affect the real possibility of articulating alternative, if "early" and precolonial, forms of political modernities fed by the vitality and originality of the process of instituting life in the ecumene, which culminated in legitimate forms of statehood. In this view, a type of statehood reflecting "the importance of being Islamic" appears not as a failed imitation of the Westphalian model but as a historically grounded configuration shaped by its own modes of mediation and instituting practices.

Notes

1. Wendy Shaw (2019, 291–335) has convincingly shown how the alleged origins of "perspective" in the Italian Renaissance are much more composite: by way of example, deeply owing to the optics of Ibn Haytham (d. ca. 1040). This approach,

however, unlike the alleged modern Western "discovery" of perspective, rests on the premise of infinite, and differently positioned, viewers, rather than one single view artificially made into the objectifying center of a world made fully observable.

2. This could be seen, for example, in an edited volume titled *Debates on Civilization in the Muslim World: Critical Perspectives on Islam and Modernity* (Sunar 2016), listing a full lineup of contributors with a Muslim background, not unlike the edited book on *Islam and Global Justice* (Safi 2023) to which I also contributed, perhaps by being considered as an "honorary Muslim," a token designation occasionally extended to non-Muslim scholars deemed unusually attuned to Islamic thought and therefore especially trusted for having gained a partial insider status. However, this is not a label I would choose for myself, given how it is still integral to a longstanding, and ultimately orientalist option for keeping a quite rigid border between insider and outsider knowledge (the "honorary Muslim" enjoying a special, if conditional, recognition within an exceptional grey zone). Chapter 1 outlines strategies for addressing—and potentially mitigating—the adverse effects of the insider-outsider dichotomy. In doing so, it seeks to loosen the epistemic constraints that such classifications impose and to open a more workable space for dialogic inquiry.
3. See, e.g., albeit from quite different perspectives, Massad (2015) and Yücesoy (2023).
4. I prefer to avoid the adjective "descriptive" since it obliterates the importance of "positions of knowledge," to quote Bryan Turner (2023), in studying Islam, a theme that will be developed further in Chapter 1 in outlining the method adopted in this volume.
5. The periodization of the history of the Islamic ecumene into High Caliphate, Earlier and Later Middle Period, and early modernity is exquisitely Hodgsonian (see also Salvatore et al. 2018, 275).

References

Ahmed, Shahab. 2016. *What Is Islam? The Importance of Being Islamic*. Princeton, NJ: Princeton University Press.

Aishima, Hatsuki, et al. 2021. "AHR Review Roundtable on *The Wiley Blackwell History of Islam*." *American Historical Review* 126 (1): 199–213.

Arnason, Johann P., Armando Salvatore, and Georg Stauth, eds. 2006. *Islam in Process: Historical and Civilizational Perspectives*. Bielefeld: Transcript; New Brunswick, NJ: Transaction (*Yearbook of the Sociology of Islam*, Vol. 7).

ʿAyyiq, Muris, 2018. "*Susyulujia al-Islam wa muʿadila al-maʿrifa wa-l-sulta*. [The Sociology of Islam and the Knowledge-Power Equation]. Review of *Susyulujiya al-Islam: al-Maʿrifa, al-Sulta wa-l-Madaniyya*, by Armando

Salvatore. Beirut: al-Shabaka al-ʿArabiyya li-l-Abhath wa-l-Nashr." *Idaʾat: Majallat al-Tanwir al-Fikri*, no. 18, 175–182.

Aydin, Cemil. 2007. *The Politics of Anti-Westernism in Asia: Visions of World Order in Pan-Islamic and Pan-Asian Thought*. New York: Columbia University Press.

Aydin, Cemil. 2017. *The Idea of the Muslim World: A Global Intellectual History*. Cambridge: Harvard University Press.

Bamyeh, Mohammed A. 2019. *Lifeworlds of Islam. The Pragmatics of a Religion*. New York: Oxford. University Press.

Dainotto, Roberto M. 2007. *Europe (in Theory)*. Durham, NC: Duke University Press.

Geyer, Michael. 2018. "The Invention of World History from the Spirit of Nonviolent Resistance." In *Islam and World History: The Ventures of Marshall Hodgson*, edited by Edmund Burke, and Robert J. Mankin, 55–81. Chicago: University of Chicago Press.

Haleh Davis, Muriam. 2022. *Markets of Civilization: Islam and Racial Capitalism in Algeria*. Durham, NC: Duke University Press.

Hodgson, Marshall G. S. 1974. *The Venture of Islam: Conscience and History in a World Civilization*, Vol. 1–3. Chicago: University of Chicago Press.

Hodgson, Marshall G. S. [1974] 2021. *Mughamara al-Islam. Al-Damir wa-l-Tarikh fi-Hadara ʿAlamiyya*. Beirut: al-Shabaka al-ʿArabiyya li-l-Abhath wa-l-Nashr.

Lawrence, Bruce B. 2021. *Islamicate Cosmopolitan Spirit*. Oxford: Wiley Blackwell.

Massad, Joseph A. 2015. *Islam in Liberalism*. Chicago: University of Chicago Press.

Menchik, Jeremy. 2017. "Review of *The Sociology of Islam: Knowledge, Power and Civility*, by Armando Salvatore. Oxford: Wiley Blackwell, 2016." *Politics and Religion* 10 (4): 919–22.

Peter, Frank, Paula Schrode, and Ricarda Stegmann, eds. 2025. *Conceptualizing Islam: Critical Approaches*. Abingdon: Routledge.

Safi, Louay, ed. 2023. *Islam and the Drive to Global Justice: Principles of Justice Beyond Dominant Ethnic and Religious Communities*. Lanham, MD: Lexington.

Salvatore, Armando. 2016. *The Sociology of Islam: Knowledge, Power and Civility*. Oxford: Wiley Blackwell.

Salvatore, Armando [2016] 2017. *Susyulujiya al-Islam: al-Maʿrifa, al-Sulta wa-l-Madaniyya*. Beirut: al-Shabaka al-ʿArabiyya li-l-Abhath wa-l-Nashr.

Salvatore, Armando, and Kieko Obuse. 2023. "Overwriting the Orient and the Islamosphere: Religio-Civilizational Imaginaries Through East-West Entanglements." In *Imaginaries in Intercultural Perspective*, edited by Lubomír Dunaj et al., 181–96. London: Routledge.

Salvatore, Armando, and Kieko Obuse. Forthcoming. *ReOrienting Islam? Cosmopolitan Refractions*. Oakland. CA: University of California Press.

Salvatore, Armando, et al., eds. 2018. *The Wiley Blackwell History of Islam*. Oxford: Wiley Blackwell.

Shaw, Wendy M. K. 2019. *What Is "Islamic Art"? Between Religion and Perception*. Cambridge: Cambridge University Press.
Sunar, Lütfi. 2016. *Debates on Civilization in the Muslim World: Critical Perspectives on Islam and Modernity*. Oxford: Oxford University Press.
Turner, Bryan S. 2023. *Understanding Islam: Positions of Knowledge*. Edinburgh: Edinburgh University Press.
Yücesoy, Hayrettin. 2023. *Disenchanting the Caliphate: The Secular Discipline of Power in Abbasid Political Thought*. New York: Columbia University Press.

1

A Southern Dialogue on the "Islamic Frame"

Instituting Life in the Ecumene

Confronting the Insider–Outsider Dichotomy in Knowing Islam

Increasingly vocal and largely persuasive arguments have been developed for the determination of observers' and researchers' "positionalities" in knowing Islam. Such claims have been advanced in the wake of the Orientalism critique, of which Edward Said was the intrepid and intellectually sophisticated hero, even though by far not the initiator. This critique is as old as the movements, which were both intellectual and political, resisting Western colonialism and imperialism. However, in the last two decades or so, we have been witnessing a new shift marked by an increasing urgency to create new frameworks that specify the positioning of authors. This has occurred between residual commitments to Western ("orientalist") hegemonic conceptual frameworks and the uncertain onset of a post-Western and decolonial scholarship, ushering in a predicament, more than a paradigm, that has been termed "post-Orientalism" (Turner 2023, 107). In this chapter, I should provide selective elements that illustrate my own trajectory within post-Orientalism. Hopefully, this will not be seen as an idly self-referential exercise. I consider this clarification essential for presenting my approach to shaping an Islamic frame in the analysis and conceptualization of the instituting process within the Islamic ecumene, reaching up to the level of statehood. This brings us to the methodological crucible of the chapter, to be built on transparency about how my trajectory of dialogic repositioning relates to the present, if unstable, epistemic conundrum of post-Orientalism. The trajectory culminates in the critical transition I underwent between the completion of Volume I and the start of work on the present one.[1]

The question of epistemic repositioning—a dynamic concept that I prefer to the more current, identitarian idea of fixed "positionalities"—has been broached by Bryan Turner, an early champion (even before Said) of a critical approach to Orientalism as well as a pioneering advocate of a sociology of Islam (Turner 1974; 1978). He has done so in a crisply written volume on *Understanding Islam*, with the eloquent subtitle *Positions of Knowledge* (Turner 2023). In this book, he provides valuable signposts for navigating the tension between purportedly "insider" and "outsider" approaches to Islam. This brings us directly to the core methodological stakes of this chapter's discussion, for in an online lecture he gave to thousands of students in Qom, Iran, in October 2021, where he first presented ideas that would then flow in the book, Turner gave Hodgson pride of place in addressing the insider–outsider dichotomy.[2] The leading British sociologist, who in his youth had authored a quite critical review article on Hodgson's trilogy (Turner 1976), now emphasized how, through his empathic historical hermeneutics of Islam, the US historian was able to challenge almost single-handedly the European exceptionalism that masqueraded as universalism.

Following Turner, I am not succumbing to a rhetoric that emphasizes the self-enclosed positionality of the researcher, as if reflecting a fixed identity. Nevertheless, I embrace the strategic importance of a sociology of knowledge approach to understanding how institutional involvements, trans-institutional collaborations, and intellectual fellowships nourish our own trajectories. The outcome is a continuous and largely open-ended process of repositioning, rather than an anchoring on identity-based and unflexible positionalities. While assuming static identities and invariable "origins" is implausible from a sociological perspective, particular moments or stations on the way can provide watersheds and sliding doors within evolving trajectories. At this juncture the conceptual implications of situating one's own trajectory come to the fore. I completed Volume I immediately after arriving at McGill University in 2014, following years of toil and tribulation spent at the Università degli Studi di Napoli "L'Orientale" in Naples, Italy. Not less notably, my time at McGill has been punctuated with an intermittent learning process about the unique, if often erratic, trajectory of McGill's Institute of Islamic Studies (IIS).[3] Only after completing Volume I, and while engaging the history of IIS, I realized that the phrasing of an "Islamic perspective" I had committed to in that volume had been famously claimed by key proponents of the broader project of Islamization of knowledge associated with leading Muslim scholars whose trajectory included important stations at McGill. They are Ismail Raji al-Faruqi, who completed his MA at McGill's IIS in 1953 with Wilfred Cantwell Smith, and returned to McGill as a Visiting Fellow between 1959 and 1961 on invitation by his mentor, and Syed Muhammad Naquib al-Attas, who earned his MA at McGill's IIS in 1962 after being awarded a Canada Council Fellowship.

Al-Faruqi's Islamic perspective (1982) was much more holistic and theologically grounded than what I had suggested in Volume I, following Hodgson's historical hermeneutics. Thanks to his seminal approach, al-Faruqi became the paramount inspirer of the International Islamic University of Malaysia (IIUM) in Kuala Lumpur in 1993 under the auspices of the Organisation of the Islamic Conference—the prominent international Muslim body (now called the Organisation of Islamic Cooperation). Alongside al-Faruqi, or perhaps even before him, and further deepening its implications via a broader philosophy of knowledge, al-Attas (1995) invoked the necessity of an Islamic perspective or worldview linking epistemology with ontology. He founded a smaller but extremely influential institution of advanced studies, today affiliated with IIUM, namely, the International Institute of Islamic Thought and Civilization (ISTAC). Together, IIUM and ISTAC are considered global strongholds of the Islamization of knowledge project, even if via different articulations of an "Islamic perspective." My usage of "Islamic frame," however, bears no relation to that programmatic effort, since it arises inductively from historical-sociological analysis rather than from a prescriptive reorganization of knowledge.

Yet, in July 2023 I visited both IIUM and ISTAC and gained insights into how working through the lens of an Islamic frame (which I now prefer to "perspective," for the reasons specified in the Introduction) can be enriched by crossing the paths and trajectories of fellow scholars across the purported insider–outsider divide in the knowledge of Islam. At IIUM, I had the privilege to engage in a discussion with several colleagues affiliated with its Sociology, Political Science, History, and the originally named "Usul al-Din and Comparative Religion and Philosophy" departments. For the methodological implications of this chapter, what made the discussion at IIUM a promising, if tentative, test of how shared an Islamic frame can be across the purported insider–outside boundary is the fact that IIUM was built and works as an intellectual powerhouse of knowledge production. This role closely reflects the complex transition from the precolonial strength of the Islamic ecumene to the world of modern capitalism and bureaucratic state steering hegemonized by the West, but within which Malaysia, both as a dynamic society and as a powerful Muslim-majority state, actively participates.[4]

While the moment of dialogue at IIUM in Kuala Lumpur included a promising, if preliminary, spell of discussion, which I hope will continue as the trilogy unfolds, it is essential to acknowledge that such occasions, regardless of their immediate results, are themselves propaedeutic to the participants' repositioning. In my case, it certainly contributed to demystifying the ghost of the insider–outsider boundary, which was explicitly addressed in the discussion. In that sense, I am joining Bryan Turner (a scholar, incidentally, with an excellent degree of familiarity with Malaysia) in questioning the rigidity of positionalities and appreciating the virtues of a continuous repositioning. On the other hand, dialogue can also nourish a shared reflexivity on the legacy of unbalanced constellations of power relations in the building of epistemic constraints, which continue to privilege anglophone academia. Therefore, it cannot be mortified into a hypocritically irenic reproduction of the same power relations. Neither can it be reduced to a sanitized mapping of dislocated positionalities, followed by theatrical manifestations of goodwill to mutual empathy and nonbelligerence. A dialogue can only be productive if it works as an epistemic trigger facilitating sound explanations,[5] even if not necessarily shared—as will be argued shortly. This shift from mere understanding to the explanatory register is crucial, and in the meeting at IIUM no participant seemed to question that—probably also thanks to the prevalence of social scientists in the meeting room, significantly named after Ibn Khaldun and underscoring the centrality of his legacy in cultivating an Islamic frame.

More than presenting, or criticizing, bits of old and new methodologies, one could detect in the flow of the discussion an emerging understanding of "method." Like in the Greek etymology of the term (*methodos*), it is a continuous, if bumpy, path to be shared with fellow travelers, rather than a prepackaged toolkit to be imposed on docile learners. Seen from this angle, the methodological focus shifts to the shared itineraries themselves, given that being together on such a path requires awareness of crisscrossing—if often contentious—routes and encounters, as well as readiness to process knowledge–power crucibles, both inherited and ongoing. To be sought is some measure of an overlapping consensus or a lowest common denominator on ways to be on this path by managing the knowledge–power entanglements. This task should be approached piecemeal, by tentative steps and small-scale practical moves, as if performed on a broad construction site where no single worker can claim to command an exhaustive view (indeed, a "perspective" of sorts) over the entirety of the site. The emphasis thus shifts from imposing an authoritative method to cultivating a disciplined readiness for situated movement along a continuous and open-ended path.

This is why integral to the dialogic reflections at the IIUM session was a first attempt to address how my process of repositioning—particularly after the publication of Volume I of the trilogy—required awareness of how one's trajectory can factor into the knowledge–power equation, especially as shaped by the postcolonial asymmetries that continue to structure "who speaks for Islam," from where, and with what authority—and so into the production, and potential sharing, of an Islamic frame.[6] This was a significant omission in the preparation and writing of Volume I. Of course, self-reflexivity cannot be a self-referential, or, worse, narcissistic exercise. In our case, it requires an empathic, if resilient, effort at reformulating the open question *What is Islam?* Once raised, and scholastically answered, by the Scottish orientalist and Presbyterian minister W. Montgomery Watt (1959), it was boldly inherited and radically cracked open by Shahab Ahmed (2016), as we saw in the Introduction. Setting on such an open-ended and shared, if bouncy, path of method seemed the only practical alternative to either taking the idea of Islam and the quality of "being Islamic" dangerously for granted or dismissing it as an essentialist ruse of the continuing Western colonial hegemony (see Introduction). It is a fair level of mutual, if contentious, recognition that keeps us together on the road and secures a shared, if at times shaky, epistemic ground. This is not tantamount to seeking a positivistic objectivity based on the binary of true vs. false, which violently conceals relations of domination, but a process that warrants a modicum of consensus on what "valid" (i.e., scholarly plausible and agreeable) knowledge is—a momentary consensus from which participants in an epistemic dialogue can again depart, individually or in smaller groups, on their own pace and in various directions.

Looking back at my trajectory of continuous repositioning on the path—often blessed by good company, even though at times solitary and jumpy—I cannot name any clear "origin" determining an unambiguous "identity." And yet, as I also shared at the IIUM dialogue session, the fact that I was socialized into academic life in Naples, while coming from its immediate surroundings (quite in the middle of the Mediterranean), did affect my sense of direction. It sensitized me to fissures in how the insider–outsider binary is artificially derived from the postulation of a selfsame "Western" orientalist perspective. This is where the epistemic implications become relevant, since my departure point affected not just my positioning in but also my appreciation of the knowledge–power equation in specific ways, given that it was geographically and historically located within and outside the West simultaneously (cf. Chambers 2008). The peculiarity of Southern Italy as a site of collective life, politics, and knowledge production is that it has been subjected to a process of inner colonization since the unification of the Italian peninsula through the armies and militias of the Northwestern Italian Duchy of Savoy. The enterprise was supported by a comprehensive Northwestern European discourse on the defectivity of the modern European credentials of Southern Europe in general and Southern Italy in particular (Dainotto 2007). This asymmetrical positioning—at once inside and at the margins of the European project—intensified my sensitivity to how epistemic authority is unevenly assigned and withheld. This tension is summarized by a joke that colleagues from the Northwestern part of Italy—from where the conquest of the South started in the 1860s, followed by a brutal repression of a fierce insurgency—often love to crack, according to which "Naples is the only Middle Eastern city without a European quarter."

The encompassing notion of Western colonialism is surely justified by its (often genocidal) techniques of exploitation and capitalist extraction, and concomitant forms of supremacism, racism, and orientalism, transcending differences between, say, British, American, and French practices of hegemony. And yet, such general notions risk concealing forms of colonial exploitation and orientalist stigmatization within the "West" itself. In the case of Italy and its "Southern question," scholars have aptly spoken of "Orientalism in one country" (Pandolfi 1998; Schneider 1998; Chambers 2008). This is why it would be a historical and cultural misunderstanding to locate Naples, its region (Campania), and Southern Italy in general (roughly matching the conquered and colonized Kingdom of the Two Sicilies) by default and without specifications within hegemonic Europe, or, even more problematically, the imperialist "West." However, it cannot be denied that Southern Italy, and more specifically Naples, as its foremost center, also operated as a site of production of both orientalist knowledge and Enlightenment thought. The former occurred most notably through the Collegio dei Cinesi, founded in 1732, which, after the forced unification of Italy in the 19th century, became first the Real Collegio Asiatico and, in the following century, the Istituto Universitario Orientale (now rebranded Università degli Studi di Napoli "L'Orientale")—nothing less than the oldest orientalist institution of higher learning in

Europe. Walking through downtown Naples, where this university is located, one can appreciate—also through the prism of a global tourist gaze on Southern exoticism—the place's living paradox of belonging simultaneously to the knowledge apparatus of the colonizers and suffering from a subaltern status derived from the structural disadvantages of life in a "domestically" colonized (and "orientalized") region. This dual role complicates any easy mapping of colonizer and colonized positions in the very context from which my own trajectory departed.

The reasons why I decided to undertake social-science-oriented Islamic Studies at the just-mentioned university in Naples were also a consequence of how as a teenager my first, uncertain steps on an educational and intellectual path were affected by a sequence of local, national, and international vicissitudes peaking in the late 1970s with the Iranian revolution. I vividly remember how the role played by Islam in that revolution and its aftermath was feverishly discussed within political and intellectual circles, most notably on the Italian left-wing spectrum. It is worth noting that, in the political context of the time, the two main Italian intellectual camps that dominated various institutions, including academia—the Catholic and the Marxist—were both mutually antagonistic and intensely intertwined and almost complicit. This intense relation reached the point of configuring an intersecting, if minoritarian, "Catholic–Marxian" (in Italian, *cattocomunista*) current that was particularly influential in public intellectual debates. It presented itself for a while as a synthesis of thought and engagement that could heal the country from its fascist past and play a role in support of anti-imperialist movements. In the Italian context of the time, this constellation rendered the Islamic dimension of the Iranian revolution—which unfolded simultaneously with the Sandinista revolution in Nicaragua, itself sustained by religious commitments through currents of Catholic liberation theology—far from contradictory or illegible. This stood in contrast to how it appeared when filtered through the intellectual and media circuits of other Western countries.

Living through such events from what is clearly a frontier zone between Europe and what Europe tagged as the Middle East (Salvatore 2022) started to sensibilize me—along with a few companions of study and discussion or fellow travelers through the events of the late 1970s and 1980s—to how our peculiar, if subaltern, situatedness in a Mediterranean frontier zone harbored an original potential to generate and cultivate a type of interstitial knowledge with border-crossing virtues that could help healing the insider–outsider fracture in knowing Islam. It is indeed intellectual forces developing in such liminal areas that often play a role in unsettling, if not subverting, dominant paradigms and facilitating new ones, also through transversal dialogues with intellectual forces from other subaltern regions of the "Global South."[7] Liminal does not mean marginal, but productively interstitial (cf. Bottici and Challand 2021). Seen in retrospect, this frontier positioning anticipated what I would later articulate, in a different register, through the notion of a *barzakh*-like epistemic stance—an intervaled way of inhabiting knowledge positions without collapsing into either side, the substance of which will be discussed in the next chapters. From this standpoint, the rise of a conceptual opportunity out of an interstitial positioning gains sharper contours.

It was probably also thanks to this unstable and liminal type of early intellectual socialization that, rather than unilaterally trashing mainstream sociological theory—and notably Weber—wholesale as irremediably colonial (which it is undoubtedly true in many crucial respects; see Bhambra and Holmwood 2021), I started to appreciate the potential upside of eccentrically navigating various straits of sociopolitical thought between the hegemonic and the subaltern. Through the long years I spent at Humboldt University in Berlin after completing my PhD at the European University Institute in Florence, I had the chance to confront leading voices within German thought and political and intellectual history. This legacy harbored a strategic value given Germany's prominent, if politically decentered, role in Western thought overall. What proved particularly instructive was how German thinkers crafted sociopolitical conceptualizations that drew on the broader Western experience while remaining, for extended periods, less directly entangled in the colonial and imperial agendas that shaped Anglo-American and French intellectual traditions. I benefited from discerning the way the sociopolitical conceptualizations produced by German thinkers ingeniously elaborated foundational themes drawn from more generally Western (or, as Weber unabashedly had it, "occidental") historical experience—while also, for long stretches, less immediately reflecting the political agendas of Western colonialism and hegemony than, say, Anglo-American or French thought.

This repositioning from dwelling in an interstitial and subaltern space to exposure to a singularly (de)centered cradle of Western thought alerted me to the ambivalence of hegemonic notions of historicity and modernity, like those that marked the rise of modern statehood, capitalism, and selfhood. In their German articulations, such concepts appeared imbued with distinctive world-historical diagnostic insights, and yet friable to the point of self-implosion. Ideas were not seldom articulated via a modicum of self-criticism and even a vein of dark pessimism on the trajectory and destiny of "the West." Seen from this angle, a further epistemic opening becomes visible, for the broader venture of German thought—Marx included, or even typically—appeared to me as quite unique for being both pivotal and liminal. It certainly did not impose itself as the unproblematic evolutionary apex of the self-complacent trajectory of modern Western rationalism. Not entirely unlike its Italian counterpart, German thought was fed by the ambivalence of the aspirations and fears of a latecomer to statehood and colonialism. This also impacted their respective, and quite thriving, orientalist traditions. As such, these peculiarly Western knowledge traditions, and even more, the ambivalent historical experiences that generated them, invited a judicious reconstruction of some of their intellectual debris—elements which, if adequately processed, could acquire a "recycling" value within the construction site hosting multiple points of departure for the envisaged post-Western epistemic dialogue.

To recapitulate, being intellectually socialized first in (Southern) Italy and then in Germany, both in Islamic Studies and sociology, I grew into occupying a doubly liminal, if complex and shifting, position toward anglophone academia. It is quite well-known that Edward Said admitted the limitation of his critique of Orientalism for not taking into account these two countries. While this applies to the knowledge of Islam discussed by Said, the same concerns *a fortiori* mainstream sociopolitical thought, which provides an essential background to their respective national orientalist traditions (cf. Stauth 1993). It is also by navigating the tricky waves of German theory, before a full immersion in what I will discuss shortly as Southern/Italian thought, as well as steering through their mutual gulfs, that I gained a healthy distance from (and a matching sensibility to cope with and process) the anglophone academic discourses on Islam, which have been ever more hegemonic in the current post-orientalist phase marked by the eclipse of classical continental European Orientalism. This equipment I took with me on the path, and it helped me take decisive, if critical, steps toward an Islamic frame.

The path, however, was far from smooth. Admittedly, and given the political–intellectual climate of the 1980s and early 1990s, I was first captured by a post-structuralist view on the production of knowledge on Islam and its purported politicization. Poststructuralism (to which also Edward Said's work should be counted) did impact some significant waves of the first tentative surge of postcolonial thought. Yet here a crucial conceptual limit emerges, for its being caught in a rather inner-Western, immanent critique of (colonial) modernity. The doctoral dissertation that I defended in 1994 at the European University Institute in Florence, Italy, with two German supervisors (a sociologist, Klaus Eder, and an Islamic Studies scholar, Reinhard Schulze), was decisively influenced by this methodological orientation. In that work, I maintained that, while Islam is not the product of essentialist abstractions and reductions, and as such cannot be just "deconstructed," its global apprehension (including, if not mainly, the view of how it may get "politicized") is the outcome of overlapping hermeneutic circles. These stretch across the purported insider–outsider boundary and are determined by imbalanced power relations largely influenced by Western imperialism, colonialism, and Orientalism.

The fact that this PhD thesis, whose topic was sharply eccentric to the mushrooming works on "political Islam" of the time, was awarded the 1994 Malcolm Kerr Dissertation Award in the Social Sciences of MESA (Middle East Studies Association of North America)[8] could be taken as a clue that, by the early 1990s, the anglophone Middle East Studies establishment had started to pay attention to continental types of "critique" (see Salvatore and Obuse 2022, 16–18). Indeed, the unexpected (and surely undeserved) recognition of my early work came at a moment when the, by that time, American-hegemonized studies of Islam appeared increasingly invested in the chimera of a paradigm change—as if one could nimbly vault beyond the European orientalist legacy by just faithfully trailing the critique launched by Edward Said. He was invited as a very special guest to the annual MESA meeting in 1998 in Chicago on the occasion of the 20th anniversary of his *Orientalism* and was celebrated as the inspirer of the coveted novel paradigm. What struck me at the meeting was the heightened, almost millenarian mood—an expectation that Said's imposing presence might somehow inaugurate a new epistemic order, embodied in his undeniable charisma and moral authority. The atmosphere at that meeting made the mood unmistakable: an innocently intense, almost messianic expectation of the coming of a new dispensation of knowledge, heralded by the intellectual stature of Said. Of course, I felt swayed too. And yet, as every even minimally self-conscious area studies practitioner is painfully aware of, in the present post-orientalist limbo a new paradigm is not in sight and is quite unlikely to see the light any time soon. The fact itself that a poststructuralist move facilitated the critique of Orientalism did not forebode the replacement of an old ideological certainty with a new one. This is also evident if we acknowledge the volatility of the new politics of positionality, which decolonial aspirations struggle to turn into consistent patterns of method. What follows is a sobering recognition: methodological heterogeneity, if not fragmentation, is the best antidote to ideological conformism. In this sense, the invocation of an Islamic frame has the potential to accommodate a healthy plurality of approaches while responding to the need to take parallel, if discreet and realistic, steps in decolonizing the global conceptualization and knowledge of Islam.

Understanding vs. Explanation?

Bryan Turner (2023) has convincingly argued that to navigate the present post-orientalist waters, one needs to develop and manage a suitable sense of distance from what we explore and engage. This modicum of distance allows us to move swiftly from understanding what we study to explaining it, but also from there back to understanding. Crucially, however, we should see understanding and explanation not as the opposite extremes of an epistemic gulf separating the understanding insider from the explaining outsider, but as a continuous spectrum of epistemic engagements. Undoubtedly, however, the understanding position requires an interpretive mode that presupposes a congruent degree of empathizing with an insider's predicament. In our case, and in analogy to Hodgson, this positioning helps weave an Islamic frame, allowing us to appreciate the world-historical "importance of being Islamic." Once such attunement takes hold, it enables a fluid shift along the spectrum, making explanation a deepening—rather than a departure from—understanding. Through this movement one can explain the dynamics of *ʿumran* and the unfolding of *maʿmura* (see Introduction), that is, the multicausal and multidimensional becoming of the Islamic ecumene, including the process of building institutions and crafting statehood.

A bright example of an explanation of the development of the Islamic ecumene grounded in a sensible modulation of empathy can be found in the work of Mohammed Bamyeh (2019, 139–190). His approach yielded an explanatory prism encompassing the three foremost and dynamic dimensions of the ecumene. They are the partial control exercised by political authorities over social relations, the long-distance movement of people, goods, and ideas, and the coexistence of several registers of speech—or heteroglossia, a term Bamyeh borrowed from Bakhtin. Seen from the vantage point adopted here, Bamyeh's prism becomes a useful prelude to grasping the salient patterning forces of the ecumene—forces we can interpret through the dynamics of *'umran* and its instituting processes. However, following Bamyeh, examining these explanatory factors will only yield deep insights into the workings of the precolonial Islamic ecumene if one apprehends the becoming of the ecumene as undeniably Islamic, while not sui generis or exceptional: as a shared patrimony of humanity. This recognition becomes all the more urgent in a moment of planetary crisis determined mainly by the Western combination of extractive capitalism and a bureaucratic, if often neo-colonially violent steering of populations. These key factors of what is generically—and confoundingly—labeled "globalization" have hollowed the historical venture of the Islamic ecumene, without, however, obliterating either its memory or the resilience of its civility patterns and instituting processes. That is, the component of understanding that plays a role in the explanation is here addressed not even to "Islam as such," which never existed, if not in many an orientalist (and, regrettably, post-orientalist) fantasy, but to Islam as an expression of the human quest for felicity. The Islam in question is not smoothly aligned, to say the least, with the historic and current "globalized" predicament of humankind, which, by contrast, has privileged the free movement of goods over people, the unlimited control of states over borders and populations, and the imposition of uniform legal codes (not least through the fictive cage of the "person": see Chapter 9).

As Turner argued, the living remedy to the (often rhetorically amplified) constraints of the insider–outsider boundary lies in a cosmopolitan vocation of border-crossing embodied by free-floating intellectuals. This is not necessarily an enviable condition, as it is often triggered by exile, persecution, or other vicissitudes accompanying repositioning processes in their life and work trajectories. Yet in the history of sociopolitical thought, scholars who were exilic, liminal, or interstitial often played a significant role. This was the case, for example, with the Jewish scholars who escaped Nazism or Muslim scholars who suffered displacement due to colonial oppression and the inequalities and injustices of postcolonial knowledge–power constellations, often reflected in authoritarian rule exercised on behalf of neo-colonial interests supportive of privileged local elites. Such conditions compelled several scholars to leave the former colonies and embark on critical intellectual paths within the former metropolises—no doubt also, if involuntarily, contributing to an impoverishment of the knowledge production in the former colonies and accruing to the bubble of global anglophone and francophone academia. I am referring to intellectual personalities of a high caliber, ranging from Hannah Arendt and Theodor Adorno, through Edward Said himself, to Ali Shariati, Mohammed Arkoun, Fatima Mernissi, Abdolkarim Soroush, and Saba Mahmood, among others. Turner (2023, 167) is therefore keen to underscore a complementary point, namely how a leading metropolitan personality like Pierre Bourdieu, throughout his stellar career at French elite academic institutions, could become, and remain, committed to migrant rights and the Algerian liberation from the French colonial yoke. While doing so, he never ceased to plead for the strategic value of explanations—even more so when one needs to stand up against oppression and exploitation. Even when starting with an empathic understanding of, and solidarity with, the pleas of the exploited and colonized, one should be able to account for plausible causalities of colonial oppression. This is a major example disproving the existence of an unbridgeable epistemic gap between understanding and explanation. Seen in this light, an Islamic frame—supported by the recognition of "the importance of being Islamic" and triggered by the pledge to an empathic understanding—can facilitate the move toward sound explanations of post-colonial conditions.

The knowledge process unfolding in such liminal spaces and the concomitant reflexive repositioning undergone by those scholars indicate why we should not view the process as centered on a type of subject safely buffered from the object of knowledge and therefore seeking "objective" knowledge. The process is inherently interactive, dialogic, but also epistemically challenging for the scholars who produce such knowledge. This is especially the case if their subject position is not institutionally entrenched and is therefore exposed to a certain degree of desubjectivation and alienation. Such recognition should help dissolve the relatively static notion of positionality within knowledge production and shift the focus to continuous processes of repositioning, of which free-floating scholars are the most extreme, yet visible, foil. Indeed, nobody can ever be a self-consistent subject dwelling in a stable position despite the illusion provided by the Cartesian fallacy that might delude us into perceiving a secure shielding, by default, of the subject position. When the illusion prevails, we pay a heavy price by abstracting subjectivity from its intrinsic impermanence and exposure to the often unsettling unpredictability of knowledge processes.

Therefore, within an approach guided by a sociology of knowledge emancipated from the ideology of subjective buffering and abstraction, what matters is less individual identity and positionality than mutual interactions and cumulative adjustments on a path. No doubt, such interactions are constrained by the spectrum of possibilities allowed within a given articulation of the knowledge–power equation discussed in Volume I. Surely, in the precolonial dynamics of the Islamic ecumene knowledge was already, and quite consciously, a fundamental source of power. However, since the rise of Europe to colonial hegemony and the imposition of modern capitalism and Westphalian statehood on the conditions for the production of knowledge, the knowledge–power equation has been subjected to unprecedented constraints that continue to bestow a superior power on Western institutions and their methodologies. These transformed conditions significantly narrow the options for a dialogic repositioning across the epistemic grid linking understanding and explanation. In a nutshell, the relatively open knowledge–power equation, which had for long fed the instituting process in the Islamic ecumene, has been transformed into a power–knowledge cage dependent on the corporate norms and institutional disciplining of a Western-dominated world order (on institution as corporation, see Chapters 4 and 9). This order is trapped in the power mechanisms that produce and legitimize the abstraction of "the knowing subject" and regiment it through unflexible institutional control and corporate forms of "line management." In this constrained landscape, what becomes imperative is a mode of inquiry capable of slipping between fixed epistemic positions and reopening the space for dialogic repositioning that Western institutional regimes have progressively eroded.

Seen also through this lens, one could discover a deep epistemic affinity between the trajectories and commitments of Marshall Hodgson and Shahab Ahmed. They shared a continuing repositioning in pursuing a study of Islam that was both empathic and critical, regardless of their diverse starting points and shifting institutional constraints. Their combined achievements suggest that embracing the importance of being Islamic should help view such binaries as insider–outsider as being themselves the outcome of exploitative orientalist views and nativist reactions against them. As stressed by Yücesoy (2023, 11), these dichotomizing categorizations end up creating an environment that "empowers oppressive practices in the misleading guise of 'socially and culturally authentic' traditions in the name of religion." In this regard, the avoidance of an objectification, if not "reification," of Islam as a "religion" was central to the attempt to harmonize insider and outsider positions that became the privileged methodological battleground in the trajectory of Wilfred Cantwell Smith and his founding of the previously mentioned McGill's IIS in 1952. He envisaged this academic institution as an epistemic laboratory radically alternative to the Centres of Middle East Studies that were mushrooming in America at the time. These institutions focused on producing knowledge, when not outright "intelligence," finalized to the domestication of what was left of the Islamic ecumene after colonialism via the imposition of capitalist patterns of dependent modernization (Salvatore and Obuse 2021; see also Brankley Abbas 2021, 52–91). Smith's critical approach survived his move to Harvard in 1964. It was enriched by his increasing interaction with the leading American sociologist and social theorist Robert Bellah, who, after postdoctoral studies at IIS in 1956–1958, inherited from the Scottish orientalist Hamilton Gibb the teaching of "Islamic Institutions" classes at Harvard. Smith's intensive exchanges with Bellah sharpened his sense of how non-objectifying approaches could sustain sociopolitical explorations and explanations—an insight that Bellah, for his part, was developing in his own work (Bortolini 2021, 65–69, 91–94).

Following this thread that reconciles understanding with explanation, even if we were to keep our original label of the "sociology of Islam," the "of" in the genitive "of Islam" should then be intended in a double sense. The first offsets the objectifying risk by having the inquirer embrace the sense-making tools developed in the trajectory of Islam's making as simultaneous with its ecumene; this would amount to a frame vowed to understanding. The second sense would result from shifting toward an explanation of the heteroglossic, if often conflicted, sociopolitical unfolding of the Islamic ecumene. In this movement between the two senses, the task and method of the inquirer are not fixed but repeatedly refashioned through an interactive engagement with Islam's protean and ever-unfinished venture. Bracketing out "Islam" altogether for fear of incurring the sin of essentialism would, instead, entail neglecting the dynamic and open-ended venture in history that elicited the importance of being Islamic across the insider–outsider divide.

Walking on such a path bridging understanding and explanation and healing the insider–outsider dichotomy, as done through different trajectories by Hodgson and Ahmad, I took further steps to inflect my own version of an Islamic frame. They were inspired by the emergent appeal of a line of Southern/Italian sociopolitical thought that has recently enjoyed increasing attention in non-mainstream anglophone academic circles, partly supplanting the attraction of French-style poststructuralism. Within the Italian thought tradition, I would like to single out three authors who are particularly well-known internationally and are linked together by their intersecting legacies, namely, the already mentioned Giambattista Vico, Antonio Gramsci,[9] and Roberto Esposito. What these three authors share, spanning a trajectory of almost three centuries—from the early 18th to the early 21st—is an emphasis on the primacy of civility and institutions over statehood, as well as the role of broader popular (including, at large, "religious") cultures in shaping civility. As a result, the type of civility they focused on cannot be reduced to a top-down civilizing process initiated by political elites, as emphasized by Norbert Elias (a stalwart in German sociological thought, whose work I profusely referenced in Volume I) when addressing Northwestern Europe. Rather, these Italian thinkers foreground a more open-ended and relational pattern of how civic and political cultures take shape—one that binds thought and experience, knowledge and life, and history and theory, without prioritizing (let alone absolutizing) either pole.[10]

Charting the Path: Conceptual Maps from Southern/Italian Thought

In Volume I, I was certainly remiss in clarifying my trajectory of repositioning. Nevertheless, I did start to draw from intellectual sources from the above-considered frontier region when I evoked counter-notions of civility elaborated by the 18th-century Neapolitan thinker Giambattista Vico (Salvatore 2016, 67–69). I compared these notions with those developed by his roughly contemporaneous Scottish authors, often labeled "Scottish moralists." This comparison has been more recently corroborated by works juxtaposing the Scottish and the Neapolitan Enlightenment currents as equally influential and sharing common themes, yet moving toward different, if not diverging, conclusions, as exemplified by Hume and Vico, respectively (Robertson 2005). In particular, I contrasted Vico with the Scottish author who incorporated ideas of human agency into a hegemonic discourse on the nature of *homo economicus* aligning with British imperial hegemony, namely, Adam Smith (Eriksson 1993). I probably do not need to spell out again, as I did in Volume I, the reasons why Vico's notion of civility should be seen as much more resonant with the conception emerging from the study of the Islamic ecumene and therefore can be counted as a potential asset in the development of a shared Islamic frame. What requires emphasis here is that my appeal to Vico—when viewed through the prism of my own trajectory—gains further weight from the often-noted affinity between his thought and that of Ibn Khaldun (Gabrieli 1975; Dayeh and Messling 2020; Trabant 2021; Messahel 2025). Whether consciously or less so, I came to treat the Vico–Ibn Khaldun constellation as a post-orientalist springboard for embracing an Islamic frame and recalibrating my own repositioning.

The Italian philosopher Remo Bodei (2017) has characterized the approach exemplified by Vico—antedating any post-structuralist "linguistic turn" by a few centuries—as envisioning concepts as metaphors and "crystals" poetically susceptible to continuous metamorphosis and qualitative leaps. This is an alternative path to considering the meaning of any key concept (say, between "life" and "politics") as ultimately sanctioned by a corporate authority, be it the Church or the state. To be sure, the intellectual posture represented by Vico was enabled by the political fragmentation of the Italian peninsula, which was only overcome with a late nation-state formation in the second half of the 19th century. This is when Italy began a tortuous process of aligning with the hegemonic structure of Westphalian nation-states—a process that was never fully completed. Its incompletion owed much to the persistent resistance to homogenization in Italy's Southern regions after they were subjected to a form of domestic colonialism-*cum*-Orientalism, as previously suggested.

The outcome of this original trajectory has been the assembling of an epistemic space that endured beyond nation-state formation, woven by a brand of Southern/Italian thought eccentric to the prevailing European understanding of the civilizing process as integral to the emergence of modern statehood, as famously theorized by Elias ([1939; 1968] 2000). Instead, this type of sociopolitical thought is invested in a civic vocation: citizenship in weak states, the carving out of spaces of autonomy vis-à-vis the Church, and, above all, a sense of the impermanence and open-endedness of instituting processes. It also exhibits a marked skepticism toward purely theoretical speculations that lack solid historical grounding. Southern/Italian thought is at its most incisive where ambivalence is operative—between the universal and the particular, the ideal and the concrete. It is vividly anti-Cartesian in its attention to the dialectic of tradition and innovation. This dialectic works through a habitus nourished by bustling life—signally, one of the key meanings of *'umran* (see Introduction). Here practice is continually enriched by renewed interpretations of the circumstances, needs, and aspirations of human life. The focus is on thought as living and lived and, most vividly in Vico, embodied—almost as a "philosophy of impure/spurious reason" (Bodei 2017, 36–37).

Broadly speaking, this was also the approach of Vico's most prominent 20th-century heir, Antonio Gramsci. Of partly Albanian ancestry, Gramsci hailed from Sardinia, an even more subaltern region than peninsular

Southern Italy. Yet, he socialized into political life in the industrial Northwestern city of Turin, which had been the capital of the Duchy of Savoy that ruled over Sardinia as its periphery for centuries before the conquest of the peninsular South. Gramsci was able to integrate the Southern Italian Enlightenment tradition (also by a critical appropriation of another towering, albeit much less progressive, Neapolitan thinker, Benedetto Croce) into the most significant international movement of liberation from imperial, colonial, and capitalist exploitation of the early 20th century, namely Marxism. Gramsci was an original Marxist thinker eager to engage in an in-depth analysis of the specific cultural configuration of post-unitary Italy, where Catholic intellectual and political forces rivalled the workers' movement in claiming to represent "the people": not only the industrial working class but the wider popular and subaltern sectors of society. Gramsci, who died in prison under the Italian fascist regime, has become a globally influential icon in the wake of the decolonization movement, including in the Muslim-majority world (see Gervasio and Teti 2024). As observed by Bryan Turner (2023, 156), he has also been increasingly influential in European postwar sociology. As previously alluded to, at the time of the revolution in Iran, a pristine moment of my intellectual socialization—with its fueling new ways of understanding Islam emancipated from colonial and postcolonial Orientalism—was represented by debates in the Gramscian Left in Italy on whether Islam could be a force of change to fight inequality and poverty—indeed, if it had the potential of a revolutionary force. While this idea was shared by several generations of anti-colonial activists from the Islamic ecumene—mirrored by the movements and political forces that in the West supported resistance to colonialism—in the late 1970s the debate took a new turn, thanks to the questions raised by Michel Foucault, the iconic critical European intellectual of the era. He did so upon visiting Iran during the revolution and commenting on what he saw and experienced on the pages of the leading Italian daily *Corriere della Sera* (Salvatore 1997, 133–161; see also Ghamari-Tabrizi 2016).

A combination of Foucauldian and Gramscian motives happened to feed into a quite standardized type of criticism within anglophone academia that peaked in the 1990s. Largely outside this trend, Southern/Italian thought experienced a new blossoming and international renown throughout the post-9/11 early 21st century—no doubt also through its original reception of several masters of French theory, Foucault included. It was in this context that the tradition acquired the ambitious label of *New Italian Theory*. Its success owed decisively to the writings of the third among the

Southern Italian thinkers I enlisted, namely Roberto Esposito, the author—among several bestsellers—of *Living Thought* (Esposito [2010] 2012) and *Vitam Instituere* (Esposito [2023] 2025a).[11] Over his trajectory, Esposito has synthesized multiple theoretical strands to develop a distinctive approach to the mutual entanglements between life, community, and the instituting process. In discreet yet strategically placed parts of this book, I will invoke Esposito's work for the way it resonates with our search for an Islamic frame. This resonance is not only due to neglected affinities with the conceptual implications of Ibn Khaldun's *ʿumran*, but also to Esposito's delineation of a path to statehood that—while often shunned or dammed in the West—flourished in the early modern, precolonial configurations of political modernity in the Islamic ecumene.[12]

Although Esposito was never directly involved in research on Islam or the Islamic ecumene, it is worth noting that he taught for a long time at the previously mentioned Università degli Studi di Napoli "L'Orientale." This might have provided him with a modicum of familiarity with both the local configuration of Islamic Studies and the decolonial perspectives that were clearly antagonistic to classical Orientalism, not least through his academic acquaintance with the leading scholar of Mediterranean coloniality, Iain Chambers, who taught at the same university for several decades and whose exquisite elaborations on decolonial Southern thought (Chambers 2008) were often inspired by thinkers of the caliber of Walter Mignolo. For this reason, despite the conspicuous absence in Esposito's work of an explicit problematization of the colonial dimension of Western modernity—or of what constitutes a distinctively Southern/Italian difference in relation to that dimension, a gap that, alongside Chambers and others, I certainly miss—Esposito's approach remains invaluable for helping, if indirectly, mediate, as I will do throughout this book and especially in its last part, between the legacy of Ibn Khaldun and an alternative view of civilizing and instituting processes resistant to the normative requirements of Westphalian nation-statehood. The centrality of life in Esposito's work, via concepts like bare life, life forms, and biopolitics (as the politics of managing life), as well as his more recent focus on instituting life (see also Esposito 2021a), has offered crucial inspiration for shaping the trajectory of repositioning that I sought to transform into a path leading to a viable Islamic frame.[13]

It should be stressed, however, that my appropriation of themes and ideas from Southern/Italian theory is not a way to claim that the above-mentioned Catholic–Marxian nexus is an antidote to the orientalist aberrations of, say, the liberal and Protestant mainstream in knowing Islam.

Quite the opposite. I regard the most recent and successful phase of Southern/Italian thought as a precious asset for inquiry into the Islamic ecumene precisely because it can help redeem our interstitial appreciation of an Islamic frame from any residual Catholic–Marxian accretions that may have been preponderant at the time of the Iranian Revolution. Embracing Southern/Italian thought in building an Islamic frame, as I am doing in this book, can function as a therapy against lingering Western hubris and conceptual complacency, from which both Catholicism and Marxism have historically been far from immune—given their deep, if often critical, involvement in the European formations of modern capitalism and statehood (see Chapters 5 and 9 in this volume).

How does this reflexive discussion of my repositioning trajectory revise or integrate the approach I followed in Volume I? While this will be progressively shown throughout the present volume, some preliminary steps are in order. In the previous volume, I relied not so much on the academically popular notion of Islam as a "discursive tradition" associated with specific practices—as defined by what is increasingly identified as Talal Asad's (or even the "Asadian") school—but rather on how its unfolding generated patterns of civility, after which I preliminarily addressed how those patterns invigorated sociopolitical institutions. As the present volume is primarily dedicated to clarifying the relationship between Islam, institution-building, and statehood, both historically and conceptually, I follow Roberto Esposito in abstaining from providing a formalized definition of what an institution is and, more importantly, what an instituting process entails. Instead, I adopt a gradual approach to elucidating the type of process at stake—one that, because it is entangled with the building of human life, cannot begin by privileging a formal institutional dimension. After all, there would be no easy consensus for such a formal definition, even among sociologists. In this respect, I take an initial clue from a notable loose end in the conceptual apparatus associated with Asad's school, which has quite radically shunned the formalism of the social sciences.[14]

A few reflections are needed to explain the significance of this loose end for the theme at hand. It is helpful to go back to Bryan Turner for a moment. He closely interacted with Talal Asad both during their shared endeavors in the 1970s to launch a critique of Orientalism (Salvatore 2021, 50–51) and more recently when both scholars held professorships at the Graduate School of The City University of New York (CUNY). This is why Turner (2023, 69) is well positioned to remind us of how Asad's criticism of anthropology as a colonial science was instrumental in launching the project of a new anthropology of Islam (Asad [1986] 2009). While the notion of Islam as a discursive tradition was its centerpiece, the project prominently included a view of "instituted practices" through which "Muslims are inducted as Muslims" (ibid., 21, also quoted in Turner 2023, 69). Now, it is well known that the approach of Asad's school has acquired merits for rightly critiquing the dominance of the Western notion of religion as well as its "secular" counterpart, exposing the way this hegemony worked not just conceptually and discursively but by being nested in colonial and orientalist institutions. However, while highlighting "instituted practices" among Muslims—rather than treating Islam as a reified "religion"—the approach tended to leave unexamined the very processes through which such practices become instituted, that is, the instituting process at the heart of this volume. This omission meant that Asad and his school implicitly relied on an inherited and largely Western notion of "institution," itself as tailormade to Western disciplining discourses as the category of "religion." Such tacit acceptance of colonial vocabulary limits the project's capacity to interrogate the specific modes of instituting practices in the Islamic ecumene.

An even more problematic consequence is the assumption that practices are already and consistently "instituted," as suggested in the very quotation Turner draws from Asad—an assumption that brackets out the instituting dimension altogether. Shouldn't this Western colonial vocabulary be unpacked and reconstructed not merely through a "smart critique" (which Asad himself often admitted was insufficient) but through the adoption of a consistent Islamic frame? This step cannot be reduced to conceptual engineering, for developing an Islamic frame makes sense only if it blurs, rather than fortifies, the insider–outsider distinction. In other words, what social space could Islam's "discursive tradition" inhabit if it had not effectively instituted practices across centuries? Surely, we should acknowledge that Asad and his school are in excellent company in taking for granted, within the study of Islam, the notion of institution and, even more, the instituting process.[15]

The comparative historical sociologist and social theorist[16] Johann P. Arnason (2003, 214) provided a preliminary, if illuminating, insight into this question. He suggested a distinction between a meta-institutional (or, we would say here more dynamically, "instituting") vs. an institutional (or "instituted") dimension of the process of creating and ordering the social bond. The process comprises imaginative and interpretative aspects, including reflections on how these two dimensions relate to one another—operations that a deceivingly compact and seemingly self-sufficient (but in fact quite tautological) concept like "practice," which became popular in cultural anthropology between the 1970s and 1980s as a reaction against overly systemic and static models of "culture," risks obscuring. Regarding this question, Asad's school has unpacked the self-sufficiency of practice by invoking a theological conceptualization of the virtuous self's dispositions, adapting it from Aquinas through the work of the Catholic moral philosopher Alasdair MacIntyre (1988). In this theological shortcircuit, the referral of practice to what Asad—largely following MacIntyre—called a discursive tradition fostered an under-conceptualization of the instituting process itself. The process of instituting practices—or, less tautologically and more sociologically, the instituting process—was particularly well defined and robust in the medieval Catholic tradition of Aquinas via the conception of the Church as a "corporate" institution (a mystical body, ultimately the instituted body of Christ) articulated through medieval canon-law jurists (see Chapter 4). By contrast, as I will argue in this book, the instituting process in the Islamic ecumene unfolded by shunning incorporation. Most crucially, it did not depend on the authority of any Church-like corporate institution, nor did it draw on the political theologies that legitimized such institutions (see Chapter 9). This is why it is highly problematic to extract the institutional bearings of the "Islamic tradition"—and the associated concept of "practice"—from a work like MacIntyre's, which is explicitly tailored to the theological and institutional universe of medieval Roman Catholicism.

Arnason's argument on the meta-institutional dimension to be distinguished from specific institutions helps fill the gap, or tighten the loose ends, left open by Asad and his school. The argument suggests that the type of socioreligious knowledge and habitus that enables "practice" in Asad's sense operates as a meta-institutional—or, better, instituting—force. Arnason's reflections thus reopen the question of the cultural and, potentially, "religious" (and in the European case, even "theological") determination of what counts as an institution. From this enlarged viewpoint, one should then be ready to hypothesize that an institution is neither the telos nor the mere facilitator of practice. It follows that, within an Islamic frame—unshaped by anything comparable to Latin Christendom's systematic theology and its nexus to a political theology that instituted the Church as a "corporation" (see Chapter 4)—what we can trace is a protean, continuous, instituting (and at times destituting) process. In other words, what matters most is the process-like dimension of what we imperfectly (and still eurocentrically) call an "institution." Following Arnason's lead, in turn inspired by scholars of the caliber of Merleau-Ponty, Castoriadis, and Mauss—who also influenced Roberto Esposito's idea of "instituting life" (2020, 179–181)—we can discern that a possible key to conceptualizing the instituting process writ large, particularly in the Islamic context, lies in a notion of habitus animated by the twin forces of affect and imagination, which I will address in Chapter 2 (see also Bottici 2019).

Such preliminary reflections on the need to stop taking for granted what is an "institution" and its process of formation should be followed by turning to a recent trilogy of Roberto Esposito, on which I will selectively, if critically, draw to clarify the very process-like character of institutional formations in the Islamic ecumene—or, to paraphrase the title of the present volume, how the ecumene itself was instituted in ways that made it "Islamic" (Esposito [2020] 2021b; [2021] 2022; [2023] 2025a). Additionally, this trilogy helps clarify—and provincialize—the meta-institutional force of conventional Western notions of religion as shaped by the institutional history of Latin Christendom and its Church. Here "the Italian difference" becomes visible in its resolute and transparent handling of a political theology deeply ingrained in the history (and success) of Latin Christendom. In parallel, and by reflex, it helps disentangle from that trajectory both "religion" and the instituting process powered by its meta-institutional force. The combined effect of critically reassessing the Latin Christian articulation of "religion" and "institution" is to open alternate vistas that resonate with the Islamic frame, within which, as we will see, it would be moot to seek a sharp distinction between "religion" and "civility." In other words, the "Italian difference" sensitizes us to recognize the "Islamic difference" in articulating—and, to some extent, amalgamating—"religion" and "civility" as the meta-institutional engines of a Janus-faced instituting process.

I am suggesting that, by embracing an Islamic frame through the helping lens of Southern/Italian theory, we are enabled to focus on the nexus—however unstable—between life, civility, and institution without needing to predetermine which meta-institutional dimensions of "religion" can support that axis. Most crucially, this nexus activates an open-ended, non-teleological instituting process. This idea can be fruitful in loosening the grip of the conceptual religio-civilizational straitjacket that Western thought (and not merely what we call Orientalism) has imposed on the study of Islam and the Islamic ecumene. Through this approach, we can understand *'umran* as the expression of a meta-institutional force working through narrative and habitus and the ensuing enactment of life forms, as I will argue in this book starting from Chapter 2. We will see how the process ultimately reflects a fundamental level of indistinction between what we have been educated to regard as "religion" versus "civility." It would make little sense to single out either component as the preeminent meta-institutional force—as if we were pitting Durkheim (who privileged religion) against Elias (who focused on civility).[17]

This is how Southern/Italian thought offers an original, if robust, conceptual framework that enables us to circumvent Western dichotomous conceptualizations. We should, however, drop the somewhat naive hope that, with just one clever move of deconstruction, we could emancipate ourselves from the Western "religio-civilizational" straitjacket. This straitjacket has long provided the main prism through which non-Western traditions were objectified as comparatively imperfect instantiations of the very model the West tailored to itself (cf. Masuzawa 2005). This is also why, while embracing an Islamic frame in pursuing an alternative approach, our minds cannot be hijacked by an obsessive search for "the right" emic terms to match what an established Western conceptual vocabulary might take as the essence of religion or the ethos of civility, and the processes of instituting them. Rather than chasing isolated concepts to be listed in static encyclopedias, we should search for dynamic networks of key ideas—no doubt associated with emic terms—that designate original, open-ended processes. As an example, while invoking the authority of key thinkers like Ibn Khaldun and drawing on the growing insights of intellectual and institutional history, one could (at least provisionally) identify *ʿumran* as the primary semantic terrain marking the instituting dimension of civility via burgeoning, shared life, given its linkages to other key concepts used by Ibn Khaldun and others. Conversely, the combined concepts of *adab–siyasa* (as alluded to in Volume I and further expounded in the present book) can be taken to represent another crucial aspect of what is meant by "civility" in its mildly instituted dimension: namely, as a habitus or cultural technique for managing self–other relations, with the potential to infuse the field of activities that we identify with governance.

As also shown by Ibn Khaldun, religion is not the primal force of social cohesion or solidarity (*ʿasabiyya*). Nevertheless, at crucial historical junctures, religion remolds and redirects it via modalities that include, by default, a "civilizing" effect (see Chapter 5). As a concrete instantiation of how to loosen the religio-civilizational straitjacket in the analysis of the Islamic ecumene, Chapter 2 will begin by identifying the religious side of the coin with a concrete corpus, namely, *hadith*, and (political) civility with a distinct body of knowledge and practice, namely, *adab-siyasa*, moving from their initial distinction toward a mutual dialectic. This process involving the two corpora turned out to ignite, in several periods and locales of the ecumene, a twinning narrative and discursive configuration feeding the fundamental grid of habitualization, which is in turn a condition for the instituting process. This process can be identified, analyzed, and tested much more directly than generic predications of Islam as religion and/or civility (or, even more bluntly and eurocentrically, as civilization) would allow for.

In parallel, one should be prepared to take a few more steps in liberating the idea of the institution and the instituting process from the strictures imposed on it by mainstream Western social theory, which has trapped it in a cloud of symbols generated from within a stubborn (if often unconfessed) Christocentric political theology. This shift is crucial if we are to avoid reinscribing in Islam the very eurocentric assumptions we seek to critique. After examining the two ubiquitous formations of the *tariqa* (Chapter 3) and the *waqf* (Chapter 4), we will turn to an appraisal of how a Khaldunian approach can contribute to reconstructing viable views of the instituting process in the Islamic ecumene (Chapter 5). We will continue by examining how, in the early modern, precolonial era, the process ushered in the production of original forms of statehood, thereby challenging the universality of the Western notion of sovereignty (Chapters 6–8). The last part of the book will deepen the key question initially broached in Volume I, namely, the reassessment of statecraft and statehood as the supposed pinnacles of the instituting process and integrators of the knowledge–power dynamics (Chapter 9 and Conclusion).

Without a focus on how statehood derives from instituting processes, any conceptualization of "sovereignty" in Islamic (or, as we will see, "super-Islamic") terms would, at best, amount to a worn-out exercise in measuring deficits against Western Westphalian standards. What follows, instead, is an attempt to account for original and multilayered conceptions of rulership whose patterns of legitimation differed from—and were in many respects more complex than—those that culminated in Europe with Westphalian state formations. The trajectories and entanglements that produced early modern sociopolitical formations in the Islamic ecumene yield a multilevel type of statehood, nourished by distinctive institutional practices and notions of sovereignty that crystallized long before Western colonial encroachments on Muslim lands. They are therefore irreducible to the patterns prevailing within a postcolonial nation-state framework struggling to mimic Westphalian norms. Given the historical and geopolitical centrality of the Islamic ecumene delineated in the previous volume, these processes offer a more plausible benchmark for interregional comparison—one that looks East rather than West. This orientation will hopefully come to fuller fruition in Volume III of the trilogy.[18]

Notes

1. This chapter provides the reflexive and methodological scaffolding for the volume. Readers primarily interested in the historical and conceptual argument may proceed directly to Chapter 2, returning here as needed for a discussion of the epistemic foundations of the Islamic frame.
2. Personal communication by the author (January 2021). See also https://www.acu.edu.au/research-and-enterprise/our-research-institutes/institute-for-humanities-and-social-sciences/our-people/bryan-turner (accessed 5 July 2025).
3. This study belongs to an intersecting yet distinct project underway (Salvatore and Obuse, forthcoming) envisioned as the volume completing our trilogy.
4. I refrain from reporting here on my visit to ISTAC solely because it pertains more directly to the book project referenced in the preceding footnote.
5. An example would be explaining how the centrality of the Islamic ecumene in human history was obliterated through its capitulation to Western colonial and imperial hegemony.
6. This was addressed even more explicitly in a paper I presented at the College of Islamic Studies, Hamad Bin Khalifa University, Doha, in February 2025, as I was completing the final stages of work on this volume (Salvatore 2025).
7. As a prominent example from among the many colleagues and friends whose trajectories likewise begin in this region, I limit myself to mentioning Gennaro Gervasio and Andrea Teti, who through their numerous co-authored works have also foregrounded the influence of Southern/Italian thought, most notably via Gramsci (see, e.g., Gervasio and Teti 2024).
8. The dissertation was later reworked and published (Salvatore 1997) without altering its basic approach.
9. Gramsci has frequently been displaced from this trajectory through an overly facile "pairing" with Foucault in early anglophone engagements with continental critical thought and, later, in some emergent decolonial approaches—including, to an extent, in Edward Said's own elaborations.
10. It cannot go unmentioned that the same historical conditions that produced the reflexivity of German and Italian sociopolitical thought—namely, their belated nation-state formation and the tension between universality and lateness—also incubated fascism in both contexts, culminating in the

Holocaust. As of autumn 2025, this unresolved legacy has resurfaced in the starkly divergent responses of the two countries to the ethnic cleansing, war crimes, crimes against humanity, and genocidal violence directed against the Palestinian people—most formally substantiated in Gaza, yet increasingly situated within a broader structure of occupation, forced displacement, and colonial erasure. On the one hand, both governments—supported by compliant media ecosystems—have distinguished themselves in Europe for adopting extreme positions that rationalize or downplay these crimes. Acting in concert, they have obstructed even minimal institutional responses, such as EU-level initiatives to suspend Israel's access to those parts of the Horizon 2020 research program that support startups involved in military-related technologies, or to reconsider the preferential trade regime afforded under the EU–Israel Association Agreement and its human-rights clauses (to say nothing of their refusal to recognize the state of Palestine). On the other hand, the most glaring sign of continuity with the fascist past in Germany has been the systematic repression of Jewish voices—including students, faculty, and activists—who have denounced the genocide. Both those subjected to repression and numerous critical observers have identified these measures as a reiteration, under formally democratic and hypocritically moralist guises, of antisemitic policies (see Jewish Solidarity Collective, 2025). Far from facilitating redemption from the crimes of national socialism, this pattern has been aptly described as a new form of state antisemitism. As eloquently formulated by Dirk Moses (2025) in a piece published on the website of the American-German Institute:

> In trying to exorcise its anti-Semitic demon, German leaders are inadvertently activating it as well as other German demons: in targeting progressive Jews and in using anti-anti-Semitism measures against Arabs and leftists, all the while undermining the *Rechtsstaat* in the name of state power and whiteness. Even Zionist Jews who oppose the Israeli government and its war are not spared. In this way, *Staatsräson* becomes a form of state anti-Semitism, driven by an army of non-Jewish, state-employed anti-Semitism commissioners.

This approach homogenizes Jews as a monolithic entity, ignoring the plurality of Jewish positions and thereby reproducing the very logic that has long underpinned antisemitism. Equally emblematic is the case of the most prominent living German thinker, Jürgen Habermas, who in 2003 helped mobilize a European intellectual front against the U.S.-led invasion of Iraq—an intervention he heralded as marking the emergence of a pan-European public sphere (Esposito 2016, 196), yet has now hastened to defend Israel's actions in Gaza. His stance reveals how the German, time-honored project of "critical reason," reaching back to Immanuel Kant, has become ensnared in a distorted ethos of *Staatsräson* and guilt management, today perpetuated with the active complicity of university leadership. On the racial underpinnings of Kant's universalism, see Bernasconi

(2011); on the neocolonial ethnocentrism in Habermas's own project, see Ahmad (2025).

In a different trajectory—and despite a government whose main coalition party's very logo, a tricolor flame, is directly linked to post-war neo-fascist movements—the Italian grassroots has displayed a markedly different sensibility. Within the stream of Southern/Italian thought that informs this volume, Roberto Esposito's latest intervention (2025b) insists that the fascist legacy cannot be sealed off as a past aberration in Western history. Rather, it must be confronted as a self-perpetuating metaphysical machine of modern power, one that captures bodies and life itself (see Chapter 9). As Rocco Ronchi (2025a) notes, Esposito descends into the darkness of these dynamics to expose an enduring matrix of Western modern rationality which, as he and others argue (cf. Chambers 2025), is inherently colonial and often genocidal. This emphasis on confronting rather than compartmentalizing the legacies of modern power directly resonates with the epistemic concern of this chapter: namely, how unresolved historical formations shape the conditions under which knowledge, critique, and political imagination become possible. This inflection of sociopolitical thought found a striking echo in Italy, the only European country where solidarity with the Palestinian people reached the scale of a national civic uprising. Early October 2025 witnessed multi-million demonstrations after the Israeli seizure of the Global Sumud Flotilla; a nationwide general strike in late November followed, with Genoa dockworkers hosting speeches by Greta Thunberg and Francesca Albanese—the Campania-born Southern Italian jurist who rose to global prominence for her unrelenting denunciation of the genocide as UN Human Rights Council Special Rapporteur. As the leading Sicily-born social scientist Donatella Della Porta emphasized in her analyses and public interventions, the mobilization brought together dockworkers, students, grassroots unions, pacifists, feminists, and faith communities (see also Ronchi 2025b). City councils—including that of Rome—raised the Palestinian flag in open defiance of the government. Such forms of civic insurgency demonstrate how alternative repertoires of political agency can emerge from subaltern or liminal sites—precisely the kinds of sites that, as argued throughout this chapter, enable epistemic repositioning beyond hegemonic frames. By contrast, the harsh repression of comparable mobilizations in Germany, as Della Porta argued, reproduced rather than overcame fascist-colonial patterns of domination (Della Porta 2024; 2025). Francesca Albanese likewise documented these dynamics in her 2025 report, identifying Germany as an "enabling" state whose military and political support for Israel contributes to what she terms a system of genocide—a characterization resonant with the ICJ case Nicaragua v. Germany, which alleges German breaches of the Genocide Convention. It is therefore unsurprising that several of Albanese's speeches in Germany, including at universities, were cancelled or obstructed. During her February 2025 visit, she reported a pervasive climate of intimidation: venues changed at the last minute, heavy policing, vandalized event sites, and threats of arrest under German laws governing speech and assembly (Steinberg 2025). These contrasting trajectories between Italy and Germany thus provide an instructive lens through which to view the broader methodological argument of this chapter: namely, that epistemic repositioning is not an abstract stance but is conditioned by concrete histories of power, repression, and civic imagination. Where the German response reveals the closure of epistemic space through *Staatsräson* and guilt-management, the Italian case—however fragile—illustrates openings for alternative frames of understanding and critique.

My main concern here lies less in chronicling these movements of resistance than in showing how they articulate the only genuinely antifascist stance capable of denouncing the crime of genocide as integral to the reenactment of fascism and antisemitism—now reconfigured within a new geopolitical constellation—as forms of organized violence against the *damnés de la terre*. The genocidal violence exercised against the Palestinian people is both a culmination and a warning of further climaxes in fascist crimes, including those directed against migrants from the Global South. It is in this context that Southern/Italian thought—also thanks to its lucidity in diagnosing fascism as the belated, if predictable, spin-off of the metaphysical machine of Western political theology—emerges as a privileged, living critique of domination. It offers conceptual resources for problematizing statehood and the lopsided colonial normativity built into Western modernity. By exposing the continuities between the theopolitical machine, fascist repression, and the biopolitical rationalities that enabled the rise of the West and its colonial–imperial domination, this trajectory of thought retains a distinctive diagnostic power. Further discussions of these continuities—including the comparable Japanese case—will be developed in Volume III of this trilogy.

11. All major works of Esposito have been translated into English. In this volume, I will quote from English translations whenever possible; otherwise, I will reference the original Italian publications.
12. Yet as a sociologist I became accustomed to bringing this stream of scholarship into dialogue with another that has only recently attracted sustained attention in anglophone circles. This is the work associated with a fellow sociologist, the late Franco Cassano ([1996] 2012) from the University of Bari in Apulia. He termed it *pensiero meridiano*—"meridional" or "Southern" thought—in a deliberately provocative pun that inverts what, after the violent Italian unification (that is, the annexation of the South), came to be known as the *questione meridionale*, the Southern question. That label encapsulated the hegemonic Northern Italian view that the South was inherently backward (rather than rendered so through domestic colonial subjugation) and therefore in need of being civilized and developed. Where the *questione meridionale* casts the South as a bundle of

deficits to be remedied, *pensiero meridiano* refigures it as an epistemic resource—a vantage point from which to rethink categories, challenge hegemonic binaries, and articulate modes of thought not predetermined by Northern or "Western" norms. In contrast to the *questione meridionale*, which positions the South as a passive object of corrective intervention, *pensiero meridiano* foregrounds the South as a locus of conceptual autonomy and as a generator of alternative intellectual itineraries capable of unsettling the inherited epistemic grid.

13. The attentive reader will have noticed that these concepts have also—if not primarily—been popularized in the English-speaking world by another Italian thinker, this time from Rome: Giorgio Agamben. My decision to focus instead on Esposito reflects both the role he has played in my own intellectual trajectory and the shared sociocultural predicament of Naples and Southern Italy outlined above. We were also affiliated with the same university in Naples, though not at the same time.
14. My experience and appreciation of the Asadian school were not only mediated by readings, but also by sustained exchanges with members of its "second generation," which proved formative for my own trajectory toward articulating an Islamic frame at a crucial stage. Foremost among these interlocutors were scholars of the caliber of Saba Mahmood, Charles Hirschkind, and Hussein Agrama, with whom I had frequent and searching conversations during overlapping periods of research in Cairo in the late 1990s.
15. A recent and particularly notable instance of this omission can be found in an otherwise valuable discussion of Sufi institutions (Green 2021).
16. Among mainstream Western sociologists, Arnason's sustained engagement with Islam (and with Hodgson) renders him comparable only to Bryan Turner. This affinity also explains why Arnason acted at various stages of my intellectual trajectory as a mentor, and why our paths intersected in several collaborative undertakings.
17. In this sense, I am revising what I wrote in Volume I (Salvatore 2016, 7), where—under the influence of Arnason, himself drawing on Durkheim—I attributed a meta-institutional force to a robustly resilient "religion" that, as it unfolded through the knowledge–power equation, generated patterns of civility only as a derivative effect.
18. An important recent contribution by Hendrik Spruyt (2020) attempts to move comparative analysis beyond Western models of statehood. Yet it does so within analytical parameters that ultimately reproduce a "religio-civilizational" straitjacket and remain calibrated to the expectations of an International Relations audience. What thereby drops out of view is precisely the instituting process: the complex sociopolitical and cultural labor through which forms of rule take shape, stabilize, and become intelligible—a labor that cannot be reduced to the classificatory schemas of International Relations nor to the abstracted comparison of "civilizations." A similar pattern recurs, albeit with different emphases, in Ayşe Zarakol's more recent reconstruction (2022) of an

"Asian" or "Eastern" international state system preceding Westphalia and structured around post-Mongol polities. Situated even more firmly than Spruyt's contribution within the disciplinary limits of International Relations, this work tends to confine the genesis of statehood to dynastic organization and elite power structures, thereby underplaying the broader sociopolitical and cultural processes from which statehood emerges. Unlike Spruyt, however, Zarakol does discern how Khaldunian questions resonated within the early modern empires of the Islamic ecumene and how they gestured toward what I will call, in Chapters 5–9, the political cosmology animating their forms of statehood. Yet even here the relevance of these questions tends to be primarily situated within the sphere of dynastic ideology, which is taken to provide the principal contours of a non- or pre-Westphalian "world order." Seen from the vantage point of an Islamic frame—attuned to the meta-institutional dynamics of *'umran* and to the instituting processes that exceed both dynastic politics and the conceptual grids of International Relations—these otherwise valuable studies highlight, by contrast, what is at stake in shifting the analytical focus from civilizations and dynasties to the open-ended processes through which life, civility, and institutions co-constitute one another.

References

Ahmad, Irfan. 2025. "Habermas as an Ethnic Thinker *Par Excellence*: On Critique, Palestine and the Role of intellectuals." *Teaching in Higher Education: Critical Perspectives* 30 (6): 1343–62.

Ahmed, Shahab. 2016. *What Is Islam? The Importance of Being Islamic*. Princeton, NJ: Princeton University Press.

Arnason, Johann P. 2003. *Civilisations in Dispute: Historical Questions and Theoretical Traditions*. Leiden: Brill.

Asad, Talal [1986] 2009. "The Idea of an Anthropology of Islam." *Qui Parle* 17 (2): 1–30.

al-Attas, Syed Muhammad Naquib. 1995. *Prolegomena to the Metaphysics of Islam: An Exposition of the Fundamental Elements of the Worldview of Islam*. Kuala Lumpur: International Institute of Islamic Thought and Civilization (ISTAC).

Bamyeh, Mohammed A. 2019. *Lifeworlds of Islam. The Pragmatics of a Religion*. Oxford: University Press.

Bernasconi, Robert. 2011. "Kant's Third Thoughts on Race." In *Reading Kant's Geography*, edited by Stuart Elden and Eduardo Mendieta, 291–318. Albany: State University of New York Press.

Bhambra, Gurminder K., and John Holmwood. 2021. *Colonialism and Modern Social Theory*. Cambridge: Polity Press.

Bodei, Remo. 2017. "Sulla forza dell'effetto." In *Effetto Italian Thought*, edited by Enrica Lisciani-Petrini and Giuseppina Strummiello, 45–60. Macerata: Quodlibet.

Bortolini, Matteo. 2021. *A Joyfully Serious Man: The Life of Robert Bellah*. Princeton, NJ: Princeton University Press.

Bottici, Chiara. 2019. "Imagination, Imaginary, Imaginal: Towards a New Social Ontology? *Social Epistemology*" 33 (5): 433–41.

Bottici, Chiara, and Benoît Challand. 2021. "Toward an Interstitial Global Critical Theory." *Globalizations* 18 (8): 1150–68.

Brankley Abbas, Megan. 2021. *Whose Islam? The Western University and Modern Islamic Thought in Indonesia*. Stanford, CA: Stanford University Press.

Cassano, Franco [1996]. 2012. *Southern Thought and Other Essays on the Mediterranean*. Translated and with an Introduction by Norma Bouchard and Valerio Ferme. New York: Fordham University Press.

Chambers, Iain. 2008. *Mediterranean Crossings: The Politics of an Interrupted Modernity*. Durham, NC: Duke University Press.

Chambers, Iain. 2025. *Lampedusa/Gaza. L'orologio coloniale e i linguaggi interrotti*. Milan: Orthotes.

Dainotto, Roberto M. 2007. *Europe (in Theory)*. Durham, NC: Duke University Press.

Dayeh, Islam, and Markus Messling, eds. 2020. "*Early Modern 'New Sciences' Inquiries into Ibn Khaldun and Giambattista Vico*." *Philological Encounters* 5 (1): 1–96.

Della Porta, Donatella. 2024. "Moral Panic? The Contentious Politics of Anti-Semitism in Germany." Free University, Berlin, 19 December. Accessed 12 November 2025. https://www.interact.fu-berlin.de/en/News/INTERACT_conversations_5_Della_Porta.html.

Della Porta, Donatella. 2025. "Eventful Protests Against the Israeli Genocide: The Italian 'Hot Summer' for a Free Palestine." *Logos. A Journal of Modern Society and Culture*. 24 (1–2) Accessed 12 November 2025. https://logosjournal.com/article/eventful-protests-against-the-israeli-genocide-the-italian-hot-summer-for-a-free-palestine/.

Elias, Norbert [1939; 1968]. 2000. *The Civilizing Process*. Oxford: Blackwell.

Eriksson, Bo. 1993. "Adam Smith and Sociology." *European Journal of Sociology* 34 (2): 303–24.

Esposito, Roberto [2010]. 2012. *Living Thought: The Origins and Actuality of Italian Philosophy*. Translated by Zakiya Hanafi. Stanford, CA: Stanford University Press.

Esposito, Roberto. 2016. *Da fuori: Una filosofia per l'Europa*. Torino: Einaudi.

Esposito, Roberto. 2020. *Pensiero istituente: Tre paradigmi di ontologia politica*. Torino: Einaudi.

Esposito, Roberto. 2021a, *Instituting Life: Essays on Biopolitics, Subjectivity, and Modernity*, edited by Ines S. Zupanov. Translated by Timothy Campbell. Cambridge: Polity Press.

Esposito, Roberto [2020] 2021b. *Instituting Thought: Three Paradigms of Political Ontology*. Translated by Zakiya Hanafi. Cambridge: Polity Press.

Esposito, Roberto [2021] 2022. *Institution*. Translated by Zakiya Hanafi. Cambridge: Polity Press.

Esposito, Roberto [2023] 2025a. *Vitam Instituere: A Genealogy of the Institution*. Translated by Zakiya Hanafi. Cambridge: Polity Press.

Esposito, Roberto. 2025b. *Il fascismo e noi. Un'interpretazione filosofica*. Torino: Einaudi.

al-Faruqi, Ismail Raji. 1982. *Islamization of Knowledge: General Principles and Workplan*. Herndon, VA: International Institute of Islamic Thought.

Gabrieli, Francesco. 1975. "Ibn Khaldun: Il Vico dell'Islam." *Bollettino del Centro di Studi Vichiani* 5: 122–6.

Ghamari-Tabrizi, Behrooz. 2016. *Foucault in Iran: Islamic Revolution after the Enlightenment*. Minneapolis: University of Minnesota Press.

Green, Nile. 2021. "Rethinking the Institutionalization of Islamic Mysticism: A Review Essay of *Sufi Institutions,* edited by Alexandre Papas, Leiden: Brill 2020." *Journal of Sufi Studies* 10 (1–2): 235–52.

Jewish Solidarity Collective. 2025. "'Nicht in unserem Namen' – Erfahrungsberichte jüdischer Studierender in Deutschland." *etos.media,* 31 October. Accessed 12 November 2025. https://etosmedia.de/politik/nicht-in-unserem-namen-erfahrungsberichte-juedischer-studierender-in-deutschland/.

MacIntyre, Alasdair. 1988. *Whose Justice? Which Rationality?* London: Duckworth.

Masuzawa, Tomoko. 2005. *The Invention of World Religions: Or How European Universalism Was Preserved in the Language Pluralism*. Chicago: University of Chicago Press.

Messahel, Fatma. 2025. "History and Cyclical Equivalence: A Comparative Approach between Ibn Khaldun and Vico." *Review of Contemporary Philosophy* 24 (1): 222–9.

Moses, Dirk. 2025. "The German Reason of State as State Anti-Semitism." *American-German Institute*, January 28. Accessed 12 November 2025. https://americangerman.institute/2025/01/the-german-reason-of-state-as-state-anti-semitism/.

Pandolfi, Mariella. 1998. "Two Italies: Rhetorical Figures of Failed Nationhood." In *Italy's 'Southern Question': Orientalism in One Country*, edited by Jane Schneider, 285–9. Oxford: Berg.

Robertson, John. 2005. *The Case for the Enlightenment: Scotland and Naples, 1680–1760*. Cambridge: Cambridge University Press.

Ronchi, Rocco. 2025a. "Roberto Esposito nelle tenebre del fascismo." *Doppiozero*, 26 September. https://www.doppiozero.com/roberto-esposito-nelle-tenebre-del-fascismo.

Ronchi, Rocco. 2025b. "Dalla politica alla geopolitica: minoranze antagoniste." *Doppiozero*, 28 October. https://www.doppiozero.com/dalla-politica-alla-geopolitica-minoranze-antagoniste.

Salvatore, Armando. 1997. *Islam and the Political Discourse of Modernity*. Reading: Ithaca Press.

Salvatore, Armando. 2016. *The Sociology of Islam: Knowledge, Power and Civility*. Oxford: Wiley Blackwell.

Salvatore, Armando. 2021. "The Sociology of Islam: Beyond Orientalism, Toward Transculturality? In *Exploring Islam Beyond Orientalism and Occidentalism: Sociological Approaches*, edited by Christel Gärtner and Heidemarie Winkel, 43–63. Wiesbaden: Springer VS.

Salvatore, Armando. 2025. "ReOrienting the Islamic Ecumene: Narrative, Habitus, and Institution." Public Lecture, College of Islamic Studies, Hamad Bin Khalifa University, Doha, 5 February.

Salvatore, Armando, and Kieko Obuse. 2021. "ReOrienting Religion? An East–West Entanglement." *Implicit Religion* 24 (3–4): 331–52.

Salvatore, Armando, and Kieko Obuse. 2022. "What Went Wrong? Western Sociology and the Fiction of the Middle East." In *The Oxford Handbook of the Sociology of the Middle East*, edited by Armando Salvatore, Sari Hanafi, and Kieko Obuse, 3–25. Oxford: Oxford University Press.

Schneider, Jane, ed. 1998. *Italy's "Southern Question": Orientalism in One Country*. Oxford: Berg.

Spruyt, Hendrik. 2020. *The World Imagined: Collective Beliefs and Political Order in the Sinocentric, Islamic, and Southeast Asian International Societies*. Cambridge: Cambridge University Press.

Stauth, Georg. 1993. *Islam und westlicher Rationalismus: Der Beitrag des Orientalismus zur Entstehung der Soziologie*. Frankfurt am Main: Campus.

Steinberg, Stefan. 2025. "Massive Police Intimidation of UN Special Rapporteur Francesca Albanese in Berlin." *World Socialist Web Site*, 20 February. Accessed 12 November 2025. https://www.wsws.org/en/articles/2025/02/20/92d0-f20.html?utm_source=chatgpt.com.

Trabant, Jürgen. 2021. "Vico and Ibn Khaldûn: Polis and Logos." *Bollettino del Centro di Studi Vichiani* 51 (1): 133–51.

Turner, Bryan S. 1974. *Weber and Islam: A Critical Study*. London: Routledge & Kegan Paul.

Turner, Bryan S. 1976. "Conscience in the Construction of Religion: A Critique of Marshall G. S. Hodgson's *The Venture of Islam*." *Review of Middle East Studies* 10 (1): 17–38.

Turner, Bryan S. 1978. *Marx and the End of Orientalism*. London: George Allen & Unwin.

Turner, Bryan S. 2023. *Understanding Islam: Positions of Knowledge*. Edinburgh: Edinburgh University Press.

Watt, W. Montgomery. 1959. *What Is Islam?* London: Longmans, Green and Co.

Yücesoy, Hayrettin. 2023. *Disenchanting the Caliphate: The Secular Discipline of Power in Abbasid Political Thought*. New York: Columbia University Press.

Zarakol, Ayşe. 2022. *Before the West: The Rise and Fall of Eastern World Orders*. Cambridge: Cambridge University Press.

2

Triggering the Instituting Process
From Narrative to Habitus

Adab and *Hadith*: Distinction of Registers Within a Narrative Continuum?

In the endeavor to contribute to spelling out what is Islamic in the Islamic ecumene, this chapter investigates the inception of the instituting process through a focus on the dynamics of narration and habitualization.[1] The chapter argues that the instituting process within the Islamic ecumene originates in an interplay of storytelling, emulation, and habitualization that both precedes and grounds the emergence of formal normativity. Against this backdrop, it maintains that *hadith* and *adab*, though distinct in register and genealogy, form a narrative continuum shaping Islamic life forms. This orientation diverges from the common strategy in Islamic Studies that turns immediately to the conceptual foundations of jurists' law (*usul al-fiqh*) when explaining the rise of Islamic normativity. *Fiqh*—including the overarching principle of *maslaha*, or "common good"—crystallized as a crucial specialized field within this broader instituting process. Yet this process clearly encompasses much more than the formation of norms, which appear not as its trigger but as belonging to its eventual products.[2]

I fully agree with Shahab Ahmed that we should avoid incurring the familiar reductionist view of "the Islamic" through the comprehensive lens of *shari'a* normativity. As is now much better recognized than a few decades ago, *shari'a* should be understood as embracing the idea of Islamic normativity issued from a divine decree, rather than bluntly defined (in reality, mistranslated) as "Islamic law" (Buskens and Dupret 2015). This expression conveys the lopsided impression of a searchable code, which *shari'a* never was. More crucially, it asserts the existence of an ostensibly Islamic instance of the general category of "law," too often understood—especially by non-specialists—through its Western genealogy and thereby taken as normative without residues. Given the centrality of law within the Western instituting process leading to statehood, the expression ultimately insinuates that "Islamic law" is what makes Islam fully—indeed politically—Islamic. This is precisely what Shahab Ahmed (2016) sought to refute through his sensibly argued and erudite book.

Therefore, we should place the emergence of normativity within the broader process through which patterns of habitualization contribute to instituting life forms, providing the means for managing the social bond and governing human relations. Put differently, the process cannot be reconstructed by presuming *shari'a* as a ready-made normative framework. It is, rather, the reverse: the key dimensions of the instituting process must first be identified in order to illuminate the logic of practicing *fiqh* and how it contributes to the importance of being Islamic. From this perspective, the process unfolds through threads of habitus formation, sustained by narratives that, in turn, feed into institutional forms and in so doing shape the production of norms. Against this backdrop, the chapter turns to two major narrative corpora: the exemplary prophetic sayings and deeds (*hadith*) and the multi-genre compendia that articulate forms of a "good life" in ways that are at once ethical and aesthetic (*adab*). While *hadith* and *adab* differ in register and formality—one canonizes exemplary conduct, the other elaborates it through worldly, literary, and courtly idioms—they nonetheless participate in a shared narrative-to-habitus continuum.

I will contend that the combined and often mutually interpenetrating dynamics of the two narrative registers provided the generative codes for instituting practices in the Islamic ecumene. In this light, such practices are neither independent of the narratives that animate them nor reducible to narrowly "pious" comportments. Rather, their exemplary force makes them pivotal in the gradual formation of proper institutions, to be analyzed in the chapters that follow. What ultimately matters is that practices innervated by habitus become adequate to the "bustling life" (*'umran*) of the ecumene—in other words, to the expectations, pressures, and needs that arose among its various groups and interlocutors. This, I argue, is where the instituting process gathers its momentum and where the narrative-to-habitus continuum becomes historically generative.

The prophetic narrative of *hadith* and the courtly narrative of *adab* began to crystallize in tandem, consistently coming into view from the 2nd century after the inception of Islam. The *hadith* corpus, composed of selected and authenticated sayings and deeds of Prophet Muhammad, furnished not only a necessary repository of precedent but also a vivid dramatization of the legitimacy and appeal of what came to be known—based on a symbolically pregnant Qur'anic keyword—as the Islamic *shari'a*. By contrast, *adab* emerged as a counterpoint to the *hadith–shari'a* complex by drawing on non-Prophetic sources of knowledge. This divergence in origin is significant; yet, as the following sections will show, the notion of *adab* eventually entered the *hadith* corpus itself, thereby further ennobling the Prophetic exemplar as the fountainhead of ethical and even beautiful conduct (*sunna*) worthy of emulation. As networked sets of narrations transmitted through variously authorized chains, both the *hadith* and the *adab* assemblages crystallized in the early 'Abbasid period, between the 8th and 9th centuries. Each tradition comprised intersecting registers of narration, habitualization, and, ultimately, the production and authorization of norms. Although *hadith* and *adab* were crafted through different forms of specialized labor, they converged in shaping codes of conduct whose exemplarity resonated across the ecumene, appealing to a broad spectrum of its members and groups. Contemporary research on both traditions is rich and thriving; yet only recently have studies begun to probe more deeply the mutual interpenetration of these narrative ensembles (cf. Sperl 2007; Alshaar 2017; al-Khatib 2023a).

Hadith (lit. "news/report," but also "occurrence/incident") is the label acquired by an increasingly systematic body of narrations originating in speeches and deeds traceable to Prophet Muhammad and His inner circle. His interaction with—and/or emulation by—His Companions often plays a crucial role in the corpus. For long after the passing of Prophet Muhammad, stories about Him and His Companions were recounted by wandering storytellers or *qussas*. Narrated in nightlong sessions held in mosques or other gathering places, these performances extended a longstanding tradition of narrative enactment popular among the Arabs, including in pre-Islamic times (cf. Khoury 2006). In this sense, what we might call proto-*hadith*, taking form prior to its consolidation into an increasingly certified corpus, was quintessentially a narrative and performative genre. As such, it set in motion discussions and reflections that, over time, prompted a systematization of both the content of the stories and the chains of their transmitters.

Once this narrative ecology had taken shape, the subsequent efforts to scrutinize narration and authenticate transmission gained a clearer rationale: they sought to stabilize the exemplary force of these stories and align them with the formative habits of life in the ecumene. However, while emphasizing the oral dimension of this genre of telling the stories of Prophet Muhammad, one should not overemphasize its pristine orality per se and so risk neglecting how this storytelling was nourished by rhetoric and poetic forms. One could surmise that even the debated question of "when exactly" the stories acquired an explicitly normative dimension (which was, supposedly, both cause and consequence of the systematic *hadith* mining, collection, authentication, and renarration/recording feeding into an incipient corpus) is ill-posed (cf. Amir 2023). This is because it would be disingenuous to suppose that a systematically normative dimension is ever, first, strategically engineered and, second, attached to the stories. The impetus behind the process that instituted the exemplary force of these narrations to enliven life forms could only result from a self-sustaining process of appropriation, via habituation, of the imitable plots of the stories. This could only occur through the work of emulation that was integral to the "bustling life" of the embryonic ecumene and, therefore, essential to the dynamism of *'umran* (Hallaq 2011, 152). Indeed, the distillation of codes of conduct from narrations was already typical of the pre-Islamic tradition of narrative performance, which legitimized local practices as *sunan* (pl. of *sunna*). Moreover, storytelling, and reflections thereupon, in mosques, like elsewhere, were essential to the early stages of forming experts in *fiqh*. This process set the precedent for the consolidation of the idea that a prophetic authorization of specific practices, via authenticated *hadith*, sanctioned a legitimate, now Islamic, *sunna* that could work as a source of *shari'a* normativity. The transformation, however, took about two centuries, while the narrative form of storytelling remained steady in supporting the process via its appeal to both specialists and laity (ibid., 153–154).

Clearly, the process could not have unfolded without the formation of an expert group specialized in selecting and authenticating *hadith*. This specialization was in principle distinct from, even though it emerged in parallel with—and ultimately supported—the development of a professionally practiced "jurists' law." On the one hand, the fields of the *muhaddithun*, as the pursuers of *hadith* knowledge, and the *fuqaha'*, as the practitioners of *fiqh*, ultimately bifurcated. On the other hand, the narrative dimension of *hadith* as stories remained the key to their plausibility and popularity in the expanding ecumene—even more so as many of the collectors, narrators, and authenticators were increasingly recruited among non-Arab and non-elite personnel. In this sense, *hadith* emerged as a crucial path to building a tradition by relying on a methodology that originally combined narration and transmission. Seen from this angle, one could argue that this breakthrough occurred before the crystallization and legitimation of a multitasking, professional method among the specialized *muhaddithun*[3] as "traditionists," who built mobile and connective networks in their hunt for authentic *hadith* across various locales of the ecumene (Şentürk 2005; El Shamsy 2013, 49–53; Karamustafa 2018, 164; Stewart 2018, 144–155; al-Khatib 2020). These developments, in turn, provide the ground for a closer examination of how narration, transmission, and embodied practice converged to habituate concrete modes of comportment, evaluative sensibilities, and relational repertoires within the ecumene—a convergence that will orient the next step of our inquiry.

If *hadith* grounded exemplary conduct in the prophetic orbit, *adab* emerged as a complementary narrative field that translated ideals of comportment into broader ethical, aesthetic, and social registers. From early ʿAbbasid times onward, *adab* works drew on an expansive archive—pre-Islamic lore, Persian courtly traditions, Hellenistic ethical vocabularies, bureaucratic and diplomatic knowledge, and everyday observations of conduct—to craft repertoires of exemplary behavior suited to a wide array of contexts. Their authority did not hinge on a chain of transmission but on the persuasive power of literary refinement, moral discernment, and worldly acumen. Yet the distance between *adab* and *hadith* should not be overstated: both circulated as narrative performances, both elicited emulation, and both nurtured the gradual sedimentation of shared habits. What distinguished *adab* was its capacity to render ethical comportment aesthetically appealing and socially desirable—mobilizing wit, eloquence, and narrative craft to shape the sensibilities of courtiers, administrators, scholars, and ordinary urban dwellers. In doing so, *adab* contributed its own trajectories of habitualization, furnishing a repertoire through which individuals could orient themselves in the ecumene's expanding sociopolitical spaces and attune their conduct to what appeared graceful, appropriate, or conducive to relational balance. The *adab* tradition thus stands not as a secular foil to prophetic exemplarity but as a complementary, if indispensable narrative engine of the instituting process, elaborating the texture of life forms before formal normativity crystallized.

A fitting way to approach the next stage of the argument is to note that the *hadith* corpus took shape as both the source and the product of what most closely approximates an Islamic "discursive-performative tradition," fed by the recording and articulation of exemplary prophetic action and speech. In terms of its integration into what we will examine as the instituting process in the ecumene, most impactful were the narrative chains and the patterns of emulation and habitualization initiated within Muhammad's inner circle. Intended as such, the corpus has a complex genealogy and an original development that unfolded through an increasingly standardized and certified methodology. This, however, did not suppress the creative work that went into reconstructing stories or the multiple uses and forms of narrativization, performance, and reasoning they could authorize. Yet too often scholars have focused primarily on what they regarded as the outcome of the process—namely, the authenticated and valid body of source data—to the detriment of the open-ended richness of the process itself, which entailed, indeed required, the combined vectors of narration and habitualization (Şentürk 2005; Fudge 2018; al-Khatib 2020).[4]

I preliminarily suggest here that the open-ended process that led to the formation of the *hadith* corpus provided a seminal, though far from exclusive, trigger for the instituting process within the Islamic ecumene. As an essential step in recalibrating inherited Western biases concerning what counts as an institution—a point whose implications will become increasingly clear as the volume progresses—we should view the indissolubly ethical, aesthetic, and sociological dimensions of *hadith* production, intrinsic to its narrative and performative forms, as one such trigger of the instituting process. In this sense, *hadith* operates as a meta-institutional force: it does not constitute an "institution" in the formal Western sense, but it generates the horizon of meanings, sensibilities, and embodied expectations within which institutions could take shape. As alluded to in Chapter 1, it is precisely this originality that enables us to adopt a capacious notion of institution—one that does not necessarily conform to conventional definitions circulating within Western sociology, political science, or legal and constitutional studies. The analytical emphasis therefore falls on the instituting process itself rather than on the consecration of its outcomes in the form of well-contoured institutions (see Chapter 4). To recapitulate, one should view *hadith* as a short narrative that enters the corpus of canonical collections after a rigorous, if complex, procedure of authentication grounded in the reliability of its chain of transmitters. What emerges is a sustained investment in assembling a treasure of relatively brief narratives consolidated through the work of several generations of scholars. Their efforts secured the bundling of these narratives into extensive collections, subdivided by the compiler into sections, usually according to topicality. This investment manifests a clear diffidence toward "grand narratives" (Sperl 2007) in favor of a comprehensive mapping of situated interactions documented through multiple—and, most crucially, traceable—lines of transmission. In effect, the preference for compact, situational accounts over synthetic or totalizing stories betrays an early intuition that the texture of exemplary conduct is best captured in concrete moments of interaction rather than in overarching historical schemes.

Accordingly, a meaningful rule—one worth following—is not established by solidifying into a brick within a massive normative edifice constructed out of edifying storytelling, but rather through the ordering of series of fragmentary episodes. These acquire normative force through their mutual, if piecemeal, consistency and through the chains of transmission that keep them alive. This consistency takes shape diachronically, as transmission over several generations embeds the stories into habitual patterns of action, and synchronically, as narrations are woven into compendia like threads in a fabric. What grants rules of conduct their meaning and authority is that they arise from narratives that can be quoted, performed, and ultimately enacted. That is, coherence arises not from a grand, hierarchical narrative structure but from the ways many short stories intersect, reinforce one another, and circulate independently. The short stories gain their traction as parts of mobile and "rhizomic" assemblages, markedly different from "arboreal" grand narratives. Here narrative condensation prevails over expansion, heightening the propensity for the emulative uptake of the story—and of the norm emerging from it—well beyond its original, situated context (Sperl 2007, 459–461). Ultimately, it is this process of validating stories through their emulative performance and circulation that institutes their normative validity. One could surmise that only those narratives (*hadith*) that passed this practical test were subsequently transmitted and subjected to the increasingly codified procedures of authentication, including the identification of a reliable *isnad* or chain of transmitters. Yet it is likely that the first level of validation resulted from the successful emulation of the conduct dramatized in a given narrative; this should therefore be regarded as the primary level of authentication. Its cumulative outcome is habitualization—the production and reproduction of a shared habitus: shared to the extent that the emulation of the narrated conduct is increasingly experienced as rewarding and effective in crafting Islamically worthy life forms.

This validation of narrative where performance precedes canonization resists the Western projection of a code-first model onto Islamic norm formation. If this cumulative work of narration, emulation, and habitualization furnished one major pathway into the instituting process, a parallel yet distinct narrative register—*adab*—performed a comparable labor of shaping forms of life, albeit through a different idiom and social ecology. Whereas *hadith* compressed exemplary conduct into brief, authenticated episodes anchored in the prophetic milieu, *adab* expanded the repertoire of exemplary comportment by drawing on literary, courtly, ethical, and worldly sources that circulated across broader strata of the ecumene. In this sense, *adab* neither competed with nor merely supplemented *hadith*; rather, it articulated another mode of narrative condensation and transmission, oriented less toward canonical authorization and more toward cultivating styles of living, modes of sociability, and sensibilities consonant with the "bustling life" of the ecumene. As we now turn to examine this second register, the continuity between the two becomes clearer: both fed into the same matrix of habitualization, enabling the formation of shared life forms through distinct but mutually resonant narrative technologies.

Compared with *hadith*, the origins of *adab* are rather fluid and protean. Moreover, *adab* did not develop into a searchable corpus but into a spectrum of cohesive genres. However, not unlike *hadith*, *adab* relied on intersecting registers of narration, habitualization, and, ultimately, the production of exemplary codes of conduct—albeit in a variety of combinations and degrees. This multi-genre and varied corpus alternately summoned pre-Islamic Arab and Persian narratives whose character was not prophetic but associated with poetry and with both elite and folk wisdom. Over time, the term *adab* became a prism that captures and reflects, quite kaleidoscopically, a broad range of meanings and nuances tied to the idea of conducting a virtuous and beautiful life. These meanings changed and multiplied across periods and regions, wave after wave, as the Islamic ecumene expanded and diversified. The scope and fluidity of these transformations make unfeasible any comprehensive genealogy or even, more plainly, a conceptual history of the multi-genre corpus of *adab* repertoires.

In the first half of the 20th century, a few European orientalists—famously fixated on proving authentic origins and tidy etymologies—insisted that in its purportedly original meaning *adab* is virtually synonymous with *sunna*, which, even in pre-Islamic usage, designated customary, normative practice (Patrizi 2023, 62–63). This claim was canonized in Francesco Gabrieli's *adab* entry in the second edition of the *Encyclopaedia of Islam* (Gabrieli 1960). Over time, however, this orientalist search for a single, authentically "original" meaning gave way to a more nuanced appreciation of a complex process of layering, partial amalgamation, and overlapping of various, if often affine, significations. Revolving around character refinement, etiquette, and generosity, such layers of meaning accumulated over generations (Salvatore 2019, 37). It became increasingly recognized that the plasticity of *adab*'s core narrative stabilized during the ʿAbbasid era into a designation of what we may call the quintessence of practical knowledge and wisdom. *Adab* so conceived needed to be exercised through a prism of conviviality and sociability, lest it lose its force as knowledge articulated through wisdom. This recognition that *adab* embraces both a diversified yet coherent bundle of meanings and a transgenerational distillation of their quintessence offers a useful port of entry for conceptualizing habitualization. It suggests that habitualization does not simply occur to *adab* as an ideal of practical wisdom codified in a literature; rather, it unfolds through its very refinement, dissemination, and social uptake, which together generated the durable habits and expectations that structured conduct across the ecumene. Once this approach is accepted, one can, with due caution, circle back to the orientalist fondness for etymologies and recall that the triliteral root of *adab* can be associated with inviting to, offering, and sharing a meal. The significance of this meaning, however, lies not in its supposed authenticity but in its recurrence as a literary trope—ranging from the image of a divine banquet, which is also Qur'anic, to the cultivated skills required for dignified, even joyful, hospitality. Seen through this lens, *adab* signals the convivial art of building communion while acknowledging (and gently smoothing over) difference—especially when the "guests" may hail from distant social worlds. Within this interpretive register, the host-in-chief, as it were, is—and can only be—Allah (Murata and Chittick 1994, 307; Alshaar 2020; Patrizi 2023).

An interesting qualification of the meaning of *adab* was provided by another Italian orientalist of an earlier generation than Gabrieli, namely Carlo Alfonso Nallino. Reading *adab* through the prism of the Latin *urbanitas* while teaching at Dar al-ʻUlum in Cairo at the end of the 19th century, he prefigured *adab* as a key aspect of what we interpreted as "civility" in Volume I (Farag 2001, 99; see also the Introduction to the present volume). This apparently mundane meaning does not contradict the more "spiritual" register just discussed. In both cases, *adab* nurtures the consciousness that we live in a world marked by difference—an awareness that calls for cultivating specific interactive dispositions, skills, and virtues, while ultimately trusting in the mercy of a shared provenance or Creator. By instilling a capacity to appreciate beauty and propriety within their social context, *adab* came to designate etiquette and "courtesy" as the norms of conduct in rulers' courts. It mandated refinement in interpersonal relations, or what we might call "social virtues": an open code guiding individuals in giving form to an ethical—both good and beautiful—life. This practical knowledge of "social commerce" enables one to enhance reputation through eloquence, effective speech, and situationally attuned communication. As such, and unlike the *hadith* corpus, *adab* narratives were only moderately "canonized," retaining a degree of openness for ad hoc reconstruction and performance in the guise of a flexible and context-sensitive *savoir faire*.

The Virtuous Habitus of Managing Difference

In the process, *adab* became the name for a discursive assemblage that was both internally coherent and strikingly protean—embracing aesthetic and entertaining dimensions alongside edifying and regulative ones. It addressed the requirements of human interaction not only within royal courts but also beyond them, in dealings with administrators and literati of other courts, religious scholars, and other notables, while also playing a crucial role in Sufi life (see Chapter 3). In other words, *adab* taught a form of know-how integral to the building and maintenance of social relations. More broadly still, it served the aims of conflict prevention and social integration. To this end, *adab* was often invested in style and distinction, in the sense famously elucidated by Pierre Bourdieu ([1979] 1984). Yet it equally emphasized the necessity of acquiring a discerning understanding of social complexity and the nuances and contingencies of human interaction—differences of taste, value, and interest that structure everyday life. As Barbara Metcalf (1984, 2) memorably put it, *adab* cultivated the "proper discrimination of correct order, behaviour and taste."

The ways of *adab* resonate with a prominent sociological—yet notably non-eurocentric—definition of civility. In her study *Bonds of Civility*, which examines medieval and early-modern precolonial Japan, Eiko Ikegami argues that civility is best understood as a microsociological, performative ritualization of interpersonal relationships, one that bridges the gulf "between the intimate and the hostile" (Ikegami 2005, 28; Salvatore 2016, 63–64). This conception identifies civility with the social and cultural techniques for managing diversity within a broader ecumene. Crucially, such techniques require navigating the fluid boundary between formalized rules and the art of reading the specificities of a situation or encounter—an art that demands adaptive, often creative improvisation rather than mere rule-following. What is particularly telling in Ikegami's sociological definition is the absence of any presumed opposition between civility and religion. Religious practices and actors certainly appear throughout her narrative, yet they move in and out of the picture without altering of how bonds of civility are generated. For Ikegami, the process combines dimensions that conventional frameworks would separate into the ethical and the aesthetic—both of which were, unsurprisingly, shaped by diverse religious ideas. But acknowledging these influences does not compel us to treat civility and religion as mutually exclusive or locked into a rigid binary. Instead, the interplay of ethical and aesthetic registers underscores why *adab*, too, can be seen as cultivating a situationally attuned, improvisational *habitus* for managing difference within an expanding ecumene.

Most conspicuously, Ikegami's work is a historical sociology of a non-Western society—Japan—anteriorly to its late-19th-century modernization, a transformation initiated in response to Western imperial and colonial pressures. This historical predicament later triggered terminological innovations that conceptually insulated "religion" from its civic nexus (Josephson 2012). Against this backdrop, it is not incidental that *Bonds of Civility* was conceived as a sequel to *The Taming of the Samurai* (Ikegami 1995), a work that explicitly engages a framework of inquiry comparable to Norbert Elias's lifelong project. The shared underlying thesis is that the civilizing process generates patterns of cultivated self-restraint among elite groups, which can then be appropriated by other strata of society—merchants, traders, and entrepreneurial groups. What Elias neglected, and Ikegami foregrounded, is the variability of the broader cultural and institutional conditions that shape such processes. In these conditions, religious traditions may influence the formation of civility through channels quite different from the top-down mechanisms explored by Elias. Ikegami highlights the decisive role played not only by established religious actors but also by marginal groups—most notably liminal and itinerant religious figures—in cultivating bonds of civility during specific stages of the process (Ikegami 2005, 76–101).

Likewise, in the *adab* discourse the boundary between religion and civility is notably porous. While stories of prophets of old (*qisas al-anbiya'*, also a Qur'anic component: see Alshaar 2017, 35) certainly play a role in the *adab* repertoire, the paramount model of wisdom that shaped the very inception of major *adab* works was provided by the administrative knowledge and associated life forms cultivated at the Sasanian Persian court before the rise of Islam. This is exemplified by a seminal work such as *Kitab al-Adab al-Kabir* by Ibn al-Muqaffa', a high-ranking officer in the late Umayyad and early 'Abbasid bureaucracies (Yücesoy 2023, 111–118). It is at this intersection—between a self-conscious professional ethos and the creative elaboration of inherited notions of wisdom—that the disciplined work of perfecting one's life form becomes a leitmotif of *adab*. In shaping the habitualization of patterns of good and beautiful living within what Hodgson (1974, I, 239) termed the "worldly culture of the polite classes," represented by high- and mid-ranking bureaucrats and literati, *adab* fuses erudition with creativity and connoisseurship with taste. The simultaneous, indeed inseparable, mastery of literary and practical life forms generates a virtue of discernment: of distinguishing what is harmful from what is valuable, and what is beautiful from what is coarse. The resulting *savoir faire* is irreducible to mere instrumentality. Rather, it is the convergence of means and meanings—of technique and significance—that facilitates the habitualization of an ability to form, sustain, and enjoy life in skilled and socially attuned ways.

Such pedagogical criteria are addressed both to the self, through the cultivation of proper conduct, and to the other, through the provision of suitable counsel. Accordingly, they operate not only through articulated instruction but also via example, complemented by registers of speech calibrated to shifting circumstances—whether serious, playful, admonitory, or conciliatory. Courtiers, secretaries, and other dynastic personnel were expected to know not only how to act on every occasion but also how to speak on every topic. Al-Muqaffaʿ himself was a bold experimenter in this requisite use of language, to the extent that he fashioned a style of prose "ready to unleash the potential of language beyond poetical expression and strictly administrative manuals" (Yücesoy 2023, 117). What ultimately shines in *adab* is that all speech and action is understood to express—and contribute to—the well-being of individuals and their interlocutors.

What is scripted in *adab* as an open-code corpus is a character-building path that equips the practitioner to internalize the code rather than merely follow rules. This code pivots on cultivating an awareness of the diversity intrinsic to social situations and encounters, thereby leaving space for negotiation as well as inventiveness. Such habitualization prefigures a distinctive mode of instituting social relations. Embedded in discursive and performative models—not unlike *hadith*, which revolves around the virtues, wisdom, and beautiful character of Prophet Muhammad—*adab* often remains under-articulated at the explicitly normative level. Its thrust lies in educating individuals into a habitus that facilitates the ongoing reconstruction of rules rather than imposing a top-down disciplining discourse. Within the articulated assemblage that *adab* became, the use of *hadith* was not uncommon, frequently in tandem with tales of non-prophetic exemplary figures. One may even discern a gradual mutual alignment between the *adab* and *hadith* traditions in the way they paired character formation with ideas of a general order—anthropological, sociopolitical, and ultimately cosmological.

It is by analyzing such trajectories—rather than searching for any purported "origin"—that we can say that *adab* became a comprehensive concept designating "performance on behalf of, and in search of, the greater good"

(Lawrence 2021, 29). In this respect, it is noteworthy that *adab*, as a discursive culture, was primarily—though by no means exclusively—cultivated by personnel engaged in statecraft. This helps explain why the ultimate "other" whom the bearers of statecraft were prepared to counsel for the sake of the common good was the ruler, on whose behalf statehood had to be crafted. While everything is ultimately willed by Allah, including who is granted ruling prerogatives at a given historical moment—as per the cosmological assumptions of the *adab* discourse—the art of counsel, and the forms of knowledge it presupposes, are necessarily autonomous, for they arise from the requirements of *siyasa*, the art and craft of government (see Chapters 5–9). This also clarifies why one key genre within the broader *adab* corpus became the "counsel to kings" (*nasihat al-muluk*), conventionally rendered in English—by analogy with a supposed European equivalent—as "mirrors for princes." More generally, as Yücesoy (2013, 133) compellingly observes, the secretarial culture of *adab* was sustained by "a cosmopolitan world-historical awareness," of which *siyasa* constituted a necessary outgrowth.

Despite the role played by the secretarial class in shaping *adab*—often in competition with the knowledge and authority of religious scholars—a consensus emerged within only a few centuries that *adab* was indeed Islamic, and comprehensively so, as persuasively shown by Shahab Ahmed (2016, 234–238). Moreover, during the height of the High Caliphate, the court culture built around *adab* genres and codes of conduct so deeply saturated the bureaucratic–literary class that it spilled outward into the social milieus of merchants, scholars, and other urbanites. At that juncture, *adab* loosened its exclusive association with the ruling elite and acquired broadly civic contours, eventually signifying nothing less than the quintessence of civility. At the same time, it came to be recognized that *adab* embodied a time-honored form of wisdom stored and transmitted over generations and across locales, thus playing a key role in the expansion of the Islamic ecumene. More broadly still, because it promoted virtue and fostered refined human interaction—regardless of its precise origins—it became increasingly implausible not to acknowledge *adab* as unequivocally "Islamic."

Indeed, one would have a hard time perusing *adab* writings and finding any claim that *adab* is not ultimately commanded by God. Pushing this further, some have asserted that *adab* forms the human character and equips it "to embody the beautiful, to bring out the inner harmony, oneness, and balance demanded by *tawhid*," the key concept of Islamic teachings (Murata and Chittick 1994, 307). Whether or not such a statement can be universally endorsed, it is clear that the process that placed *adab* at the center of Islam was integral to how Islam itself came to encompass far more than what the Western notion of "religion" usually denotes. It reaches into—and finds its practical anchor within—the semantic sphere we may designate as "civility." This expanded understanding, however, is the cumulative outcome of a long-term twinning process with the *hadith* body. Recognizing this does not deny the principled autonomy of *adab* as a discourse that developed outside the scriptural corpus. It merely alerts us to how the distinction between the *adab* assemblage and the *hadith* corpus—understood as the database of *shari'a*—is soft and reflexively ambivalent rather than hard and categorical, like in any purported differentiation between "religion" and "civility" (or, even less plausibly, "secularity": Salvatore 2019).

This process of mutual interpenetration between *hadith* and *adab* was facilitated by the way *hadith* itself offered guidance for shaping one's conduct and life form. It did so by foregrounding the charisma of Prophet Muhammad as both practitioner and teacher of *adab* (*muaddib*). Through His teaching, a layered set of narratives crystallized into an exemplary portrait of prophetic wisdom—an ideal model to be emulated and internalized through habituation. In this manner, portions of the *hadith* corpus, already during its formative stage, and through the practices of sharing and testing, explicitly contributed to articulating the multifaceted nature of the *adab* paradigm—not only in the ethical sphere but also in matters of skilled communication. Particularly notable is the attribution to Prophet Muhammad of the virtue of being fluent in speech yet extraordinarily concise (Alshaar 2017, 30–31). Here we encounter an aesthetic canon of persuasive utterance that directly resonates with the very form of *hadith* as an assemblage of "little narratives" (Sperl 2007, 463–465). Seen from another angle that strengthens the previous point, one is reminded of Shahab Ahmed's argument that the capaciousness of Islam rests partly on its ability to accommodate what may appear—especially from external, predominantly Western vantage points—as contradictions or ambivalences (see also Bauer 2011). In this light, the *hadith* and *adab* corpora can be conceived as branching off a single, broader Islamic narrative continuum (Sperl 2007, 466; see also al-Khatib 2023b; Alshaar 2023). Most notably—and even though this was not explicitly addressed by Shahab Ahmed—within this continuum *hadith* may also be viewed as sharing in the open-ended and creative character that typifies *adab* (Sperl 2007, 472). This holds even though the narrative force of *hadith* derives not only from the *matn* as transmitted content but equally, and inseparably, from the *isnad* as its chain of transmission (ibid., 474; see also Şentürk 2005).

As suggested by Sperl, the trigger and raison d'être—rather than the form or content—of narrative in this continuum is an intrinsic tension between desire and norm (Sperl 2017, 475). Most strikingly, the function of little narratives, rather than a grand narrative, is not to dialectically resolve this tension into a stabilizing synthesis but, on the contrary, to keep ambivalences ongoing, open-ended, and productively edging toward new narrative horizons. This dynamic unfolds precisely because these little narratives are habitually performed in practitioners' retellings of the prophetic stories to ever-new audiences, as if re-enacting the moments when Prophet Muhammad spoke to his Companions (see Aishima 2016, 111–118). Narrative so conceived is neither oracular nor cathartic but "characterizing," that is, literally character-building (*ta'addub*, from the same root as *adab*). The character of Prophet Muhammad radiates across a field of potentialities that unfold and branch through a continuous layering of micronarratives. This occurs through a compression of time that condenses exemplary action—even when accidentally triggered by a question or incident—into the state of grace of an eternal present, an effect heightened by the intergenerational bridging performed by the *isnad* transmission device. This eternity distilled into exemplarity modulates and tempers the desire embedded in human temporality through the ways generations of narrators, interpreters, and performers replotted the stories in response to the expectations, aspirations, and pains of their audiences.

The shared form of little narratives helps sustain the process of mutual interpenetration between *hadith* and *adab*. This, however, does not dilute the principled autonomy of *adab* or the formal divergence between the two corpora, their constituencies, and their institutional fields. On the contrary, the prescriptive strength of the *adab* tradition was reinforced by the recurring judgment—voiced by cultural elites across epochs and locales—that the normative import of *shari'a* was insufficient to govern the expanding complexity and diversity of the Islamic ecumene, particularly in matters of governance. Moreover, one could even suggest that *adab* renders the implementation of *shari'a* gentle, measured, and at times "spiritual" (Murata and Chittick 1994, 307). Implementing *shari'a* without *adab* risks precipitating human beings into a delirium of omnipotence as holders of the deputyship (*khilafa* = Caliphate; see also Chapter 7) of Allah—as if they possessed the keys to a flawless reading of *shari'a*, while forgetting that it ultimately reflects the inscrutable will of God (*shar'*).

From the peak of ʿAbbasid rule onwards, the two traditions of *adab* and *hadith* consolidated their regulative impact upon differentiated social strata while developing in parallel. In doing so, they progressively extended their initially tenuous mutual imbrications. No doubt, one can—and should—in principle distinguish the culture and knowledge of the *fuqaha*ʾ, who relied on *hadith* as *fiqh*'s most capacious database, on the one hand, and the court-centered secretarial culture organized around *adab* as an assemblage of stories and teachings, on the other (Salvatore 2019, 39). In this sense, as two complementary ways of turning exemplary narratives into a lifelong habitus, *hadith* and *adab* also traced lines of mutual demarcation. This is conspicuously shown both by scholars who considered themselves adept in both domains and by those who occasionally—and often polemically—emphasized, like the leading polymath al-Jahiz (d. 869), how the scribal class's social positionalities and life forms weakened their appreciation of *hadith*. Yet, most tellingly, al-Jahiz also lamented the limited potential of *adab*, as primarily an elite-oriented cultural code, to appeal to the common folk (Yücesoy 2023, 130–131). What this double gesture signals, however, is that the narrative intersections of the two corpora—and their competitive permeability to non-elite strata—were strengthened by the fact that their habitualizing power was oriented toward distinct sociopolitical milieus. Following Bourdieu, and as adumbrated by al-Jahiz, cultural distinction is the sociological precondition of cultural diffusion. Far from being situated passively at the receiving end of both sets of narrations, non-elite strata benefited from how the mutual competition between *hadith* and *adab* reduced the likelihood that either would crystallize into a rigid, uniform, top-down disciplining machine.

It should be noted that *hadith* often entered *adab*-related genres—particularly anthologies—through the main door. Within *adab* works, quoting *hadith* was far from rare and often combined with tales of non-prophetic exemplary characters. An early, if prominent, example is found in the work of the polymath Ibn Qutayba (d. 889), especially his *ʿUyun al-Akhbar* (Bellino 2023). Most cogently, the earlier mentioned praise of Prophet Muhammad's beautiful, noble, and beneficial conciseness of speech, famously argued by al-Jahiz among others, underscored the legitimacy of *hadith* within *adab* (Sperl 2007, 465). On the one hand, this interpenetration was reflected in the growing conviction that the training of scribes in acquiring the requisite linguistic and communicative skills could not be nourished solely by the terminology specific to the bureaucratic craft and the cultured life form of literati, but required substantial exposure to the teachings of the

Qur'an and *hadith* (Heck 2018, 186–190). On the other hand, the idea and practice of *adab* were eagerly appropriated by several religious scholars, whose activities in turn enlivened strategically salient parts of the *hadith* corpus itself. Not only, as previously noted, did one *hadith* present the Prophet as a paragon of *adab*; another depicted the entire *hadith* corpus as a form of knowledge that is nothing but "Allah's *adab*," through which He educated His Prophet and through which the Prophet trained His community. Here *adab* appears as the very gist of divine knowledge that protects humans from errors in speech and action, and from defects of character. This recruitment of *hadith* to legitimize *adab* contributed to making the latter less elitist and, at least potentially, more inclusive (Alshaar 2023).

This co-optation of *adab* into divine wisdom was certainly rooted in the already noted conviction that it does not—and indeed cannot—contradict divine teachings. More specifically, however, it derived from the authoritative intergenerational chain linking Prophet Muhammad, a champion of *adab*, to the *'ulama'* as the religious personnel who inherited His prerogatives. Consequently, those charged with studying and applying the *shari'a* as the manifestation of divine wisdom and mercy were also understood to benefit greatly from *adab*. This was visible in the success of sub-genres such as the *adab* of listeners of *hadith*, the *adab* of senior and junior jurists (*adab al-faqih wa-l-mutafaqqih*), and their professional specifications in forms such as *adab al-qadi* and *adab al-mufti*. It was further claimed that the commitment of the *fuqaha'* to *adab* did not merely enhance their capacities to read and interpret the Qur'an and *hadith* but comprehensively strengthened their professional skills (Masud 1984; Caeiro 2006; Salvatore 2019, 41; al-Khatib 2023a, 2).

Overall, the broader field of *shari'a*—resolutely fed by *hadith* and projecting a virtuous prophetic ethos—on one hand, and of *adab*—providing both a habitus for virtuous conduct and a professional code for ruling bureaucracies—on the other, did not constitute a statically symmetric binary, as if reflecting a neat differentiation or mutual mirroring between a religious and a civic (or even "secular") normativity. Rather, the two streams were caught in a continuous, mutual process of accommodation and cross-pollination, through which each could function as an internal control code for the other. *Adab* could not contradict the rules of *shari'a* if it was to harmonize with divine will, while *shari'a* needed to conform to the codes of *adab* so as not to transgress divine wisdom. Yet even more fundamental than this normative entanglement was the symbiotic growth of the narrative patterns of *hadith* and *adab* themselves. Crucially, this affinity did not arise from a preexisting shared ethos but from the shared practice of storytelling—above all from the ways in which narrative performance contributed to the formation of habitus. The very act of "telling a story" thus became pivotal in shaping two diachronically sustainable and mutually enlivening traditions. It is also important to acknowledge that it is not "outsiders" who attribute to *hadith* and *adab* the fashionable label of "narratives," as if squeezing them into a post-structuralist script. It was the makers and carriers of *hadith* and *adab* who worked on their selection and transmission in full consciousness of their narrative structure and power. What allowed the insights of ancient Greek sages, old Sasanian kings, and Prophet Muhammad to work isomorphically was not any agreed-upon point of doctrine, but precisely the plastic narration of their exemplary feats, regardless of their different chains of legitimation. In the progress of the interpenetration of the two narrative ensembles, we see a living epistemology in full becoming—one supported by a shared program of embedding sound knowledge in life and thus instituting life in the ecumene.

Bruce Lawrence has invoked the concept of *barzakh* as the marker of such an original and living epistemology. Referenced in the Qur'an as simultaneously a border and a bridge, the simile of *barzakh* has been frequently mobilized in Sufi thought to describe a liminal space between the human and the divine. This space is often called *'alam al-mithal*, a world intermediate between the human and divine planes, filled with "imaginal" forms of subsistence—forms that are other than imaginary, since they possess a real mode of existence. While Chapter 3 will provide a concrete instance of how this world of intermediacy is characterized as a *barzakh*, Lawrence has suggested that the latter—whose meaning in Islamic thought oscillates between ontological, eschatological, and epistemological planes—can be understood as the centerpiece of an even broader type of logic. This logic of intermediacy is at work wherever the apprehension and practice of "religion" (via *hadith*) and "civility" (via *adab*) depend on a shared affective and cognitive process. Such a process, in turn, presides over the formation and transformation of life forms while eschewing dichotomies defined by impermeable borders.

Rather than enforcing an impenetrable boundary against a religious tradition imagined as external to it, the champions of the *adab* assemblage cultivated a habitus that penetrated deeply into the religious field of knowledge production. Within that field, *adab* undoubtedly operated as a factor of differentiation among social specializations, functions, and intellectual milieus; yet it did so without fracturing the (however "ambivalent" or "contradictory") comprehensiveness of "being Islamic." A particularly influential articulation of this differentiation appears in al-Mawardi's (d. 1058) celebrated *Adab al-dunya wa-l-din*, where *adab* is applied simultaneously—albeit with distinct emphases—to "the world" (*al-dunya*) of life conduct and relationality and to "the religion" (*al-din*) as the soteriological pursuit of felicity in the hereafter. At the same time, in al-Mawardi's elaboration, *adab* emerges as a holistic discipline for cultivating a habitus of awareness and vigilance addressed to the fairness of economic transactions oriented toward human welfare (Al-Daghistani 2022, 72).

On the one hand, in the famous *Ihya' 'ulum al-din* of al-Ghazali (1058–1111), *adab*-related chapters were divided into discrete sections, differentiating, for example, between *adab al-akl* (food), *adab al-nikah* (marriage), and *al-adab fi-l-mujalasa* (conduct in courtly and polite society), but also *adab tilawat al-Qur'an* (Qur'an recitation). Alongside these, as earlier authors had already emphasized, one could also encounter the *adab* of playing—whether chess or the lute. On the other hand, the protean capaciousness of *adab* carried within it a promise of reconciling differences, evident when the *adab* of the self and the *adab* of socioeconomic welfare and political cohesion were understood as overlapping, if not effectively coinciding. In this vein, *adab* addressed rulers and their key advisers and viziers, with a recurring stress on the virtue of self-restraint and the rational control of passions as prerequisites for viable statecraft. Accordingly, we find *adab al-muluk* (kings), *adab al-sultaniyya* (the sultanate), *adab al-wuzara'* (ministers), and *adab atba' al-a'imma* (the elites). And yet, the wellspring of all forms of *adab* remains the art of storytelling (Hartung 2011, 302–303; Walker 2011, 106; Yavari 2014, 45–60; Al-Daghistani 2022, 76; Mayeur-Jaouen 2020, 5–6).

The Combined Instituting Force of *Maslaha* and *Adab*

Thus far I have tried to show that one cannot begin an analysis of the instituting process by presupposing the existence of a well-contoured normative system—defined by the work of *fiqh*—that would, in turn, determine what counts as a legitimate institution at various social and political levels. And yet, taken together, the dynamics I described still leave us with a crucial question: how do such narrative-driven forms of habitualization feed into the larger instituting process of the Islamic ecumene—especially once we move beyond the narrow presupposition that normativity and institutionality are anchored primarily in juristic method? In this light, after examining *adab* as a relational and habitualizing force, we must now consider *maslaha*, a notion mainly—though far from exclusively—associated with *fiqh*, and expressing the principle that mediates between embodied practice and broader visions of welfare. Their coupling illuminates how the instituting process in the Islamic ecumene cannot be mapped onto Western legal-formal categories but emerges instead from a fluid interplay of cultivated dispositions and purposive judgments. If *adab* alerts us to the insufficiency of conceiving institutions through the narrow lens of juridical norm-production, *maslaha* underscores the need to view the instituting process as oriented toward the unfolding of benefit in living contexts rather than toward the enforcement of codified rules.

Therefore, we must descend into a broader process in which narrative and *habitus* furnish the initial impulse for institution-building. Within this wider horizon, normativity—including but never reducible to *fiqh*—appears as only one dimension of a more capacious bio-epistemic code through which life forms are shaped via bodies of knowledge and their habitualized enactment. *Adab*, as a key contribution to such a code, was recognized even by religious scholars as showing a purchase not subsumable under the juridical ambit of *fiqh*, precisely because it was understood to emanate from the ultimate host of *adab*, namely Allah. In this sense, *adab* did not stand apart from *shari'a* but contributed to its elucidation by bundling forms of practical wisdom not directly derived from the canonical sources. It is therefore unsurprising that *fuqaha'* steeped in *adab* were often said to be better equipped to read and interpret Qur'an and *hadith*. At the same time, because *adab* articulated the art of relationality, its habitualizing effects always required differentiation and contextualization through grids of life forms and social tasks—precisely the terrain on which *maslaha* would come to operate. This is not to deny the importance and sophistication of the Islamic legal tradition, but to situate it within a larger ecology of narrative-based praxis.

So understood, *adab* facilitated a recognition and appreciation of the diversity (and, we may add, mutability and impermanence) of social positions and epistemic positionalities. Within this background, we may suggest that the formation of *fiqh* was the crystallization of a crucial, if specialized, field of normative regulation within the broader bio-epistemic process of shaping human relations and habitualizing life forms, which found a secure anchoring in the multi-genre discourse of *adab*. In this vein, *shari'a*-minded currents of thought and fields of activity, as well as the sociocultural carriers who sustained them, appear in a different light from what transpires through conventional identifications of *shari'a* as a compound of moral-legal doctrine and practice. In other words, the *shariʿa* discourse should be situated within the same bio-epistemic framework that links narrativity to habitualization, producing what we might call an art of relationality enlivening the ecumene. Normativity is one, albeit prominent, outcome of the process, but should not be insulated and therefore overestimated or misapprehended, as if taking the part for the whole.

We envisioned the development of *hadith* as the primary source of *shariʿa* not only for providing it with the needed sheer data but because of the decisive pull exerted by emulating the exemplary conduct of Prophet Muhammad through the power of micronarratives. These narratives typically condensed into the concept of *sunna nabawiyya*. In this context, one should heed the subtle dialectic that arose between the development of *hadith* science and *fiqh*. This dialectic unfolded after *fiqh* emerged from still uncodified legal practices—indeed, prior to the completion of the canonization of *hadith*. At that germinative stage, *fiqh* had not yet produced a full-fledged, specialized practice of jurisprudence (al-Khatib 2023b). Even once such specialization took form, the normative (and even the more technically "legal") dimension of *fiqh* continued to derive from its being a practice of discerning the "good" in each relation or transaction, approached through relationally trained judgment and practical reason (Salvatore 2007, 142–144). Nevertheless, it is undeniable that, over time, the work of *fiqh* was fueled by an unceasing activity of systematization performed by its emerging schools. Through these developments, *fiqh* became a privileged instrument for governing multiple levels of relationality in the life of the ecumene.

Such developments notwithstanding, the impact of *hadith*'s micronarratives vastly exceeded its function of providing "source materials" for legal regulation and adjudication. In the development of *fiqh* from inherited local practices or *sunan*, beginning in key locales such as Medina and Kufa, the narrations of the sayings and deeds of Prophet Muhammad played more than an ancillary role, as we have seen. Narration decisively facilitated the absorption of a variety of pre- or non-Islamic practices into the prophetic *sunna*, as reflected in the *hadith* corpus (Hallaq 2011, 153). More generally, within the unfolding of *fiqh* activities, practical reason emerged not as an abstract capacity cultivated solely through specialized training, but as a skill that continued, over time, to rely fundamentally on emulative performance guided by the exemplarity of *hadith* as narrative—arguably even increasingly so, given the key role played by *hadith* in shaping and regulating Sufi life (see Chapter 3).

Moreover, one should consider that, despite the conventional orientalist reductionism that identifies the core of the *'ulama'* class—the producers of knowledge (*'ilm*)—with the practitioners of *fiqh*, the notion of *'ilm* in fact evolved to denote knowledge in the broader sense of learning, rather than as a fixed "body" of specifically "religious" knowledge. In this expanded sense, *'ilm* often served as the ultimate source of *adab* and its pedagogical reach. In parallel, the activity of *fiqh* denoted the capacity to comprehend a situation and apply practical reason to it, as one particular—if crucial—articulation of *'ilm* understood as a vast and variegated know-how. This is also why the standard translation of *fiqh* as "jurisprudence" risks failing to capture its many shades (Rahman [1966] 1979, 103; Lapidus 1984, 39). The ongoing practice of *fiqh* as a refined form of know-how generated reflections on its conceptual foundations in the form of *usul al-fiqh*, which decisively relied on the relational dimension of human action. Within *usul al-fiqh*, beginning in the late 10th century, the idea of *maslaha* began to attract sustained attention from legal theorists. Derived from the triliteral root *s-l-h*, denoting being or becoming good, *maslaha* is most commonly translated as "common/social good" (or, though misleadingly, "public interest/weal"). As the most general principle underlying all rulings—understood as Allah's commands—it gradually gained traction, albeit unevenly, among the legal schools, often in tandem with the related notion of *istislah*, derived from the same root. This latter term designates the actual process, conducted through practical or (juris)prudential reasoning, of finding the best attainable good in any given situation, relation, or transaction. Being sophisticated conceptual tools, it is not surprising that neither *maslaha* nor *istislah* appear in the Qur'an. However, *istislah* does surface in the *hadith* corpus and, no less most notably, made its earliest recorded appearance in the emerging *adab* corpus, particularly in the work of Ibn al-Muqaffa', centuries before it was appropriated by *fiqh*. In his usage, *istislah* carried a more broadly political than strictly legal meaning, expressing the pursuit of the welfare of ordinary people. Nonetheless, a legal dimension was already implicit: Ibn al-Muqaffa's appeal to *istislah* formed part of his critique of the inconsistency of *fiqh* across different locales of the ecumene in his time—well before the consolidation of the *hadith* corpus and, even more so, before the emergence of *usul al-fiqh* (Masud [1977] 1995, 119–137; Opwis 2010, 9–15; Yücesoy 2023, 155).

Admittedly, the importance of the *maslaha*/*istislah* semantic and operational field may have been overamplified by the emphasis that various generations of Muslim reformers have placed on it since the colonial era

(Salvatore 2016, 264–265). Yet it remains undeniable that, beginning no later than the 9th century and culminating in the work of the eminent 14th-century Andalusi jurist al-Shatibi (d. 1388), this field succeeded in establishing a general principle for applying practical reasoning to the pursuit of the common good. This principle was to be employed in discrete cases where specific goods were at stake. Along this trajectory, *maslaha/istislah* came to be theorized as more than a merely supplementary device within *fiqh*, invoked only when the scriptural sources were silent or the consensus of the jurists unavailable. Drawing on the Hanafi method of induction and the Maliki emphasis on communal welfare, al-Shatibi famously argued that *maslaha* is the very foundation of all *shari'a* rulings. *Maslaha* was understood to embody Allah's legislating will and thus to encompass the overarching "purposes of the law" (*maqasid al-shari'a*; Masud [1977] 1995, 118–119; Salvatore 2007, 156–157).

Al-Shatibi inherited this type of approach from theorists active between the 11th and 14th centuries. He posited that *maqasid al-shari'a* are intrinsically oriented to *maslaha* as the welfare of the people. In this way, he forcefully argued that the purpose of *shari'a* is ultimately aligned with promoting *maslaha*. This, in turn, highlights the law's role not merely as a set of rules but as a system designed to facilitate well-being through fairness in human relations. This perspective marks a critical juncture in al-Shatibi's legal philosophy, for it integrates the principles of Islamic jurisprudence into a broader sociopolitical thought that clarifies how norms enter the process of instituting human and social life rather than being imposed on it as if from the outside. Precisely because *maslaha* was deemed essential for fostering human flourishing in diverse aspects of life—including dimensions we tend to see as far apart, like the economic and the spiritual—it became a seed of the flourishing of the ecumene, the "bustling life" of *'umran*. Far from being an abstract or merely convenient jurisprudential tool, *maslaha* can thus be viewed as inherent in the very idea of a divinely ordained *shari'a* for the benefit of humankind within a living cosmos (Salvatore 2007, 155–162; Fadel 2023).

One step forward, one can detect an interpretative trend that firmly situates *maslaha* within the same capacious compass of meanings that *adab* had acquired as a regulative code for a life of virtue and felicity. This trend culminates in the moment when *maslaha* attained prominence as reflecting a habitualized "holistic vision of human nature" (Al-Daghistani 2022, 58). This dimension lies at the epistemological core of al-Ghazali's work, which straddles the purported borders between the experiential, ethical, and legal dimensions of Islam, and which was also influential on conceptions of what we would call economic conduct. Al-Ghazali's holistic view of *maslaha* as the purpose of *shari'a* resonates with the work of *adab* (via *ta'addub*, or teaching) within the corpus of *hadith*. Here the imitation of Prophet Muhammad embodies divine mercy as the origin of all goods (*masalih*, pl. of *maslaha*). Understanding the emergence of *maslaha*—from within *usul al-fiqh* and beyond—thus requires placing it within the same bio-epistemic field that animated the holistic vision of *adab*, situated at the intersection of ethical, aesthetic, and economic values, and therefore resistant to any utilitarian reduction of the common good (Opwis 2010, 67–80; Al-Daghistani 2022, 59–65).

Seen retrospectively, *maslaha* appears not merely as an ingenious legal device dear to the Maliki school of *fiqh*—to which al-Shatibi (and Ibn Khaldun: see Chapter 5) belonged—but as a pillar of the social and communicative infrastructure of the ecumene, well beyond the formal status that other leading scholars or legal schools were ready to attribute to the concept. Thus understood, *maslaha* becomes synonymous with "flourishing" itself, in its intrinsically relational foundations (Fadel 2023). It is remarkable how this idea of *maslaha* is both foundational to *fiqh* as a practice and to the broad public advocacy of all the goods and good practices evoked by the triliteral root *s-l-h*. This semantic complex is expressed, together with *maslaha/istislah*, through such keywords as *sulh*, *salah*, and *islah* (denoting what is whole, proper, and incorrupt) as purposive conduits toward *sa'ada*, i.e., felicity, in the key vocabulary of a champion of *adab* like Ibn al-Muqaffa'—long before any crystallization of the overarching field of *usul al-fiqh* (Yücesoy 2023, 309n20). The conceptual constellation built around *s-l-h* therefore prefigured a social philosophy of harmony, repair, and flourishing that would later find legal theorization in *usul al-fiqh* but was never exhausted by it.

Discussing this broader notion of *maslaha* allows us to recognize a remarkable alignment among the key notions of habitus, practical rationality, and sound—i.e., relationally effective—communication. For in al-Shatibi's conception, it is not that *maslaha* (or *masalih*) are first ascertained by applying practical reason and then communicated efficiently; rather, the rationality of finding the best possible good in any given situation is premised upon human actors seeking mutual understanding—an inherently communicative process—about how to define the situation and identify the good(s) to be found within it. This transcends any utilitarian balancing of competing interests among discrete legal subjects. Integral to *maslaha* is the previously noted *istislah*, the process through which a shared understanding of the goods at stake, and the means for securing them, is cultivated. Crucially—albeit ideally—the communicative and reflective activities of the *fuqaha'* are possible only as a specialized extension of the practical reason of the common folk. One of the jurists' key functions is therefore to ensure that the flow and rationality of communication remain sufficiently inclusive (Masud [1977] 1995, 181). The primary outcome of this approach is an inherently relational view of the subject, integrally involved with interactants and interlocutors in the ongoing process of building a habitus that nourishes the social bond (Salvatore 2007, 171).

Taken together, this trajectory suggests the need to situate normativity—including *shari'a*—within a process marked by the rise of an original type of narrativity that, through habitualization, elevates the power of relationality. *Adab* plays a paramount role in this process, both as a label for a multigenre corpus and as a key idea that permeates *hadith* and contributes to the formation of an overarching, shared conception of the common good. This is not a process of secularization *ante litteram*, but rather the rise of a culture of "civility" that overlaps with—and at crucial junctures harmonizes with—"religion." Such a culture did not merely infuse but often amalgamated with the professional expertise of legal practitioners within the broader *shari'a* field, refining legal activities from within. *Adab* promoted models of conduct that equipped one to be a good religious practitioner and a skilled professional, and—at a deeper level—enhanced the understanding, practice, and implementation of *shari'a*. I have warned against the conceptual trap of tagging *adab* as either "religious" or "secular," since both terms are anachronistic and eurocentric. Instead, I have advocated seeing a twinning—at times a mutual mirroring, often an intertwining—between two fundamentally distinct registers of habitualization, constituted by *hadith* and *adab* and their broader fields of operation. This soft distinction matched an institutional differentiation of personnel across various fields of activity within the Islamic ecumene.

In conclusion, as clarified by Al-Daghistani (2022, 78), both *adab* and *shari'a* configure spaces of discourse and practice that are far from monolithic or self-referential, even as they entail cosmological and anthropological understandings of comprehensive life. They should be viewed as mutually interpenetrating discursive assemblages that provide nerve, affect, and discipline to multiple practices associated with the overarching idea of Islam. Admittedly, the modes of their interpenetration vary across time and locale and must be contextually reconstructed. Yet as a general proposition, one may suggest that *adab* functioned as an intensely narrative counterpoint to *shari'a* as the manifestation of divine will (*shar'*), which humans seek to apprehend and implement with the crucial support of the micronarratives of the *hadith* corpus. Their combined effect—via narrativity, habitualization, and relationality—supplied the principal axis of the instituting process in the Islamic ecumene. Their meeting point—the isthmus, both sweet and brackish—conveyed by the image of *barzakh* constituted a meta-institutional level of habitus formation (see Chapter 1), which in turn served as the fundamental trigger of the instituting process.[5]

Notes

1. Berger and Luckmann (1967, 53–57) offered a landmark sociological account of "habitualization" as the patterning of conduct that can be repeated and refined over the life course, thereby making social action and interaction increasingly efficient and predictable. Following Marcel Mauss, Pierre Bourdieu ([1972] 1977, 72) defined habitus as generating "systems of durable, transposable dispositions."
2. Here I am also responding to the justified criticism that Shahab Ahmed (2016) directed at my early work (Salvatore 1997), written long before I began the present trilogy on the sociology of Islam. At that time, my contribution to the field—despite adopting a markedly poststructuralist approach (see Chapter 1 of this volume)—remained somewhat trapped in conventional views of Islam. As Ahmed (2016, 123) observed, "the insistence on locating *fiqh* as the centre of Islam has the analytical effect of radically diminishing the very qualities of plurality, complexity, and flexibility that Salvatore is seeking to recuperate." In my subsequent book (Salvatore 2007), I clarified that *fiqh* manifests a sophisticated understanding of practical reason (broadly comparable to *phronesis* in Aristotelian parlance), although at that stage I did not yet venture into analyzing the underlying habitualizing process.
3. They shouldn't be confused with the *ahl al-hadith*, the movement that directly shaped the theory and practice of jurisprudence, even though the two groups may at times have overlapped (Heck 2018, 190; Stewart 2018, 137–138).
4. For more contemporary instances, see Aishima 2016, 208–268.
5. Unfortunately, scholars of Islamic literature and Islamic law have, for too long, treated narrations and norms as if they were mutually insulated rather than interpenetrating within an open-ended process. On occasion, a rather oblique

glance has been cast toward Norbert Elias's notion of the civilizing process—as though it could simply be "applied" to anything "Islamic" (see Mayeur-Jaouen 2020)—without attending to earlier critical sociological engagements with the question, such as the one offered in Volume I of this trilogy. This tendency is itself an unmistakable symptom of the methodological constraints affecting the present post-orientalist predicament (see Chapter 1).

References

Ahmed, Shahab. 2016. *What is Islam? The Importance of Being Islamic*. Princeton, NJ: Princeton University Press.

Aishima, Hatsuki. 2016. *Public Culture and Islam in Modern Egypt: Media, Intellectuals and Society*. London: I.B. Tauris.

Al-Daghistani, Sami. 2022. "Beyond *Maṣlaḥah*: *Adab* and Islamic Economic Thought." *American Journal of Islam and Society* 39 (3–4): 57–86.

Alshaar, Nuha. 2017. "Introduction. The Relation of *Adab* to the Qurʾan: Conceptual and Historical Framework." In *The Qurʾan and Adab: The Shaping of Literary Traditions in Classical Islam*, edited by Nuha Alshaar, 1–61. Oxford: Oxford University Press.

Alshaar, Nuha. 2020. "Reconstructing *Adab* in Islamic Studies." In *Deconstructing Islamic Studies*, edited by Majid Daneshgar and Aaron W. Hughes, 167–203. Cambridge, MA: Harvard University Press.

Alshaar, Nuha. 2023. "Ḥadīth and the Concept of *Adab* as Moral Education." In *Ḥadīth and Ethics through the Lens of Interdisciplinarity*, edited by Mutaz al-Khatib, 30–47. Leiden: Brill.

Amir, Safwan. 2023. "The Ethical in the Transmission of Sunna: Rethinking the *ʿUlamāʾ-Quṣṣāṣ* Conflict." In *Ḥadīth and Ethics through the Lens of Interdisciplinarity*, edited by Mutaz al-Khatib, 198–220. Leiden: Brill.

Bauer, Thomas. 2011. *Die Kultur der Ambiguität. Eine andere Geschichte des Islams*. Frankfurt: Verlag der Weltreligionen.

Bellino, Francesca. 2023. "Developing a Knowledge System Based on *Adab*: Birds Fluttering from Ibn Qutayba's *Adab al-Kātib* to the *ʿUyūn al-Akhbār*." In *L'*Adab*, Toujours Recommencé. "Origins", Transmissions, Metamorphoses of* Adab *Literature*, edited by Francesca Bellino et al., 216–35. Leiden: Brill.

Berger, Peter L., and Thomas Luckmann. 1967. *The Social Construction of Reality: A Treatise in the Sociology of Knowledge*. New York: Anchor Books.

Bourdieu, Pierre [1972]. 1977. *Outline of a Theory of Practice*. Translated by Richard Nice. Cambridge: Cambridge University Press.

Bourdieu, Pierre [1979]. 1984. *Distinction: A Social Critique of the Judgement of Taste*. Translated by Richard Nice. Cambridge, MA: Harvard University Press.

Buskens, Léon, and Baudouin Dupret. 2015. "The Invention of Islamic Law. A History of Western Studies of Islamic Normativity and Their Spread in the Orient." In *After Orientalism: Critical Perspectives on Western Agency and Eastern Re-Appropriations*, edited by François Pouillon and Jean-Claude Vatin, 31–47. Leiden: Brill.

Caeiro, Alexandre. 2006. "The Shifting Moral Universes of the Islamic Tradition of *Iftāʾ*: A Diachronic Study of Four *Adab al-Fatwā* Manuals." *The Muslim World* 96 (4): 661–85.

El Shamsy, Ahmed. 2013. *The Canonization of Islamic Law: A Social and Intellectual History*. Cambridge: Cambridge University Press.

Fadel, Mohammed. 2023. "*Maṣlaḥa* as 'Flourishing' and Its Place in Sunnī Political Thought." *Journal of Islamic Ethics*: 7: 1–31.

Farag, Iman. 2001. "Private Lives, Public Affairs. The Uses of *Adab*." In *Muslim Traditions and Modern Techniques of Power*, edited by Armando Salvatore, 95–122. Hamburg: Lit New Brunswick; NJ, and London: Transaction (*Yearbook of the Sociology of Islam*, Vol. 3).

Fudge, Bruce. 2018. "Scholarship, Speculative Thought and the Consolidation of Sunni Authority." In *The Wiley Blackwell History of Islam*, edited by Armando Salvatore et al., 215–33. Oxford: Wiley Blackwell.

Gabrieli, Francesco. 1960. "*Adab*." In *Encyclopaedia of Islam*, edited by H. A. R. Gibb et al., Vol. 1, 2nd edition, 175–6. Leiden: Brill.

Hallaq, Wael B. 2011. "Islamic Law: History and Transformation." In *The New Cambridge History of Islam*. Volume 4: *Islamic Cultures and Societies to the End of the Eighteenth Century*, edited by Robert W. Hefner, 142–83. Cambridge: Cambridge University Press.

Hartung, Jan-Peter. 2011. "Enacting the Rule of Islam: On Courtly Patronage of Religious Scholars in Pre- and Early Modern Times." In *Court Cultures in the Muslim World. Seventh to Nineteenth Centuries*, edited by Albrecht Fuess and Jan-Peter Hartung, 295–325. London: Routledge.

Heck, Paul L. 2018. "Contested Fields, Knowledge Mobility, and Discipline Crystallization." In *The Wiley Blackwell History of Islam*, edited by Armando Salvatore et al., 177–94. Oxford: Wiley Blackwell.

Hodgson, Marshall G. S. 1974. *The Venture of Islam. Conscience and History in a World Civilization*. Chicago: University of Chicago Press.

Ikegami, Eiko. 1995. *The Taming of the Samurai: Honorific Individualism and the Making of Modern Japan*. Cambridge, MA: Harvard University Press.

Ikegami, Eiko. 2005. *Bonds of Civility. Aesthetic Networks and the Political Origins of Japanese Culture*. Cambridge: Cambridge University Press.

Josephson, Jason Ānanda. 2012. *The Invention of Religion in Japan*. Chicago: University of Chicago Press.

Karamustafa, Ahmet T. 2018. "Shiʿis, Sufis and Popular Saints." In *The Wiley Blackwell History of Islam*, edited by Armando Salvatore et al., 159–76. Oxford: Wiley Blackwell.

al-Khatib, Mutaz. 2020. "*Hadith* Criticism between Traditionists and Jurisprudents." In *Modern Hadith Studies: Continuing Debates and New Approaches*, edited by Belal Abu-Alabbas et al., 129–150. Edinburgh: Edinburgh University Press.

al-Khatib, Mutaz. 2023a. "Introduction: Ḥadīth and Ethics." In *Ḥadīth and Ethics through the Lens of Interdisciplinarity*, edited by Mutaz al-Khatib, 1–7. Leiden: Brill.

al-Khatib, Mutaz. 2023b. "*Ḥadīth*-Based Ethics *Ḥadīth* as a Scholarly Sub-discipline of Islamic Ethics." In *Ḥadīth and Ethics through the Lens of Interdisciplinarity*, edited by Mutaz al-Khatib, 8–29. Leiden: Brill.

Khoury, Raif Georges. 2006. "Story, Wisdom and Spirituality: Yemen as the Hub between the Persian, Arabic and Biblical Traditions." In *Islam in Process: Historical and Civilizational Perspectives*, edited by Johann P. Arnason et al., 190–219. Bielefeld: Transcript.

Lapidus, Ira M. 1984. "Knowledge, Virtue, and Action: The Classical Muslim Conception of Adab and the Nature of Religious Fulfillment in Islam In Moral Conduct and Authority." In *Moral Conduct and Authority: The Place of* Adab *in South Asian Islam*, edited by Barbara Daly Metcalf, 38–61. Berkeley: University of California Press.

Lawrence, Bruce B. 2021. *Islamicate Cosmopolitan Spirit*. Oxford: Wiley Blackwell.

Masud, M. Khalid. 1984. "*Adab* al-Mufti: The Muslim Understanding of Values, Characteristics, and Role of a Mufti." In *Moral Conduct and Authority. The Place of* Adab *in South Asian Islam*, edited by Barbara Daly Metcalf, 124–51. Berkeley: University of California Press.

Masud, M. Khalid [1977]. 1995. *Shatibi's Philosophy of Islamic Law*. Kuala Lumpur: Islamic Book Trust.

Mayeur-Jaouen, Cathérine. 2020. "Introduction." In Adab *and Modernity: A "Civilising Process"? (Sixteenth–Twenty-First Century)*, edited by Cathérine Mayeur-Jaouen, 1–45. Leiden: Brill.

Metcalf, Barbara Daly. 1984. "Introduction." In *Moral Conduct and Authority: The Place of* Adab *in South Asian Islam*, edited by Barbara Daly Metcalf, 1–20. Berkeley: University of California Press.

Murata, Sachiko, and William C. Chittick. 1994. *The Vision of Islam*. St. Paul, MN: Paragon House.

Opwis , Felicitas. 2010. *Maṣlaḥa and the Purpose of the Law: Islamic Discourse on Legal Change from the 4th/10th to 8th/14th Century*. Leiden: Brill

Patrizi, Luca. 2023. "From Education to Etiquette: An Attempt to Reconstruct the Semantic 'Enlargement' of the Term *Adab*." In *L'* Adab, *Toujours Recommencé. "Origins", Transmissions, Metamorphoses of* Adab *Literature*, edited by Francesca Bellino et al., 346–77. Leiden: Brill.

Rahman, Fazlur [1966]. 1979. *Islam*. Chicago: University of Chicago Press.

Salvatore, Armando. 1997. *Islam and the Political Discourse of Modernity*. Reading: Ithaca Press.

Salvatore, Armando. 2007. *The Public Sphere: Liberal Modernity, Catholicism, and Islam*. New York: Palgrave Macmillan.
Salvatore, Armando. 2016. *The Sociology of Islam: Knowledge, Power and Civility*. Oxford: Wiley Blackwell.
Salvatore, Armando. 2019. "Secularity through a 'Soft Distinction' in the Islamic Ecumene? *Adab* as a Counterpoint to *Shari'a*." *Historical Social Research* 44 (3): 35–51.
Şentürk, Recep. 2005. *Narrative Social Structure: Anatomy of the Hadith Transmission Network*, 610–1505. Stanford, CA: Stanford University Press.
Sperl, Stefan. 2007. "Man's 'Hollow Core': Ethics and Aesthetics in *Ḥadīth* Literature and Classical Arabic *Adab*." *Bulletin of the School of Oriental and African Studies* 70 (3): 459–86.
Stewart, Devin. 2018. "Developments Within the Religious Sciences During the Rise and Decline of Empire." In *The Wiley Blackwell History of Islam*, edited by Armando Salvatore et al., 137–57. Oxford: Wiley Blackwell.
Walker, Paul E. 2011. "Social Elites at the Fatimid Court." In *Court Cultures in the Muslim World. Seventh to Nineteenth Centuries*, edited by Fuess Albrecht and Jan-Peter Hartung, 105–22. London: Routledge.
Yavari, Neguin. 2014. *Advice for the Sultan: Prophetic Voices and Secular Politics in Medieval Islam*. London: Hurst.
Yücesoy, Hayrettin. 2023. *Disenchanting the Caliphate: The Secular Discipline of Power in Abbasid Political Thought*. New York: Columbia University Press.

3

Connecting Spaces and Bodies on the Way (*Tariqa*)

The Connective Habitus of Wayfaring (*Suluk*)

Over the last few decades, we have witnessed various critiques addressed to the Western orientalist propensity to encapsulate Sufism into a confined set of practices and orientations subsumed under the category of "mysticism." Most of this criticism has targeted how that category was imbued with a distinctively Christian, or even more narrowly Protestant, sense of differentiation between institutional power—located in the Church—and the longing for a genuine, unmediated union with God (*unio mystica*). This union was presumed to occur within the secluded chamber of individual consciousness. Embracing this critical angle is an indispensable first step[1] in the task of elucidating Sufism's distinctive social moorings and institutional articulations against any reductionism. Yet further steps are necessary, including revisiting the meaning of "mysticism" prior to its Christian/Protestant hijacking. The term no doubt originates—like most words used in Western languages to describe religious, social, and political life and institutions—from a Greco-Roman conceptual dictionary that decisively influenced Latin Christianity and its sequential developments.

And yet, mysticism derives from *mystes*, which in Greek means "initiate," a term used in the "mystery religions" of ancient Greece. These religions rested on confraternal bonds and a capacious notion of membership in religious communities that transgressed the political boundaries of the Greek *polis*. These boundaries were relatively narrow, even when the *polis* took on a democratic form—contrary to common assumptions, democratic *poleis* were far from dominant in ancient Greece, whereas mystery religions were far more pervasive. Most notably, the type of initiation characteristic of the mystery religions placed a premium on fostering a deep sense of connectedness among their members, supported by transformative practices, rather than on producing the static identity and individualized interiority of the "believer." The latter crystallized only with the institutionalization of Christian churches, and most consistently after the Protestant Reformation. One cannot fail to notice how several features of the "mystic" way associated with Greek mysteries—especially its strongly relational and initiatory dimension—resonate with Sufism, as we will see, far more than does the mainstream Western Christian understanding of the term.

Having determined that there are ways to rescue "mysticism" from its confinement to an individual realm of the spirit, one can turn to Michel de Certeau's alternate and more transversal understanding of the concept. Here mysticism takes the form, in French, of *mystique*, understood as a process that generates a distinctive, mobile, and yet sociopolitically ingrained space. This process relies on producing life forms oriented toward cultivating a specific type of habitualized, embodied knowledge (de Certeau 1992, 16). No doubt, in de Certeau's analysis of early-modern France, such dynamics were entangled in the tension between lived experience and institutional theopolitical power that conventionally characterizes "mysticism." Nonetheless, his shift of focus toward a fully embodied and socially layered set of teachings and practices provides a compelling parallel to the development of Sufi life forms. Its merit—counter to the Western restrictive channeling of "mysticism"—lies in apprehending a genuine capacity to institute a habitus sustained by multiple modes of connectedness, which often blur standardized distinctions between mundane and divine planes. This understanding of mysticism turns the Western, Protestant-biased emphasis on individual spirituality upside down. It offers a first conceptual window for grasping the relational and connective dimensions of Sufi-inflected instituting and instituted practices. This is because, far from reducing mysticism to a solitary quest of the spirit, de Certeau's idea helps us appreciate the kind of civility Sufism was able to articulate—and institute—across a variety of geocultural settings. The institutional matrix most closely associated with Sufism is a dual type of bond. The first connects master and disciple vertically; the second is a confraternal nexus created through horizontal ties of mutual support among members of a Sufi group. While the vertical axis pivots on the authority of the master, the horizontal one cements links among disciples, who metaphorically recognize one another as brothers and sisters despite the absence of consanguineous ties (Salvatore 2016, 89). Often referenced as "brotherhood" (ibid., 73–104), this institutional matrix is characterized by a plastic organizational grid—rooted in specific locales, urban as well as rural, yet extensible across regions. As will be seen shortly, this matrix is essentially a result of the combined habitualizing (and meta-institutional) power of *hadith* and *adab* explored in Chapter 2.

This chapter argues that the *tariqa*—the Sufi organizational structure often reduced to a religious or mystical institution—constituted the primary matrix of embodied sociopolitical formation in the Islamic ecumene. Over time, the term *tariqa* came to encompass the complex bond and designate the institutional matrix itself. It metaphorically signals a mystical path or wayfaring, often referred to more specifically as *suluk*, which also means conduct. The combination of these meanings connotes a journey across space by a *tariqa*'s members—or, more precisely, as will be seen shortly, by their bodies. Yet we should see the "path" also, and indissolubly, as a method, in its original Greek sense (see Chapter 1), for achieving unity with the ultimate dimension of the Real, or Divine. As used by Kharraz (d. ca. 899), one of the earliest Sufi teachers, *tariqa* is "the journey toward the state of harmony with God that is Islam" (Green 2012, 31). Even more fundamentally, the idea reflects the *hadith* in which Prophet Muhammad intimates: "Be in this world as if you were a stranger or a wayfarer." One could also suggest a parallel with the Chinese concept of *Dao*, in which the idea of the "way" combines cosmological and existential dimensions.

While Western understandings of mysticism are often associated with a struggle against bodily desires in order to attain purely spiritual states conducive to a unitive experience with the Divine, in the Sufi inflection of Islam—and its organized modes—it is the bodily dimension of connecting vertically and horizontally in the process of wayfaring that takes center stage. Here, like elsewhere, a "view from the East" (i.e., from traditions other than the Abrahamic ones), rather than the flat lens of the hegemonic Latin (post-)Christian West, may yield more suitable insights into the process. The Japanese philosopher Yasuo Yuasa is especially helpful in this regard. He not only stressed the centrality of the body in East Asian traditions (including those that could be dubbed "mystical") but also specified that "[the] body lives in relation to things in space, and it itself exists spatially" (Yuasa [1987] 1993, 127). It is the very idea of a human aggregation living through "bodies in space" that, as will be seen shortly, conveys a strategic understanding of the instituting process vectored by the *tariqa*. This process involves more than an appropriation of space, whether locally or across long distances; it unfolds through the mutual linking of bodies, something that can occur only *through* space—indeed, via a piecemeal "corporealization" of space. Such a dynamic is far removed from the model of a "collective body" coming into being by fiat, as in the top-down corporate institutionalization characteristic of medieval Europe, where a "corporate" bond (from *corpus*, body) was legally and symbolically imposed (see Chapters 4 and 9).

By contrast, the *tariqa* grows through the gradual, ongoing work of connecting discrete bodies into a web or tissue of embodied networks that stretch across space. Connective and mobile bodies, on the one hand, and collective and corporate bodies, on the other, thus instantiate different—indeed, opposite—models of institution. The idea of a journey of connecting bodies is a fitting simile for Islam's historical venture. It reflects how the unfolding of the Islamic ecumene cannot be reduced to a strategic, militarily driven model of empire-building. Especially after the collapse of the centralized authority of the Baghdad Caliphate in the 10th century CE, the continued flourishing and expansion of the ecumene depended on partnerships in the circulation of goods, people, and ideas along multiple long-distance routes—continental and maritime alike. Sufi *turuq* (pl. of *tariqa*) stood at the forefront of this networking process, providing both leadership and know-how. Concomitantly, the expansion of trade networks promoted by Persian and Arab merchants entered into a positive loop with the propagation of Islam, which in turn generated codes regulating a wide range of relations and transactions (see Chapter 2). As Nile Green has succinctly put it, Sufism functioned as a "technology of inter-regional connection and exchange." (Green 2012, 12).

The first shoots of what over the centuries flourished as a comprehensive and translocal Sufi movement were already, if ambivalently, entangled with the development of urban forms of Islam under the Umayyad imperial program. Its centralized court balanced Arab hegemony with a creative appropriation of Byzantine and Sasanian administrative, aesthetic, and material cultures (see Chapter 5). While the Umayyads' interpretation of the caliphal institution folded the idea of succession to prophetic authority into the prerogatives of imperial rule, surging oppositional movements—some of which fed into the 'Abbasid revolution of 747–750—became invested in a grass-roots reconstruction of community life oriented to the prophetic example. In the interstices of the entanglements between court-centered *adab* and the popular devotion that fed into the process of collection and authentication of *hadith* (see Chapter 2), initial seeds of alternative life forms came to fruition. Sprouting in the very middle of the new

'Abbasid capital of Baghdad, these seeds gave life to a self-feeding movement that, over time, happened to be mostly (though far from exclusively) identified with *tasawwuf* as the "emic" word imperfectly translated as "Sufism" which reifies a form of life into a systematic doctrine and formation.

Developing in tandem to similar movements in the strategic Eastern region of Khorasan, the narratives and practices of surging Sufi life were nested within what, following Japanese sociologist Eiko Ikegami, we may call "enclave publics." In her work on comparable developments in premodern and early-modern Japan (see Chapter 2) Ikegami (2005, 39) emphasized how such milieus were "unconnected with the hierarchical order of the dominant publics." The emerging life forms and underlying communicative, connective, and ritual practices did not produce formal identities and often required the bracketing out of social roles (Ridgeon 2015, 4–12; Rahimi and Salvatore 2018, 255–258). In this sense, these enclaves constituted both a critique of prevailing patterns of authority and an incubator of novel relational, ethical, and embodied modes of living. During the Umayyad and early 'Abbasid eras, Sufi circles remained relatively marginal and localized, still lacking definite organizational profiles. Yet as the 'Abbasid capital of Baghdad grew into a vast and dynamic metropolis, these enclave publics increasingly served as hubs for more sophisticated mystical practices and reflections, enabling the blossoming of several genres of Sufi literature (Rahimi and Salvatore 2018, 259). In parallel with Baghdad's rapid urbanization, comparable groups emerged in other regions of the empire—most notably in Khorasan, and especially in the city of Nishapur[2]—where distinct local formations became entangled in translocal connections.

While Sufi groups and publics continued to spread across the Islamic ecumene during the 10th century, it was particularly in the 11th—and even more successfully in the 12th—century that the *tariqa* developed the full institutional matrix of a confraternity. During this period, it began to formalize its practices and to place them at the center of the socioreligious life of overlapping social groups and cultural milieus. As the 'Abbasid order of what Hodgson termed the High Caliphate fragmented into various autonomous principalities, Sufi networks completed their transformation from loose associations into stable—if mobile and translocally networked—*turuq* (Rahimi and Salvatore 2018, 260). Typically organized around the authority of a master or *shaykh* (lit. "elder"), the confraternities refined their methods for initiating followers and for structuring their activities in the aftermath of the High Caliphate's collapse. The *turuq* steadily gained influence, financial support, and a form of organizational sophistication matched by a remarkable institutional nimbleness. Their expansion was further propelled by social and geographical mobility: an increasing number of wayfarers sought out masters for instruction, while masters themselves traveled frequently to connect with other masters and obtain authorization to transmit particular ways of *tasawwuf* distinctive of different *turuq*.[3]

This momentum of the *tariqa* as an institutional matrix was further amplified through the integration of Turkic nomadic populations into the Islamic ecumene, beginning with their warrior elites, who frequently went on to found ruling dynasties (Salvatore 2016, 107–109). In this context, the *turuq* played a pivotal role in facilitating integration, acting—alongside long-distance trade networks—as primary conduits of Islamization. Throughout this trilogy, Islamization is understood not as a unilinear process of conversion, but as the formation of an ecumene or cosmopolis radiating from core regions such as the Fertile Crescent, the Iranian plateau, and the Syr-Oxus basin, and binding together self-renewing Arabic traditions with emerging Persianate forms of cultural expression and social organization. Within this expanding ecumene, the confraternities demonstrated a distinctive capacity to operate across vast distances by generating dense, replicable networks of connection. In doing so, they gradually nourished a translocal Sufi movement that linked metropolitan centers to their hinterlands and to other urban nodes. The instituting process did not involve only masters and their immediate disciples, but drew in a wide range of social groups, including merchants, townspeople, farmers, and nomadic populations. Under conditions of intensified mobility, the teachings and practices of a *tariqa* were deliberately shaped to be portable, allowing them to be reproduced in new settings by a master's authorized representatives, who were often dispatched to establish new branches (DeWeese 2018, 335). At the same time, it should be noted that not all *turuq* pursued expansive networking strategies. Some preferred to remain closely tied to particular localities, flourishing within specific cities or surrounding regions without becoming integrated into broader initiatic circuits or organizational frameworks (ibid., 345).

Surging as a fluid institutional matrix articulating a shared path of communion with the Divine, the *tariqa* played a pivotal role in the intricate tapestry of Islam's historical venture. Regarded by Hodgson as a vector of an "institutionalized mass religion" and a conduit for combining and harmonizing diverse facets of popular piety (Hodgson 1974, II, 210–218), the bundling of Sufi teachings and practices within the matrix of the *tariqa* offered individuals and groups viable—if locally adaptable—pathways for aligning their lives with the exemplary *sunna* of Prophet Muhammad. This alignment unfolded through varying modalities and degrees of participation in increasingly organized groups. At the core of the practices that cemented the associational bond, however, stood the pivotal relationship between master and disciple. Initiatory oaths and the investiture of new initiates with the *khirqa* (a white woolen cloak) ritualized the transmission of a form of knowledge that was, paradoxically, both esoteric—accessible only through the mediation of the master—and broadly inclusive. Even as initiatory procedures became more demanding during the transition to the early-modern era, the associational bond sustained a remarkable degree of openness, allowing the *tariqa* to remain a capacious and socially integrative institutional form.

Conventional orientalist tropes, forged by scholars such as the Anglican minister and missionary J. Spencer Trimingham (1971), tended to portray the institutionalization of Sufism through the *turuq* as the imposition of masterly authority over the alleged mystical fervor of earlier Sufis, exemplified by figures such as Mansur al-Hallaj (857–922). While it is undeniable that several emerging masters hailed from urban propertied elites and thus often promoted forms of regulation of Sufi life, recent historiography—also building on Hodgson's insights—has decisively challenged this reductive reading. Rather than endorsing a monolithic narrative, scholars have reappraised the multifaceted and internally differentiated evolution of Sufism. With the flourishing of the *tariqa*, initiatory rituals, mystical poetry, and communal gatherings multiplied and interwove, enriching the texture of Sufi life. Far from signaling the triumph of a top-down authority promoting a sanitized and inward-looking "mysticism," the rise of the *turuq* diversified practices and modes of participation by instituting durable bonds of fellowship, loyalty, and mutual allegiance across a wide range of social milieus.

While Baghdad played a seminal role in the blossoming of an embryonic Sufi life form, the model of relations between Sufi masters and disciples that later set standards for the ecumene-wide development of the *tariqa* was first articulated in Nishapur, Khorasan. The nexus between the Baghdadi and Khorasani formative milieus was embodied by the travels of Abu Bakr al-Wasiti (d. 932) between the two centers. These journeys crystallized the indissoluble link between the instituting power of the *tariqa* and the practice of travel—not merely as a metaphor for spiritual wayfaring, but as its very pedagogical and experiential lifeline (Rahimi and Salvatore 2018). It should also be noted that the process leading to the consolidation of the *tariqa* matrix initially involved seekers engaging with multiple masters. Aspirants would travel to different teachers in search of initiation, authorization to instruct others, or licensure to interpret Sufi treatises. As the field of Sufi adepts expanded, debates within Sufi literature increasingly focused on defining the profile of an ideal master capable of offering comprehensive guidance to followers. Gradually, this discussion favored the institution of more organic and durable bonds between master and disciple, thereby limiting the number of masters an aspirant could legitimately consult.

The need to impose limits on the entropy of seeking and journeying reflected broader concerns about organizing mystical pursuits and instituting Sufi life. As recognition grew for the diversity of holy figures, pressing questions emerged: who was entitled to attract followers, and who was capable of providing comprehensive training to seekers? The most typical pattern that took shape consisted of programs overseen by a master (*murshid*) vying for the allegiance of aspirants (sing. *murid*), both through personal knowledge or other merits rooted in forms of "charisma,"[4] and by demonstrating an unbroken chain (*silsila*) of initiations—each link transmitting spiritual authority—leading back to none other than Prophet Muhammad. Significantly, this lineage model was inspired by the authentication procedures of *hadith* transmission (Green 2012, 53)—even if, in the context of a *tariqa*, it supplemented scriptural anchoring with a focus on ultimate truth (*haqiqa*) as illuminated by the prophetic example. Most importantly, as the initiatory dimension of the Sufi path gained prominence, earlier instructional patterns—more closely modeled on the study of *hadith* or *fiqh*—gradually gave way to a more intimate master–disciple bond, known as *suhba*. This bond should be understood as a form of "conversational" companionship, one that remains attentive to the vertical differentiation of status along the path while intensifying embodied proximity and shared practice.

Regardless of the degree of commitment to *hadith* and its study, which retained its importance across regions and over the ages in many *turuq*, the common thread in this instituting enterprise and related life forms was an unwavering commitment to embody the exemplary patterns set by prophetic conduct, drawing inspiration from the resplendent model of Prophet Muhammad. Likewise, and notwithstanding any potential parallels of the early Sufi movement with the ascetic models of Christian mysticism, Sufism was firmly rooted in the Qur'an. Moreover, while pivoted on the injunction to "remember" God (central to the practice of *dhikr*, on which more below),

Sufi practice aligned closely with what Hodgson famously—yet vaguely—dubbed "*hadith* moralism" (Hodgson 1974, I, 393), enshrined in the corpus of transmitted and authenticated prophetic reports. The emerging Sufi groups skillfully crafted a specialized vocabulary that harmonized with the cultured environments they inhabited, drawing deeply from the ethos of *hadith*, whereby the prophetic model served as a guiding light. However, the term "moralism" may be simplistic and misleading. The focus should be on the habitualizing process unfolding at the intersection between *hadith* and *adab* explored in Chapter 2. As will be seen shortly, the Sufi movement was at the vanguard of blending the two traditions in setting standards for a simultaneously bodily and spiritual training. This was oriented to attaining harmony with the multifaceted beauty of creation—as the cosmic reflection of Allah's love for His creatures.

One should also consider that ordinary Muslims, including recent converts, often encountered Islam first through the examples of itinerant renunciants (proto-Sufis, so to speak), preachers, and proponents of the centrality of *hadith* for determining the prophetic *sunna*, commonly known as the *ahl al-hadith* (see Chapter 2). Their embodied modes of life and conduct frequently exerted a stronger formative influence on everyday practices than did the scholarly treatises produced by urban religious specialists (Karamustafa 2018, 163–165). At the same time, much like the notion of "moralism" in Hodgson's terminology, the category of "piety" proves too narrow to capture the instituting process associated with the *tariqa* and the forms of wayfaring it enabled. Precisely in response to this limitation, an emergent Sufi urban intelligentsia elaborated a more refined vocabulary of holistic training. This vocabulary was increasingly attuned to broader audiences already familiar with narratives and tropes drawn from the Qur'an and the *hadith*, while seeking to animate and encompass ever more diversified life forms on that shared narrative ground (Green 2012, 42).

Equipped with such a fast-developing toolkit of knowledge and practice, the Sufi circles frequently intersected with Sunni legal schools and interfaced with their approach to teaching and knowledge transmission. For example, direct synergies were established between the emerging Shafi'i school of jurisprudence and the Khorasani strand of Sufism, particularly in cities such as Nishapur. By maintaining an adaptable yet foundational connection to the instituting prism linking narrativity to norm-formations via habitualization, Sufism played a central role in the unique blurring of "religion" and "civility" within the broader culture of the Islamic ecumene (Green 2012, 42–51; Karamustafa 2018, 167). Put differently, the form of civility generated in this process was better described as "enchanted" rather than "secular" (Rahimi and Salvatore 2018, 264). Most significantly, in the pursuit of inner truth (*haqiqa*) the Sufi movement facilitated a convergence of the two narrative streams of *hadith* and *adab*, a trajectory that reached a point of consolidation on the threshold of the early-modern era. *Adab* progressively entered the life of various Sufi brotherhoods, shaping practice and pedagogy by assuming a pivotal role in instructional manuals for aspirants and practitioners alike. While even the earliest Sufi handbooks displayed a marked concern with questions of etiquette and ceremony, Sufi *adab* was increasingly codified as a mode of governing the individual body in its interaction with other bodies, through a flexible modulation of the wayfaring self.

From the 11th to the 13th century, *tariqa* manuals increasingly articulated codes of conduct and explored how lay members of Sufi associations could participate in the embodied enactment of Sufi narratives and habitus. Among the most influential contributions to this genre is *Kitab Adab al-Muridin* ("The Book of the *Adab* of the Disciples"), authored by Abu-l-Najib al-Suhrawardi (1097–1168). This formative work offered aspirants concrete guidance in matters of everyday conduct and spiritual practice, while also responding to significant transformations in Sufi organizational patterns. Most notably, it accompanied the consolidation of the dyadic relationship between master and disciple and facilitated the inclusion of individuals and groups that had previously remained at the margins of the Sufi path.

In this context, Abu-l-Najib creatively reworked the juridical concept of *rukhsa* (dispensation) to accommodate evolving modes of participation. Whereas the rigor of earlier Sufi circles had rendered such dispensations suspect, they now served to recalibrate the authority of masters over expanding and increasingly diverse circles of followers. The manual thus went beyond merely specifying permitted dispensations for lay participants. It examined the conditions under which the relaxed imitation practiced by the lay affiliate (*mutashabbih*) of the disciplines incumbent on the *murid* (the full disciple) could sustain a more articulated, if flexible, organizational structure (DeWeese 2018, 331–332). Through this codifying effort, the *tariqa* took shape as a malleable and ramified institutional matrix, structured both horizontally and vertically. The systematic articulation of relations linking masters to their disciples, and further to wider circles of affiliates, emerged as a central outcome of this process. Significantly, the prominence of *adab* in the very title of Abu-l-Najib's work signals its growing practical relevance within a pedagogical program that extended well beyond strictly spiritual exercises. The manual addressed the habitualization of conduct in everyday social life, encompassing matters of etiquette, attire, food and drink, and, above all, travel. Journeying was treated as quintessential to Sufi wayfaring, a privileged conduit for integrating body and mind. In this holistic perspective, mundane activities were recognized as decisive components of a path that was at once bodily and spiritual (Rahimi and Salvatore 2018, 267).

Abu-l-Najib's nephew and disciple Shihab al-Din Abu Hafs ʿUmar al-Suhrawardi (1145–1234) deepened this enterprise and brought it to a new level of organizational sophistication and sociopolitical relevance (DeWeese 2018, 333–335). His approach affected not only the institutionalization of the Sufi movement itself but also the wider institutional landscape of the Mongol and post-Mongol eras (see Chapters 5–8). During this period, various Sufi groups became closely associated with local communities, both nomadic and sedentary, mobilizing them either in support of or in resistance to the military and political projects of Turko-Mongol ruling elites. While lay members did not necessarily aspire to the full realization of *adab* as required by the strictest Sufi disciplines, their affiliations nonetheless provided a durable framework for negotiating social ties within shifting political constellations, particularly under Mongol rule. The conceptual groundwork laid by Abu-l-Najib proved decisive in this development, insofar as it acknowledged that the aspiration or desire (*irada*) of a lay affiliate might diverge from that of a conventional novice (*murid*, literally one who possesses or manifests *irada*). The legitimation of such a differentiated lay status reflected a longer-term evolution of Sufi ritual and disciplinary practices, enabling their partial displacement into more public and shared ceremonial forms across diverse social milieus. Rather than signaling a dilution of Sufi rigor, this inclusive strategy undercuts the orientalist trope—common in earlier Western scholarship—that the emergence of a mass following marked a decline from a supposed golden age of mystical purity.

Additionally, Abu-l-Najib emphasized the strategic importance of cultivating Sufi life in urban contexts. This orientation facilitated the diffusion of spiritually imbued manners across the major cities of the ecumene while simultaneously reinforcing their vital links to the countryside. The subsequent work of comprehensive reconstruction of Sufi life undertaken by his nephew ʿUmar al-Suhrawardi, by contrast, stands out as an articulation of a mystical framework that consecrates the city as a privileged space of divinely assisted growth and communal connectedness. In this perspective, the city emerges as a conduit for achieving unity and cohesion within a fractured world. The concept of *adab* became increasingly central to sustaining fraternal discipline and solidarity, harmonizing the inner and outer dimensions of existence—the mundane and the spiritual. In this way, it functioned as the driving force of a profoundly embodied process, through which the Sufi movement operated simultaneously on the instituting and the instituted planes of life in the ecumene. By the onset of the Mongol era, Sufism had effectively become a mainstream force within Islam and one of the most vital institutional formations of the Islamic ecumene.

The Intercorporeality of *Walaya*

The blossoming of the institutional chrysalis of the *tariqa*, drawing on a significant amalgamation of the two meta-institutional repertoires of *hadith* and *adab*, continued to pivot on the imitation of the exemplary virtues of Prophet Muhammad. While such an emulative pursuit was intensely subjective and profoundly bodily, it did not unfold as a solitary journey. Membership in a *tariqa* provided a supportive framework for embodying the Prophet's virtues through ritual performances, disciplines, and, more broadly, processes of habitualization that remained open to continuous reinterpretation and debate among competing confraternities and lineages. A constant factor within this dynamic process, however, was the role of prominent masters who were seen as capable of walking in the prophetic footsteps by cultivating a special closeness to Allah. This was articulated through their recognition as God's "friends" (*awliya'*, sing. *wali*) in post-prophetic times: saintly wayfarers entrusted with carrying forward Muhammad's charismatic legacy.

While not every master of a *tariqa* qualified as a *wali* in the burgeoning hagiographic literature, *walaya* nevertheless provided the shared model that masters were expected to approximate. The intermediation of a *wali* as the ultimate lynchpin in human relations with the Real or the Divine was sought not only by disciples, but also by rulers and a wide range of patrons. The designation of *wali* as a uniquely gifted figure enjoying proximity to Allah was extended retrospectively to the Companions of Prophet Muhammad, the first four Rightly Guided Caliphs, and, in some cases, selected rulers, urban scholars, and judges. Their authority, understood as persisting beyond death, carried far-reaching social, political, and even economic implications. Their shrines became major pilgrimage hubs, drawing increasingly diverse populations—urban and nomadic alike—who sought access to their *baraka*. This was conceived as a fluid force traversing the material and spiritual divide, capable of conferring comprehensive benefits upon its recipients (Karamustafa 2018, 173).

In order to appreciate the prerogatives and powers of the *awliyya'*, one needs to gain a more precise understanding of their fundamental attribute based on *walaya*. This quality inflected the deepest possible embodied habitualization of relationality between the human and divine planes. This understanding is crucial for our exploration, given that the inherently relational dimension of the concept of *walaya* became central to the instituting process within the Islamic ecumene, extending up to the level of rulership.[5] While often—if inadequately—translated as "saintliness," a term heavily burdened by Christian connotations, *walaya* is better understood as proximity, friendship, or clientship with Allah, as in the witnessing phrase *inna waliyya Allah* ("My protecting *Wali* is Allah"). One should further note that the term *wali* belongs to the canonically recognized Divine Names of Allah, who in the Qur'an is named the *Wali* of the *mu'minun* (sing. *mu'min*), that is, the active subjects of *iman* (commonly rendered as "faith"). As *Wali*, Allah assists them, as well as the *muttaqun* (those endowed with *taqwa*, or God-consciousness) and the *salihun* (the righteous), in accessing divine light. Yet, to grasp the attribute of *walaya* more fully, as Elmore (1999, 111–116) argues, one must recognize the exquisitely relational character of being a *wali* in its most general sense—that is, not only at its most elevated level, namely the proximity between the divine and human planes. Like the attribute of *walaya* itself, being a *wali* denotes an intensely binding form of relational power, applicable to Allah as well as to humans, and one that establishes a robust tie of reciprocity. At a purely human and broadly social level, *walaya* was already attested in pre-Islamic Arabia, where it designated the inclusion of out-group members into a tribe. After the advent of Islam, it commonly underpinned the legal figure that enabled the co-optation of non-Arab converts, thereby configuring a relationship of clientship.[6]

Unabashedly translated either as "saint" or, more faithfully (yet still incompletely), as "friend," in the case of Sufi saintly leaders the specification "of Allah" was always implied, the full expression being *wali Allah*. The power of *walaya* in instituting social relationships thus made it a key component of the *tariqa*. What was instituted was not merely a social bond, but the very possibility of life in the ecumene—or even the ecumene's capacity to exist as a human assembly bustling with life. The cosmos itself was understood as unable to persist, or even subsist, without the *awliyya'*, who were conceived as manifestations—indeed, as an institution—of the divine mercy that generates life. A fundamental layer of meaning derives here from the fact that, while sustaining the world's existence, the *awliyya'* were thought to live essentially ordinary human lives, albeit enlivened by divine blessing (*baraka*). By infusing this vital force into the social bond, they were imagined as forming a hierarchy culminating in the figure of the *qutb*, the Pole representing the ultimate microcosmic mirror of Allah. Disputes over who the Poles were in a given age, and over the relative ranking of subordinate figures among the *awliyya'*, generated contentious and often sharply divergent hierarchies in hagiographical literature. Yet these works shared a common endeavor: to construct taxonomies of *walaya* "as a Sufi institution" (Bashir 2011, 15). Such classifications were intended to offer seekers reputational parameters, encouraging them to enter discipleship with masters occupying higher ranks in the hierarchy of friendship and proximity to Allah. A recurring image expressing this form of relational intermediation was that of an ocean branching into rivers and rivulets—a networked geometry that integrated the hierarchical verticality of *walaya* with a decentralized horizontality. The latter secured fraternal mutuality along the path among those who undertook their journeys in search of intimate closeness to highly ranked masters (ibid. 85–87).

Therefore, *walaya* combines cosmological and social forms of relationality in the figure of the *tariqa*'s master. While *walaya* is no doubt ontologically inflected, it is the *tariqa* that renders it sociologically effective. *Tariqa* practices and ritual disciplines transform *walaya* into embodied habitus and patterned sociability via *adab*. While *adab* handbooks for Sufis were primarily concerned with the conduct of disciples, masters entered the picture insofar as *adab* was indispensable to their task of attracting and forming suitable disciples. Most notably, masters were expected to display sincerity and humility toward their followers, despite the authority they exercised over them. This trained relationality, supported by configurations of overlapping dyads, should not be reduced to the empathy-based intersubjectivity often posited by Western phenomenology. Rather, it is generated and governed by intercorporeal affectivity. From this perspective, understanding the significance of the body of the *wali* or master becomes critical. It was, above all, their capacity to work upon and attune the bodies of their disciples that constituted them as masters, enabling them to direct *adab* and radiate *baraka*. Even more fundamentally, the dynamic intercorporeality of bodies in perpetual motion—characteristic of a Sufi life of wayfaring—proved essential to instituting social connectedness and solidarity. In turn, as emphasized by the leading Sufi thinker Najm al-Din Razi (ca. 1177–1256), these dynamics depended on the *wali*'s ability to "read" the bodies of adepts—a condition, we might say, for allowing social *adab* and spiritual *baraka* to enter into productive synergies (Yuasa [1987] 1993, 195n18; Salvatore 2007, 97; 2016, 88; Bashir 2011, 12, 20–21, 46, 80–81).

While we prefer not to rely on the nebulous and biased concept of "charisma" to summarize the master's authority over disciples, it is nonetheless worth noting a set of recurring hagiographic motifs that give bodily consistency to the habitualizing force of *adab* and prepare the terrain for the deployment of intercorporeal affectivity. Of particular salience is the appeal of the master's face and speech to the heart of the disciple. This combined efficacy of visage and utterance signals the master's disciplined command of his own body and its capacity to generate affects that remold the bodily habitus of disciples and redirect the course of their lives (Bashir 2011, 82–83). Seen in this light—and without subsuming *baraka* under any ethereal, preconstituted notion of charisma—it is more apt to understand it as a kind of life force: the condensed expression of intercorporeal affects at work within the Sufi instituting process.

The understanding of *baraka* that emerges from the preceding discussion can be reinforced, rather than contradicted, by approaching habitus directly at the level of embodiment. In developing this argument, I have drawn primarily on Shahzad Bashir's work, which focuses on a decisive period and central region of the Islamic ecumene, namely the Persianate zone of the Middle Periods. At the same time, while learning selectively from Bashir's insights, I also seek to reformulate some of their implications by turning to Eastern, rather than Western, theories of the body that Bashir seems quite eager to reference. Such non-Western views are better suited to clarify the radiating luminosity attributed to the body and bodily practices in Sufism. It should be noted that Bashir is far from isolated in his reliance on Western theoretical lineages. The notion of habitus, discussed in Chapter 2, is often grounded in the body through appeals to the idea of a "habitual body," as articulated by figures such as Bergson or Merleau-Ponty. Bashir follows this interpretive line with little reservation: the habitual body appears as the instrument through which the body's life as a "subject" in the world is enacted over time (Bashir 2011, 15).[7]

However, non-Western scholars have criticized this position for depending on what is, in effect, an overly academic and predictable critique of disembodied Cartesian models of subjectivity. While such a corrective gesture was long overdue, it arrives too late to undo the early-modern Western conception of the subject and its problematic relation to embodiment—a conception that continues to structure Western instituted life (see Chapters 4 and 9). The central limitation of allegedly anti-Cartesian approaches such as Merleau-Ponty's lies in the fact that their turn to embodiment remains tethered to an essentially individual notion of the body. The critique of Cartesian dualism proceeds without a radical interrogation of the modern Western subject itself and the attendant body–mind divide. This limitation is especially evident insofar as the individual body's relation to other bodies is insufficiently traced through space, via what we have previously termed the "corporealization" of space. Yet it is precisely this connective dimension—bodies linked to other bodies across space—that Bashir emphasizes in his analysis. His insights would gain additional clarity, I suggest, if reframed through conceptual resources that do not inherit, even if critically, the historical biases of Western theories of the subject.

This is why I have been considering the approach of the Japanese thinker Yasuo Yuasa ([1987] 1993), who—significantly—developed a constructive critique of Merleau-Ponty while drawing primarily on inherited East Asian understandings of the body. Read through Yuasa's lens, Bashir's findings suggest that, rather than reflecting the body–mind dualism that continues to haunt Western phenomenology, Sufi conceptions point to a layered understanding of the body, produced through the tethering of an "imaginal" dimension to its underlying physical substrate, with the *qalb* (heart) occupying a strategic position at their intersection. The heart here functions as an organ of intellection that bridges inner states and the outer world. At the same time, it serves as a vessel for apprehending the interconnectedness of bodies through the love it captures and absorbs by revolving around the divine plane. Ultimately, the heart emerges as "a shadow body within the body" (Bashir 2012, 43–44), the seat of a deep intellect capable of harmonizing microcosmic and macrocosmic powers.

This is what makes the body, with the heart at its center, an interface or gate between interior and exterior, neither of which exists *per se*—unlike what is implied by the familiar Western subject–object dichotomy. Cosmologically, this entails a blurring of boundaries between the physical and the metaphysical, between the human microcosmic and the divine macrocosmic planes. At the same time, the affective dimension of the body, functioning as a revolving door between interior and exterior, enables masters to deploy their capacities so as to access, affect, and recalibrate the bodily habitus of their disciples. This is the key to triggering and governing the habitualizing—and, ultimately, instituting—process. The engine of this process is neither the individual body nor the body as such, but the intercorporeality expressed in the dyadic relation between master and disciple and the circulation of *baraka* through it. The movement proceeds, as it were, from the bodily "skin," standing for the more material strata of habitus, inward toward what is too readily labeled the "spiritual" realm, yet finds in Sufi thought a comprehensive and non-dual conceptual articulation (Bashir 2021, 20–32). Indeed, the body and its corporeality are not purely material, as they are inscribed within an imaginal dimension whose knowledge is essential to a deeper understanding of the connective dynamics of bodies, that is, their affective intercorporeality. The term designating this in-between space is *barzakh*, briefly introduced in Chapter 2 and described in the Qur'an as "[t]he confluence of the two seas (*marj al-bahrayn*), the one potable and sweet, the other salty and bitter" (Q. 25:53). As previously noted, this vivid image encapsulates a paradox: a border that is also a bridge, or a passage that connects. Correspondingly, the most venerated and feared among the *awliyya'* were understood as living doorways between the human and divine planes.

The notion of *barzakh* is often combined with the idea of *'alam al-mithal*, the imaginal world. This is a liminal space sharing in the intermediateness of the *barzakh*. It is an ontological level situated between the sensible and the intelligible, where material bodies are conjoined with their spiritual qualities. Dwelling in this space could be considered as tantamount to accessing extraordinary states of consciousness, like visions, states of trance, and dreams. Given that the *'alam al-mithal* consists of imaginal forms of material bodies, Bashir has suggested that it is "corporeous rather than corporeal since it can be described in the language of everyday experience, but without the kind of limitations that impinge on action in the material sphere" (Bashir 2021, 37). In other words, the experience of exceptional states of consciousness presupposes a physical body. Here we can resort to Yuasa's notion of the "quasi-body" for clarifying that such states are not mental fabrications (Yuasa [1987] 1993, 118–121). This is because the corporeous body, or "second body," is tethered to the material body in experiencing sensual states, like hearing or tasting. Again, leaning on Yuasa, the existence of such a second, corporeous body is not just postulated for theoretical convenience. It is rather the outcome of a type of experience, shared among several (mostly non-Western) traditions, that suggests how the mind, rather than unfolding as if against a bodily substratum, is tethered to a multilayered corporeality.[8] This experience, in turn, is acquired through advancing on the path toward the realization of a microcosmic, that is, human, alignment with the divine, macrocosmic plane—across the strait (but also bridge) of the *barzakh* (Bashir 2021, 38–39).

Some pivotal Sufi practices should be understood as integral to such conceptions of intercorporeal affectivity. Foremost among them is *dhikr*, which underwent several contested specifications across the history of the *turuq*. At its most basic level, however, *dhikr* takes the form of a meditative practice that generates awareness—through "remembrance," its primary meaning—of the divine plane by the repeated utterance of the name of Allah. Different Sufi *turuq* elaborated *dhikr* through a variety of bodily performances, including patterned movements, breathing techniques (whether focused and rhythmic or more spontaneous), and vocal utterances, whispered or voiced aloud. Through adherence to instructions governing these techniques—entailing intense modulation and coordination of the body–mind, or more precisely of different dimensions of the body—practitioners sanctioned their belonging to a specific *tariqa*. Such belonging ultimately consisted in inhabiting a distinctive way of being on the path, defined by particular lineages of masters and "friends," and by the patterns of intercorporeality they transmitted (Bashir 2021, 68). The related practice of *sama*ʿ, that is, "audition," involving music, singing, and recitation—and at times also bodily movement or "dance"—further exalted patterns of intercorporeality through the coordination of multiple bodies responding to the power of sound as it acts upon the heart. The practice often entailed graceful movements and spinning or "whirling," whereby the inner microcosmic journey mirrored macrocosmic cycles spiraling toward union with the Divine (Bashir 2021, 51, 77). Manuals of *adab* frequently played a crucial role in detailing the proper performance of such intercorporeality, providing a privileged avenue for articulating the requisite modes of habitualization and, thereby, instituting a *tariqa* that traced the specific wayfaring expected of Sufi practitioners.[9]

To recapitulate, Sufi life, as guided by *adab*, is best understood through the prism of the cultivation of bodily and perceptive experience. Along the path of imitating the exemplary life of Prophet Muhammad, techniques for embodying harmony with the Divine became intrinsic to life forms shaped by wayfaring within a *tariqa*. The process pivoted on the "friends" and their bodies, whose interlacing proximity indexed a seeker's advancement on the path. The engine of the process is *irada*, understood as a properly oriented desire, with the master as its object. This is why the agent of this desire is called the *murid*, the key term designating the disciple, while the target of desire, namely the master, is the *murad* (Bashir 2011, 136). The process unfolding through the dyadic, intermirroring, and intercorporeal affectivity between master and disciple presages the triangulation with every *tariqa*'s telos, that is, divine love. It acts as a catalyst for instituting the connective bond, unfolding over time through the *silsila*, the unbroken chain of transmission of the essential equipment for building habitual bodies and their attendant repertoire of socioreligious powers (ibid., 109–30).

The Confraternal Bond of *Futuwwa*

The weaving of a rich associational embroidery through the matrix of the *tariqa* multiplied the avenues and social loci for instituting the powers of bodily *habitus* via connectedness, intercorporeality, and patterns of civility. As these powers intensified and diversified while radiating outward from urban centers, it is hardly surprising that Sufi *turuq* developed organic—and often symbiotic—relations with two major forms of non-elite urban association. On the one hand stood craft and trade guilds; on the other, the "youth clubs" known as *futuwwa* (literally "young manliness" in Arabic, with the Persian counterpart *jawanmardi*).[10]

Uncertain are the links between professional guilds and any pre-existing craftsmen's associations in the Sasanian Empire, whose members largely belonged to religious—especially Christian, and more specifically Nestorian—minorities (Hatke 2018, 49), as well as with their Roman or Byzantine counterparts. Likewise, assimilating these formations to European organizational models—whence the very term "guild"—is implausible. Craft and trade guilds in the Islamic ecumene appear instead to have developed as part of the distinctive amalgams of urban life that flourished especially during the Middle Periods. They contributed to instituting the lives of their members as craftsmen and tradespeople on multiple levels by articulating—much like the *turuq*—a relatively low degree of formal organization. They supervised markets, worked to protect both the material and immaterial standards and secrets of the trades, and represented the interests of their affiliates vis-à-vis public authorities. Over time, particularly in the Ottoman Empire, guilds came to enjoy a considerable degree of autonomy in overseeing marketplace fairness and equality and in curbing excessive gains by their members (Arjomand 2004, 230–231; see also Faroqhi 2009).

Organizationally distinct from the *turuq*, the guilds nevertheless absorbed a range of values and symbols drawn from Sufi life, which often helped shape their collective rituals, not least through the centrality of the dyadic master–apprentice relationship. Not only were many guild members also affiliated with Sufi *turuq*; masters from these confraternities frequently acted as spokespersons or mediators on behalf of guilds in their often tense relations with public authorities, for instance on matters of taxation. Most significantly, guild members were expected to conform to a specifically professional *adab*, articulated and transmitted through manuals often condensed into the genre of *resaleh*. This genre, which delineates the virtuous habitus of the marketplace, proved especially popular across large parts of the Persianate zone, including Central Asia, Northwestern India, and Kashmir. Although written down only in relatively recent centuries, such works were traditionally transmitted orally. They were continuously adapted to shifting audiences and milieus, while remaining deeply influenced by Sufi teachings, particularly those associated with the *tariqa* Naqshbandiyya. These texts not only articulated models of exemplary conduct for craftsmen and tradespeople—grounded in respect for customers and a principled aversion to unlawful or excessive gain—but were also ritually recited, as they often derived from holistic conceptions of purity encompassing both body and mind (Dağyeli 2018, 215–220).

The *resaleh* genre and the life forms it was meant to institute and transmit emerged through a process in which the grid of civic associations was enriched by a further component whose links to pre-Islamic precursors in the Sasanian Empire remain debated. This component is *futuwwa*, an Arabic term derived from *fata*, meaning "youth." The term has often been made to resonate—especially through an orientalist lens—with the European idea of "chivalry," though the parallel is at best partial. As Scott Ridgeon notes, in pre-Islamic poetry *fata* designates the perfection of tribal virtues, indexed by commitments to solidarity, bravery in the defense of one's kin, and hospitality. In the Qur'an, by contrast, words derived from the same root sometimes associate youth with loyal servanthood, as in the case of Abraham (Q. 21:60), thereby reconfiguring *futuwwa* within a different ethical and relational horizon (Ridgeon 2010, 6–8).

A significant clue to how *futuwwa* could be integral to Sufi life—including its introspective methods—prior to its organizational differentiation with the *tariqa* comes from none other than Mansur al-Hallaj, as famously argued by Louis Massignon, who elevated this figure to a martyr of faith for a Western orientalist public. In this interpretation, the value of connectedness and loyalty associated with *futuwwa* was redirected toward Allah Himself. It made al-Hallaj a champion of a trope that unsettled formal theological conventions by radicalizing the dyadic relationship between Creator and creature (Ridgeon 2010, 28–30). Al-Hallaj's life spanned the final stretch of the High Caliphate, and Massignon's interpretive move also reflects the difficulty of tracing ideas and practices of *futuwwa* to a period preceding the Middle Periods, when prescriptive *futuwwa* manuals began to proliferate. This new phase was heralded by the work of the Sufi al-Sulami (973–1021), who was, significantly, also a scholar of *hadith*. In a work devoted to the earliest generations of Sufis, al-Sulami explicitly portrayed them as consciously and deliberately articulating the ideal of *futuwwa*.

While this retrojection of *futuwwa* to the very origins of Sufism is debatable—though not sociologically implausible (Arjomand 2025, 28–29)—al-Sulami's move marked only the beginning of a well-documented race to define *futuwwa* through a Sufi lens. This dynamic intensified to the point that the self-understanding of the "path" increasingly came to depend on the articulation of *futuwwa*. In a work encompassing the biographies of several generations of early Sufis, al-Sulami presents the leading master al-Junayd (ca. 830–910) defining *futuwwa*, subtly yet forcefully, as the virtue of seeking justice while renouncing one's personal claim to it. Other early Sufi leaders also figure prominently in al-Sulami's narrative, as they elucidate *futuwwa* by coupling rigorous self-introspection with unwavering dedication to others (Ridgeon 2010, 32–33). One can thus discern a clear trajectory whereby *futuwwa* was appropriated as a method for intensifying connectedness and intercorporeality into durable forms of group solidarity and cohesion. It should be noted, however, that in a manual al-Sulami specifically dedicated to *futuwwa*—one that meticulously traced chains of transmission of the various understandings of the ideal—the initial distillation of the quintessence of *futuwwa* found in early Sufi biographies exploded into a fantasmagoria of competing or overlapping definitions. A scholar of the caliber of Annemarie Schimmel counted more than two hundred such definitions. Among them stands out a striking tendency: the near-collapse of the meaning of *futuwwa* into a highly sophisticated technique of Sufi *adab*. In this register, *futuwwa* reflects the idea that in each situation or station on the Sufi path there is a particular habitus to be formed or a specific rule to be followed. This understanding presupposes a supple Sufi body, one adaptable to an indefinite range of social situations. Two articulations of this principle emerge, both of which became increasingly prominent during the Middle Periods. The first institutes *futuwwa* as conviviality: the joy of sharing actions and celebrations within a confraternal setting. The second sublimates this rule of exalted brotherhood through the saying that "the eyes that shine with the light of Allah will give light to the eyes that look upon them." Here the body shaped through Sufi *futuwwa* is understood as a medium of light. The intercorporeality of dyadic relationships relativizes not only individuality but also the organic character of

Sufi bodies. As bodies of light, their organs—including the heart and the eyes—are submerged in their mediating gifts, which are themselves gifts of light (Ridgeon 2018 with ibid.).

Likewise, al-Sulami's manual succeeds in authenticating *futuwwa* in Islamic terms in an unusually comprehensive way. It posits *futuwwa* as originating with Adam and being transmitted through the entire prophetic chain to Muhammad, before being sealed with 'Ali as its custodian. Overall, *futuwwa* is validated through a multiplication of the hermeneutic and practical horizons of *adab*. This is achieved by delving more deeply into dyadic ego–alter relationships and the habitualization of the mutual bond among wayfarers (Ridgeon 2010, 36–39). In this regard, Ridgeon also presents the view of Kharaqani (963–1033), a Khorasani scholar who unabashedly understood *futuwwa/jawanmardi* as a "sublime rank of wayfaring and traversing the path" (ibid., 46). Ultimately, the intimacy that members of *futuwwa* acquire with Allah may even dispense them from the mediation of the *awliyya'*, when it does not elevate such members to the rank of elites among the "friends." This theme is echoed by none other than Ibn 'Arabi (1165–1240) in his treatment of *futuwwa* across three chapters of his *al-Futuhat al-Makkiya*. For the Greatest Master (*al-shaykh al-akbar*), *futuwwa* ultimately amounts to a kind of cosmological super-*adab*. Through its practice, adepts acquire a form of absolute ethical autonomy that shields them from the judgment of fellow humans. This is because *futuwwa* is, in the final instance, a divine attribute nourished by Allah's mercy in creating a cosmos, despite His exclusive autonomy of Being—an idea resonant with the famous dictum where creation unfolds from the divine "love to be known" (ibid., 51–54).

To recapitulate, it is usually held that, prior to the surge of prescriptive texts, *futuwwa* groups expressed the autonomous collective power of youth "clubs." They emphasized values such as hospitality, generosity, and solidarity, but also bravery and masculinity.[11] These values were often mobilized in struggles against institutional power centers deemed oppressive and unjust, and therefore fundamentally un-Islamic. The emergence of such groups reflected the multifaceted nature of urban life, particularly during the phase that marked the beginning of the end of the High Caliphate in the 10th century and the onset of the Middle Periods. This also explains why no synthetic definition of *futuwwa* can fully capture its cultural multivalence and social versatility. As noted above, the first fully fledged tract on *futuwwa* by the Sufi and *hadith* scholar al-Sulami included as many as two hundred definitions. These were drawn from an assortment of sources, ranging from the *hadith* of Prophet Muhammad to sayings of his Companions and of five generations of Sufi masters. The cumulative effect of this operation was to fold *futuwwa* into a distinctly Sufi inflection of *adab*. In this way, *futuwwa* mediated a highly consistent amalgam of *hadith* and *adab*, serving the strategic goal of co-opting wider—and often socially lower—groups into the path.

Less clear, however, is the extent to which *futuwwa* became imbricated with trade associations or guilds, as well as when and where this occurred. The earliest source that appears to establish such a nexus is a late 11th-century treatise (Ridgeon 2010, 19, 43). Even so, any institutional cross-fertilization between *futuwwa* and the guilds seems to run against the common assumption that *futuwwa* originally expressed the ethos of non-established groups that deployed and mediated violence—the *'ayyaran*—for a variety of purposes, including extortion and coercion. It is difficult to assume that such practices would have been conducive to the stability and security of market activities—unless one stretches the notion of the market to include protection rackets. A more plausible reading is that the virtues later associated with *futuwwa* reflect the figure of the *'ayyar* "turned good," that is, transformed from a mobster into a defender of the weak and a promoter of civic solidarity. In any case, a consistent degree of mutual collaboration, if not outright symbiosis, between *futuwwa* groups and guilds likely had to wait until the Later Middle Periods, as will be seen shortly. Indeed, it is far more plausible that, both as an ideal and as a form of social organization, *futuwwa/javanmardi* first emerged in interstitial social spaces rather than within the structured milieu of professional guilds. *Futuwwa* provided cohesion and a measure of voice and power primarily to what may be described as an urban proletariat of wage earners, variably connected to—or disconnected from, depending on context—the craft professions. More often still, it comprised a subproletariat or "mob" inclined to self-organization in armed gangs (Ridgeon 2018, 12–13).

At the same time, a process of value convergence unfolded, grounded in a "civilizing" principle that sought to tame violence while promoting trust and solidarity. This process was frequently conducted under the aegis of Sufi masters and gradually secured a progression toward a habitus broadly shared with craftsmen and merchants. It appears to have operated by channeling lower-class rebellions and wider class conflicts into forms of social power and autonomy for the downtrodden, anchored in ideals of courage and compassion, but also confidentiality—that is, the safeguarding of secrets vital to the group, or the gathering and selective circulation of information, if not intelligence. Among those who explicitly framed this development as a process of sublimation into the "values" of *futuwwa* stands out the towering scholar al-Biruni (973–1048). He emphasized tenderness and malleability of character, dispositions especially prone to habitualization in ways resonant with Sufi virtues—above all those conducive to generosity, non-harm, or at least the grassroots control of violence. In this vein, *futuwwa* functioned as a decisive conduit for instituting the power of Sufi life among non-elite groups, often in symbiosis with the *tariqa*—all the more so because it did not thrive in sanitized enclave publics (Ridgeon 2010, 22).

The previously mentioned ʻUmar Suhrawardi played a significant role in providing a normative framework to *futuwwa* at the beginning of the 13th century. This intervention complemented the process—associated with him and his uncle—of formalizing, via *adab* rules, the training of a variety of constituencies in Sufi life. As we saw, this operation aimed at integrating into the Sufi fold broader social circles beyond disciples proper. The role ʻUmar Suhrawardi played both as an envoy of Caliph al-Nasir (1180–1225) and as a Sufi author and leader marked a watershed, through which *futuwwa* clubs were hierarchically folded into governmental institutions. This occurred during a major attempt to revive the institutional purchase and power of a long-enfeebled Caliphate, only a few decades before its suppression at the hands of the Mongols. ʻUmar Suhrawardi composed two *futuwwa* tracts (*fotovvat-nama*), notably in Persian rather than Arabic—the language typically used for *adab* manuals on Sufi organization—as if deliberately targeting a different urban audience (Hodgson 1974, II, 130–131, 292; Ohlander 2008, 26).

In parallel, and as a necessary premise to his more theoretical effort to establish the complementarity of *shariʻa* and *tariqa*, ʻUmar Suhrawardi emphasized the centrality of craftsmanship and industry within the Allah-willed order of society. Most crucially, *futuwwa* was instituted within the same synchronic and diachronic patterns of connectedness he recommended in his *adab* manuals, namely the master–disciple dyad and the chain of transmission (*silsila*) originating from Prophet Muhammad—both consecrated through initiatory power. It is symptomatic that the process began with Caliph al-Nasir himself being initiated into a *futuwwa*, before he went on to found new ones and initiate various elite members into them. The process culminated when al-Nasir proclaimed himself the master of all *futuwwa* associations across the regions belonging to the Caliphate. His choice of *futuwwa* as the vehicle to revive the agonizing power of the Caliphate indicates that he perceived it as the most potent and versatile Islamic institution. Its power was appropriated to secure not only social cohesion but also political stability, on which the very survival of the Caliphate as an institution depended. What stands out in this program is that the integration of new groups and classes into *futuwwa* began at the very top of society, among the elite personnel of the caliphal court (Arjomand 2004, 224–228; Ridgeon 2018, 4–6).

We have here the singular case of how the institutionalization of *futuwwa*, which had long functioned as a tool for self-organization and for channeling the violence of predominantly lower social strata, was taken over from the very pinnacle of ruling legitimacy in Islamic terms, namely the Caliph (Hodgson 1974, II, 282–283; Salvatore 2016, 85–87; see Chapter 7 in the present volume). The attempt was short-lived, as it was crushed by the Mongol takeover. And yet, it set the stage for streamlining the instituting power of the tripartite pool represented by Sufi life, the ethos of professional craftsmen, and the virtues of *futuwwa*. This amalgam would continue to play a seminal role in the Later Middle Period, albeit in a more pronounced oppositional vein vis-à-vis the rising Mongol type of statehood (Arjomand 2025, 177–200). The success of this post-caliphal triangular amalgamation became particularly visible in the organizations known as *akhi*, which spread from Anatolia and Western Iran beginning in the 13th century. ʻUmar Suhrawardi himself played a key role in this process as an envoy of al-Nasir to Syria and Egypt, tasked with promoting the standing of this emerging institution, including in its relations with ruling elites (Yıldırım 2018, 79–80).

Akhi means "my brother" in Arabic, but concurring meanings in Turkic idioms have been proposed to account for its usage, such as "knightly" or "generous" (Ridgeon 2010, 86–87fn34). The label surfaced, already in a mildly formalized form, in the works of ʻUmar Suhrawardi to designate membership in the Sufi–*futuwwa* at the time of al-Nasir. This occurred after comparable appellatives had appeared in earlier instantiations of both *tariqa* and *futuwwa*, in various guises, to designate masters and leaders of these associations. One should also consider that ʻUmar Suhrawardi's intervention took place at a moment when the cumulative migration of Turkic nomadic groups out of Central Asia, and particularly into Anatolia—a movement that long predated Mongol pressure—was triggering further transformations in socioreligious movements. Most notably, this development facilitated additional permutations within the growing amalgam linking *futuwwa* associations, the self-organization of market forces in professional associations, and the Sufi path. Turkish Sufi masters such as Ahmad al-Yasawi (1093–1166) contributed decisively to rearticulating Islamic associational life across Anatolia and Central Asia. Their distinctive *turuq*, culturally and linguistically Turkish, promoted forms of popular mysticism that bridged folk poetry with urban religious cultures and practices. It was at such crossroads that *akhi* associations flourished and came to assume a pivotal role within the *tariqa–futuwwa* nexus, remaining urban-centered while reaching deeply into tribal zones among nomadic populations. Following the 13th-century Mongol conquests, a thoroughly amalgamated institution—often referred to as *al-akhiyat al-fityan*[12]—fully captured the ethos of Central Asian steppe warriors. It blended their horseback valor with the urban egalitarianism and messianic fervor of Irano-Semitic traditions (Rahimi 2004, 67).

The renowned traveler Ibn Battuta (1304–1369), writing in the aftermath of the Mongol expansion into the Islamic ecumene, clearly included both craftsmen and "young men" within this type of organization. He observed that it played significant roles in the civic and political life of Anatolian, Iranian, and Central Asian urban centers. By this time, *akhi* had increasingly become the label of choice for such associations. Ibn Battuta, who often lodged in *akhi* hospices during his travels, reported their egalitarian and wealth-sharing practices, which combined forms of self-organization with a strong professional ethos, cutting across class divides. This outcome was facilitated by a cosmologically inflected and initiatically ritualized emphasis on a confraternal life form. Its bodily dimension found expression in the cultivation of competitive activities, such as wrestling, which exalted traits of masculinity and bravery. Most crucially, these associations played a strategic role in reconciling local and translocal expressions of "the importance of being Islamic" (Arjomand 2004, 228–229; Ridgeon 2010, 69, 75, 82; Rahimi 2018, 320–321).

We can infer that the social articulation of the Sufi-inflected *futuwwa/jawanmardi*, culminating in the *akhi*'s absorption of professional representation, reflects in full the close nexus between intercorporeality and the institution of a multifunctional type of social body. Through this development, the wayfaring path was fully folded into a civic space indissolubly linked to a precapitalist marketplace. These associations exhibited flexible—if often mutating—yet internally consistent organizational modes, whose instituted forms solidified and reached their zenith during the critical phase of the Islamic ecumene's historical venture that, with Hodgson, we identify as the Middle Periods. This versatile institutional framework enabled Sufis to cultivate a lasting sense of mutual trust and belonging within the ecumene, while integrating informal patterns of interaction and association drawn from a plurality of social worlds. Most notably, *futuwwa* was also inclusive of non-Muslims. At the same time, however, it tended to exacerbate patterns of gender segregation, insofar as the frequent gender exclusivity of emerging organizational forms replaced the earlier, milder inclusivity of women in Sufi life.[13] Nevertheless, the resulting form of civility not only accommodated diverse loyalties but also facilitated deliberate options for overlapping affiliations. Such affiliations could extend across long distances without the need for formal institutional charters or statutes, as was the case in medieval Europe (Salvatore 2016, 99–100; Chapter 4 in this volume).

It remains that the process by which increasingly organized Sufi enterprises extended their influence across broader social networks decisively owed to the codification and popularization of relationships between Sufi masters and their disciples. These relationships were crucially reflected in narratives of bodily connectedness within the vast and impactful literature conventionally dubbed "hagiographical" (Bashir 2011, 215). Such narratives are not merely records of exemplary lives but function as enactments of the habitualization process itself—much as, and on a par with, the work performed by the *hadith* and *adab* corpora examined in the previous chapter. This process could successfully unfold because, contrary to the idea of "mysticism" as requiring strict seclusion, Sufi life forms actively encouraged engagement with urban existence. Here desires and their channeling into habitualized forms amenable to subtle institutionalization contributed to the construction of what we may term an "enchanted city" (Rahimi and Salvatore 2018, 264), echoing de Certeau's understanding of mysticism as an alternative epistemic and social space. Along this trajectory, Sufism facilitated the flourishing of affective connections within civic life, codifying—rather than repressing—the pleasurable, the earthly, and the erotic. Such experiences point to a holistic, divinely inspired quest for what may be described as poetic reconfigurations of sublime enchantment enacted through a variety of practices (Arjomand 2025, 201–219). This perspective also resonates with the notion of civility articulated by Eiko Ikegami (2005; see Chapter 1 in this volume): a form of sociability imbued with aesthetic sensibilities that sustain the ever-fragile social bond, distilled from medieval and early-modern Japanese contexts that are, in significant ways, comparable to those examined in this chapter and the preceding one.

Wrapped in a web of reciprocity and manners, this idea of civility has a deeper sociological purchase than the "moral" sensibilities advocated by Scottish theorists of civil society, or the subjective dispositions produced through the work of a discursive tradition, as proposed by Asad's school in analogy with European Catholic medieval patterns (Salvatore 2016, 43–71). More than anything else, this type of civility was associated with the power of a continuous instituting process. The shared expectations underpinning these civic bonds presupposed familiar narratives, infused with soteriological orientations and a quest for beauty. As a richly cultural practice, Sufism most vividly embodied this civilizing-*cum*-instituting process without ever monopolizing it. In the increasingly fragmented social world of the Middle Periods, exacerbated by the arbitrary character of post-caliphal military rule (see Chapter 5), the affective and bodily dimensions of civic ties found support in the poetic reimagining of communion on a divine plane. And yet, unsurprisingly, the hard realities on the ground dented the enchantment of civic entanglements. As reliance on patronage from political and economic elites intensified, a delicate—if unstable—balance between patron–client and master–disciple relationships emerged. Intermediate forms of civil arrangements, marked by a combination of interest and affection, market partnership and lifeworldly companionship, played an increasingly vital role in shaping local knowledge–power constellations and long-distance networks. In turn, these networks extended their reach by including ordinary Muslims, itinerant preachers, and warrior-scholars operating in frontier regions. The interplay of enchantment and practical wisdom thus wove a complex tapestry of associational life, in which spiritual aspirations were pressed to align with, or respond to, worldly dynamics.

Notes

1. For a good summary, see Green (2012, 2).
2. Arjomand (2025, 17–38) has forcefully reiterated an assessment previously advanced by other scholars, according to which Khorasan—or, more precisely, Greater Khorasan, understood as including Transoxiana—was the primary cradle of the broader movement that came to be known as *tasawwuf*. Situated on the frontier with Central Asian regions where Buddhism had long flourished, Arjomand's focus on Khorasan also yields valuable insights into possible

Buddhist influences on Sufism (ibid., 18–22). This question will be addressed in the previously mentioned, co-authored third volume of the trilogy (Salvatore and Obuse, forthcoming). Here it suffices to note that the never-extinguished controversy over whether Sufism entered Islam "from the outside" or is genuinely Islamic "from the beginning" is itself symptomatic of the shortcircuit produced by the orientalist obsession with authentic origins, often mirrored by a "nativist" response asserting an uncontaminated authenticity of the tradition from its inception. Such interpretive patterns do not exclusively affect the study of Islam and Sufism but extend across the entire spectrum of traditions examined by Western Orientalism. A more adequate approach to the complex historicity of these processes must therefore relinquish any illusion of "authentic origins" and accept the normality of incessant interreligious becoming, involving both major and minor traditions.

3. These forms of itinerancy of adepts and masters were codified into practices like *siyaha* and *rihla*.
4. After conducting a critical review of the notion of "charisma" in Volume I (Salvatore 2016, 92–100), I will further develop the implications of this ambiguous and ultimately misleading term in Chapter 4 of the present volume. For the time being, its place is taken by the master's knowledge and power, associated with merits recognized by the circle of active followers and, as we will see, by broader publics of sympathizers.
5. While postponing to Chapter 7 a clarification of the importance of the duplication of the concept through a different vocalization of the first syllable (*wilaya*), I am here discussing *walaya*, the attribute of being a *wali*, through the lens of the fundamental assumptions guiding the use of this attribute.
6. For an extended and more historical analysis of *walaya*, see Ghofrani (2023).
7. A conceptually even more sophisticated grid of references to Western—also sociological and anthropological—theorists of the body is found in the brilliant work of Scott Kugle (2007, 10–16), which may also have inspired Bashir's analysis of Sufi bodies. I nevertheless found Bashir's work more suitable as a foil for the questions addressed in this chapter, given its sociohistorically grounded and theoretically expansive treatment of embodiment within specific institutional contexts.
8. One should consider the explanatory power of an approach to Islam nurtured by sensibilities and insights acquired through familiarity with Eastern, that is, non-Abrahamic traditions. The entire intellectual trajectory of Toshihiko Izutsu exemplifies this potential (Salvatore and Obuse, forthcoming). An additional reason for invoking Yuasa is that, as a scholar and thinker, he engaged many of the same themes addressed by Izutsu, yet did so by centering his analysis on the body—an aspect that Izutsu, still constrained by the horizons of Western Orientalism, appeared more hesitant to foreground. It is telling, in this regard, that Izutsu and Yuasa jointly occupy a central place in what is arguably the most

authoritative anthology to date of writings, in English translation, by Japanese philosophers active in the last third of the 20th century (Krummel 2019).

9. It is worth noting that, as a more theoretical counterpart to the manuals, al-Ghazali's science of unveiling (*'ilm al-mukashafa*), which he developed in his masterwork *Ihya'*, foregrounded a practice of self-examination oriented toward spiritual proximity to the Divine. This practice was identified as pivotal both to the *adab* of the inner self and to the *adab* governing the life of a broader community (Al-Daghistani 2022, 77).
10. According to Arjomand (2025, 27–32) one may even posit the existence of a pristine form of *futuwwa–tariqa* association prior to their later differentiation and to the full emergence of the *tariqa* well into the Middle Periods. This urban *futuwwa–tariqa* would then constitute what we have called the instituting "matrix," providing an initial crystallization of the "enclave publics" of the enchanted civility of early Sufi life. Moreover, as will be seen in Chapters 5 and 7, the *tariqa–futuwwa* nexus prefigured associative forms of sovereignty that would later contribute to the early modern *dawla*.
11. This last set of virtues was also related to how *futuwwa* overlapped in meaning with pre-Islamic *muruwwa*, or manly valor (Schimmel 1975, 134–136). Hodgson suggested that *futuwwa* provided an all-male hub of socialization for young men that functioned as a counterpart to the all-female space of the harem (Hodgson 1974 II, 143), a point sensibly noted by Jocelyn Dakhlia (2018, 124–141). While the latter was a segregated—if often extensive—domain of domestic space mainly comprising upper-class women, the former was exclusive in terms of membership yet situated within a much broader civic space. It was open—if not especially catering—to lower-class men and, moreover, relatively porous and inclusive toward visitors such as travelers. While this comparison may appear far-fetched, it should be recalled that Hodgson was a pioneer in addressing sociocultural dimensions of gender relations in the Islamic ecumene. He particularly emphasized the prominent role played by many women in the Sufi path and in other teaching capacities, while also noting how this role was progressively eroded with the institutional entrenchment of segregated spaces during the Middle Periods.
12. Here *fityan* is the plural of *fata*, meaning young man, from the same root of *futuwwa*.
13. The previously mentioned work by Kugle (2007, 81–121) provides a uniquely insightful treatment of the crucial, if eccentric, place of the female body in Sufi life, through a literary and psychoanalytic lens that foregrounds the symbolic and affective dimensions of the saintly body, especially in connection with gender, memory, and devotional imagination. Nonetheless, *futuwwa* did not exclude women in principle. As noted above, al-Sulami's work emphasized a female equivalent (*niswan*) to the male *futuwwa* and listed several female figures as paragons of this gender-specific mode of generosity and "chivalry" (Ridgeon 2010, 33–34).

References

Arjomand, Said Amir. 2004. "Transformation of the Islamicate Civilization: A Turning Point in the Thirteenth Century? In *Eurasian Transformations, 10th to 13th Centuries: Crystallizations, Divergences, Renaissances*, edited by Johann P. Arnason and Björn Wittrock, 213–45. Leiden: Brill.

Arjomand, Said Amir. 2025. *Kings and Dervishes: Sufi World Renunciation and the Symbolism of Kingship in the Persianate World.* Oakland, CA: University of California Press.

Bashir, Shahzad. 2011. *Sufi Bodies: Religion and Society in Medieval Islam*. New York: Columbia University Press.

de Certeau, Michel. 1992. *The Mystic Fable*, Vol. 1. Chicago: University of Chicago Press.

Al-Daghistani, Sami. 2022. "Beyond *Maṣlaḥah*: *Adab* and Islamic Economic Thought." *American Journal of Islam and Society* 39 (3–4): 57–86.

Dağyeli, Jeanine Elif. 2018. "*Adab* in the Workshop: Concepts of *Fotovvat*, Proper Conduct and Moral Economy in Central Asian Craftsmanship." In *Javanmardi: The Ethics and Practice of Persianate Perfection*, edited by Lloyd Ridgeon, 215–31. London: Gingko.

Dakhlia, Jocelyne. 2018. "Harems and Cathedrals: The Question of Gender and Sexuality in the Work of Marshall Hodgson." In *Islam and World History: The Ventures of Marshall Hodgson*, edited by Edmund Burke III, 117–44. Chicago: University of Chicago Press.

DeWeese, Devin. 2018. "Organizational Patterns and Developments within Sufi Communities." In *The Wiley Blackwell History of Islam*, edited by Armando Salvatore et al., 329–50. Oxford: Wiley Blackwell.

Elmore, Gerald T. 1999. *Islamic Sainthood in the Fullness of Time: Ibn al-ʿArabī's Book of the Fabulous Gryphon*. Leiden: Brill.

Faroqhi, Suraiya. 2009. *Artisans of Empire: Crafts and Craftspeople Under the Ottomans*. London: I.B. Tauris.

Ghofrani, Shayesteh. 2023. *Walāya in the Formative Period of Shiʿism and Sufism: A Comparative Analysis*. Abingdon: Routledge.

Green, Nile. 2012. *Sufism: A Global History*. Oxford: Wiley Blackwell.

Hatke, George. 2018. "Agrarian, Commercial, and Pastoralist Dynamics in the Pre-Islamic Irano-Semitic Civilizational Area." In *The Wiley Blackwell History of Islam*, edited by Armando Salvatore et al., 39–58. Oxford: Wiley-Blackwell.

Hodgson, Marshall G. S. 1974. *The Venture of Islam. Conscience and History in a World Civilization*, Vol. 1–3 . Chicago: University of Chicago Press.

Ikegami, Eiko. 2005. *Bonds of Civility: Aesthetic Networks and the Political Origins of Japanese Culture*. Cambridge: Cambridge University Press.

Karamustafa, Ahmet T. 2018. "Shiʿis, Sufis and Popular Saints." In *The Wiley Blackwell History of Islam*, edited by Armando Salvatore et al., 159–76. Oxford: Wiley Blackwell.

Krummel, John W. M., ed. 2019. *Contemporary Japanese Philosophy: A Reader*. London: Rowman & Littlefield.

Kugle, Scott. 2007. *Sufis and Saints' Bodies: Mysticism, Corporeality, and Sacred Power in Islam*. Chapel Hill: University of North Carolina Press.

Ohlander, Erik. 2008. *Sufism in an Age of Transition*. Leiden: Brill.

Rahimi, Babak. 2004. "Between Chieftaincy and Knighthood: A Comparative Study of Ottoman and Safavid Origins." *Thesis Eleven* no. 76: 85–102.

Rahimi, Babak. 2018. "The Consolidation of Sunni and Shi'i Legitimacies." In *The Wiley Blackwell History of Islam*, edited by Armando Salvatore et al., 311–28. Oxford: Wiley Blackwell.

Rahimi, Babak, and Armando Salvatore. 2018. "The Crystallization and Expansiveness of Sufi Networks within the Urban-Rural-Nomadic Nexus of the Islamic Ecumene." In *The Wiley Blackwell History of Islam*, edited by Armando Salvatore et al., 253–72. Oxford: Wiley Blackwell.

Ridgeon, Lloyd. 2010. *Morals and Mysticism in Persian Sufism: A History of Sufi-Futuwwat in Iran*. London: Routledge.

Ridgeon, Loyd. 2015. "Mysticism in Medieval Sufism." In *The Cambridge Companion to Sufism*, edited by Lloyd Ridgeon, 3–23. Cambridge: Cambridge University Press.

Ridgeon, Lloyd. 2018. "The Felon, the Faithful and the Fighter: The Protean Face of the Chivalric Man (*Javanmard*) in the Medieval Persianate and Modern Iranian Worlds." In *Javanmardi: The Ethics and Practice of Persianate Perfection*, edited by Lloyd Ridgeon, 1–27. London: Gingko.

Salvatore, Armando. 2007. *The Public Sphere: Liberal Modernity, Catholicism, and Islam*. New York: Palgrave Macmillan.

Salvatore, Armando. 2016. *The Sociology of Islam: Knowledge, Power and Civility*. Oxford: Wiley Blackwell.

Salvatore, Armando, and Kieko Obuse. Forthcoming. *ReOrienting Islam: Cosmopolitan Refractions*. Oakland, CA: University of California Press.

Schimmel, Annemarie. 1975. *Mystical Dimensions of Islam*. Chapel Hill: University of North Carolina Press.

Trimingham, J. Spencer. 1971. *The Sufi Orders in Islam*. Oxford: Clarendon Press.

Yıldırım, Rıza. 2018. "From Naserian Courtly-*Fotovvat* to *Akhi-Fotovvat*: Transformation of the Fotovvat Doctrine and Communality in Late Medieval Anatolia." In *Javanmardi: The Ethics and Practice of Persianate Chivalry*, edited by Lloyd Ridgeon, 66–97. Edinburgh: Edinburgh University Press.

Yuasa, Yasuo [1987] 1993. *The Body: Toward an Eastern Mind-Body Theory*. Translated by Shigenori Nagatomo and Monte S. Hull. Albany, NY: State University of New York Press.

4

THE *WAQF*
Circulating the Gift, Resisting Incorporation

The Mainstream Channel in Instituting the Ecumene

In the previous two chapters, we first explored the evolving and often strategically intertwined *hadith* and *adab* corpora as carriers of the force of narration. We saw how, through habitualizing patterns of exemplary relationality, they fed into the instituting side of the civilizing process. We then identified the *tariqa* as the main converter, via purposeful networking, of the instituting power of *hadith* and *adab* into the instituted landscape of the ecumene. In this chapter, we turn to the *waqf*, which played a crucial intermediary role in the instituting process across virtually all its aspects. Owing to this role, it deserves to be called the wellspring of the entire instituting process in the Islamic ecumene. The *waqf* provided the financial channeling and managerial infrastructure for all fully articulated socioreligious institutions, such as the Sufi lodge (*khanqa/ribat/zawiya*), the school or college (*madrasa*), and the mosque (*masjid*), which should be viewed as an institution in its own right. The *waqf* proved to be a thriving, if highly versatile, instituting channel. Variously (mis)translated as charitable trust or philanthropic foundation, a *waqf* consisted of an endowment of wealth pledged by any member of the community who could afford it, with the intention of pleasing Allah and doing good to fellow humans. The pivotal condition for the legal validity of a *waqf* endowment was its perpetuity, insofar as its benefits could not be subjected to arbitrary human termination and thus had to reflect the eternal aspect of divine mercy.

While legitimized by various occurrences in the *hadith* corpus referencing the obligation to give, the *waqf* began to acquire precise contours in the final stage of the High Caliphate. This occurred at the point of convergence between diverse practices of donation and the work of the *fuqaha'*, particularly those of the Hanafi school, who pragmatically synthesized what the leading historical sociologist Said Amir Arjomand (2004, 218) has defined as a "civil law" of *waqf*. These regulations covered a field of practices of heterogeneous provenance, some of which antedated the rise of Islam, both within the broader Irano-Semitic area and beyond it (Arjomand 1998, 110–111; Çizakça 2000, 5; Hennigan 2004, 52–70). In this process, the *waqf* emerged as the paramount financial and managerial infrastructure of the Islamic ecumene and as a warrant of its remarkable degree of societal autonomy. It experienced continuous growth, especially through the Middle Periods, until the colonial penetration of Western powers heralded its gradual erosion (Hofer 2021, 58–59). Even under the umbrella of relatively consistent jurisprudential frameworks, the development of the *waqf* reflected a striking richness and variety of financial arrangements, strategies of wealth preservation, and patterns of social patronage across the ecumene. This has been amply documented by a field of dedicated *waqf* studies that has particularly flourished over the last few decades. Beyond elucidating the originality of the *waqf*, this scholarship has raised broader questions about its adaptive and protean rationality, which may serve as a cipher for what should be considered specifically Islamic in the process of instituting its ecumene (see Chapter 1).

The outcome of this cumulative literature is a sustained emphasis on the significance of the *waqf* as situated at the strategic intersection of most—if not all—processes of funding and managing institutions in the ecumene. Far from being an unchanging "institution," as the term is commonly (and eurocentrically) understood, the *waqf* functioned as a multipurpose instituting conduit or channel, adaptable to a wide range of intentions and strategies (Ghazaleh 2011, 2–4). Most importantly, this chapter will show how the *waqf* provides a crucial foil for deepening the question of why the instituting process in the Islamic ecumene should not, by default, be measured against Western sociological standards. Rather, the *waqf* furnishes its own criteria for appreciating the distinctive process through which Islam, in the course of its historical venture, contributed to instituting the ecumene.

While the term *waqf* conveys the meaning of stopping (the suspension of the circulation of wealth), its outcome is, in many ways, the very opposite. The "stop" concerns only direct market transactions, whereas the act of giving, or gifting, wealth through a *waqf* operates as a powerful instrument of sharing and connecting. Endowing a *waqf* entailed a purposeful alignment of the giver or endower—more precisely, of the gifting intention, reflecting a benefacting disposition of the body-mind—with Allah's mercy. The intended effect was to do good for fellow human beings by redistributing wealth and by creating new spaces, services, and even forms of employment. In effect, an endowed good or property—whether immovable, such as real estate and agricultural land, or movable, such as equipment and, at a later stage, cash—generated ripple effects that nourished the connectedness underpinning the Islamic ecumene, both within urban spaces and in their relations with the countryside. This connectedness, closely associated with mobility, was integral to a dense grid of exchange, or what we may call the "market," and contributed to the need for its continual adaptability to local conditions and translocal dynamics. Clearly, this was a precapitalist form of market organization, whose functioning depended on the habitualizing and instituting processes examined in the previous chapters and which often responded to general notions of *maslaha* (Singer 2018, 703; Al-Daghistani 2022, 57–65).

Nada Moumtaz (2018, 7) has suggested that the *waqf* should be studied in the guise of what Marcel Mauss called a "total institution," whose rationality cannot be confined to a specific, differentiated social field. While this view helps counter critiques of the *waqf*—critiques we will examine shortly—that are articulated from the standpoint of a fully fledged capitalist rationality, the *waqf* was never meant to fulfil, we must nevertheless warn against treating it as a jellied "institution" rather than as an instituting (or meta-institutional) conduit. Accordingly, Mauss' definition of a "total" institution can only partially, and provisionally, function as a corrective to modernist anachronisms and Westernist bias in understandings of the *waqf*. I would instead stress the versatile, supple, and adaptive character of the *waqf* as the most comprehensive manifestation of the orientation to *maslaha* in the unfolding of *'umran*. Concurrently—and evoking another key theoretical contribution by Mauss—the *waqf* should be viewed as a gifting channel whose dynamics would be obscured if giving and circulating were treated as separate and successive acts. In the *waqf*, these are intrinsically and mutually entangled. Whether this configuration reflects Mauss' approach or, more probably, exceeds and ultimately disproves it, the *waqf* is a gift that does not entail an obligation of return. Rather, it sets in motion an open-ended and—despite the often detailed provisions of *waqf* deeds—largely unpredictable circulation of effects, especially over the long term, ideally extending into eternity or to the end of the world. This indeterminacy is reinforced by the mutability of the *waqf*'s very understanding as a major channel of the instituting process in the ecumene. For this reason, in precolonial contexts the *waqf* can scarcely be squeezed into modern Western categories such as "charity" or "philanthropy," which only acquire partial analytical traction within capitalist economies and Westphalian states, with their opposition between a "non-profit" sector and profit-oriented corporations—a development that will be discussed at length in the final part of this chapter.[1]

One could say that the endowing act inflects the way the multi-sided prism of religion-*cum*-civility channels a compassionate form of solidarity in addressing multiple others. Summing intention and effect, one should see in the *waqf* a trigger for circulating gifts. This operation fits a category of exchange that is foundational not only to the construction of the social bond but also to the way the self simultaneously triangulates with the earthly other and the heavenly Other (Salvatore 2007, 54–56). The other is identified with legal precision in the gifting deed (*waqfiyya*) as the beneficiary of the income generated by the donation, whether the urban poor of a city or quarter; all the members of a given community or neighborhood; or, most prominently, a congregation of worshippers, scholars, or Sufis on whose behalf a mosque (*masjid*), a school (*madrasa*), or a Sufi lodge (*khanqa/ribat/zawiya*) was funded, instituted, and maintained. The beneficiaries could also include, for example, the endower's family members or manumitted slaves. No less crucial were the specifications, laid out in the deed, concerning how and by whom the *waqf* was to be administered. These provisions shaped the strategic orientation of the *waqf* as an endowing act within its specific sociohistorical context, no less decisively than the selection of the beneficiaries themselves (Ghazaleh 2011, 7–12).

As an instrument for strategically instituting bonds of connectedness and relations of patronage—ranging from benefitting one's enlarged family to servicing urban infrastructure by funding squares, hospitals, and caravanserais—any splitting of *waqf* into the categories of "public" versus "private" would be artificial. More to the point, such a dichotomy would obscure the protean adaptability of this instituting channel. In most circumstances, *waqf* yielded unequivocally dual advantages, benefiting both the endower's family and the designated recipients. One may therefore state that the instituting process triggered by *waqf* systematically blurs a distinction—private versus public—that is intrinsic to the legacy of Roman law and that Westerners—and, owing to Western legal and political hegemony, often people elsewhere as well—tend to take for granted and to apply backwards and universally in an anachronistic fashion.

On the one hand, it is undeniable that the *waqf* was often used to serve specific interests, not least the protection of property from state intervention and confiscation. On the other hand, precisely as an instituting channel, the *waqf* funneled resources into services of broad social utility and decisively contributed to the institution of health, educational, and infrastructural provisions. These included schools and colleges, libraries, Sufi lodges, markets, squares, bridges, soup kitchens, Qur'an schools for disadvantaged boys, residences for single women, fountains, underground wells, dams, bathhouses, caravanserais, cemeteries, burial societies, as well as farms, gardens, shops, movable equipment for coffeehouses, lodgings and facilities for urban dwellers, travelers, and traders, ships, harbor-related services and infrastructure, and even entire new neighborhoods and commercial centers (see also Chapter 5). In this way, the *waqf* actively shaped urban space and the built environment, even when it was initially designated to advance particular interests. Whether a given endowment ultimately benefited more the endower's family or the "common good" could only begin to be assessed over the course of several generations.

Moreover, *waqf*-funded and administered infrastructure facilitated long-distance trade, including—quite spectacularly—by feeding into major exchange hubs such as Samarkand and Bukhara along the Silk Road, across the Sahara into the Sudanic lands of Africa, and along the commercial sea routes of the Indian Ocean linking East Africa to India and the Malay archipelago. Through these interconnected circuits, the *waqf* contributed decisively to establishing the historical and geopolitical centrality of the Islamic ecumene. Belonging to this ecumene, whether as a Muslim or as a member of recognized minorities (*dhimmis*), became not a marker of exclusivity but a condition broadly synonymous with what we would today call being global: enjoying recognition as a legitimate partner in the hemisphere-wide circulation of goods, people, ideas, and healing practices. At the same time, while operating as a pan-Islamic instituting channel, the *waqf* retained a remarkable capacity to respond to local needs, contingent circumstances, and shifting balances of power. Despite vulnerabilities—on which more will be said shortly—its wide reach did not rest on the imposition of normative or institutional uniformity detrimental to local aspirations and interests. Rather, the *waqf* channeled investments into shared goods and material conditions that sustained the unfolding of *'umran*, especially in its sense of inhabiting, cultivating, and building. In this way, it became a signature infrastructure of a flourishing ecumene, simultaneously local in articulation and global in scope.

As to the endowers, they were mainly—though not exclusively—members of various segments of the political, bureaucratic, and economic elites, including women and non-Muslims. Over time, however, they also increasingly included artisans and traders, whether acting individually or through guilds and *akhi* organizations. That said, the founders of the most substantial *waqf*s typically hailed from ruling families or from among courtiers and wealthy commercial entrepreneurs. Endowing a *waqf* certainly accrued to the endower's *qurba* (closeness) to Allah and was understood to attract *baraka*. At the same time, and no less significantly, it functioned as a privileged avenue for establishing durable bonds of patronage and loyalty with lower classes, disadvantaged groups, and the urban poor, who were the beneficiaries of many *waqf*-funded services. In this capacity, the *waqf* partly compensated for the chronically fragile legitimacy of those who occupied privileged positions in the control of wealth and/or power after the dissolution of caliphal charisma (see Chapter 6). It thus became the main instituting channel through which elites, in a precolonial setting, demonstrated—or failed to demonstrate—their accountability to commoners, while also serving as a key arena of intra-elite competition for influence and leadership.

The competition was measured by the capacity of endowers to mobilize resources dedicated to caring for the good of significant segments of the common folk—whether defined by social condition, such as the poor or orphans, or by spatial belonging, as the inhabitants of a specific neighborhood. Unsurprisingly, the modalities of endowment and administration of *waqf*s, as well as the identification of their beneficiaries, varied sharply—often creatively and adaptively—across regions and periods (Ghazaleh 2011, 7–13; see also Bamyeh 2019, 146–147; Safi 2022, 147–150). At the same time, rulers were expected to create practical conditions for fair competition among potential endowers and to prevent, or at least limit, abuses of the *waqf*. It would therefore be misleading to celebrate the flexible character of the *waqf* without qualification. Violations of its institutional, civic, and service-oriented scope were at times widespread. Quite often, one motivation for endowing wealth was to evade taxation or to provide stable employment for family members or clients. Yet the very fact that the *waqf* continued to thrive across regions and epochs, despite such distortions, is itself a powerful sociological indicator of its long-term viability as a foundational instituting route of civility in the Islamic ecumene—largely irrespective of the sincerity of individual endowers or the honesty and competence of a given *waqf*'s administrators.

The *waqf*'s pivotal role in the institutional landscape of the Islamic ecumene made it a key venue for collectively and reflectively pursuing a variety of specific or shared goods, closely aligned with the notion of *maslaha* (pl. *masalih*) outlined in Chapter 2. This idea, far from legitimizing a top-down imposition of what counts as a good, benefit, or legitimate interest, relied on continuous, decentralized interpretations of such goods by the individuals and groups involved in their production, safeguarding, and distribution. Within this framework, jurists—acting simultaneously as administrators and adjudicators in *waqf*-related affairs—played a crucial role in balancing and negotiating the interests of multiple legitimate stakeholders, always with reference to the endower's intentions. Achieving workable outcomes required a calibrated blending of equity, relationality, and reflexivity, one that could inclusively weigh competing claims and incline toward context-sensitive, and at times creative, determinations of *maslaha*. This mode of operation fostered a form of social consensus around the *waqf*'s living goals, ideally ensuring a degree of inclusion whereby commoners appeared not only as beneficiaries but also as participants capable of articulating interests and influencing how resources were allocated. In certain contexts—notably in the Ottoman Empire—this logic extended further, evolving into mechanisms that granted any subject the right to file a lawsuit in the name of a shared interest when *waqf* properties were improperly managed. Such extensive, if weakly formalized, forms of civil monitoring did not replace strictly legal liability; rather, they thickened it by generating broader and more diffuse structures of accountability (Isin and Lefebvre 2005; Salvatore 2016, 121).

One should consider that the application of the *maslaha* principle required attending to the needs and voices of social groups well beyond the elites. The legal discourse guiding its implementation was, at least in principle, a practical manifestation of connective reflexivity oriented to fairness and equity, even when specific regulations—such as those developed by the schools of *fiqh* for the *waqf*—did not explicitly invoke *maslaha*. Beyond its direct juridical application, notably in the management of *waqf*, the diffusion of the principle's normative impact enabled a broad range of subjects to articulate consent or dissent regarding the scope of collective responsibility in supervising *waqf* use, thus exceeding the confines of mere legal scrutiny. Famously, in a *fatwa* related to a *waqf* controversy, al-Shatibi applied the *maslaha* principle to ensure that a *waqf* served a shared good while remaining specific in its purpose (e.g., funding a particular mosque or school). Quite symptomatically, this ruling opposed the widespread practice of using *waqf* revenues to fund general services indiscriminately—i.e., without specification of beneficiaries—since such practices could indirectly replenish the ruler's treasury (Masud [1977] 1995, 93).

This intervention by one of the foremost legal thinkers of the ecumene illustrates how the *waqf* was designed to protect and promote social autonomy against abuses deriving from its subordination to state policies. Nonetheless, Arjomand has argued that, particularly with the strengthening of statehood that accelerated during the Later Middle Periods (see Chapters 5 and 6), the *waqf* did, to some extent, become an instrument of what he terms "public policy" in the hands of rulers and their administrators (Arjomand 1998). While—for the reasons already explained—I would strongly caution against the anachronistic application of the categories "private" and "public" to the *waqf*, it is nonetheless useful to situate the trajectory outlined by Arjomand within the broader process of instituting statehood and the expansion of the prerogatives of *siyasa* as government, which will be examined in the second part of this volume. Indeed, even the aforementioned *fatwa* by al-Shatibi points to an emerging tendency whereby rulers sought to introduce mechanisms of top-down control over the funding flows generated by *waqf*—while simultaneously provoking principled resistance to such attempts.

More plausibly—and as previously anticipated—Arjomand (1999) has argued that the minimal yet functional formalization of the *waqf* through legal practice and theory amounted to the emergence of a de facto "civil law" of *waqf*. This body of norms was interpretively developed and administered by the various legal schools through the day-to-day work of juristic interpretation and adjudication amidst shifting power balances. Such a civil law was less the linear outcome of abstract legal doctrine than the cumulative, pragmatic product of evolving—if often precarious—post-caliphal equilibria, grounded in compromises negotiated between ruling military elites and the social patriciate. These balances were famously captured by Hodgson's concept of the *amir-a'yan* system (1974 II, 62–68), itself a synthetic formulation grounded in emic categories. The arrangement enabled the largely autonomous flourishing of vital social institutions beneath the level of sultanic rule. Pushing this argument further, Arjomand (1999, 266) has emphasized that under Seljuq rule, and as a culmination of the Earlier Middle Periods, Persian viziers consciously mobilized this civil law of *waqf* to secure a workable blend of stability and equity within the governance framework sustained by the *amir-a'yan* system. In this sense, even practices retrospectively described as "public policy" could operate only insofar as they were filtered through the *waqf*'s deeper status as a central marker of civility articulated in Islamic terms.

There is no doubt that, during the transition from the Earlier to the Later Middle Periods, particularly in the wake of the Mongol conquests, the *waqf* played an increasingly significant role in funding and integrating school-colleges and Sufi lodges. These lodges had emerged as early as the 9th century, likely originating in Khorasan, and their diffusion across the ecumene was especially successful during the Earlier Middle Period, above all within the Seljuq realm (see Chapter 3). By the late 11th century, the Sufi lodge (*khanqa*) had crystallized as a durable—if flexible and decentralized—institution. As a multifunctional hub, the *khanqa* hosted Sufi learning and socialization, supported the destitute and the sick, and provided services for long-distance traders. Lodges also expanded beyond major urban centers, thereby facilitating the formation of translocal Sufi lineages (Salvatore 2018, 164–165). Significantly, the take-off of the *waqf* economy and the instituting of Sufi life on a mass scale, explored in the previous chapter, largely coincided. Funding these Sufi spaces enabled adepts to congregate, receive food, and find lodging; learning was complemented by connective rituals, punctuated by celebrations and meditation sessions. Throughout the Middle Periods and into early modernity (ca. 1453–1683), the lodges enjoyed growing support from ruling families and were particularly favored by Islamizing Mongol elites.

The most powerful Sufi lodges were often centered on the tomb or shrine of a *wali* and his descendants, attracting followers and pilgrims of diverse loyalties, including non-Muslims, who performed *ziyara*, or "visitation," in order to partake in the *baraka* of the "friend." During the Later Middle Period, these lodges became the pivots of larger architectural and institutional complexes endowed by the Turko-Mongol ruling and military classes. From post-Mongol Iran, they spread to other parts of the ecumene, most notably to Mamluk Egypt and Syria (Arjomand 1999, 276–278). As pilgrimage sites, shrines played a crucial role in connecting urban centers with peripheral rural areas, reaching illiterate peasants and nomadic populations. At the same time, they often functioned as key hubs for the long-distance circulation of goods and knowledge, thereby reinforcing the habitualization of exemplary modes promoted by the *hadith–adab* complex (Salvatore 2018, 160–161). The rising significance of the shrine of a *wali* as a point of convergence of multiple instituting and instituted complexes thus underscored the singular relationship between a compassionate, socially produced form of connectedness and military power centers within the evolving *amir-a'yan* system of the Middle Periods.

Facilitated by these organizational patterns, the translocal expansion of Sufi institutions spurred by *waqf* was continuous and consistent throughout the period. It reached a peak under the conditions of *Pax Mongolica*, as vividly documented in the travelogue of Ibn Battuta discussed in Chapter 3. During his journeys—especially through Anatolia—he was most often hosted in lodges, including, notably, those associated with the *akhi*. His travels were therefore sustained, directly or indirectly, by a dense web of *waqf* infrastructures and revenues: both those catering to wayfarers in general and those, such as schools and colleges, that favored itinerant scholars in particular (Safi 2022, 149). Most remarkably—and in sharp contrast to the radically local rooting of European municipalities in the late Middle Ages, to be discussed shortly—the *waqf*, though locally endowed, frequently funded infrastructures of long-distance connectedness. This support often went well beyond mere utility. For example, the Turko-Mongol ruling elites lavishly endowed major Silk Road centers such as Samarkand and Bukhara, thereby spectacularly amplifying the flourishing of the ecumene through a multisensory experience offered to travelers by a monumental architecture of singular majesty and refinement.

Articulating the Islamic Difference via *Waqf*

While it is broadly correct to consider the *waqf* endower's intent "pious" (to please God) and "charitable" (to benefit various categories of others beyond the endowing self), its effects were more broadly relational and civic. The *waqf* became the backbone of the ecumene's cosmopolitan civility and precapitalist exchange economy. Large service complexes functioned as strongholds of connective power, both in urban settings and across translocal networks. This model not only enhanced the prestige of endowers drawn from various elite segments but also, increasingly, expanded the agency of traders and less affluent groups and individuals. Most significantly, it avoided rigid institutionalization through statutes and charters, relying instead on the civil law of *waqf* for a pragmatic, limited degree of formalization. At the same time, while feeding into a process of proto-globalization within and beyond the Islamic ecumene, the adaptability of the *waqf* was reinforced by its capacity to encompass a plurality of interests and practices encountered along the ecumene's paths of expansion. One should also recognize that the *waqf* facilitated long-distance trade in ways that supported hemisphere-wide capital accumulation even within a fundamentally precapitalist—if proto-global—economy. Such accumulation remained compatible with the integration of production and trade into the ecumene-wide rationale of promoting *'umran*. The resulting process fostered the flourishing of a relational civility in which a reasonably inclusive notion of welfare was continuously negotiated against shifting power balances among social classes. At the same time, it allowed for a degree of social mobility sustained by a fundamentally egalitarian ethos unknown in other precolonial civilizational realms of the Afro-Asian landmass, Europe included, as Hodgson repeatedly emphasized.

From this perspective, it would be not only ideologically and colonially biased, but also profoundly unhistorical, to regard as a deficit the fact that the conditions for a hyper-calculative, individualistic, and highly exploitative capitalist system—toward both labor and the environment—did not develop endogenously in the Islamic ecumene as they did in parts of Europe. If any retrospective and ultimately anachronistic judgment were to be passed, one should instead acknowledge that the absence of such an endogenous capitalism signaled not a systemic limitation but a form of foresight in protecting and promoting *'umran*, owing to the relational, civic, and reflexive mode characterizing the instituting process of the ecumene. On the positive side, and most notably, as shown above, a significant portion of *waqf* investment was directed toward circulation nodes not merely as a matter of "state policy," but also—and often primarily—through the grid of motivations underlying the endowment of urban infrastructural facilities. Given the high risks associated with investing venture capital in such nodes, the sociocultural attractiveness of much of the endowed built environment, including its sophisticated and imposing architectural complexes, would have been severely undermined without the *waqf*, either remaining underfunded or not funded at all. The instituting strength of the *waqf* becomes even more evident when one considers that long-distance trade was interwoven with the circulation of intellectual, artistic, and scientific ideas across multiple borders, including those conventionally associated with distinct religious traditions such as various forms of Christianity, Buddhism, Hinduism, and Chinese folk religions.

Whoever slips, consciously or not, into the anachronizing posture of decrying the purported deficits of *waqf* can only do so by assuming a capitalist property-development rationality. What such a restrictive—and ultimately rapacious—rationality is unable to integrate is the key institutional upside of the *waqf* exchange economy. This economy contributed to building what we might call a "knowledge ecumene," one that promoted social, managerial, and scientific competencies. These competencies were essential not only to improving the effectiveness of service delivery and the pursuit of general welfare, but also to advancing the careers of talented individuals from lower social strata. Seen from this angle, the *waqf* exchange economy also accommodated a set of institutional constraints in the production of knowledge that, as discussed in Chapter 2, fed into the processes of habitualization, civility, and, ultimately, institution-building. These constraints become clearer if one recalls that, in the early Islamic ecumene, scholarly activity was rarely a full-time vocation. Being a scholar was often a "second job," pursued alongside other forms of employment. The gradual professionalization of education that followed was therefore not a simple rationalization, but a response to the saturation of loosely organized practices of collecting and transmitting knowledge. Most crucially, this knowledge included the *hadith* corpus, which provided the indispensable database for the development of *fiqh*, to the point that one can speak of a *hadith-shari'a* complex (see Chapter 2). Usually—and reductively—translated as "jurisprudence," *fiqh* evolved into an increasingly elaborate science, progressively differentiated from *hadith* scholarship while continuing to support the relationally grounded processes of habitualization. At the same time, *fiqh* scaled up its function and became a key instrument of regulation, administration, and governance.

It is in this context that the rise of the school-college (*madrasa*), first in Khorasan by the 10th century and often centered on the teaching of *fiqh*, should be understood. Earlier, many of these functions had been fulfilled by the mosque, which served as a multipurpose site of community learning. As Caterina Bori (2018, 225–228) has argued, the *madrasa* represented a major institutional innovation in that it provided scholars with a stable income and facilitated a rich and diversified professionalization—not only in legal fields (as judges or *muftis*) or as *waqf* administrators, but also in education and health, for instance through contributions to regulating medical provision and patient care. This was all the more the case when *madrasa*s were funded by *waqf*, whose management itself required legal and administrative expertise. The professionalization of knowledge production and transmission associated with the *waqf* exchange economy thus generated a significant degree of formalization, without eliminating informal channels of learning. These informal channels continued to benefit lower social strata and helped diffuse knowledge among those excluded from formal curricula. Moreover, alongside mosques and Sufi lodges, *madrasa*s often functioned as communal hubs within their neighborhoods.

Yet this same process of professionalization also created new dependencies on patronage from ruling and military elites, exercised through their strategic use of *waqf*. Such dependence threatened to compromise what was widely perceived as the pristine autonomy of the scholarly field and its carriers, the *'ulama'*. It is therefore unsurprising that the need to protect scholarly autonomy from political interference deeply concerned figures such as al-Ghazali, who sensed that the institutionalization of teaching and learning facilitated by *waqf* might constrain the role scholarship needed to play in the life of the ecumene (Bori 2018, 227–228). And yet, a substantial degree of autonomy was in fact preserved precisely through the *waqf*. It enabled scholars, including jurists, to cultivate a measure of collective identity and solidarity by giving rise to relatively informal interpretive schools (*madhhab*, pl. *madhahib*). These schools often competed fiercely with one another in elaborating *fiqh* and exercising sociopolitical influence, while never crystallizing into corporate bodies in the strict sense (Schacht [1935] 1950; Rahman [1966] 1979, 261; Salvatore 2007, 141). In this light, the degree of formalization and rationalization introduced into the instituting process by the *waqf* produced a more powerful, yet also more realistic, configuration of the knowledge–power relationship. This configuration became integral to the fragile equilibria of the *amir–a'yan* system. Overall, that system proved effective in preventing the equation from being absorbed and distorted as a mere instrument of "public policy"—or, worse still, as a mechanism for disciplining and managing populations, groups, and individual subjects.

As such—and as will be elucidated shortly—the instituting process in the Islamic ecumene was quite at odds with the juridical fiction of a corporate personality that proved essential to the development of the disciplinary grids of modern capitalism and statehood in Europe. This difference was preserved also, if not mainly, thanks to the operational versatility of the *waqf*. If we are allowed to counter the abysmal anachronism of the "critics" of the *waqf* by borrowing just a modicum of the same anachronism, one could surmise that the juridical fiction of a "corporation" was shunned simply because it was not needed to legitimize the scholars' professionalization in the production of knowledge in the ecumene. As it might have dawned on the most sensible spirits, such as al-Ghazali, the adoption of such a fiction would have precipitated knowledge production and transmission into a spiral of commodification. What rendered the fiction of a corporate identity superfluous was precisely the way the institutionally multilayered, yet conceptually straightforward, logic of *waqf* configured one of its main products—in this case, knowledge—as other than a commodity. Knowledge, as an output of scholarly activity funded by *waqf*, warranted the pivotal role of the *'ulama'* in freely returning to the ecumene the gift of a given endowment by recirculating it, as it were, in the form of shareable knowledge.

Here Allah's invisible yet ubiquitous "thirdness" in the circulation of the gift mediated what appeared, and indeed was, a licit form of exchange. This exchange was blessed precisely insofar as it protected the gift tangibly, on behalf of the "common good"—and therefore regardless of the real intent of the giver—from both commodification and incorporation. One can see here how, even ideologically, the twin register of religion and civility within the Islamic ecumene produced and legitimized a system of exchange compatible with, yet not reducible to, the rules of a precapitalist market. The process steered clear of the type of legitimation that Max Weber famously identified with the Protestant, puritan "ethic" of escaping frivolous consumption by reinvesting wealth into production and taking success in the form of profit as the index of predestination. This ethic was one of the factors that pushed Europe toward the development of a juridical theology establishing the corporate personality of an abstract entrepreneurial subject, as will be discussed below.

Despite the successful record of the *waqf* in contributing to prosperity and circulation, and in safeguarding the integrity and balance of the knowledge–power equation, an argument has nonetheless been advanced according to which the *waqf* constituted the main institutional deterrent to the rise of capitalism in the Islamic ecumene, because it allegedly inhibited the accumulation and circulation of potential investment capital (Kuran 2001, 2005, 2011). No doubt, as noted at the beginning of the chapter, the primary literal meaning of *waqf* does indicate the stopping of wealth's circulation. In practice, however, the *waqf* initiated and sustained a singular dynamism by not only catering to local needs but also promoting the formation of transregional exchange hubs and nodes. The resulting circulatory networks played a salient role in supporting long-distance trade, which was the sine qua non of all hemisphere-wide capital accumulation. In nodal cities, markets often overlapped with Sufi shrines and centers of learning, which frequently clustered together with multifunctional complexes providing a wide range of material and immaterial services to traders. More locally, the *waqf* evolved beyond an exclusive focus on immovable property and came to fund a broad array of income-generating activities that accrued to the purchasing power of non-elite individuals, including populations living in the countryside. In this way, it operated countercyclically as a seminal and solidly institutionalized source of welfare provision, both protecting—and being protected from—the hazards of political instability and economic cyclicality (see Chapter 5). Clearly, *'umran*, including the *waqf* exchange economy, even while allowing for and mediating class and income differentials, was not grounded in a heteronomy of goals of the sort that emerges when profit is allowed to trump welfare.

Admittedly, the argument championed by Kuran, which posits the long-term institutional failure of *waqf* in promoting corporate capitalism, does not fundamentally deny its centrality within the specific dynamics of the Islamic ecumene. However, his diagnosis rests on a path-dependent approach grounded in the idea of "endogenous growth." This perspective flagrantly neglects the extent to which colonialism contributed to the rise of European capitalism and, conversely, the thwarting effects that the same colonial processes had on economic development in the Islamic ecumene, like elsewhere. The result is a striking anachronism, depicting *waqf* as the signature of a timeless Islamic institutional inflexibility that allegedly prevented the ecumene from adapting to the new realities of modern capitalism. These realities were, in fact, decisively facilitated by the idea of incorporation as the sole harbinger of the type of large-scale enterprise we now identify as the capitalist "corporation." In other words, *waqf* is anachronistically evaluated in terms of purely economic efficiency measured against a system—modern capitalism—that did not exist anywhere globally at the time of *waqf*'s flourishing during the Middle Periods.

Seen from this angle, discussing Kuran's approach opens the way to a broader question: incorporation as the quasi-exclusive mode of instituting processes in Europe. This includes a consideration—largely omitted by Kuran—of how the "corporation" (in its original and much broader sense than today's usage) came to be legitimized as the paradigmatic model for institutions as such. This problem was only cursorily addressed in Volume I of this trilogy. To pursue it further, we need to revisit key arguments on incorporation developed by both Weber—an author whom Kuran selectively invokes or criticizes, while missing the coherence of his broader sociological framework—and Hodgson, whom Kuran ignores altogether.

At this point, it is useful to observe that the move, initiated by Weber and followed, if in original ways, by Kuran, to single out *waqf* as the main culprit for the absence of an endogenous capitalism in the Islamic ecumene is at once logically correct but historically wrong. It is correct insofar as it identifies *waqf* as the pivot of an original and, for long periods, relatively prosperous non-capitalist form of exchange—based, as we saw, on intensifying the anthropological constant of gift circulation—and therefore not readily susceptible to capitalist metamorphosis. Yet it is wrong in denouncing *waqf* as the paramount cause of a deficit or lag in a supposedly "proper" capitalist spirit and its associated legal innovations. To avoid a profoundly neo-eurocentric anachronism, the *waqf* must instead be situated within its proper sociohistorical context, as we have done throughout this chapter, by appreciating how it instituted a sophisticated and largely effective set of organizational responses to the demands of the ecumene. From here the comparison must shift toward the European introduction of the juridical fiction of the corporation, which resulted from a chain of theological interventions in the imaginative and motivational prism of social and political agency. These interventions altered the texture of socioeconomic relationality that the Islamic ecumene shared—also through a form of soft hegemony—with the broader, precolonial Afro-Eurasian oikumene, of which Europe was for a long time an integral, if peripheral, part.[2]

It is precisely at this juncture that we need to approach the theological transformations that ushered in what Weber famously theorized as occidental exceptionalism, generating the twin modern rationalities of capitalism and bureaucratic steering. I will begin by focusing on a step in Weber's theorizing that general commentators often overlook. For our purposes, this step offers the opportunity to develop a more balanced—and, crucially, non-anachronistic—comparative perspective. Such a perspective allows us to grasp the instituting power of *waqf* alongside the way confraternal bonds, decisively facilitated by *waqf*, provided the principal instituting matrix for the binary—though non-dichotomic—meta-institutional dynamics of religion and civility (see Chapter 2).

We should therefore start by critically revisiting, and expanding on, discussions first undertaken in Volume I (Salvatore 2016, 89–92), concerning Weber's identification of *Verbrüderung*—literally, "confraternization," or the process of creating a confraternal bond—as the vital patterning principle of both associational life and fully fledged institutions in a wide range of premodern societies (Weber [1921–1922] 1980, 425–437). To clarify this patterning within instituting dynamics, we cited a succinct formulation by a commentator on Weber's oeuvre, according to whom the confraternal bond is "based on artificially created and freely willed mutual ties, not on consanguinity" (Nippel 2002, 132). This notion resonates strongly with what we examined in the previous chapter through the *tariqa* model and its capacity to combine with the dynamics of *futuwwa* and professional guilds.

The more specific question we must now confront is why, in late medieval European cities—the primary empirical ground of Weber's argument—this pattern of *Verbrüderung* was transformed into the theologically intensive model of the corporation. This is the model that would later propel both modern European bureaucratic steering, associated with Westphalian statehood (see also Chapter 9), and capitalism, whereas in the Islamic ecumene a comparable process of forging non-consanguine confraternal bonds generated a different typology of associational forms, institutions, and even modes of rulership, as will be shown in the second half of this book.

Weber was, in fact, fundamentally right in singling out the exceptional character of the dynamics of *Verbrüderung* in late medieval cities within Latin Christendom, most typically in what is now Central and Northern Italy. This is particularly true insofar as the outcome of the process in that specific sociohistorical context was the production of the idea of what, in Western languages, happens to be called an institution (*Anstalt*, as used by Weber in German). Weber's primary focus in his exploration of the European case was on "lay," that is, non-monastic confraternities—often grounded in devotional practices while generating strong ties of solidarity among their members—which mushroomed in Europe's late-medieval cities (Salvatore 2016, 144). As Weber explained, an *Anstalt* or institution was the outcome of a process of incorporation. This process came to dominate the instituting dynamics in Europe and was activated through instruments of juridical and political theology. These instruments—particularly sophisticated, albeit at times to the point of abstruseness—must be evaluated in their own context. That context was shaped not by Christianity *per se*, but by the specific, indeed exceptional, sociopolitical configurations of Western or Latin Christendom in the Late Middle Ages, above all in urban settings. According to Weber, the initial impulse in the instituting process pivoting on incorporation was the communal act of taking an oath. Through this act, what he called a *schwurgemeinschaftliche Verbrüderung* ("sworn confraternization"; Weber [1921–1922] 1980, 748; see also Salvatore 2020, 22–23) was called into being. This constituted the first, and decisive, step in making "one," that is, a unitary juridical personality, out of "many," namely a scattered multiplicity of associates or members of a confraternity.

This wider unity, transcending the participating individuals, formed the first nucleus of what came to be known as a corporate personality. Weber was explicit in describing the procedure as "magical," and therefore "sacramental," a point to which we will return shortly. This procedure was foundational for bestowing juridical personality on an association. It was replicated in the institution—indeed, the incorporation—of a city as a municipality, conceived as a form of "representative" government of the members of the city. The argument was crucial to Weber's understanding of the European city as the cradle of what he regarded as the exceptional character of modern Western socioeconomic and political institutions. The point, for Weber, was that representation could only emerge once a corporate, supra-individual unity had been constituted out of the aggregation of individuals. The "magico-sacramental" procedure thus referred to ritual-symbolic acts that transformed a group of persons into a legally recognized entity.[3] In other words, representative government—whose earliest European instantiations appeared at the municipal level—presupposed that the collective itself had first been juridically created as a "person" (see also Chapter 9).

In a nutshell, incorporation involved crossing a threshold: from a scattered aggregation of individuals to the sacramental authorization of a collective body and personality. Full incorporation replaced the previously decentralized connective bond among "brothers" with a higher-order unity. The magico-sacramental turning of the many into one collective personality or body (*corpus* in Latin) allowed this new entity to transcend the fragmented motivations and interests of its members, along with their individual bodies. The corporation is precisely what transforms and supersedes the confraternal bond by instituting such a higher, collective personality. The ritual emphasized by Weber revolved around a collective oath, which consecrated an institution in the form of a corporation, that is, instituted a novel type of *corpus* or collective body. This oath was often called *coniuratio* (in Latin), meaning a collective act of swearing commitment to a confraternity. Such sworn associations frequently took the form of "city leagues," which provided the initial nuclei from which municipalities were later instituted. The term *coniuratio* came to designate not only the act of swearing but also the sworn confraternity or commune itself. While every oath rests on magical presuppositions, its specifically "sacramental" character derived from its affinity with the central Christian sacrament of the Holy Communion, through which the individual is incorporated into the body of Christ by sharing in it—ultimately, and literally, by "eating" it. Weber assumed that sacraments could be understood as a ritually and theologically refined form of magic. From *coniuratio* derives the verb "to conjure," meaning to bring something into being as if by magic. In the model of institution of a collective body or corporation that Weber examined, we thus encounter a magico-sacramental transformation of multiple subject positions into the cohesive body of a corporate institution, ultimately mirroring the Church as the body of Christ (Salvatore 2013; 2020).

Weber was guided in his argument by an attentive study of the history of the Church, which decisively rests on an understanding of its sacraments as sanctioning an individual's membership—via incorporation—in it, by entering, if not becoming, the body of Christ, ultimately consummated in the sacrament of Holy Communion. To proceed further, we need to extend our critical discussion to Weber's notorious, if ambiguous, concept of "charisma," which occupied a central place in Volume I of my trilogy (Salvatore 2016, 92–96). As Weber well knew, this notion is itself part and parcel of the history of the Church. Charisma is the "stuff" that produces the sacraments that hold the Church together. No doubt—and as discussed in Volume I—his effort to establish a viable sociological concept of charisma faced the difficult task of rendering plausible what was, and in principle still is, a fundamentally theological idea. And yet, Weber undertook an original leap by extending and transforming the Church's notion of charisma so as to explain, from a comparative perspective, nothing less than what he saw as the unique patterns of rationalization unfolding in the modern West. This move allowed him to avoid directly addressing questions of political theology, which, as he probably assumed, belonged to the domain of legitimizing ideologies of Church and state and therefore lay beyond the theoretical scope of the social sciences.

Nevertheless, Weber's concept of charisma was significantly inspired by theological debates of his time, particularly those concerning the bestowal of grace as a charismatic gift (charisma stemming from *charis*, meaning grace or gift in Greek) through the Church's ministering of sacraments (Salvatore 2020, 25–26). Weber sought to de-theologize, but also de-institutionalize, the concept of charisma by associating it with specific "personality types," such as the military hero and the gifted magician, but also the prophet (and, even more, the messiah, or, by reflex, the saint). By drawing from fields like anthropology and mythology, he thought he was able, at least momentarily, to distance himself from the Church as the proper institutional framework of the sacraments and their working, while still distilling "charisma" as the sociologically plausible, quintessential condition for the magico-sacramental procedure of incorporation to work. In other words, according to Weber, charisma is first produced through exceptional personalities (which also include prophets) and only later, thanks to their actions, becomes the "stuff" to build corporate institutions, on the model of the Church.

In this way, Weber transformed charisma from a cornerstone of a Euro-Christo-centric discourse on the formation of legitimate collective bodies into a universal, if pristine, factor of social mobilization, cohesion, and the legitimation of authority. Charisma, so construed, was meant to convey the power of non-material factors in instituting society and the state. In what appears as a daring conceptual shortcut from theology to sociology, Weber located the production of charisma in the personality of extraordinary leaders capable of building constituencies in ways that significantly altered the knowledge–power dynamics prevailing in specific sociopolitical contexts, insofar as their mobilizing projects resisted and opposed the inertia of dominant material or "structural" factors, as reflected in the power and wealth of reigning elites. Invoking charisma thus allowed Weber to highlight processes unfolding beyond formal rationalization understood as the management of material factors and resources. Charisma so constructed becomes a kind of "anti-structure," or even, as it were, a "transcendent structure"—a sociological oxymoron. He intimated that while the rationalization of law, economy, and state bureaucracy is the primary driver of sociopolitical change, this rationalization itself requires explanation by factors of an essentially immaterial, cultural, or religious nature. Even if Weber analytically distinguished personal charisma from incorporation by superimposing these two strands of theorization within what he construed as the exceptionalist occidental trajectory of Latin Christendom, one can discern how personal charisma is invested into magico-sacramental procedures. These procedures proved productive of institutions affiliated with or modeled on the Church—imitating its corporate structure while competing with it, or even aspiring to replace it, as will be addressed shortly (see also Chapter 9). In Weberian terms, then, the magico-sacramental procedure of incorporation is what transforms "fluid" charisma into a "jellied" institution, thereby preparing the terrain for a subsequent process—characteristic of what he regarded as genuinely occidental, that is, Western modernity—of the formal rationalization of institutional structures.

Seen from this angle, the contrast with the Islamic ecumene becomes sharper. If Weber identified the magico-sacramental procedure of incorporation as the mechanism that converted charisma into durable corporate bodies in Latin Christendom, the instituting process in the Islamic ecumene unfolded along a different trajectory. Here the stabilization of authority, knowledge, and social bonds did not require the juridical fiction of a corporate personality like the one that in Europe was modeled on the Church.

Instead, it relied on a dispersed yet resilient assemblage of instituting channels—most notably the *waqf*—that sustained connective life without crystallizing it into a singular, self-standing institutional subject. In other words, what incorporation achieved in the Christian West through the sacralization of a corporate body was accomplished in the Islamic ecumene through relational, circulatory, and gift-based mechanisms that remained structurally open, reversible, and plural. This difference is not merely institutional but reflects a deeper divergence in how religion and civility jointly configured the very grammar of social cohesion. Indeed, the most consequential twist in Weber's argument for our purposes—one that is already implicit in his theoretical architecture—concerns how he understood the instituting process as transforming the immaterial and ultimately "irrational" dimension of charisma into the "rational" constitution of a fully instituted juridical personality. This transformation was decisively grafted onto both the corporate nature of modern capitalism and the Westphalian model of state-building (see Chapter 9).

Ultimately, Weber located the genesis of this rationalizing machine in the inscription of charisma into institutional charters, such as those regulating and legitimizing urban municipal powers and city autonomies. The phenomenon encompassed a wide range of groups and organizational forms, from local municipal associations (including trade guilds) and universities to the royal courts of emerging states. It also included trading and business companies that would later appropriate the label of "corporation."[4] Yet—and this is an additional, and even more revealing, twist, albeit one less explicit in Weber's analysis—incorporation pertains not to the structural and material pole of his theory but to its immaterial opposite. This pole has a primarily theopolitical, rather than economic, genealogy (Weber [1921–1922] 1980, 425–446). The fundamental mechanism at work here is the magico-sacramental incorporation of individual subjects into a collective body designated as a *corpus mysticum*. This process ultimately reflects a specific political theology originating in the notion of the Church as the body of Christ.

The "stuff" of charisma that fueled incorporation could only, in the final instance, be Christ's. The long and uneven process through which this fuel ignited the juridical construction of a corporate personality—understood as a collective subject of rights—drew on Roman law as transmitted through Justinian's *Corpus Iuris Civilis*. Medieval European jurists, led by the glossators of the University of Bologna, elaborated this legacy at the very moment canon law was being consolidated as the law of the Church. Canon law, in turn, proved formative for the rise of modern civil law (Berman 1983, 120–164; Brundage 2010, 75–125). What is often perceived as a secular and positive legal order was thus robustly underwritten by a medieval political and juridical theology—beginning with incorporation and corporate personhood. The Church as *corpus mysticum* ultimately provided the model not only for affiliated institutions but also, as will be argued in more detail below and in Chapter 9, for both the modern body politic and the capitalist corporation.

To recapitulate the Weberian argument, the process of institutionalization is fulfilled to the extent that it reflects the ultimately "rational" redemption, via legal techniques, of an underlying—elementary yet implicit and fundamentally "irrational"—magico-sacramental theology of making the one out of many, fueled by the charisma of a leader, whether magician, hero, prophet, or saint. This transformation is typically effected through the utterance of "sacral words"—paradigmatically, in the Christian case, those pronounced by Christ at the Last Supper. The procedure derives from Latin Christian theology's reliance on the idea of the body of Christ and on the magico-sacramental formula through which a member of the Church joins this body by the act of eating (and drinking) from it, in accordance with the words pronounced by Christ in the Last Supper. This logic became a shared meta-institutional matrix for legitimizing a collective body—the corporation—and, through it, the juridical personality of institutions, both civil and ecclesiastical (Salvatore 2020, 27).

The Alternate Instituting Power of Relationality

Weber had the merit of excavating the instituting process down to the level of a magico-sacramental, theopolitical machine of modernization as rationalization. This was the essence of his intervention in explaining the exceptional character of the Occident of modern capitalism and bureaucratic statehood. A sociology of Islam (in the double sense elucidated in Chapter 1, yielding an "Islamic frame"), however, cannot be built on the same premises, which in Weber remained irredeemably "exceptional" and, ultimately, "irrational." He struggled to provide a sociological rephrasing of what he rightly identified as a theologically predetermined and teleologically oriented—hence far from open-ended—instituting process. His nebulous sociologization of "charisma" failed to square the circle. The bottom line of the Weberian argument is that institutionalization, even if (or perhaps precisely because) it requires sacralization, can reclaim a rational character only by establishing the limited accountability of a collective subject in the form of a unified, corporate person. Yet the crucial point—well captured by Weber, though less so by many of his interpreters—is that such a corporate personality is only one, and a quite peculiar, outcome among several possible transformations of the initial associative matrix represented by the confraternal bond. Missing this open-ended spectrum of outcomes of *Verbrüderung* leads to a normatively eurocentric bias, one that generated a long series of orientalist distortions, most notably the category of the "Islamic city." Defined through a catalogue of deficits measured against European norms—especially the absence of municipal incorporation and corresponding public accountability—the "Islamic city" was misconstrued as lacking a rationally instituted "public policy," even when key services were in fact provided through the non-incorporated *waqf* (Abu-Lughod 1987; Zubaida 2006).

Accordingly, in elaborating our Islamic frame, the versatile and unconsecrated character of the confraternal bond in the ecumene should be explained through relationality, including bodily connectedness or intercorporeality, as identified in the previous chapters. This cohesion depends decisively on *adab* as a mastery of forms, harmonizing rational and sensorial dimensions. It also rests on networking and gift circulation, supported on the one hand by access to *baraka* and on the other by the normative force of *maslaha*. Seen from this angle, what Weber imperfectly captured under the label of "charisma" derives from knowledge of forms and from the capacity—not merely a set of skills, but a quasi-poetic talent or genius—to reshape and master them. Ideally, this form of knowledge culminates in *walaya*. Charismatic masters should thus be understood as masters of intercorporeal relational forms. Charisma is here transformed into a fully relational concept, extending far beyond the unilateral model—postulated by Weber and his epigoni—of followers recognizing a leader's authority. *Baraka* must be harnessed through the habitualizing force of *adab* to enable such mastery of forms, which are ultimately life forms. Reformulated in this way, charisma is not an exceptional personal magnetism subsequently routinized into institutions, but a fluid component of a continuous process of recreating confraternal bonds, and thus of instituting life itself.

Seen in this light, there is no "pure" eruptive charisma opposed to a later "jellied" institutional form; life forms are permanently in the making through instituting processes.[5] Such dynamics dispense with any sacralization of the confraternal bond into a corporate personality. Instead, they rely on patterns of "spiritual seniority," measured by degrees of mastery of forms. This is condensed in the figure of the master as *shaykh* or elder, indeed, an elder brother more than a "spiritual father" to his disciples, among whom gradations of brotherly seniority also develop. While this model shares patriarchal features common to other regions of the precolonial Oikoumene, it avoids the logic of incorporation by fiat that prevailed in Latin Christendom. There the confraternal nexus was redirected into a magico-sacramental format privileging a different patriarchal subtype, one centered on the father–son relationship. This model transcended relational and intercorporeal mediation, condensing authority into a compact symbol that enabled incorporation. Sacred sonship—rooted in pre-Christian myth—was reactivated within Christian dogma through a theology of incarnation and hypostatic personalization, rather than through the mediating, relational role played in the Islamic ecumene by the "friends" of God.

In the Islamic ecumene, the cohesion of a confraternity ultimately depended on the assent of its members. This assent was secured through a charisma embedded in chains of initiation rather than through the figure of an "exceptional personality" invoked by Weber's sociology—a move that barely disguised a secularized transposition of Latin Christian theology centered on the redemptive sonship of Christ's persona. By contrast, in the ecumene the *silsila* linking masters secured the transmission of a charisma of spiritual seniority and constituted an open-ended instituting alternative to the incorporation model, which—ironically, as Weber himself decried—erodes and routinizes charisma into a stable (and, we might add, rigid) institutional form. These patterns of *silsila* prevailed even where a ritual act was required—one that has been quite imperfectly labeled, on the basis of weak analogies with medieval Europe, an "oath of allegiance." The term used in the ecumene for such a vow of acceptance of a master's guidance is *bay'a*. Not restricted to a Sufi context, *bay'a* is, not by chance, a metaphor drawn from marketplace transactions (Salvatore 2020, 23–24). In this sense, it stands at a considerable distance from an oath imbued with magico-sacramental power, such as the one exemplified by Weber's model of European medieval urban confraternities. Taken from the vocabulary of sale, *bay'a* signifies an act of "buying into" authority rather than of "swearing" submission to it—whether to a master of a Sufi brotherhood, a guild leader, or a military commander (an *amir* or even the

Caliph). The need to renew *bay'a* upon a change of leadership further underscores the fundamentally "lay" character of the confraternal bond. Solid yet flexible, it did not require the magico-sacramental summoning of a transcendent corporate personality. The fact that *bay'a* within a brotherhood was often ritualized does not negate this point; rather, it situates the practice beyond the rigid lay–sacral binary that crystallized only after the protracted modern European process of institutionalization. One should also recall that in the ecumene commercial transactions themselves could assume ritualized forms, particularly insofar as a trader's conduct—especially when embedded in a guild or *akhi* association—was governed by *adab*. What appears, retrospectively, as a sharp divide between mystical union and commercial interest is thus better understood as the product of a later European epistemic rupture, projected backwards through an inevitably eurocentric vocabulary.

Across the proliferation of local transformations linking *tariqa* and *futuwwa*, both urban and rural, the confraternal bond retained permeable institutional boundaries, deliberately avoiding the corporate exclusivity of a singular collective personality. Because there was no personal charisma to be incorporated, there was also no charisma to be routinized. Transmission through spiritual lineages generated recurring cycles of the emergence of great masters rather than a single charismatic climax followed by institutional normalization. This dynamic enabled patterns of civility that were remarkably inclusive across social strata and receptive to informal modes of influence and patronage emanating from diverse milieus. The associational model that emerged was instituted gently, dispensing with the symbolic violence inherent in the instantaneous, magico-sacramental reduction of multiple individualities into an abstract and transcendent collective personality—one directly or indirectly modeled on the mystical body of Christ (Salvatore 2016, 89–100).

The rather supple, elegantly simple, and adaptable model that prevailed in the Islamic ecumene eschewed the far more rigid mechanisms through which, in late medieval Europe, charters and statutes instituted municipalities and kingdoms, along with their offices. Because connective charisma did not need to be locked into charters—whether bestowed by royal or ecclesiastical authorities or self-authorized by urban groups—the lineage-supported confraternity could be deployed across long distances. This open-ended and, in principle, reversible instituting process facilitated the emergence of overlapping patterns of connectedness over expanding spatial horizons, rather than producing, as in Europe, a tightly regulated hierarchy of loyalties entrenched in city-bound associations and institutions. Accordingly, the prevailing pattern in the ecumene fostered a proliferation of local ramifications of confraternities, as well as the merging of different brotherhoods across wide regions. This dynamic decisively supported Islam's diversified expansion over vast territories by land and sea (Salvatore 2018, 164–165).

What emerges from this contrastive analysis is a clarification of the convoluted nexus in Weber between the idea of charisma—intended to exalt human freedom and commitment to change—and its ultimately conservative, if not oppressive and repressive, outcome in the form of an opaque, magico-ritually consecrated institution. It thus becomes necessary to recognize not only that the instituting process and its outcomes mediated by *waqf* in the Islamic ecumene diverge sharply from Weber's European case, but also that any attempt to project a Weberian notion of charisma onto prophecy or *walaya* is deeply misleading. Authority in the ecumene—whether that of a brotherhood's master or of an "elder" (*shaykh*) more broadly—rests, as seen in the previous chapter, on webs of intercorporeal connectedness extending across space. The originality of these patterns should therefore be safeguarded against their recurrent dilution through loosely transposed notions of charisma, which only compound the misappreciation of the sophistication, malleability, and resilience of the ecumene's instituting process. A typically Weberian misapprehension of this process surfaced in the way earlier Western scholars of Sufism—from Nicholson and Arberry to Trimingham (see Chapter 3)—distinguished an allegedly "authentically spiritual" Sufism of the origins from what they decried as its authoritarian, populistic, and superstitious degeneration at the so-called *tariqa* stage. On this view, the *tariqa* appeared as an oppressive institutional cage constraining a supposedly pristine charisma, rather than as a nuanced model of creative adaptability rooted in softly instituted confraternal bonds. Yet the consolidation of the *tariqa* was embedded in its horizontal networks and vertical hierarchies, which supported some of the most "charismatic" Sufi leaders—both intellectually and organizationally—who emerged precisely in the Middle Periods, especially in the 12th and 13th centuries, as Hodgson repeatedly emphasized (Hodgson 1974 II, 203–240).

Likewise, as previously noted, a Weberian strand of neo-orientalist reasoning cast the *waqf* as the focal point of an alleged array of institutional deficits attributed to "Muslim" or "Islamic" societies. The *waqf* was blamed for the supposed failure to generate civic autonomies comparable to those of European cities, for inhibiting the rise of intermediate associations between individuals and rulers, and ultimately for obstructing capitalist enterprise by constraining the use of "private" wealth as investment capital. In this account, the *waqf* became emblematic of a fundamental institutional shortcoming—quite simply, the absence of incorporation (Kuran 2001, 2011). Notably, while the *waqf* was accused of blocking incorporation, *shari'a* law more broadly was faulted for preventing the development of civil law. This interpretive syndrome reflects less a neutral analytical bias than a distinctly "occidentalist" methodology functioning as the concealed armature of classic orientalist arguments. By mirroring the half-disguised political theology of Latin Christendom as the prehistory of the "West," such readings effectively de-sociologize and de-civilize the cosmopolitan, relational, and reflexive modes of institutionalization characteristic of the Islamic ecumene. Against these skewed comparisons—which either bracket out the impact of colonialism or openly celebrate it as the vehicle for exporting Western rationalization through incorporation—we contend that the vitality of *waqf*, as a marker of "the importance of being Islamic," emerged along a trajectory virtuously porous to pre- and non-Islamic traditions This trajectory rendered the *waqf* a highly original instituting channel, one that protected institutions from being cleaved into the polar domains of private versus public reason or religious versus civil ethics. Most importantly, it carefully avoided sanctioning chartered, unilinear chains of command, favoring instead overlapping relationalities and loyalties.

Truly, the *waqf* secured functions that in medieval European cities were increasingly taken over by municipalities. It did so, however, in conformity with the relational and civic ethos of the instituting process in the ecumene—that is, in a markedly decentered way. This held true even when, as was often the case, rulers, their families, bureaucratic elites, and other notables figured prominently among the wealthy endowers of *waqf*, and even when, for that reason, *waqf* arrangements could be mistaken for instruments of "public policy." Yet, as the generative source of virtually all Islamic institutions, the *waqf* proved far more versatile as an *'umran*-enabling mechanism. It facilitated worship, knowledge production, education, health care, spiritual cultivation, and community life. Grounded in a solid legal framework and supported by a rich and adaptable jurisprudential practice, *waqf* regulations and modes of administration could also withstand—even if they do not need to be subjected to—a rigid Weberian test of "legal rationality."

From this perspective, the *waqf* emerges as the crucial precolonial instrument of urban development and translocal exchange in the ecumene, which in turn generated wealth that could be partly redistributed through new endowments. Remarkably, its legal status, administrative practices, and socioeconomic impact proved capable of adaptation to widely varying historical and geographical circumstances. Its non-incorporated status, rather than weakening it, reinforced this adaptability, alongside a scalable formalization of rules and accountability patterns (Hennigan 2004). It should be stressed that this was not merely a regulative achievement. It reflected a foundational "theological" orientation—one that, as will become clearer in the following chapters, was inseparable from a broader sociopolitical cosmology—according to which a single *waqf* originated in a pious commitment to doing good for others in need. The beneficiaries, in turn, were less the recipients of an individual endowing act than of the mercy of the ultimate Other, God.

For this reason, and as reflected in its legal articulation, the *waqf* was neither private nor public in any strict sense—not even juridically—but instead functioned as an instituting channel occupying a distinctive "third" space (Salvatore 2016, 119). This positioning resonates directly with the *barzakh*-inspired epistemology discussed in the previous chapters. Weber himself, in a series of scattered but suggestive remarks, gestured toward viewing endowments as a third comparative genus, positioned alongside private corporations and public institutions and occupying a grey zone between them. He even cited the *waqf* as a prominent example of this category. Yet he did not pursue this line of thought further, and the insight remained submerged within an argument otherwise tilted toward demonstrating the exceptionalism of occidental institutions (Weber [1921–1922] 1980, 429; see Salvatore 2020).

Finally, it bears emphasizing that my relatively upbeat assessment of the instituting force of the *waqf* is not meant to idealize the instituting process in the Islamic ecumene, which undoubtedly involved contextual weaknesses and, at times, outright abuses—as is the case with such processes everywhere. Rather, the point has been to explain, in a sociopolitically grounded manner, the *waqf*s long-term success, which would otherwise remain sociologically unintelligible—at least until the historical moment when the aggressive nexus between Westphalian states and colonial corporations began to erode *'umran* in the ecumene. In this regard, it is worth reiterating, as felicitously formulated by John Hall and cited earlier (Salvatore 2016, 123), that in the precolonial world "Islam was so advanced as to disallow some of the social institutions involved in the European dynamic" (Hall 1985, 99).

Notes

1. It remains perplexing to see such categories still being flashed in the titles and headings of several recent studies on *waqf*—studies that are often remarkable for providing new and critical insights (see Singer 2008; 2018; Moumtaz 2021; Zencirci 2024; even Arjomand 1998).
2. This point echoes what we saw when commenting on the, in principle, universal—rather than merely Islamic—character of *'umran* as theorized by Ibn Khaldun (Chapter 1; see also Chapter 5).
3. Contemporary citizenship oaths are the residue of that procedure in a world that, both politically and economically, has retained and further developed the model of incorporation as the primary—if not exclusive—mode of the instituting process.
4. While the label "corporation" has a broader scope within civil codes, business companies have de facto monopolized it in general parlance, thereby rendering the corporate nature of most social and state institutions scarcely recognizable to non-specialists.
5. No doubt *baraka* provides a compelling emic counterpart, one that sidesteps the Latin Christian theopolitical implications embedded in Weber's notion of charisma—provided, however, that we do not orientalistically overinvest the emic term with a fixed and unilateral authenticity, something that no concept, when approached sociologically and historically, has ever possessed.

References

Abu-Lughod, Janet. 1987. "The Islamic City – Historic Myth, Islamic Essence, and Contemporary Relevance." *International Journal of Middle East Studies* 19 (2): 155–76.

Al-Daghistani, Sami. 2022. "Beyond *Maṣlaḥah*: *Adab* and Islamic Economic Thought." *American Journal of Islam and Society* 39 (3–4): 57–86.

Arjomand, Said Amir. 1998. "Philanthropy, the Law, and Public Policy in the Islamic World before the Modern Era." In *Philanthropy in the World's Traditions*, edited by Warren F. Ilchman et al., 109–32. Bloomington: Indiana University Press.

Arjomand, Said Amir. 1999. "The Law, Agency and Policy in Medieval Islamic Society: Development of the Institutions of Learning from the Tenth to the Fifteenth Century." *Comparative Studies in Society and History* 41(2): 263–93.

Arjomand, Said Amir. 2004. "Transformation of the Islamicate Civilization: A Turning Point in the Thirteenth Century? In *Eurasian Transformations, 10th to 13th Centuries: Crystallizations, Divergences, Renaissances*, edited by Johann P. Arnason and Björn Wittrock, 213–45. Leiden: Brill.

Bamyeh, Mohammed A. 2019. *Lifeworlds of Islam. The Pragmatics of a Religion.* New York: Oxford. University Press.

Berman, Harold J. 1983. *Law and Revolution: The Formation of the Western Legal Tradition.* Cambridge, MA: Harvard University Press.

Bori, Caterina. 2018. "Religious Knowledge between Scholarly Conservatism and Commoners' Agency." In *The Wiley Blackwell History of Islam*, edited by Armando Salvatore et al., 291–310. Oxford: Wiley Blackwell.

Brundage, James A. 2010. *The Medieval Origins of the Legal Profession: Canonists, Civilians, and Courts.* Chicago: University of Chicago Press.

Çizakça, Murat. 2000. *A History of Philanthropic Foundations: The Islamic World from the Seventh Century to the Present.* Istanbul: Boğaziçi University Press.

Ghazaleh, Pascale. 2011. "Introduction. Pious Foundations: From Here to Eternity? In *Held in Trust: Waqf in the Islamic World*, edited by Pascale Ghazaleh, 1–21. Cairo: American University in Cairo Press.

Hall, John A. 1985. *Powers and Liberties: The Causes and Consequences of the Rise of the West.* Oxford: Basil Blackwell.

Hennigan, Peter C. 2004. *The Birth of a Legal Institution: The Formation of the Waqf in Third-Century A.H. Ḥanafī Legal Discourse.* Leiden: Brill.

Hodgson, Marshall G. S. 1974. *The Venture of Islam: Conscience and History in a World Civilization*, Vol. 1–3. Chicago: University of Chicago Press.

Hofer, Nathan. 2021. "Endowments for Ṣūfīs and Their Institutions." In *Sufi Institutions*, edited by Alexandre Papas, 58–80. Leiden: Brill.

Isin, Engin F., and Alexandre Lefebvre. 2005. "The Gift of Law: Greek Euergetism and Ottoman *Waqf*." *European Journal of Social Theory* 8(1): 5–23.

Kuran, Timur. 2001. "The Provision of Public Goods under Islamic Law: Origins, Impact, and Limitations of the *Waqf* System." *Law and Society Review* 35(4): 841–97.

Kuran, Timur. 2005. "The Absence of the Corporation in Islamic Law: Origins and Persistence." *American Journal of Comparative Law* 53 (4): 785–834.

Kuran, Timur. 2011. *The Long Divergence: How Islamic Law Held Back the Middle East.* Princeton, NJ: Princeton University Press.

Lev, Yaacov. 2005. *Charity, Endowments, and Charitable Institutions in Medieval Islam.* Gainesville: University Press of Florida.

Masud, M. Khalid. [1977] 1995. *Shatibi's Philosophy of Islamic Law*, Kuala Lumpur: Islamic Book Trust.

Moumtaz, Nada. 2018. "Theme Issue: A Third Wave of *Waqf* Studies." *Islamic Law and Society* 25 (1–2): 1–10.

Moumtaz, Nada. 2021. *God's Property: Islam, Charity, and the Modern State.* Oakland, CA: University of California Press.

Nippel, Wilfried. 2002. "*Homo Politicus* and *Homo Oeconomicus*: The European Citizen According to Max Weber." In *The Idea of Europe: From Antiquity to the European Union*, edited by Anthony Pagden, 129–38. Cambridge: Cambridge University Press.

Rahman, Fazlur [1966] 1979. *Islam*. Chicago: University of Chicago Press.
Ricci, Ronit. 2011. *Islam Translated: Literature, Conversion, and the Arabic Cosmopolis of South and Southeast Asia*. Chicago: University of Chicago Press.
Safi, Louay M. 2022. *Islam and the Trajectory of Globalization: Rational Idealism and the Structure of World History*. London: Routledge.
Salvatore, Armando. 2007. *The Public Sphere: Liberal Modernity, Catholicism, and Islam*. New York: Palgrave Macmillan.
Salvatore, Armando. 2013. "Islam and the Quest for a European Secular Identity: From Sovereignty through Solidarity to Immunity." *Politics, Religion & Ideology* 14 (2): 253–64.
Salvatore, Armando. 2016. *The Sociology of Islam: Knowledge, Power and Civility*. Oxford: Wiley Blackwell.
Salvatore, Armando. 2018. "Sufi Articulations of Civility, Globality, and Sovereignty." *Journal of Religious and Political Practice* 4 (2): 156–74.
Salvatore, Armando. 2020. "East of Westphalia: Shaping the Body-Politic Via Institutional Charisma." In *Political Theologies and Development in Asia: Transcendence, Sacrifice and Aspiration*, edited by Giuseppe Bolotta et al., 18–39. Manchester: Manchester University Press.
Schacht, Joseph [1935] 1950. *The Origins of Muhammadan Jurisprudence*. Oxford: Oxford University Press.
Singer, Amy. 2008. *Charity in Islamic Societies*. Cambridge: Cambridge University Press.
Singer, Amy. 2018. "Replace Stasis with Motion to Fathom the Persistence of *Waqf*: The Complex Histories and Legacies of a Muslim Institution." *The Muslim World* 108 (4): 702–16.
Weber, Max [1921–1922] 1980. In *Wirtschaft und Gesellschaft: Grundriß der verstehenden Soziologie*, edited by Johannes Winckelmann, 5th edition. Tübingen: J.C.B. Mohr (Paul Siebeck).
Zencirci, Gizem. 2024. *The Muslim Social: Neoliberalism, Charity, and Poverty in Turkey*. Syracuse, NY: Syracuse University Press.
Zubaida, Sami. 2006. "Max Weber's the City and the Islamic City." *Max Weber Studies* 6 (1): 111–8.

5

INSTITUTING GOVERNANCE

A Khaldunian Inflection of the Knowledge–Power Nexus into the Adab–Siyasa *Complex*

Understanding *Dawla*'s Formation Through (and Beyond) *'Asabiyya*

While Ibn Battuta was the gifted chronicler of the transition from the Earlier to the Later Middle Period, it was Ibn Khaldun (1332–1406) who, from the vantage point of the unfolding latter epoch that was inaugurated by the Mongol conquest of Baghdad, famously diagnosed the dynamics of *'umran* in the ecumene—both its strengths and bottlenecks. He did so not only in his deservedly famous *Muqaddima*, which provided the conceptual armature to his historical work, but through his rich political biography, which reflected the quandaries and the promises of the epoch (Fromherz 2010; see also Salvatore 2016, 110). From this point onward, the Mongol conquest of the Abbasid capital in 1258 can be understood as the zero ground for the inception of a process that gradually—though not linearly—ended up instituting more consistent patterns of rulership and governance after several centuries of agony of caliphal rule, which Hodgson tagged as the Earlier Middle Period. It is precisely within this unstable interval that Ibn Khaldun's intuitions and systematizations opened a space for reflection that benefited, if intermittently, generations of scholars within the Islamic ecumene—most notably extending into the era of the Ottoman state's most extraordinary splendor in early modernity. At this juncture, however, the resulting synthesis of knowledge cannot be reduced to any of the extant fields or genres of intellectual production. Its innovative impetus is undeniable, even if attempts to anachronistically describe it as sociology or social theory are far-fetched.[1] This is not because of Ibn Khaldun's being a personality of the Later Middle Period and therefore "premodern," but rather because of the partiality and limitations of such disciplinary fields when they are uncritically valued, by default, as modern and Western—and therefore of the highest standards—while remaining not only eurocentric but also, inevitably, colonial (see Chapter 1; see also Salvatore and Obuse 2022).

Seen from within the instituting dynamics of the ecumene, while Ibn Khaldun's oeuvre and historical role can hardly bear a univocal tag, it has been convincingly argued—as we will discuss shortly—that he should be seen as a highly innovative practitioner of *adab*. This should be understood both in the broadest sense of the umbrella category and in the more pointed signification indicated by what we described in Chapter 2 as the practice underlying the broader knowledge–power complex of *adab–siyasa*, whose cumulative enrichment marked the transition from the Later Middle Period to early modernity (see also Chapters 6 and 8). In this capacity, the *adab–siyasa* complex was finely ingrained in the self-understanding of political and intellectual elites of the ecumene, who were tasked not only with comprehending but also with managing the increasingly intricate unfolding of *ʿumran* and the challenges it posed to governance.

This is why, before turning directly to Ibn Khaldun, we need to take stock and gain a clearer view of the *adab–siyasa* complex, which Hayrettin Yücesoy introduced by suggesting that "the worldly tenor of *siyasa* cannot be appreciated without regarding the *adab* tradition and its worldly and cosmopolitan character" (Yücesoy 2013, xiii). This formulation is both a recognition and a warning. It signals, first, that looking at *siyasa* as a self-sustaining or autonomous field—as a stand-alone art of government, or even statecraft—would be moot. Rather, it presupposes the habitualizing narrative of *adab* that we explored in Chapter 2. Relying on the multifaceted know-how of *adab–siyasa* thus appears as a fundamental, rather than specialized, human practice. It helped sociopolitical actors of the ecumene balance life forms and commitments with what we might call "political civility"—a possible, if imperfect, translation of *adab–siyasa* as a complex inflecting the knowledge-power equation in specific ways. In practical terms, these inflections were meant to equip rulers, administrators, scholars, and a variety of other intervening subjects to navigate wisely—but also astutely—a multiplicity of situations encountered in sociopolitical life, amidst the open-ended unfolding of *ʿumran* in all its impermanence. For this reason, *adab–siyasa* cannot be viewed as grounded either on personal virtues alone or on an impersonal and faceless machine of governmentality.[2]

Historically, Yücesoy shows how the discourse of *siyasa* was born out of a growing disenchantment with somewhat unrealistic visions of rulership, most notably the juridical theory of the Imamate that crystallized as a by-product of the consolidation of the Sunni doctrine of the four Rightly Guided Caliphs (designating the Prophet Muhammad's successors from Abu Bakr to ʿAli). This doctrine became a rather abstract benchmark of legitimacy, increasingly in competition with the Shiʿi chain of Imams, legitimized by their belonging to the House of the Prophet via ʿAli (Yücesoy 2023, 111–114). What matters for our purposes is that, after starting to challenge the discourse of the Imamate, *siyasa* did not settle into a specific field or discipline in the manner of Aristotle's *Politics*. Instead, it functioned as a spinoff of the broader *adab* narrative. Not only did it provide a key staple in the output of leading, if eclectic, *adab* scholars such as al-Jahiz (d. 869) and Ibn Qutayba (d. 889), whom we mentioned in Chapter 2. Over time, religious scholars also appropriated the term and the concept—not merely as a concession to their challengers, but as part of their own analytical repertoire (Heck 2018, 182; Yücesoy 2023, 3). Thus framed, the *siyasa* component of the broader complex further articulated a capacity that was already central to the *adab* narrative: the ability to adapt to circumstances, manage complexity, and adjust strategy according to context and necessity. In this sense, *siyasa* reflected a paramount capacity typically associated with ruling prerogatives, namely a principled unboundedness aligned with the wise and strategically oriented modulation of sovereign command, making authority both compelling and legitimate.

Here a brief clarification of approach is in order. Based on such insights, this chapter follows the thread of reflections and systematization that articulate a core concern of the Southern/Italian sociopolitical thought outlined in Chapter 1, namely, how the process of instituting human life captured and legitimized the dimension that we routinely reference as "politics." From Machiavelli to Vico, it did so, quite unlike its Northwestern European counterparts, by paying attention to the concrete, bodily, and impermanent dimension of human existence and the social bond. This approach reflects a recurrent skepticism toward theorizations of principled forms of "sovereignty." As suggested by my broader methodological reflections, I am not participating in a putative scholarly competition about how to interpret Ibn Khaldun "correctly." Like elsewhere in this volume, I elaborate on his conceptual legacy through the prism of my own trajectory of repositioning as a scholar and participative interpreter of the Islamic frame.

Read through this lens, Ibn Khaldun's thought sharpens our sensibility to how the fragility of the social bond can be built into an instituting process that deliberately shuns constructing sovereignty, as understood in the

European Westphalian trajectory, as both absolute and corporate (see Chapters 4, 9, and Conclusion). Accordingly, statehood itself appears as continuously reconstructed within the parameters of an instituting process that, as the term *dawla* aptly conveys, unfolds as a "turn of good fortune," but also, since the advent of the ʿAbbasids, as a "revolution" (Arjomand 2022, 24). A *dawla* is thus associated with a particular conquering and ruling dynasty and with a concomitant momentum sanctioned by what we call here a political astro-cosmology, rather than, unlike the European case, a political theology. From this perspective, the denouement and effects of a *dawla* result from an alchemy of targeted arrangements and alignments of propitious constellations, often intended quite literally in their astrological sense (ibid., 295). As with everything else in *ʿumran*, impermanence and prosperity are inseparably bound together, as two sides of the same incessantly rolling coin.[3]

The key concept developed by Ibn Khaldun to make sense of this process is the idea of a recurring sociopolitical cycle, which he theorized by studying—but also actively participating in—the political vicissitudes of the Later Middle Period in North Africa and further east. Fed by the dynamics of *ʿumran*, the cycle consisted of a build-up of mobilization sustained by the connective and cohesive power of tribal formations, which Ibn Khaldun called *ʿasabiyya*, developing on the nomadic side of *ʿumran*. This mobilization harbored the potential to ignite the rise and flourishing of a new *dawla*, which in turn would be followed by a gradual decay of its stability and prosperity. This downward spiral was associated with the dissipation of the very connective power, or *ʿasabiyya*, that had triggered the *dawla* in the first place.

This, at least, is the conventional—and somewhat simplified—understanding of the Khaldunian cycle. Yet the leading innovation and forward-looking explanatory potential of Ibn Khaldun's diagnosis should be located elsewhere, namely in a distinctive epistemic opening through which he powered up a key dimension of an Islamic frame in the making. This opening relied on what Bruce Lawrence, one of the most perceptive contemporary interpreters of Ibn Khaldun, has described as an interstitial mode of insight facilitated by a *barzakh*-inspired focus on in-betweenness (Lawrence 2021, 33), to which we have already alluded in the previous chapters. Approached from this angle, the Khaldunian cycle yields a finer and more nuanced reading than one that merely offers a ruthless diagnosis of the inherent fragility of institutional integrity and ruling legitimacy in the ecumene.

A more integrated reading suggests that, within the Islamic frame of the ecumene, what we have called the instituting process cannot be neatly split—pace Weber and much of Western sociology—into the discrete conditions and outcomes of the rise of a fully fledged, self-reliant "statehood," as reflected in the dualism examined in the previous chapter between "charisma" and "institution." A merely conceptual scrutiny of Ibn Khaldun's rich terminology would not suffice to unsettle this dichotomization. What is required instead is an empathic and well-situated effort to grasp how Ibn Khaldun's intellectual genius conveyed a partially hidden—or *batini*—yet holistic logic of the instituting process. He did so by mobilizing epistemic insights deeper than those available within the framework of standard sociological explanation. These insights amount to an original mode of sociopolitical thought, which some authors have interpreted as a kind of philosophy of history (Mahdi 1957). The core epistemic intuition, consonant with the *barzakh*-inspired epistemology highlighted by Lawrence (2021), carries far-reaching cosmological implications. It can be summarized in the idea that the source of a process and its manifestation—in this case, the instituting process—are at once identical and divergent.

Let us take stock and extrapolate the idea of an instituting power or potentiality, which is crucial for grasping the *barzakh*-oriented logic underlying the process. First, we should appreciate the force of *'asabiyya* not only as the key factor of the ascending phase of the cycle, but also as the latent instituting power within the unfolding of *'umran* overall. It is a form of connective, pristine force that trains humans to cooperate and thus give form to bare life. Yet it is not an Aristotelian notion of a natural human sociability. Rather, it is necessarily contextual, both socially and environmentally. At its most extreme, *'asabiyya* develops within the harsh nomadic habitats of desert or steppe. It is therefore most typically tribal, nomadic, and pastoral life that, under favorable conditions, allows *'asabiyya* to form and flourish, and thereby to generate *'umran*. Given that *'asabiyya* typically arises within a specific form of life and flourishing or civility, Ibn Khaldun termed this *'umran badawi*, the civility of nomads or Bedouins. This life form appears, at first sight, as the opposite of refinement and ease. It produces the skills required for the daily, piecemeal constitution of human life and connectedness under environmental duress, and hence the necessity to forge strong ties of trust and cooperation. The tribe itself emerges as a particularly ingenious form of connectedness which, long before being dissected by generations of anthropologists (see e.g. Eickelman [1987] 2002, 115–139), imposes itself as a primary, or "primordial," outcome of civility.

At the risk of overinterpreting Ibn Khaldun—or consciously extending his theory—one could say that while *'umran badawi* is the condition for *'asabiyya*, *'umran* in general, that is, any form of *'umran*, cannot exist without a spark of *'asabiyya*.

From this angle, *'asabiyya* can be understood as sufficiently plastic and protean to engender a mutation from *'umran badawi* to *'umran hadari*, the urban mode of flourishing or civility, when sociopolitical conditions—ideally complemented by religious factors—align with propitious astro-cosmological, that is, divinely sanctioned, constellations. *'Umran hadari* is what, in our distorted conceptual vocabulary, might sound like the tautology of a "civilized civility": a sedentary life marked by urban comfort, refinement, and prosperity. A more finely tuned lens, however, allows us to see *'asabiyya* not merely as the remote nomadic origin of a *dawla* that, once instituted, erodes the cohesive force of tribal life—this being the *zahiri*, or manifest and exoteric, sense of Khaldunian *'asabiyya*. It should also be understood as playing an essential role across the entire arc of the instituting process, at a broader social level and throughout the whole cycle. In this perspective, *'asabiyya*, precisely because it is a protean force, mutates through the articulations of urban life rather than simply being eroded by them.

For sure, sedentariness can be highly challenging for most social classes if no adequate forms of relationality and mutual support are developed in the environments in which they settle. The knowledge–power equation with which *'asabiyya* must cope in an urban context includes many more variables and is therefore far more exposed to dissipation. Ibn Khaldun's assessment of the number of generations needed for the cycle to degenerate into a full decay should thus be taken as an estimate or an average, rather than as an iron sociopolitical law. Our attention should instead be directed to how *'asabiyya*, in its fluid and dynamic becoming, provides the actual engine of the instituting process, including its dimension of *tamaddun*, the term Ibn Khaldun used to refer to the urban articulation of this process. This dimension is, in turn, the outcome—and largely the merit—of an accomplished *dawla*. But it is precisely for this reason that *'asabiyya* should be seen as playing a role in producing fundamental social institutions, including urban ones, rather than being one-sidedly bent on triggering the rising stage of a *dawla* through military might alone. In its continuous metamorphosis, one instantiation of *'asabiyya* may even be more a consequence than a cause of *dawla* formation, insofar as it creates the conditions for urban life and solidarity to thrive. This Khaldunian paradox, or hidden—if not esoteric—meaning of the "cycle," was already captured by an orientalist and historian of a past generation such as Claude Cahen (1954; 1981), who identified urban *futuwwa* (see Chapter 3) as a manifestation of *'asabiyya*. Here a transposition of tribal solidarity into urban civility instituted mechanisms through which city dwellers recreated forms of cohesion and loyalty that can be understood as functionally equivalent to—albeit more complex and therefore more fragile than—those found in nomadic settings. I would not interpret this as a mere analogy or imitation, but rather as the manifestation of the same "source" of social cohesion inherent in *'umran*, namely *'asabiyya*. This source is most visible and powerful where the reconstruction of life forms out of bare life is most demanding, that is, within *badawa*. There we can observe the institution of "elementary forms" of *'asabiyya*, but by no means its full spectrum.

I would, in any case, preemptively downplay any resemblance between this interpretation and Durkheim's distinction between "mechanical" and "organic" forms of solidarity, which is very much a by-product of a European-style civilizing process such as the one described by Elias. That framework is associated with a fundamentally different type of instituting process and state formation, which we will address shortly (see also Chapter 9). The Khaldunian approach is characterized precisely by its refusal to treat the civility of the *dawla* as the apex of human development, unlike Durkheim's organic solidarity in modern societies. Instead, it emphasizes the impermanence and vulnerability of refinement and complexity. Within the *barzakh*-inspired epistemology highlighted by Lawrence, we can surmise that Ibn Khaldun's two signature concepts, *'asabiyya* and *'umran*—which we may provisionally describe as, respectively, the foundation and the manifestation of the instituting process in the ecumene—can, and indeed should, be analytically distinguished. Yet they cannot be epistemically split, since they belong to one and the same comprehensive instituting process. The *barzakh*-oriented logic suggests, after all, that the strait is identical to the bridge. Ultimately, to focus exclusively on the inherent instability of any "institution" or "state" within the cycle is to miss how the intrinsic impermanence of any institutional achievement functions as the essential lubricant of a diversified and open-ended instituting process. This reading of *'asabiyya* and *'umran* accords with Lawrence's observation that Ibn Khaldun relied on a supple, metaphorically extended use of his key categories (Lawrence 2021, 38). Such nuancing is itself a gift of *adab* and, as we will see further, a requirement of *siyasa*. In other words, the "theory" provided by Ibn Khaldun could only have been produced by a subtle practitioner of *adab-siyasa* and is therefore far removed from the hubris of an "objective social science" fashioned by "outsiders" situated at a safe distance from their supposed object of knowledge.

'Asabiyya's Sublimation into *Adab-Siyasa*

The power of the conceptual pair of *'umran* and *'asabiyya*, the crown jewels of Ibn Khaldun's "new science," resides in the way their meaning and valence shift according to circumstances—namely, according to the stages and forms of the instituting process, which cannot be reduced to the trajectory of a *dawla* alone (Lawrence 2021, 34–35). *'Asabiyya* appears as a kind of spark that triggers the instituting process from a "ground zero," or inertial state of *'umran*, when a life prone to inhabiting and building the earth exists in a condition of pure potentiality, ready to burst into motion. In this sense, *'asabiyya* should be understood as the capability, inherent in the intrinsic precariousness of the social bond, to unleash an exceptional momentum in the life of a tribe still aloof from urban refinement. The ensuing articulation of *'umran*, with its industrious prosperity and refinement unfolding under the aegis of a successful *dawla*, owes to one exemplary and "pristine," yet not exclusive, form of *'asabiyya*—and, most crucially, to its capacity for metamorphosis. The prototypical process manifests itself through a sequence of military conquests carried out by a tribal coalition or confederation whose cohesion is forged through gifted leadership capable of actualizing latent *'asabiyya*. This leadership often intervenes from outside the immediate tribal constellation of forces. Such "raw" dynamics of *'asabiyya* thus appear almost as the inverted image of courtly *adab*, which instead cultivates differentiated repertoires of *savoir faire* and *savoir vivre*.

For this reason, *'asabiyya* cannot be adequately understood—pace several generations of interpreters, including some who, like Ernst Gellner (1981), sought to place Ibn Khaldun within a general theory of statehood—by focusing exclusively on movements arising from beyond urban centers, driven by a fresh *esprit de corps* and replacing crumbling dynasties. To magnify Ibn Khaldun's key intuition about the nature of *'asabiyya* should not entail diminishing the habitualizing prism of *adab*, which gives shape and firmness to the instituting process (see Chapter 2). The *adab-siyasa* complex is not the antithesis or depletion of *'asabiyya*; rather, it is its paradoxical culmination, fully consistent with the *barzakh*-oriented logic of the instituting process. Not only does *adab-siyasa* share the impermanence that characterizes everything in *ʿumran*; it also functions as the cognitive mirror of that impermanence. *Adab* reflects and absorbs the connective power of *ʿasabiyya* within an urban context, culminating in ruling courts instituted by formerly nomadic warriors and leaders: the erstwhile "wolves," to use Ibn Khaldun's metaphor, transformed into "watchdogs," now trained to detect the fragility of sociopolitical cohesion and its myriad sources of subversion.

Giving meaningful form to life—instituting worthy and refined life forms—is only possible on the basis of an already existing, and at times revolutionary,[4] type of connectedness shaped by *ʿasabiyya*. Its underlying power ultimately yields the art of governance (*siyasa*) through the kind of refinement reflected in the protean, multi-genre literature gathered under the umbrella of *adab*. This corpus ranges from allegorical representations of human desires, including the struggle for power (often staged through animal figures), to mirrors for princes. Yet the full actualization of *ʿasabiyya* is also what consumes it. *Siyasa* as statecraft therefore includes a crucial craft: a wisdom of power that trains its holders to manage the intrinsic impermanence of the *dawla* that has subsumed—and is in the process of exhausting—the *ʿasabiyya* of a given sociopolitical and astro-cosmological constellation. It is no accident that Ibn Khaldun's diagnostics of the knowledge–power nexus, crystallized in the concept of *ʿasabiyya*, were themselves a product of the courtly *adab–siyasa* complex, within which he was an accomplished and active practitioner throughout his life. The "new science" itself—the reflection on the process or "cycle," culminating in the animal metaphor of the *kalb al-hirasa* ("watchdog")—could only have been produced from within that complex. *Siyasa* thus appears as a craft capable of doubling as a science, practiced by and about the watchdogs themselves, who write their own story. Without this articulation, *ʿasabiyya* would remain condemned to pure potentiality without realization: resentment without martial vigor, energy without prudent administration.

To recapitulate, building on Ibn Khaldun yet moving beyond the letter of his teaching through the approach adopted in this volume, it would be reductive to confine *ʿasabiyya* to the type of power deployed by the tribal–nomadic–pastoral trigger of the broader civilizing process and attributed to those holding the force of *badawa* (the "Bedouins"). Its static opposition to urban *hadara*, understood as a life form grounded in culturedness and etiquette—in other words, already molded by *adab*—would be moot in Khaldunian terms. Yet it is precisely such a rigid contrast that risks feeding the one-sided cliché opposing the alleged instability of the *dawla* to the presumed stability of the European "state" (see e.g. Badie 1986). No doubt, the cycle largely consists in a build-up of instituting power generated by *'asabiyya*. Its climax, however, lies in the strategic lucidity required to conquer and rule. In this sense, *'asabiyya*'s primordial, heroic, and connective virtue is sublimated through the appropriation of *adab* and, even more decisively, of its indispensable spinoff, *siyasa*, whose deployment marks the crowning of the trajectory of a *dawla*. If the cycle endures, this is not because of any inertial inflation and deflation of an immutable *'asabiyya*. Nor does *adab–siyasa* simply replace an invariable and now expendable *'asabiyya* once the task shifts from conquest to governance. Rather, *adab–siyasa* itself should be understood as the outcome of a metamorphosis—indeed, a refinement—of *'asabiyya*. This is most clearly illustrated by the prime example and first consistent crystallization of an *adab–siyasa* complex in the wake of the 'Abbasid "revolution" (that is, *dawla*), as reconstructed by Hayrettin Yücesoy (2023, 82–105).

Arjomand (2022, 30; 2023, 6) aptly characterizes this transformation as an "integrative revolution," insofar as the new *dawla* could not be consolidated without the cooptation, into its highest ranks, of a Persianate secretarial class—a point to which we will return shortly. This outcome, associated with what remains, alongside the later Ottoman state, the most renowned *dawla* in the history of the ecumene and the apex of the High Caliphal era, simultaneously expressed a new self-understanding of the ruling elite and initiated the formation of a self-feeding know-how of government that, in turn, accrued to the *dawla*'s legitimacy. This result may be understood as a fully instituted, rather than pristine and heroic, form of *'asabiyya*. It is manifest in the *esprit de corps* of an administrative body—a secretarial class of increasingly Persianate inspiration—ever more conscious of its role in securing the stability and prosperity of the empire (see also Chapter 7). These actors operated by cultivating refined life forms grounded in a cosmopolitan awareness of the continuous differentiation and growing complexity of the ecumene, in ways unknown to the school of life that is *badawa*. Yet *adab–siyasa* retains and redeploys, within the context of *hadara*, the quintessence of *'asabiyya*'s power originally produced and nourished under the conditions of *badawa*. It thus constitutes a field of knowledge–power cultivation in which practitioners learn, from a different school of life, a protean adaptability to mutating circumstances and to new challenges unfolding at higher levels of complexity—though not of a radically different nature from those faced in nomadic life forms, if understood as responses to *'umran*'s intrinsic impermanence.

Viewed from this angle, the alleged seeds of the dissipation of *'asabiyya* do not lie in the sophisticated life forms of urban and court-based *hadara* as such. The social bond is always, by definition, fragile and exposed to decay. What changes within *hadara* is that this vulnerability becomes directly proportional to the degree of complexity of the life challenges to which *'asabiyya* responds. Instituting *'asabiyya* through *adab-siyasa* renders it both more powerful and more exposed to endemic pressures. The persistence and circulation of *adab-siyasa* across different locales and courts, as a meta-institution (see Chapter 2), are therefore crucial to the maintenance of the cycle itself: the exhaustion of a given *dawla* becomes the premise for the rise of a new one, rather than the implosion of *'umran*. What stabilizes the cycle as a cycle is nothing less than the self-perpetuation of *adab-siyasa* across successive formations—first in the fragile yet resilient institutional arrangements of the Earlier Middle Period, to which we will return shortly, and then more stringently in the Later Middle Period through the armature of the Mongol patronage state. In its unfolding, the cycle thus resembles a spiral. Each new *dawla* retraces the steps of previous formations, yet the outcome is always at least partly new, at each astro-cosmologically determined "turn of fortune." A corollary of impermanence is difference and novelty—even in the degree of impermanence itself.[5]

Adab-Siyasa Between Communication and Administration

To gain a sufficient understanding of the trajectory of *adab-siyasa* and its adaptation to the instability of the Earlier Middle Period, one needs to refocus on the increasing importance of *adab* in court milieus and, more generally, in high-cultural settings at the hands of the intellectual leaders of state administrative bodies. The unmatched champion of this high culture was Ibn al-Muqaffa' (d. ca. 759), who laid the groundwork of *adab-siyasa* in his famous *Epistle*. He was the exponent of a rising secretarial class of Persian origin, formed in the wake of the Caliphate's imperial expansion, particularly during the transitional phase between the Umayyad and 'Abbasid dynasties. It is essential to note that a growing self-awareness within the administrative estate was achieved by enhancing the quality and sociopolitical impact of communication as a core component of *adab* training (see Chapter 2). The political prose cultivated in the epistolary genre pioneered by Ibn al-Muqaffa' became one of the main engines of this communicative transformation, improving both the modulation and accessibility of the political lexicon beyond the mere mastery of inherited aesthetic canons.

Building on this insight, Yücesoy moves beyond Hodgson's nomenclature and identifies *adab–siyasa* as nothing less than the formula of a new type of governance. Rather than juxtaposing two oddly paired fields, conventionally (and misleadingly) translated as "literature" (*adab*) and "politics" (*siyasa*), the *adab–siyasa* complex came to occupy an increasingly coherent and expanding space within the statecraft of the High Caliphate. Its reach grew further within the far more fragmented institutional constellations of the Earlier Middle Period, not least through the multiplication of rulers' courts. Work on language thus became much more than an instrument of *siyasa*; it was its very lymph. Its sophisticated—if often crafty—inflections enabled the formulation of administrative procedures and the training of rulers in competent, prudent, and, ideally, just decision-making. These reflections and prescriptions cannot be fully subsumed under the genre of so-called mirrors for princes, which themselves underwent multiple shifts, mutations, and revivals across different regions of the ecumene from the late 8th century onward (Yücesoy 2023, 94–105). Overall, *siyasa*, far from being confined to a narrow technique of government or statecraft, or to a corpus of prescriptive manuals, emerged as the cosmopolitan culmination of the rapid and spectacular flourishing of the Islamic ecumene, shaped by an emerging elite intent on inscribing its narratives, skills, and interests into the very texture of the instituting process, from life forms to rulership.

At the same time, as Yücesoy perceptively notes, the discourse of *siyasa* inaugurated by Ibn al-Muqaffaʿ was also a marker of the precariousness of both the emerging elite of court officials trained as literati and of their craft itself. Not by chance, Ibn Khaldun later acknowledged that Ibn al-Muqaffaʿ's work inspired crucial insights of his "new science," which we have interpreted as a science of impermanence (Yücesoy 2023, 94–105). Yet the self-imposed limits of *siyasa* as envisioned by Ibn al-Muqaffaʿ mirrored its emergence amid the upheavals of the ʿAbbasid revolution. His reflections preceded by some six centuries Ibn Khaldun's diagnostic science, whose emphasis on impermanence was forged in the aftermath of the collapse of the High Caliphate and the prolonged crises of the Earlier Middle Period. In Ibn al-Muqaffaʿ, the sense of fragility conveyed by *siyasa* remained primarily anchored in individual life forms rather than extended to the instituting process as such or to the full trajectory of a *dawla*. A salient dimension of Ibn al-Muqaffa''s political wisdom relied on animal narratives, enabled by translations from non-Arab sources and adapted to an audience centered on the high-cultural milieu of the 'Abbasid court. This strategy revealed a seminal—if elegantly domesticated—human–animal analogy, grounded in the author's perception of the intrinsic exposure of the ecumene in general, and of sociopolitical actors in particular, to untamed, poorly channeled, and often fragmented drives. With Ibn al-Muqaffa', it is as if the transposition of *'asabiyya* from the conquering dynasty to its indispensable secretarial class produced a reflective, if vulnerable, "double" at the heart of the state. On the one hand, this duplication of *'asabiyya* generated a commitment to effectiveness and stability through the management of passions by means of *siyasa*. On the other hand, the reflective dimension inherent in *adab* amplified its exposure to the very drives that emanated from the untamed sphere in which *'asabiyya* constituted both a promise of cohesion and, frequently, a source of uncontrolled anarchy.

While the diagnosis of the fragility of the social bond was a primary feature of *adab–siyasa*, its foremost focus lay in the strategic value of communication as a means of stabilizing and redirecting human impulses and desires. This realization propelled *adab–siyasa* into becoming a major—and, over the long term, effective—factor in the entire threading of the instituting process of the ecumene. As we saw in Chapter 2, the appeal of the *adab* narratives spilled over into the *hadith* corpus and its uses, including by jurists. One could even argue that, by developing a form of human eloquence suited to managing the diverse and often unpredictable circumstances of urban and civilized life, *adab–siyasa* simultaneously drew on the language of animal–human drives and on divine speech. This privileged, if precarious, positioning proved decisive for improving social relationality, managing prosperity, and facilitating administration. Its complexity accelerated rapidly with the growth of the Islamic ecumene, beginning with the expansive phase of the High Caliphate that followed the 'Abbasid revolution and the interventions of Ibn al-Muqaffa'. One central communicative task of administrators concerned the composition of correspondence. The literary genre of the epistle was only the most refined expression of a broader craft aimed at persuading interlocutors of the congruence between means and ends and, ideally, of their alignment with the common good. This art of persuasion required the ability to deploy registers of speech appropriate to shifting circumstances—within the court, between courts, and across different sociocultural milieus: "whether a diplomatic missive, a response to sectarian controversy, a resolution of a tax grievance, or a sublimely worded statement that the ruler's decisions not only found favor with God but also reflected the auspicious conjuncture of the celestial bodies" (Heck 2018, 179). What was at stake here was a combination of specific technical expertise and comprehensive high-cultural competence, yielding an overarching knowledge of social complexity as it manifested itself in the nuances and contingencies of human interactions "under Heaven," so to speak. This knowledge was accumulated not only through formal learning but also, and perhaps primarily, through the formation of daily habitus, *savoir faire*, and the modulation of affects.

In Hodgson's view, this advanced cultural know-how articulated a framework in which Islam was perceived not merely as a transformative episode in human history but as its ultimate fulfillment. Such a framework displayed a marked vocation to integrate all forms of knowledge, including mundane and non-scriptural domains, into the overarching "venture of Islam." Within this venture, carried forward by the cultural and administrative agents of *adab–siyasa*, grew the awareness of what we defined in Volume I as the knowledge–power equation, namely the mutual constitution of acquiring and administering knowledge and transforming it into the capacity to govern both the self and the ecumene. This consciousness found paradigmatic expression in the life and work of al-Jahiz, whom we discussed in Chapter 2, and was magisterially condensed in his formulation: "Affairs lie in their consequences . . . and these affairs are intelligible, form the basis of social intercourse, and make governance (*siyasa*) upright" (Heck 2018, 179).

During the Middle Periods, within the context of what Hodgson termed the *amir–aʿyan* system, introduced in Chapter 4, political fragmentation further intensified the demand for *adab* and reinforced its ties to *siyasa*. The multiplication of ruling courts generated by political fragmentation fostered the proliferation of *adab* works and mirrors for princes that increasingly included sections devoted to questions of *siyasa*. These works offered guidance to rulers on acquiring and maintaining power, cultivating prudence and self-mastery, and enabling effective governance oriented toward shared well-being. Crucially, while often invoking the pre-Islamic Persianate ideal of kingly justice (Arjomand 2023; 2025), the discourse of *siyasa* frequently intersected with, and even encompassed, the religio-juridical trope of *maslaha* (Al-Daghistani 2022, 76). This nexus was already clearly articulated in Ibn al-Muqaffaʿ, who in his *Epistle* invoked *maslaha* and related notions precisely to link *siyasa*'s attention to circumstantial relations with a broader concern for welfare. This occurred well before *maslaha* was formally canonized as a juridical principle within some of the leading schools of *fiqh* (Yücesoy 2023, 14 and 274n52).

The initial polemical inflection of *siyasa* by Ibn al-Muqaffaʿ, who sought to sever statecraft from the grip of what he regarded as an abstract juridico-theological discourse, helped him and his successors—acting as the intellectual leaders of the secretarial class across the ecumene—to gradually forge the *adab–siyasa* complex as a kind of golden safe, guarding the knowledge–power equation against hypocrisy, lack of realism, and abuse (see Yavari 2014, 41–44). Over time, such pointed interventions opened *siyasa* to a process of mainstreaming beyond the boundaries of any single genre, style, or agenda, allowing it to assume a central role in reflections on the instituting process and on sociopolitical arrangements more broadly. In this sense, *siyasa* became a treasured resource for managing the peculiar dynamics of the *amir–aʿyan* system, as identified by Hodgson. This system rested on a balance of power between a political elite of increasingly martial origin, presided over in each principality by an emir (*amir*), and the urban notables (*aʿyan*), including leading *ʿulama*' and Sufi masters, landowners, and traders. The manner in which the *adab–siyasa* complex refined the predominantly military character of political rule during the Middle Periods contributed decisively to managing its vagaries during the transition to the early-modern era. It gradually nourished a more self-aware and assertive bureaucratic culture, thereby preparing the terrain for the articulation of increasingly compelling conceptions of legitimate rulership, which went beyond the largely pedagogical texture of premodern mirrors for princes (see Chapter 8).

In this context, the profile of Ibn Khaldun emerges as that of a grand master of *adab–siyasa* and as an architect of coherent justifications of statehood in the early-modern ecumene. He was able to play this role thanks to a singular scholarly and political trajectory that seamlessly integrated practice and knowledge, following centuries of crisis and experimentation throughout the Middle Periods. The *adab–siyasa* complex is pervasive, though often muted, in his work, precisely because he adopted an innovative analytical method that avoided static models of wisdom liable to become captive to the ideal and the abstract. In a seminal study, Miriam Cooke (1983) emphasized that Ibn Khaldun's orientation to *adab*, and even his sociocultural identity as an *adib*—a practitioner and master of *adab*—was foundational to his intellectual project. This orientation is evident in the way he creatively applied the science of language in the *Muqaddima*, reflecting on the social functioning of language and insisting on contextual sensitivity. Ibn Khaldun's *adab*, and its service to *siyasa*, was thus deeply reflective and conceptual rather than merely refined and discursive. His methodological innovations could only emerge at the most fertile intersection between what we would today call the humanities and the social sciences, between understanding and explanation (see Chapter 1).[6] As perceptively formulated by Bruce Lawrence (2021, 34), Ibn Khaldun's "deep *adab*" relied on injecting a *barzakh*-inspired epistemology into a new research methodology. As we have seen, Lawrence includes in this methodology Ibn Khaldun's remodulation of key terms such as *'umran* and *'asabiyya*. To condense a series of Khaldunian interventions and their contemporary reinterpretations—including those advanced in this volume—into a single synthetic formula, one could say that *adab–siyasa* is what becomes of *'asabiyya* once its nomadic life forms are filtered, rather than destroyed, through the grid of urban life forms oriented toward managing complexity and conflict.

It is worth adding that, as a well-versed *faqih*, Ibn Khaldun acted and wrote at a historical juncture when the rising *adab–siyasa* complex partly overlapped with a renewed appreciation of the versatility of Islamic jurisprudence. This development was epitomized by the towering legal theorist al-Shatibi, roughly contemporary with Ibn Khaldun, whose work we discussed in Chapter 2. *Fiqh* increasingly came to be regarded as serviceable not only for regulating social relations but also for the tasks of governance in post-caliphal courts and their bureaucracies, including those of the Egyptian Mamluks, whom Ibn Khaldun served during the final phase of his life. This shift in the fortunes of *fiqh* relied in large part on the ascent of the Hanafi school of jurisprudence, which also benefited from its engagement with *hadith*. In this sense, the simultaneous principled distinction and partial—often intertextual—amalgamation of *hadith* and *adab*, as delineated in Chapter 2, directly benefited the highest intellectual strata of the *amir–a'yan* system.

No doubt, regardless of the readiness of jurists, particularly of the Hanafi school, to integrate *siyasa* into *fiqh*, administrators retained a closer cultural affinity to the broader *adab* corpus than to the *hadith–shari'a* complex (Yücesoy 2023, 76–81). Nevertheless, not unlike the practical reason inherent in the notion of *fiqh* itself (see Chapter 2), the foremost task of *siyasa* was the calibrated management of a reticulate set of multipurpose relations (ibid., 5). This property of *siyasa* relied on cultivating a prudent sense of proportionality between means and ends. The reappropriation of *siyasa* within *fiqh* may have facilitated the long-drawn-out eclipse of the prevalently juridical inflection of the Caliphate as succession to Muhammad as God's Messenger, epitomized by the trope of the four Rightly-Guided Caliphs. This process unfolded through the increasing exposure of this conception of the Caliphate to new interpretations relying on the *hadith–adab* amalgam, while also retrieving the meaning of key Qur'anic passages that articulated the Caliphate in more expansive terms. In doing so, it eroded the rather minimalist, if rigid, legitimism that had prevailed in the first centuries of the development of mainstream *fiqh* (Arjomand 2023, 99). The trend progressed further in the Later Middle Period and culminated during early modernity in a conception of the Caliphate solidly aligned both with the *adab–siyasa* complex and with the Qur'anic idea of the Caliphate rooted in the terrestrial mandate of humans as the most beloved—and conditionally entrusted—of Allah's creatures (see Chapters 6 and 7).

Before this shift was fully consummated, however, a bifurcation emerged between the mainstream legalistic conception of the Caliphate, which emphasized legitimate succession to the Prophet Muhammad, and the Sultanate, a ruling prerogative resting on sheer military power. This separation was legitimized through political theories that developed during the decline of the 'Abbasid Caliphate (Yavari 2014). The bifurcation between Caliphate and Sultanate crystallized first with the Buyids (934–1062), and later with the Seljuqs (1037–1194), who imposed their military might on the 'Abbasid Caliphs in Baghdad. The new power came to be recognized as a Sultanate, initially entailing the possession of de facto authority to rule, whose legitimacy was limited to its effectiveness. From there the Sultanate underwent an increasing—if non-linear and locally diversified—process of institutionalization across various realms of the ecumene. Even scholars of the calibre of al-Mawardi (972–1058), al-Juwayni (d. 1085), and the already mentioned al-Ghazali (see Chapter 2) were challenged to provide a conceptual and legitimating framework for this institutional split, according to which the leading commander or emir (*amir al-umara'*) could be identified with the Sultan as the holder of effective political power (*sulta*), acting as a delegate of the Caliph (Bennison 2018, 204–205). In other words, despite repeated efforts at systematization, the de facto acceptance of the bifurcation could never be consistently recognized de jure.

The full practical implications of this constellation became evident under Seljuq rule by the second half of the 12th century (Arjomand 2004, 223).

This occurred less through theoretical systematization than through the actual working of what was by then a well-oiled *amir–aʿyan* system, accompanied by the rise of Sufi institutions (see Chapter 3), which helped fill the gap of legitimacy left by the imploding Caliphate and the rising Sultanate. This emerging, if ambivalently legitimized, arrangement represented the apex of the sheer capacity to control military garrisons within the hierarchy of emirs, yet it was constantly tempered and balanced by the socioreligious power of the *notables*. The functioning of the *amir–aʿyan* system frequently depended on Sufi masters, who came to play a key role as an increasingly authoritative component of the "notables," or *aʿyan*, thereby contributing to the stabilization of sultanic authority during the Middle Periods. They did so by mediating civic disputes and offering guidance to Muslims facing uncertainty in both rural and urban settings (Fromherz 2010, 8; Salvatore 2016, 84)). As lucidly formulated by Amira Bennison (2018, 202) this form of political devolution enabled local communities to negotiate arrangements that could prove more advantageous than paying taxes to representatives of the Caliph, while also fostering levels of political maturity and civic identity unattainable under the High Caliphate.

The relative success of the *amir–aʿyan* system was closely tied to the increasing legitimacy accruing to the *adab–siyasa* complex. Its production of narrative, habitus, and norm was far from becoming monopolized by a bureaucratic class; rather, it was selectively appropriated by the *aʿyan* themselves, who had a vested interest in denying full de jure legitimacy to any given military ruler. In this way, the complex increasingly functioned as an emollient for the shortcomings of the *amir–aʿyan* system, including the arbitrary and often violent effects of a conditionally legitimized military power. The process ushered in an unstable quasi-institutionalization of relations between the de facto legitimacy of emirate rule by seizure—culminating in the authority of a hierarchy of local emirs with the Sultan at their head—and the semi-autonomy of the social body led by the *aʿyan*. Yet the chronic precariousness of the system, together with its lack of solid legitimacy, worked against any full stabilization of the institutional dualism between Caliphate and Sultanate. This is why, toward the end of the Later Middle Period, both the Caliphate and the Sultanate came to occupy positions within more complex and increasingly versatile tableaux of titles and attributes of rulership, which first relativized and eventually dissolved the usefulness of that dualism. By the end of this process, a new, encompassing understanding of the Caliphate emerged, lending coherence to those tableaux (see Chapter 7).

Notes

1. For such criticism, see—even if from quite different, if not opposite, angles, Irwin (2018) and Tabatabai ([1995] 2024).
2. Here I may beg to differ from Yücesoy's tendency to identify *adab-siyasa* with a sort of governmentality *avant la lettre*.
3. Precisely due to the approach adopted here, we refrain from delving into a discussion of a purportedly "correct" translation of the term *dawla*, whose meaning continuously shifted from the High Caliphate through the time of Ibn Khaldun and into the early modern period. It suffices to foreground the dimensions of precariousness and change—but also of *kairos* (the Greek term for an exceptional or propitious moment)—rather than stability, that are intrinsic to *dawla*. This semantic constellation stands in sharp contrast to the European idea of the "state." At the same time, it would be disingenuous—as several Orientalists have tended to do, not least Bernard Lewis (1991, 53–66)—to infer rigid institutional implications from a merely etymological or lexical comparison between *dawla* and "state," especially in the absence of a fully contextualized conceptual and discursive analysis.
4. Please note that, developing some thoughts by Arjomand (2023), we understand "revolution," a plausible translation of *dawla*, as a simultaneously astro-cosmological and sociopolitical metaphor. This interpretation is not intended as a piloted anachronism applied to the modern Western notion of revolution—which, however, one should not forget, was itself borrowed from astronomy.
5. This spiral-like unfolding of the instituting process is probably the paramount idea that Ibn Khaldun and Vico share in common.
6. Ibn Khaldun himself might have been influenced by the work of his paternal great-grandfather, Abu Bakr Muhammad, who was a high-ranking fiscal administrator during the late Almohad period and the author of a manual for the secretarial class (*Adab al-Katib*), reportedly well respected in its time.

References

Arjomand, Said Amir. 2004. "Transformation of the Islamicate Civilization: A Turning Point in the Thirteenth Century? In *Eurasian Transformations, 10th to 13th Centuries: Crystallizations, Divergences, Renaissances*, edited by Johann P. Arnason and Björn Wittrock, 213–45. Leiden: Brill.

Arjomand, Said Amir. 2022. *Messianism and Sociopolitical Revolution in Medieval Islam*. Oakland, CA: University of California Press.

Arjomand, Said Amir. 2023. *Revolutions of the End of Time: Apocalypse, Revolution and Reaction in the Persianate World*. Leiden: Brill.

Arjomand, Said Amir. 2025. *Kings and Dervishes: Sufi World Renunciation and the Symbolism of Kingship in the Persianate World.* Oakland, CA: University of California Press.

Badie, Bertrand. 1986. *Les deux États: Pouvoir et société en Occident et en terre d'Islam.* Paris: Fayard.

Bennison, Amira K. 2018. "The Trajectory of the High Caliphate: Expansion and Contraction." In *The Wiley Blackwell History of Islam*, edited by Armando Salvatore et al., 117–36. Oxford: Wiley Blackwell.

Cahen, Claude. 1954. "Un aperçu sur les institutions musulmanes." *Arabica* 1 (1): 1–16.

Cahen, Claude. 1981. "*Futuwwa*." In *The Encyclopaedia of Islam*, edited by H. A. R. Gibb et al., 2nd edition, vol. 2, 961–6. Leiden: Brill.

Cooke, Miriam. 1983. "IbnKhaldun and Language: From Linguistic Habit to Philological Craft." *Journal of Asian and African Studies* 18 (3–4): 179–88.

Al-Daghistani, Sami. 2022. "Beyond *Maṣlaḥah*: *Adab* and Islamic Economic Thought." *American Journal of Islam and Society* 39 (3–4): 57–86.

Eickelman, Dale F. [1987]. 2002. *The Middle East: An Anthropological Approach*, 4th edition. Englewood Cliffs, NJ: Prentice-Hall.

Fromherz, Allen James. 2010. *Ibn Khaldun: Life and Times.* Edinburgh: Edinburgh University Press.

Gellner, Ernest. 1981. *Muslim Society.* Cambridge: Cambridge University Press.

Heck, Paul L. 2018. "Contested Fields, Knowledge Mobility, and Discipline Crystallization." In *The Wiley Blackwell History of Islam*, edited by Armando Salvatore et al., 177–94. Oxford: Wiley Blackwell.

Irwin, Robert. 2018. *Ibn Khaldun: An Intellectual Biography.* Princeton, NJ: Princeton University Press.

Lawrence, Bruce B. 2021. *Islamicate Cosmopolitan Spirit.* Oxford: Wiley Blackwell.

Lewis, Bernard. 1991. *Islam and the West.* New York: Oxford University Press.

Mahdi, Muhsin. 1957. *Ibn Khaldūn's Philosophy of History: A Study in the Philosophic Foundation of the Science of Culture.* Chicago: University of Chicago Press.

Salvatore, Armando. 2016. *The Sociology of Islam: Knowledge, Power and Civility.* Oxford: Wiley Blackwell.

Salvatore, Armando, and Kieko Obuse. 2022. "What Went Wrong? Western Sociology and the Fiction of the Middle East." In *The Oxford Handbook of the Sociology of the Middle East*, edited by Armando Salvatore et al., 3–25. Oxford: Oxford University Press.

Tabatabai, Javad [1995] 2024. *Ibn Khaldūn and the Social Sciences: Discourse on the Condition of Im-Possibility.* Translated by Philip Grant. Foreword by Milad Odabaei. London: Polity.

Yavari, Neguin. 2014. *Advice for the Sultan: Prophetic Voices and Secular Politics in Medieval Islam.* London: Hurst.

Yücesoy, Hayrettin. 2023. *Disenchanting the Caliphate: The Secular Discipline of Power in Abbasid Political Thought.* New York: Columbia University Press.

6

After the Mongols
Instituting Modern Statehood in the Ecumene

A Sufi Lens on the Khaldunian *Dawla*

Nobody better than Hodgson could appreciate Ibn Khaldun's diagnosis of the ambivalent developments of the Middle Periods. He valued it as the most comprehensive sociohistorical explanation of the dynamics of the Islamic ecumene under the shadow of the *amir–a'yan* system, with particular attention to the processes of instituting governance. Hodgson championed an understanding of this era not as a period of decay of "classical" cultural and political forms, but as a period marked by the formation and crystallization of key institutions of the ecumene, including statehood. What rendered the Middle Periods—stretching from the end of the High Caliphate to the rise of the great bureaucratic empires of early modernity—uniquely formative of the social bond was precisely the extent to which the socioreligious institutions examined so far bore the main burden of sustaining cohesion and vitality across the ecumene. In many respects, Hodgson's approach, and his predilection for the Middle Periods, helps explain the continuity of *'umran* and the ecumene (*ma'mura*) despite the impermanence of the *dawla* and its exposure to cyclical dissipation. And yet, as we saw in the previous chapter, the seeds of *'asabiyya* were implanted and metamorphosed at the very core of statehood through the *adab–siyasa* complex. In other words, even while compensating for the absence of a fully legitimized statehood, the *amir–a'yan* system slowly, if steadily, prepared the terrain for the later instituting of modern statehood, particularly after the Mongol irruption onto the scene.

Let us take stock of Hodgson's seminal contribution on this matter. He placed particular emphasis on how, especially in the Earlier Middle Period, "[o]pen structuring might preclude strong central power and what that power could provide, but significant structuring there was, all the same.

Hence, the reduction of central political power did not usually result in a reduction of general social complexity" (Hodgson 1974, II, 68). As depicted by Hodgson, the *amir-a'yan* system offered a continuous—and, paradoxically perhaps, relatively predictable—institutional environment for the cyclicity of the *dawla* theorized by Ibn Khaldun. Both this institutional setting and its cyclical volatility were sustained by the *adab* wheel of the *hadith-adab* amalgam. This meta-institutional engine provided a habitualizing prism for the broader instituting process, fostering ideas and practices of *siyasa* as governance. Seen from this angle, the following well-known assessment by Hodgson aptly captures the centrality of the Middle Periods in the longue durée of the instituting process:

> In a long-run perspective, one may almost regard the High Caliphal state as an interlude, a means of transition from the aristocratic agrarian monarchy of Sasanian times to a social order at once more urbanized and more decentralized, which was emerging in the region as a result of millennial forces in the hemisphere at large. Such a social order was congenial to the distinctive creativity of the Irano-Semitic society as well as to its expansion. In this long-run cultural development, the Mid-Islamic Periods would not show a breakdown but rather a culmination.

Yet this diagnosis, compelling as it is, does not by itself resolve the enduring question of the legitimation of rulership in the longer-term denouement of state formation. While the dynamics of the Middle Periods indeed represented a culmination of a long-term instituting process rather than its collapse, the institution of the Caliphate was far from a mere interlude reflecting a lack of realism on the part of the core intelligentsia among the *a'yan*, particularly the jurists. Quite the contrary: the arduous challenge posed by interpreting and enacting the roles and tasks of the time-honored caliphal institution was precisely what stimulated, in the run-up to early modernity, a political culmination of the instituting process of the Middle Periods. The outcome was the formation of powerful and increasingly stable institutions of governance at the threshold of the early-modern era. What was at stake was not only a *dawla* less exposed to the hazards of a Khaldunian cycle, but also a Caliphate articulating quintessentially Qur'anic conceptions of legitimate authority—far removed from merely replicating the sacralized wisdom of power associated with pre-Islamic Sasanian kingship, as a superficial reading of the *adab-siyasa* complex might suggest.

While the climax leading to a renewed and stable form of the Caliphate will be addressed more directly in Chapter 7, the present chapter is primarily devoted to laying out the key developments that marked the exit from the era of the High Caliphate and the entry into the dynamics of the Middle Periods. In their later phase, these dynamics were given a decisive new impetus and direction by the Mongol conquests. While Hodgson fully acknowledged the diagnostic power of Ibn Khaldun's work in conceptualizing the sociopolitical quandaries of the Earlier Middle Period and the difficult transition to the Later Middle Period, he did not criticize the Khaldunian focus on the Maghreb. On the contrary, this focus helped preserve conceptual consistency. Far from being peripheral, the Maghreb produced a variety of alternative caliphal traditions, including that of the Fatimids—an Isma'ili branch that openly challenged the 'Abbasid Caliphate—and the Caliphate of Cordoba, established by an Umayyad branch that had escaped suppression after the 'Abbasid takeover and came to rival Fatimid claims. The apparent downside of Ibn Khaldun's not directly covering the vast and central regions of the Islamic ecumene east of Egypt—the areas devastated by the Mongol invasions—was offset by the fact that the early-modern reception of his work vastly transcended the geopolitical limits of its original focus. Indeed, Ibn Khaldun's thought was received far more productively in the wider Persianate zone, and especially in the Ottoman Empire, than in Arabic-speaking regions (Hodgson 1974, II, 55, 476–478).

Although Ibn Khaldun lived in the Later Middle Period, it is difficult to overlook how his reading of the dynamics of the Islamic ecumene decisively relied on the cumulative experience of the Earlier Middle Period. In the Maghreb, this experience was marked by the formation of formidable tribal confederations, often with Berber groups playing a leading role, which in turn triggered the rise of a sequence of remarkable *dawla*s. To grasp the full analytical force of Ibn Khaldun's insights, it is therefore useful to revisit what he himself regarded as a paradigmatic case: the formation and trajectory of the Almohad *dawla*, known in Arabic as *al-muwahhidun*, "those who proclaim *tawhid*," the oneness of Allah as the central article of Islamic faith (Salvatore 2016, 111–116). Extending from the Maghreb into al-Andalus, the Almohad *dawla* emerged from a tribal movement forged under a gifted leadership that succeeded in giving institutional form to a composite and largely original political landscape. This leadership crystallized around the extraordinary figure of Ibn Tumart (1080–1130), who articulated with particular force the gifts of knowledge–power subsumed under the notion of *walaya*, examined in Chapter 3 and to be further developed in Chapter 7. Most significantly, the Almohads' ascent to power appeared to embody a synthetic vision of knowledge placed at the service of the ecumene's welfare. This vision resonated with the thought of one of the towering intellectual figures of the Earlier Middle Period, Muhammad al-Ghazali (see Chapter 1), who was reportedly consulted by Ibn Tumart during one of his journeys to the Mashreq.[1]

What Ibn Khaldun captured more clearly than any other voice of the ecumene was how the Almohad *dawla*, across successive generations and up to its demise roughly a century after Ibn Tumart's death—that is, toward the end of the Earlier Middle Period—largely replicated the trajectory of the *dawla* it had overthrown, namely that of the Almoravids, while adding to it a distinctive alchemy of motivation and power. The revolutionary dimension of the Almohad movement was evident in Ibn Tumart's call to subvert the prevailing class structure in Almoravid territories, coupled with an appeal to *jihad* against what the Almohads regarded as the iniquity of Almoravid rule. This call was inscribed within a strongly messianic horizon, in which Ibn Tumart's leadership (*imama*) was reinforced by his appropriation of the epithet Mahdi, the "rightly guided" figure of Islamic eschatology expected to appear at the End of Time (*akhir al-zaman*) to restore justice and eliminate tyranny and iniquity (Arjomand 2022, 262).[2] The analogy between the Almoravid and the Almohad *dawla* reflected the central tenet of the Khaldunian cycle: originating in nomadic milieus through tribal confederations, these formations instituted their power in major cities. Ibn Tumart's trajectory was almost paradigmatically geared toward establishing a tribal–urban connection. Born in the High Atlas region of Morocco within a Berber tribal environment, he traveled eastward in his youth in search of knowledge, studying in Mecca, Baghdad, and perhaps Damascus or Alexandria. Not a typical product of the institutional college system, after completing his studies he operated primarily in nomadic contexts, where he established what would later become a Khaldunian textbook case of a gifted and knowledgeable scholar gradually winning the loyalty of an expanding constellation of tribes and clans. At the same time, he attracted students, whom he personally taught through texts tellingly entitled *al-Tawhid* and *al-Murshida* ("The Guide"; Arjomand 2022, 267).[3] Through an astute and energetic combination of education and organization—including the establishment of a hierarchy of councils as well as the execution of ruthless revolutionary "purges" (ibid., 272–274)—he mobilized the force of group cohesion, or *'asabiyya*, within a powerful tribal confederation led by highly motivated and well-trained cadres. Most notably, and as observed by Ibn Khaldun, under Ibn Tumart's leadership the Almohad movement invested *'asabiyya* in the creation of a *dawla* in a manner that consciously retraced the emergence of Islam under the leadership of the Prophet Muhammad.

Remarkably, Ibn Khaldun famously compared the Sufis to the early Muslims surrounding the Prophet (Fromherz 2010, 124). While Ibn Tumart was more than a Sufi master, he clearly shared in the type of activist *walaya* that would later be claimed by several other rebels and aspiring founders of new *dawla*s, often associated—more or less directly—with the broader Sufi movement, particularly in the Later Middle Periods and early modernity. As more than one commentator has observed, when viewed from the Prophet Muhammad through Ibn Tumart and the various movements and insurrections of the Later Middle Periods, *'asabiyya* proves particularly effective, and capable of yielding longer-term institutional outcomes, when powered by prophecy or *walaya* (Irwin 2018, 46). If we recall how, in Chapter 3, we unpacked and reformulated—or rather replaced—Weber's garbled and unsociological notion of charisma from within an Islamic, yet fully sociopolitical, frame, *'asabiyya* should be seen as providing the nerve (*'asab*) of the confraternal bond, while itself being nourished by *'umran*—whether *badawi* or *hadari*, or combinations thereof—in its ceaseless unfolding. This perspective corrects one-sided, disembodied, and overly spiritualized views of individual *walaya* that fail to account for the dynamics of intercorporeality outlined in Chapter 3, which are among the most tangible and bodily manifestations of the connective *'asab* underpinning group cohesion.

This also explains why the frequently used translation of *'asabiyya* as "solidarity," evoking a Durkheimian conceptual register, remains too ethereal and disembodied to do justice to its meaning (see also Chapter 5). One might describe the *'asabiyya* at work in the exemplary case of Ibn Tumart—a scholar straddling nomadic and urban milieus, and a Mahdi endowed with a form of intensified *walaya*—as an upgraded, non-eruptive modality of *'asabiyya*, produced through meticulous labor in forging connectedness and coalitions among tribal groups, while relentlessly confronting both internal and external enemies across nomadic and urban settings. As I suggested in Volume I (Salvatore 2016, 110), this is precisely the form of *'asabiyya* that can operate countercyclically, functioning as a stabilizing factor at the level of the production and maintenance of *'umran* within the broader ecumene or *ma'mura* (see Introduction). *Walaya* intervenes here to cement intercorporeality and connectedness, operating as a factor of cohesion and "partisanship" that is not inherently subject to routinization or dissipation, unlike Weberian charisma (see Chapters 3 and 4).

The typification of inspired leadership, ultimately approximating *walaya*, that was required to trigger the trajectory toward a new *dawla* can be further explored through an examination of Ibn Khaldun's multifaceted relationship with Sufi life across different periods of his existence. His engagement with Sufism was far from superficial; it encompassed multiple dimensions of sociability intrinsic to the Sufi-led habitualization process. Nor did he neglect the epistemic contribution of Sufism to the knowledge–power equation. On the contrary, Ibn Khaldun regarded Sufism as a vital source of insight, providing a form of intuitive knowledge capable of disclosing hidden (*batini*) laws and truths. Most significantly, however, he appears to have viewed this Sufi methodology as consonant with the principles underlying his own sociohistorical approach, which sought to uncover the "hidden laws" governing the instituting process in the ecumene (Ahmad 2014, 65–76; see also Morrissey and Nettler 2019, 414–418). From this perspective, a leadership oriented toward articulating *walaya* seemed uniquely equipped to apply the knowledge–power equation to refining what we might be tempted to call the source code of a successful instituting process in the Islamic ecumene.[4]

By acting as far more than spiritual guides, representatives of this type of leadership—epitomized by Ibn Tumart in the Earlier Middle Period—secured cohesion among diverse tribal groups while simultaneously bridging the divide between nomadic life and urban civility. This mode of action enabled the upgrading of tribal *ʿasabiyya* into a far more versatile formula for governing the social bond, one that, during the Later Middle Period and into early modernity, became crucial for transcending the structural limitations of the *amir–aʿyan* system. As suggested in Chapter 5, this was achieved by sublimating *ʿasabiyya* into the forms of life and administrative practices prevailing in rulers' courts. At this stage, several Sufi masters came to see themselves as particularly well equipped to exercise influence on the *adab* side of the *adab–siyasa* complex, which they had substantially appropriated through the developments discussed in Chapter 3. As shown there, a holder of *walaya* could aspire to the title of Pole (*qutb*), which may be understood sociologically as encompassing the full range of capacities and virtues required to activate *ʿasabiyya*. The knowledge–power inherent in *walaya* could thus be deployed by translating a Khaldunian-type of revolution into a robust and enduring *dawla*. This is precisely what occurred in the case of one of the great early-modern empires of the ecumene, the Safavids, who replicated—under new historical conditions—the success of the Almohads (Arjomand 2023, 86–106). Yet *walaya* could also, and perhaps even more impressively, be mobilized to stabilize forms of rulership that depended on domesticating and integrating the challenge posed by Sufi-inspired movements, as in the paradigmatic case of the Ottomans, with the Mughals occupying an intermediate position between the Safavid and Ottoman models (ibid., 11–119; see Chapters 7–9).

For these reasons, the *walaya* of Ibn Tumart should be seen as providing a crucial nexus, during the Middle Periods, between the dynamics of the ʿAbbasid revolution and the early-modern legitimations of statehood in the great Muslim empires. This nexus becomes particularly visible in the messianic attribute of the Mahdi, which assumed a central role in the processes of instituting and stabilizing the *dawla* in the Later Middle Period and into early modernity. Through his original reinterpretation of Ibn Khaldun, combined with insights drawn from Western sociopolitical theory, Arjomand (2022) has convincingly shown that the long arc of *dawla* formation in the ecumene was decisively sustained by the messianic idea of a restorer of justice at the End of Time—a trope deeply rooted in the Qur'an and, more broadly, in key strands of Abrahamic scripture. Without entering here into the complex genealogy of the protean figure of the Mahdi, which Arjomand reconstructs in detail, it suffices to note how this character dynamizes and "finalizes" the attributes of *walaya* in ways that effectively bracket the diagnosis of the impermanence of the *dawla*. Associating a *dawla* with the End of Time offers a powerful means of pre-empting anxieties about its dissipation while maximizing—and often diversifying—the recruitment and cohesion secured through *ʿasabiyya*.

The Recalibration of *Dawla* Via Turko-Mongol Power

While Ibn Khaldun's model was predominantly anchored in the Maghreb and in the role often played there by Berber tribes, long before the arrival of the Mongols the Mashreq—or what Hodgson termed the Nile-to-Oxus region—had already witnessed successive waves of incursions and conquests by predominantly Turkic-speaking horsemen and warriors. These groups were sustained by the ethos of nomadic pastoralism rooted in the steppes of Inner and Central Asia. Not coincidentally, such movements were often interpreted by settled populations of the Nile-to-Oxus region through a messianic lens, associated with signs of the End of Time. By the period of the collapse of the High Caliphate and its bureaucratic apparatus, nomadic pastoralism had become a sociopolitical force in its own right. By providing the military armature and leadership of the Sultanate (see Chapter 5), which came to eclipse the Caliphate, it gradually forged a powerful connection with urban economies and long-distance trade networks throughout the Earlier Middle Period. Steppe herders from Inner and Central Asia formed large and highly mobile groupings, accumulating a military potential far greater than that achieved by nomadic populations in other mountainous or arid regions, such as those that framed Ibn Khaldun's own life and work, or even the Arabian Peninsula, the cradle of Islam.[5] Over time, these pastoral nomads learned to appropriate and deploy urban skills, thereby enhancing both their wealth and their military technologies.

During the Earlier Middle Period, these developments unfolded in parallel with the consolidation of the *amir–a'yan* system. They fed into the emergence of military dynasties presiding over multiple *dawla*s or subordinate principalities, under whose shadow the broader *amir–a'yan* system ultimately flourished. In this context, Sufi masters played a decisive role in integrating entire Turko-Mongol tribal groups and confederations into the Islamic ecumene, often beginning with their leaders. These dynamics, well documented in Central and Inner Asia (see DeWeese 1994) and later replicated westward in Iran and Anatolia along the main axes of migration, highlight the seminal role of Sufi masters in a typically Khaldunian instituting cycle conducive to the establishment of a *dawla*. Throughout the Middle Periods, Turko-Mongol formations supplied the bulk of the ruling military class—from local commanders to amirs and sultans—across the Eastern reaches of the Islamic ecumene. This process also generated patterns of mutual solidarity among these formations, amounting to a kind of super-*'asabiyya*. Remarkably, this solidarity coexisted with recurrent internecine warfare, which itself conformed, on both larger and smaller scales, to the Khaldunian cycle of *dawla* formation and collapse (Hodgson 1974, II, 397).

This reconfiguration of power did not simply override earlier institutional arrangements; rather, it forced a recalibration of the very logic through which a *dawla* could be instituted and stabilized. The military patronage state initiated a new modulation of the knowledge–power equation, one in which the nomadic foundations of *'asabiyya* were neither fully dissolved nor allowed to operate autonomously. Instead, they were selectively absorbed, disciplined, and redirected through administrative and symbolic mechanisms that had matured during the Middle Periods. At this juncture, the legacy of the *adab-siyasa* complex proved decisive. Precisely because Turko-Mongol rulers lacked an inherited legitimacy rooted in the classical caliphal tradition, they depended heavily on preexisting repertoires of governance, communication, and ethical self-fashioning. Persianate secretarial elites, jurists, and Sufi masters thus became indispensable intermediaries in translating military dominance and dynastic law into recognizable and workable forms of rulership. In this sense, the Mongol moment did not suspend the Khaldunian logic of instituting power but displaced its center of gravity. What had previously unfolded as a cycle driven primarily by tribal *ʿasabiyya* now increasingly depended on the orchestration of multiple sources of legitimacy, none of which could operate in isolation. Accordingly, the military patronage state redefined the relationship between coercion and consent. While coercive capacity reached unprecedented levels, especially through the scale and mobility of steppe warfare, it could not by itself secure durable rule over sedentary populations embedded in complex urban economies. The need to govern cities, manage taxation, regulate trade, and arbitrate disputes compelled rulers to rely on institutional know-how that had been refined long before the Mongol conquests. This dependence reinserted *adab-siyasa* into the heart of governance, even when sovereignty appeared to rest overwhelmingly on military foundations.

At the same time, this configuration altered the temporal rhythm of a *dawla*. The Mongol and post-Mongol polities did not eliminate impermanence; rather, they sought to buffer it. By multiplying channels of recruitment into the ruling elite—through slave households, bureaucratic training, and Sufi-mediated loyalties—they aimed to prevent the rapid dissipation of power characteristic of earlier cycles. Yet this strategy came at a cost. The diffusion of authority across heterogeneous elites increased the complexity of governance and intensified the need for continuous mediation among competing interests. Stability, when achieved, was therefore contingent and negotiated, not absolute. This helps explain why the Later Middle Period witnessed not a resolution but a transformation of the Khaldunian problematic. The question was no longer how a tribal coalition could seize power and found a *dawla*, but how a ruling formation could continuously reproduce legitimacy across generations without relying exclusively on the volatile energies of *ʿasabiyya*. The answer, as the subsequent chapters will show, lay in increasingly sophisticated syntheses of military patronage, bureaucratic rationalization, Sufi mediation, and symbolic claims to universal authority. These syntheses did not abolish the cycle; they bent it into a spiral, extending its duration while raising the stakes of failure. In this light, the Turko-Mongol recalibration of *dawla* appears less as a deviation from Ibn Khaldun's model than as its historical intensification. By pushing nomadic power to its zenith and forcing it into sustained interaction with urban institutions, the Later Middle Period revealed both the resilience and the limits of the instituting process in the Islamic ecumene. It is precisely this tension—between unprecedented capacities for domination and the intrinsic impermanence of legitimacy—that set the stage for the early-modern rearticulations of Caliphate, sovereignty, and governance to which we now turn.

A remarkable corrective to the downward trend of Khaldunian *dawla* formation was the emergence of "slave" elite corps—often, though not exclusively, of nomadic-pastoral and predominantly Turkic origin. These corps, which will be discussed in greater detail in Chapter 8, were deployed by rulers as a means to halt, or at least slow down, the dissipation of ruling power caused by the loosening of tribal *'asabiyya*. When Ibn Khaldun himself encountered the growing tendency toward the self-perpetuation of military rule through slave households—most notably in Mamluk-ruled Egypt and Syria—he tended to evaluate it negatively, regardless of its potential to counter the downward spiral of *dawla* power. In his assessment, elite slave households entailed not only an erosion of the role of *walaya* but also, more fundamentally, the near-total annihilation of *'asabiyya* itself. This was because they lacked, by definition, a primordial and heroic esprit de corps and were likewise ill-suited to generating its urban counterpart through the *adab–siyasa* complex. As a result, the impact of elite slaves on the *dawla* appeared labile and unpredictable. This ambivalence may have become particularly acute in the final phase of Ibn Khaldun's life, when he was directly involved with the Mamluk Sultanate in Cairo—a paradigmatic instance of rule exercised by freed slave soldiers presiding over slave households.

The decisive moment of reckoning arrived with the irruption of the Mongols into the ecumene, marking the onset of the Later Middle Period. This event overlaid and amplified the cumulative rise of Turkic nomadic patterns of military and political power that had already characterized the Earlier Middle Period. The Mongols forged a new military and ruling elite through alliances with, and the subordination of, large Turkic nomadic populations from the steppe regions. Initially, this emerging Turko-Mongol military–political synthesis did not fit smoothly within the Persianate tradition of imperial bureaucratic rule that had developed under the banner of *adab-siyasa*. On the contrary, Mongol momentum often proved profoundly destabilizing, at times devastating urban equilibria and unsettling the balances of the *amir-a'yan* system. Yet this system, together with the *adab-siyasa* know-how mediated by the Persianate secretarial class, displayed a notable resilience over the longer term.[6]

The Mongol conquests thus constituted both a rupture and a continuation of earlier trajectories, bringing nomadic power to the peak of its historical potential. It is for this reason that Hodgson interpreted the Mongol conquests as inaugurating what he called the "military patronage state" within the Islamic ecumene. Even when power continued to be devolved to local emirs, Mongol rulership reflected a heightened awareness of how military might could be aggregated on a transregional, even global, scale and mobilized toward ambitions of world conquest and universal rule—on a scale comparable only to the legendary exploits of Alexander the Great (356–323 BCE). Whether in Ilkhanid, Timurid, or Ottoman form, the Turko-Mongol military patronage state rested directly or indirectly on a political myth of universal rulership. These new dynasties strengthened and expanded their administrative apparatus, eventually absorbing it into the ruling military elite. At the same time, they extended systems for recruiting and training slave elites who were not bound to local interests or to the power balances mediated by the *amir-a'yan* system.

A salient trait of these new patterns was the conception of the state as an integrated military power that controlled the resources necessary for the patronage and support of select socioeconomic and cultural forces. This highly consistent ideology of centralized power reshaped the entire cluster of socioreligious institutions examined in the previous chapters, without, however, undermining their resilience or their reliance on conditional autonomy and reflexive relationality. On the one hand, the backbone of centralized rule remained the civilian bureaucracy, largely of Persianate inspiration. On the other hand, after an initial phase of relative segregation from the Mongol military elite, civilian officials increasingly came to be integrated into the military estate in terms of rank, function, and privileges. This convergence enabled them to provide rulers with ever more essential services in sustaining legitimacy and projecting charisma—a development to which we will return shortly (Hodgson 1974, II, 404–407). Most notably, Mongol ruling elites consolidated and displayed their authority through adherence to the nomadic code known as the *yasa* (or *yasaq*) of Chingiz Khan. At first sight, this normative framework had no close equivalent in earlier nomadic formations of *dawla* either in the Western or Eastern reaches of the ecumene. The *yasa* originated in tribal and shamanic practices of Inner and Central Asian steppe societies. By the time of the Mongol conquests, it consisted largely of the decrees issued by a reigning ruler, yet it also encompassed articulated rulings governing rights and obligations in both civil and criminal matters. The authority of the *yasa* derived from an original—and, within the Islamic ecumene, unprecedented—form of what may be described as a "sacred right" of rule. Although grounded in Mongol custom, this normative authority was rapidly reframed, as we shall see, within the workings of *walaya*, thereby facilitating its accommodation within the broader religious–civic grammar of the ecumene. In this mediated form, the Mongol *yasa* also exercised influence beyond Mongol polities proper, inspiring other Turkic-influenced *dawla*s, most notably that of the Mamluks in Egypt and Syria.

It was symptomatic of the authority of the *yasa* that a leading scholar of the age, the Mamluk historian Maqrizi (1364–1442), whose life trajectory partly overlapped with Ibn Khaldun's, coined a critical pun by suggesting that *siyasa* derived from *yasa* (Darling 2013, 122). This rhetorical move expressed an anxiety—if a relatively short-lived one—among some scholars that, following the Ilkhanid model, rulership in the Later Middle Period was drifting inexorably away from the canonical standards of the Imamate, even among the Mamluks, who were otherwise the Mongols' most determined rivals. Yet Maqrizi's polemic also betrays, on closer inspection, that the imposition of Mongol dynastic law was not an isolated novelty within the ecumene. At least in part, it could be absorbed quite smoothly into earlier amalgamations of *adab* and *siyasa*, within the framework of the emerging dual structure of Turko-Mongol military command and Persianate bureaucracy. In this sense, the rise of the *yasa* ultimately contributed to further integrating the *adab–siyasa* complex into an increasingly seamless legitimacy of the ruler, his court, and the administrative apparatus. From this angle, one can discern a trajectory in which the Khaldunian cycle is, as it were, redeemed through *adab–siyasa* and *yasa*, understood together as a process that institutionally supported emergent formulas for legitimating and centralizing rulership. These formulas will be examined in greater detail in the final chapters of this volume. It is precisely for this reason that the Later Middle Period marked a level of institutional integration that enabled the unprecedented flourishing of the ecumene in the subsequent early-modern era. And yet, as Yücesoy (2023, 24) has observed, much of the recent scholarship on the early-modern empires of the ecumene has tended to underestimate—or simply to take for granted—the longevity and structuring power of the ʿAbbasid-derived, and therefore caliphal, *adab-siyasa* complex in articulating the knowledge-power equation.

Despite the more than symbolic deposition and execution of the last ʿAbbasid caliph in Baghdad, the post-Mongol synthesis did not obliterate the pragmatic foundations of the institutional formations that had crystallized during the Earlier Middle Period. These formations still included the Caliphate as a superordinate, if largely ineffective, institution. Rather than being erased, they were indirectly set on a path toward rejuvenation. Before this process could fully unfold, Amir Timur (1336–1405)—the Turko-Mongol conqueror who rose from the status of a modest sheep raider—had already ascended to the pinnacle of power bearing the simple title of *amir* (commander), characteristic of the Earlier Middle Period and closely aligned with the Seljuq model of legitimizing the sultan as a leading *ghazi* raider. Yet Timur's extraordinary military feats transformed him from a regional commander into a new type of universal ruler, bringing to fruition the combination of dynastic law and the *adab-siyasa* complex as a basis for instituting statehood on increasingly solid foundations.

While the Mongol expansion reshaped some of the primary factors governing the movements, institutions, and forms of government that had crystallized in the Earlier Middle Period, Ibn Khaldun could not directly address the full ramifications of the dynamics of *ʿasabiyya* and *ʿumran* that propelled the Mongols toward an unprecedented form of universal rulership. Nevertheless, even while remaining largely focused on the Maghreb, he was able to grasp the long-term momentum unleashed by the Mongol conquests. This occurred through a remarkable episode late in his life, noteworthy even if it came too late to decisively reshape his theoretical synthesis. When the Maghrebi scholar met and interviewed Amir Timur in 1401 outside besieged Damascus, he was acutely aware of the world-historical significance of the Turko-Mongol conqueror's imperial advance. Through his campaigns, Timur revived the legacy of Mongol universal rulership at a moment when the Later Middle Period was giving way to new political configurations, after the Mongol heritage had already undergone substantial Islamization. For all the geopolitical limitations of his work, Ibn Khaldun could not ignore the decisive role played in the Eastern reaches of the ecumene by Turko-Mongol tribal formations as paradigmatic carriers of *ʿasabiyya* and agents of state renewal. He may even have recognized that a denouement of the Khaldunian cycle could be achieved through the thickening of nomadic *'asabiyya* into an institution of legitimate rulership—one comparable to, yet capable of remedying, the inherent fragilities and tensions of the High Caliphate of the first centuries of Islamic history (cf. Arnason and Stauth 2004, 39).

We should therefore examine the extent to which Amir Timur's reenactment of Mongol ambitions to universal rulership inaugurated a new dispensation capable of tempering—and partially domesticating, though not eliminating—the volatility of the Khaldunian cycle of flourishing and dissipation. On the one hand, this requires considering how Timur's highly flexible modalities of rule redeployed attributes of sovereignty already present among the Seljuqs and within the Ilkhanid Empire, the first Mongol polity to consolidate its rule in the Nile-to-Oxus region. On the other hand, it calls for tracing how the Timurid model became a source of inspiration for most subsequent Islamic empires, most notably the Safavids (1501–1722), the Mughals (1526–1858), and the Ottomans (1281–1924), whose distinctive and extended trajectory of state formation had begun well before the rise of the Timurids themselves (Melvin-Koushki 2018). The encounter between Ibn Khaldun and Amir Timur took place outside Damascus in 1401, one year before the Battle of Ankara (1402), which dealt a crushing blow to the then-ascending Ottoman polity. The Ottomans will occupy much of our attention in the final part of this volume, where we analyze the refashioned instituting process and institutional landscape of early modernity. By the time of his encounter with Amir Timur, the Maghrebi scholar had lived through much of the 14th century—the core of the Later Middle Period—while serving a succession of unstable principalities in North Africa, each caught within the very cyclicality he so lucidly theorized. Ibn Khaldun arrived in Damascus in 1400–1401, either as part of the entourage of the Mamluk sultan Faraj during a military campaign or in connection with his scholarly and judicial engagements, given his long-standing service in Cairo as a *qadi* under Mamluk patronage.

When Damascus came under siege by Timur, Ibn Khaldun remained in the city while the Mamluk sultan and army retreated to Egypt. As the Damascene population sought to negotiate terms of surrender, envoys were dispatched to Timur's camp, and Ibn Khaldun volunteered to join the delegation. He subsequently spent more than a month in the conqueror's camp, leaving behind an invaluable firsthand account of Timur's character, strategic acumen, and rhetorical self-presentation. Beyond the anecdotal richness of this episode, the encounter is analytically significant.

Ibn Khaldun reportedly shared with Timur his reflections on the cycle of the *dawla*, and he could scarcely have failed to perceive in Timur's achievements a potential to transcend, or at least reconfigure, the institutional impasses generated by that cycle. What may have appeared at the time as an exceptional deviation can, in retrospect, be recognized as the sign of a genuine breakthrough (Lawrence 2005, x; Alatas 2013, 12–13). From this perspective, the same dynamics that Ibn Khaldun theorized—while privileging the Maghreb over the Eastern reaches of the ecumene devastated by the Mongols—can be reinterpreted in ways that remain faithful to his insights while accounting for novelties he could not fully assimilate. Such a reinterpretation must return to transformative factors that were already present within Ibn Khaldun's conceptual horizon, not least the enduring and periodically resurgent messianic dimension of *walaya*. This was a form of authority that might appear "charismatic," while being profoundly relational and socially embedded. It played a decisive role in the transition to the early-modern empires of the ecumene and was later retroactively incorporated by Timurid court scholars into the repertoire of legitimating prerogatives attributed to the former sheep raider who had risen to claim universal rule.

Endowing Universal Rulership

More immediately, and in response to newly emerging patterns of validation of universal rulership—while continuing to build on practices already established in the Seljuq and Ilkhanid empires—Amir Timur fully invested in a powerful idiom of monumental architecture. This was the model that gave life to what Arjomand (1999) has termed the educational-charitable complex. Here the shrine of the saint, a veritable embodiment of *walaya*, was nested in the fabric of the cityscape and reflected back upon the ruler, whose role as endower of the complex became a foundational pillar of his ruling legitimacy. The topographic centrality of Sufi shrines and lodges became a monumental constant, particularly in the cities of Iran and Central Asia, after their reconstruction following the Mongol destruction. This process perfected, but also subtly altered, the role of *waqf* through the mediation of the military patronage state. The construction of such complexes provided architectural consistency to the self-sustaining cluster of urban services facilitated by the *waqf* system. Now an entire complex could originate from a single deed of *waqf* issued by the ruler. This was also the case in a paradigmatic instance inaugurating the early-modern era in the Islamic ecumene: the foundation of a new central neighborhood, Fatih, in the newly conquered Constantinople—now Istanbul—endowed by the Ottoman sovereign Mehmed II the Conqueror (r. 1444–1446; 1451–1481; Abdul Salam 2024, 25–26).

In such new settings, the shrine and the lodge—sometimes supplemented in major cities by an astronomical observatory—could overshadow the school or *madrasa*. These shifts did not fail to influence the types of knowledge produced and transmitted within institutions of Islamic learning, given the increased capacity of ruling families and elites to monitor and direct higher education (Moin 2018, 379). The semi-autonomous urban notables, who had previously exercised substantial control over educational and charitable institutions—also thanks to the juridical and administrative skills of religious scholars acting as *waqf* administrators—were now compelled to compromise that control. To be sure, the broader scholarly class retained important prerogatives in the production of knowledge entering the knowledge–power equation, and it contributed decisively to articulating and debating the new patterns of legitimacy associated with the institutional network of the military patronage state and its modes of sovereignty. Yet the wide margins of autonomy enjoyed within the *amir–a'yan* system of the Earlier Middle Period gradually gave way to a more vertical system of promotion, patronage, and governance of knowledge production and dissemination. This system became increasingly subsumed within projects of political stabilization and governmental centralization (Salvatore 2018).

At this juncture, we need to examine how these developments affected what we have identified as the primary matrix (the confraternity or *tariqa*; see Chapter 2) and the principal channel (the endowment or *waqf*; see Chapter 3) of the instituting process. As the conditions for its unfolding changed during the Middle Periods and in the transition to early modernity, both *waqf* and *tariqa* were subject to significant transformations. To clarify this development, Hofer (2020, 62) identifies a watershed not only in the dynamic interaction between *waqf* and *tariqa* but in the history of the Islamic ecumene as a whole. This was the epochal event that symbolically marked the end of the Middle Periods according to our periodization, and with it the onset of early modernity in the ecumene. It occurred almost half a century before the conventional European marker of modernity's inception in 1492, still commonly—and eurocentrically—described as the "discovery of the Americas." The event in question was the conquest of

Constantinople by the Ottoman ruler Mehmed II in 1453.[7] While marking a messianic zenith, given the symbolic weight of capturing the imperial seat of "Rome," which allowed Mehmed the Conqueror to appropriate the epithet of Mahdi, the victory also enabled him to posture as the endower of the city as a whole, and particularly of the new quarter dedicated to the conquest, Fatih. What became Istanbul was thus literally instituted as a new and powerful center of Islamic learning. Fatih was the first in a series of monumental building complexes (sing. *külliye* in Ottoman Turkish) staffed by scholarly personnel largely drawn from the culturally leading, Persianate regions of the ecumene (Abdul Salam 2024, 26–36). In the deed of trust, or *vakıfname* (*waqfiyya* in Arabic), that endowed the new central neighborhood and monumental complex named after Mehmed's distinctive appellation as Conqueror, the endowing act already bore the marks of an upgraded form of instituting sovereignty. After the lesser *jihad* of conquest, the erection of this unprecedented *külliye* signaled the onset of the greater *jihad*: the task of transforming Istanbul not merely into the capital of the Ottoman Empire but into a major cosmopolitan hub of the ecumene. Fatih was consciously planned and built by creatively folding inherited aesthetic standards into new, early-modern canons of architecture and urban design. Most notably, it brought to the very center of the ecumene the concept of the *imaret* as the core of the *külliye*. An *imaret* (Ottoman Turkish, sharing the same root as the Arabic *ʿumran*) was symbolically and practically organized around a soup kitchen mandated to reproduce, quite literally, the life of the complex and its inhabitants, including students, Sufi adepts, travelers, and traders. As the centerpiece of the educational-charitable complex, it matched Mehmed II's program as endower to channel wealth into a form of urban prosperity that enhanced the cosmopolitan connectedness of the ecumene.

As a corrective to the Weberian notion of a patrimonial state—according to which the state is an extension of the ruler's household—and also, in part, to Hodgson's revised concept of the military patronage state, one should note how Mehmed the Conqueror conceived of himself primarily as a super-endower rather than as an owner or mere patron of the city. It was in this capacity that, beyond directly endowing Fatih, he supervised the entrusting of high administrators with the task of endowing buildings and complexes across different neighborhoods of the new capital. These included commercial centers, caravanserais, and residential quarters, all contributing to the repopulation of the city and its opening to long-distance trade, while also facilitating the circulation of ideas, scholars, and students.

Unsurprisingly, and despite Mehmed II's personal reluctance to directly endow Sufi lodges—unlike several of his predecessors and his son Bayezid II after him—the synergy between *waqf* and *tariqa* played a decisive role in this process (Abdul Salam 2024, 21–30).

As will become clearer shortly, Ottoman state-building relied on a capillary instituting process in which Sufi masters played a central role from its very inception. Coming on the heels of nearly two centuries of Ottoman *dawla* formation, the conquest of Constantinople allowed Mehmed II to posture as a messianic ruler who fulfilled the long-awaited Islamization of the East Roman capital, thereby acquiring the credentials of a universal sovereign (Yılmaz 2018, 31). The symbolic and practical operation of positioning the ruler as the tangible apex of an instituting process extending all the way down to Sufi-style confraternal bonds was further cemented by the role of court scholars. Chief among them was ʿAli al-Bistami, also known as Musannifek (1403–1470), a figure marked by a clear Sufi orientation. Originating from Transoxania, Musannifek became a close adviser and confidant of both Mehmed II and Mahmud Paşa, the grand vizier and head of the bureaucracy of the emerging world empire. This position, once monopolized by Ottoman grandees, was now increasingly reserved for personnel trained through the *devşirme* system of elite slavery (see also Chapter 8). Musannifek's *Tuhfa-i Mahmudiyya* (1456), composed for Mahmud Paşa, functioned as a manual for the new vizierate, offering guidance for navigating the complexities of the executive arm of imperial power. Mahmud Paşa fulfilled the expectations attached to this role by acquiring the intellectual sophistication required by the *adab–siyasa* complex. Most significantly, he inflected his office in a manner that demonstrated that *walaya* was not the monopoly of the supreme ruler but could—and ideally should—permeate the highest echelons of the bureaucracy itself (ibid., 33–37). The work of Musannifek was echoed by the anonymous author of the *Mukhtasar fi-l-Siyasa wa-Umur al-Saltana* ("Compendium of Governance and the Affairs of Rulership"). Written for Mehmed's successor Bayezid II, this text even more clearly redirected the *adab–siyasa* discourse away from the moral character of the ruler, as foregrounded in the mirrors-for-princes genre, toward the primacy and solidity of the institutional apparatus itself. This shift was further reinforced under Bayezid II's successor Selim I by a treatise authored by Şemseddin Jahrami, which succinctly bound together—and explicated in strikingly practical terms—the governance of the self (*siyasat-i nafs*), of the ruling elite (*siyasat-i khassa*), and of the commoners or general public (*siyasat-i ʿamma*). This work departed markedly from the ornate literary texture of classical advice literature, approaching what might be described as a *siyasa* stripped of *adab* in its more literary sense (Yılmaz 2018, 37–40).

Mehmed the Conqueror's new order thus represented the first culmination of a long trajectory in the formation of an unparalleled Afro-Eurasian state, alongside—and initially, at least in part, under the umbrella of—the rise of Mongol rule. Its origins long predated the watershed marked by the ascent of Amir Timur, who came close to crushing the Ottoman rise to world empire. The Ottoman trajectory toward an empire of extraordinary longevity (1281–1924) began with a frontier *ghazi* chieftaincy in 13th-century Western Anatolia. It rested on the capacity to weave together coalitions among heterogeneous groups, including Byzantine defectors. Most significantly, the Ottomans invested in their nomadic traditions of steppe warfare, occupying the interstitial spaces between competing empires. At the head of an interconfessional tribal confederation, early Ottoman chiefs projected a composite form of authority combining shamanic and messianic elements, embodied in the figure of the paternal guide or *baba*. This configuration closely resembled that of several other leaders and movement founders who, particularly in the Later Middle Period, gravitated toward Shiʿi-leaning idioms during what Arjomand has described as an age of "confessional ambiguity" (Arjomand 2023, 34–35). The early Ottoman polity gradually evolved into a dynastic order under Osman I (r. 1299–1326), marking the emergence of a more centralized administration under a military ruler. Yet it is plausible to suggest that the shamanic dimension of frontier lordship, which animated the *ghazi* ethos, survived this transition into a more formalized stage of the Ottoman sultanate. This primal dimension of power became progressively less visible, while remaining tangibly operative, as it was wrapped in successive layers of *walaya* transmitted by the earliest Sufi masters of the Ottoman age, known as the *abdalan*. These loosely organized yet "charismatic" itinerant figures transformed pre-Islamic and shamanic rituals into an increasingly articulated Sufi political cosmology. They played a crucial role as cultural mediators in early Ottoman state formation and maintained an intimate relationship with the earliest sultans (Kafadar 1995).

The traits of what may be termed, in Khaldunian parlance, *ʿumran badawi*—which moved with frontier *ghaza* and Sufi forms of life from the Central Asian steppe into fertile Anatolia—were most clearly expressed in a warrior ethos centered on bravery and honor, accruing to the authority of the chief (Rahimi 2004, 67–69; Yılmaz 2018, 96). This combination of fluidity and institutionalization of leadership depended on the role of masters in generating the degree of *ʿasabiyya* required to sustain diverse, even heteroglossic, coalitions underpinning frontier chieftainship. The most influential among these masters, including figures associated with the Yasawiyya and Kubrawiyya orders, amplified their *walaya*—often gesturing toward the status of *qutb*—to construct a political cosmology that was readily absorbed by the rulers of Rum, including the rising Ottomans, during and after the collapse of Seljuq authority in the region (ibid., 112). Most significantly, the Ottoman *dawla* took form in an interstitial time between the still recent memory of the 'Abbasid Caliphate and the gradual erosion of Mongol hegemony, a conjuncture that expanded the space of Sufi practices and imaginaries in construing the legitimacy of rulers (ibid., 97–98). While appropriating for the Ottoman *dawla* some of the regalia and symbols of the Seljuqs of Rum, the leading scholar and Sufi thinker Davud-i Kayseri (d. 1350) celebrated Orhan, the second ruler of the Ottoman *dawla* (r. 1323/1324–1362), as a new Anushirvan—the Sasanian monarch who occupied a central place as an exemplary ruler not only within the *adab-siyasa* complex but also in some *hadith*s (ibid., 99). Crucially, however, Orhan was portrayed not merely as a just ruler but as the inheritor of the *dawla* itself: the divinely blessed and astrologically determined turn of good fortune in power whose conceptual emergence coincided with the 'Abbasid revolution, as discussed in Chapter 5 (ibid., 102; Arjomand 2022, 24). In this sense, Davud-i Kayseri's construal of Orhan's ruling prerogatives positioned him as the inheritor of the 'Abbasid *dawla* through the Seljuqs (Yılmaz 2018, 107).

Huseyin Yılmaz has convincingly spoken of a "mystical turn" in the con struction and legitimation of the Ottoman Caliphate, a development that will be examined in greater detail in the next chapter. While this turn had unfolded across the broader Islamic ecumene already in the Earlier Middle Period, it proved particularly successful in the Ottoman transition from frontier chieftainship to world empire. For this reason, the Ottomans became an ideal laboratory for the passage from the instability of a Khaldunian world to one increasingly dominated by centralizing states animated by aspirations to universal rulership. The Ottomans inherited this mystical turn as it had taken shape in the 13th century with figures such as Ibn 'Arabi and Rumi (1207–1273), both highly influential in Anatolia, as well as the slightly earlier Yahya Suhrawardi (1154–1191), whose work proved especially resonant for what Yılmaz has described as the uncharted frontier of Ottoman state-building. The intervention of Davud-i Kayseri, a leading Ottoman follower of Ibn 'Arabi, must be situated against this background. Here the mystical turn enabled the fusion of the Persianate *adab-siyasa* complex with the shamanic traditions and horseback-warrior ethos of the Turkmen. To be sure, early Ottoman state formation also echoed earlier models, including Ibn Tumart's Almohad *dawla* of the Earlier Middle Period, which played a constitutive role in Ibn Khaldun's theorization (see Chapter 5). Yet the net result of the Anatolian experience was distinctive. Nowhere else in the ecumene did rulers adopt and adapt, with such continuity and consistency, the ideas, symbols, and titulature articulated by Sufi masters, who played an essential role in the effervescent *'umran* of the frontier (Yılmaz 2018, 112–123).

Symptomatically, the centrality of the *dawla* and the conditions for deserving and safeguarding its good fortune in power reached a critical threshold during the early 15th century civil war that followed the ruinous defeat of Bayezid I (r. 1389–1402) at the hands of Timur. At that moment, the Ottoman *dawla*—still a fledgling yet promising form of statehood—underwent a severe trial by being confronted with the overwhelming power of the rising world conqueror. Retrospectively, Ahmedi's *İskendername* ("The Book of Alexander") mystified Bayezid I's reckless and failed preventive blitzkrieg, which had provoked Timur's furious response, by casting it as an emulation of Alexander the Great's feats of world conquest. The epic thus ushered the Ottoman *dawla* onto the stage of universal rulership as the embodiment of justice resisting an overpowering oppressor. For this very reason, despite military defeat, it was portrayed as destined to endure and ultimately outlive the oppressor's *dawla*. More than a piece of self-serving propaganda, the *İskendername* provided a powerful literary canvas for inscribing legitimacy into an institutional apparatus grounded in the *adab-siyasa* complex, linking the ruler to administrative and scholarly elites. Yet the decisive adhesive of this emerging formula of statehood was supplied by a Sufi-inflected *walaya*. As we will see in the next chapter, this became the primary instrument through which Ottoman rulers advanced their claim to be the sole legitimate inheritors of the 'Abbasid Caliphate (Yılmaz 2018, 228–232).

It was the scholar Bidlisi (1457–1520)—to whose pivotal role as an Ottoman court intellectual a brilliant monograph has been devoted (Markiewicz 2019)—who, shortly before the onset of the Suleymanic age, completed this legitimating construction. He did so by decisively trumping earlier formulations by scholars at Mongol courts who had identified the Mongol rise to power with divine will. Several strategic moves stand out in

Bidlisi's intervention. First, he contrasted the Mongols' allegedly crude ambitions to world domination with the Ottomans' devotion to the success and expansion of Islam. Second, he grounded Ottoman claims in a radically different, and much more ancient, non-Mongol legacy of world empire—one that metonymically appropriated the seat and charisma of the Roman Caesars while, as only the Ottomans had done, dislodging them from their imperial center. Finally—and this was the most ingenious twist—Bidlisi emphasized that these infidels were followers of the Prophet Jesus, that is, adherents of a faith that Islam was destined to supersede rather than annihilate. In this way, the Ottoman takeover of Caesarship appeared not only legitimate but providential, whereas the much-despised Mongols, who had never threatened the Christian imperial center in this way, could never aspire to such a succession (Yılmaz 2018, 236). To sum up, beginning in the Later Middle Period, Sufi leaders and thinkers—following the pattern traced earlier by Ibn Tumart in the Maghreb during the Earlier Middle Period—increasingly combined spiritual (and at times explicitly messianic) authority with military leadership. In doing so, they either challenged existing polities or contributed decisively to the creation of new ones, as will be examined in greater detail in the next chapter. As eloquently noted by DeWeese (2018, 345–46), the Later Middle Period

> saw the routinization, in imagery and titulature, of the "royal" equivalences of Sufi masters. *Shaykhs* of various sorts were styled *shah* ("king"), and the communities they led went about with banners and drums and other trappings of royalty. That the titles and pageantry were not mere theatricality, much less purely metaphorical, is suggested by the genuine concern evoked among actual ruling elites regarding the potential threat posed by such figures and their adherents among the people.

The prestige, wealth, and power of Sufi organizations—in their dual capacity as movements and as established institutions—not only mirrored those of the empires of the Later Middle Periods but also furnished them with some of their most effective formulas of legitimation. It has often been observed that it is difficult to determine univocally who was mimicking whose sovereignty in the interaction between Sufi leaders and dynastic rulers. Nonetheless, whether in cases of Sufi-led rebellions or in episodes of active support for existing regimes, it is hard to overlook a certain primacy of Sufi masters and ideas, especially given the growing centrality of *walaya* as a legitimizing idiom (Green 2012, 125–127). In many respects, Sufi actors filled the legitimacy gap left by the collapse of caliphal authority by constructing dense grids of relations that balanced vertical authority—embodied in charismatic masters and living saints—with horizontal cohesion, structured through confraternal forms of association. Oscillating between the defense of the oppressed and the endorsement of the powerful, the Sufi master often appeared as a functional double of the ruler, who in turn frequently sought the master's counsel and blessing. This pivotal nexus between spiritual authority and political power was destined to be integrated into a broader trope of associative and circular sovereignty in the early-modern era, a development that will be examined more closely in Chapter 8.

Notes

1. The story of their encounter, most likely a fabrication, is nevertheless relevant for establishing an intellectual and political connection between the Maghreb and the Mashreq within this exemplary process of *dawla* formation (Hodgson 1974, II, 269).
2. The trope of the Imamate of the Mahdi may have been borrowed from, or at least significantly shaped by, the Fatimid Caliphate (Arjomand 2025, 268).
3. Their exact authorship is still debated in scholarly circles.
4. There is a documented instance in which Ibn Khaldun issued an extensive *fatwa* delineating the boundaries and permissible expressions of Sufism, reflecting his nuanced grasp of its spiritual and social implications. At the same time, the *fatwa* reveals his unease with what he perceived as esoteric deviations from Sufism's constructive orientation—deviations that, in his view, could nourish movements liable to derail a sound instituting process (Ib Khaldūn 2017). *Pace* Ibn Khaldun and his decidedly orthodox stance, however, it was precisely from among these more heterodox currents that the Safavids emerged as the historically most successful Sufi *tariqa* in founding a durable *dawla* (see Chapter 8).
5. Hodgson was keen to note how symbiotic—if complex—patterns of connectedness between steppe nomads and mercantile cities had evolved since the establishment of commercial networks linking China and Western Eurasia during classical antiquity, networks later subsumed under the misleading label of the "Silk Road." These long-distance configurations far exceeded, in scale and impact, the nomadic–urban nexus forged between the Quraysh and the Hijaz Bedouins in pre-Islamic Arabia.
6. Here, too, Hodgson emphasized how this build-up to nomadic supremacy starkly contrasted with the degree of control that the urban Quraysh merchant elite had been able to retain over the early Islamic conquests and the state-building process that culminated in the High Caliphate (Hodgson 1974, II, 402).
7. This is the same periodization adopted in Salvatore et al. (2018).

References

Abdul Salam, Fawaz. 2024. *Architectural Mediations: The Reconfiguration of Muslim Urban Life in 20th Century Istanbul*. PhD thesis, McGill University.

Ahmad, Syed Naeem. 2014. "Between Spiritual Authority and Temporal Power. Ibn Khaldūn's Views on Sufism." *Shajarah: Journal of the International Institute of Islamic Thought and Civilisation* 19 (1): 55–84.

Alatas, Syed Farid. 2013. *Ibn Khaldun*. New Delhi: Oxford University Press.

Arjomand, Said Amir. 1999. "The Law, Agency and Policy in Medieval Islamic Society: Development of the Institutions of Learning from the Tenth to the Fifteenth Century." *Comparative Studies in Society and History* 41 (2): 263–93.

Arjomand, Said Amir. 2022. *Messianism and Sociopolitical Revolution in Medieval Islam*. Oakland, CA: University of California Press.

Arjomand, Said Amir. 2023. *Revolutions of the End of Time: Apocalypse, Revolution and Reaction in the Persianate World*. Leiden: Brill.

Arjomand, Said Amir. 2025. *Kings and Dervishes: Sufi World Renunciation and the Symbolism of Kingship in the Persianate World*. Oakland, CA: University of California Press.

Arnason, Johann P., and Georg Stauth. 2004. "Civilization and State Formation in the Islamic Context: Re-Reading Ibn Khaldun." *Thesis Eleven*, no. 76: 29–47.

Darling, Linda T. 2013. *A History of Social Justice and Political Power in the Middle East: The Circle of Justice from Mesopotamia to Globalization*. London: Routledge.

DeWeese, Devin. 1994. *Islamization and Native Religion in the Golden Horde: Baba Tükles and Conversion to Islam in Historical and Epic Tradition*. University Park, PA: Pennsylvania State University Press.

DeWeese, Devin. 2018. "Organizational Patterns and Developments within Sufi Communities." In *The Wiley Blackwell History of Islam*, edited by Armando Salvatore et al., 329–50. Oxford: Wiley Blackwell.

Fromherz, Allen James. 2010. *Ibn Khaldun: Life and Times*. Edinburgh: Edinburgh University Press.

Green, Nile. 2012. *Sufism: A Global History*. Oxford: Wiley Blackwell.

Hodgson, Marshall G. S. 1974. *The Venture of Islam: Conscience and History in a World Civilization*, Vol.1–3. Chicago: University of Chicago Press.

Hofer, Nathan. 2020. "Endowments for Ṣūfīs and Their Institutions." In *Sufi Institutions*, edited by Alexandre Papas, 58–78. Leiden: Brill.

Ibn, Khaldūn. 2017. *Ibn Khaldun on Sufism. Remedy for the Questioner in Search of Answers* Translated, introduced, and annotated by Yumna Özer. Cambridge: The Islamic Texts Society.

Irwin, Robert. 2018. *Ibn Khaldun: An Intellectual Biography*. Princeton, NJ: Princeton University Press.

Kafadar, Cemal. 1995. *Between Two Worlds: The Construction of the Ottoman State*. Berkeley: University of California Press.

Lawrence, Bruce B. 2005. "Introduction." In *The Muqaddimah: An Introduction to History, by Ibn Khaldūn*. Translated by Franz Rosenthal, edited and abridged by N. J. Dawood, vii–xix. Princeton, NJ: Princeton University Press.

Markiewicz, Christopher. 2019. *The Crisis of Kingship in Late Medieval Islam: Persian Emigres and the Making of Ottoman Sovereignty*. Cambridge: Cambridge University Press.

Melvin-Koushki, Matthew. 2018. "Early Modern Islamicate Empire: New Forms of Religiopolitical Legitimacy." In *The Wiley Blackwell History of Islam*, edited by Armando Salvatore et al., 353–76. Oxford: Wiley Blackwell.

Moin, A. Azfar. 2018. "The *'Ulama'* as Ritual Specialists: Cosmic Knowledge and Political Rituals." In *The Wiley Blackwell History of Islam*, edited by Armando Salvatore et al., 377–96. Oxford: Wiley Blackwell.

Morrissey, Fitzroy, and Ronald L. Nettler. 2019. "Ibn Khaldun on Sufism: A Story of Truth vs. Falsehood in Three Parts." *The Maghreb Review* 44 (4): 403–26.

Rahimi, Babak. 2004. "Between Chieftaincy and Knighthood: A Comparative Study of Ottoman and Safavid Origins." *Thesis Eleven*, no. 76: 85–102.

Salvatore, Armando. 2016. *The Sociology of Islam: Knowledge, Power and Civility*. Oxford: Wiley Blackwell.

Salvatore, Armando. 2018. "Civility and Charisma in the Long-Term Genesis of Political Modernity within the Islamic Ecumene." In *Islam in der Moderne; Moderne im Islam. Eine Festschrift für Reinhard Schulze zum 65. Geburtstag*, edited by Monica Corrado et al., 267–83. Leiden: Brill.

Salvatore, Armando et al., eds. 2018. *The Wiley Blackwell History of Islam*. Oxford: Wiley Blackwell.

Yılmaz, Hüseyin. 2018. *Caliphate Redefined: The Mystical Turn in Ottoman Political Thought*. Princeton, NJ: Princeton University Press.

Yücesoy, Hayrettin. 2023. *Disenchanting the Caliphate: The Secular Discipline of Power in Abbasid Political Thought*. New York: Columbia University Press.

7

A Saint–Philosopher–King?

The Workings of Walaya *in the Early-Modern Caliphate*

Restituting the Caliphate

The last vestiges of the ruling charisma of the time-honored "peak" institution of the ecumene, the Caliphate, were exhausted at the end of the Earlier Middle Period with the short-lived caliphal renaissance attempted by al-Nasir in ʿAbbasid Baghdad (see Chapter 3). This ultimately doomed intervention unfolded alongside the erosion and collapse of the powerful Ismaʿili alternative to the Caliphate in Fatimid Cairo and of its rival Sunni Caliphate of the Umayyads in Cordoba. In this sense, the disintegration of caliphal authority was not an isolated failure but part of a broader, ecumene-wide transformation of the institutional landscape. Yet this was not the end of the Caliphate as an instituting horizon. On the contrary, during the Later Middle Period a process was set in motion that enabled a deep reinterpretation—and, eventually, a new implementation—of the caliphal institution after its mainstream Sunni embodiment, identified with the ʿAbbasids, had been deliberately and strategically discontinued by the Mongols. As succinctly but forcefully put by Hüseyin Yılmaz (2018, 277), on whose seminal *Caliphate Redefined* this chapter substantially relies, "the void created by the collapse of the Caliphate could only be filled by the Caliphate itself, albeit in a different form."

Paradoxical as it may sound, this "different form" was itself, at least in part, a metamorphosis of the "old" Caliphate, now unfolding within a drastically transformed, post-Khaldunian ecumene. What was required was not a simple revival but a dedicated, if circuitous, process of re-institution—or, more precisely, restitution. The possibility for the Caliphate to blossom again depended on the activation of resources that had long been embedded in the ecumene's instituting dynamics. Among these, a decisive role was played by the *adab-siyasa* discourse, whose rise, as we saw in the previous chapter, was coeval with the transition from the Umayyads to the ʿAbbasids and thus integral to the effectiveness, prestige, and durability of the High Caliphate. Accordingly, while the meaning, scope, and functions of the Caliphate were profoundly reworked in the Later Middle Period and beyond, the main line of continuity between its "old" and "new" dispensations lay precisely in the persistent role of the *adab-siyasa* complex and of the personnel trained to operate within it. It was through this medium that caliphal authority could be reimagined, translated into new institutional arrangements, and ultimately restituted in forms compatible with the transformed conditions of governance in the early-modern ecumene.

The first wave of the instituting process in the ecumene corresponded to what Hodgson famously labeled the High Caliphate. This phase extended until the Buyid takeover of power in Baghdad in 945, an event that, in Hodgson's chronology, marked both the onset of the Earlier Middle Period and the decisive bifurcation between the Caliphate and the de facto power of the Sultanate discussed in the previous chapter. At this juncture, what came to the fore was not a sudden evaporation of caliphal authority, but rather the remarkable resilience of the idea and prestige of the Caliphate itself. This resilience manifested on several interconnected levels. On the one hand, the Caliphate retained a firm place within juridical theory, where it was articulated through the doctrine of the Imamate. On the other hand, it survived as the living specter of its former power and, no less significantly, as a symbolic and practical titulature increasingly available not only to rulers but also to spiritual masters. In this respect, caliphal legitimacy continued to circulate well beyond the effective control of ruling institutions. Crucially, this trend did not come to an abrupt halt with the formal discontinuation of the ʿAbbasid Caliphate at the hands of the Mongols in 1258—an event that, for Hodgson, marked the beginning of the Later Middle Period. Rather, the Caliphate entered an erratic yet consequential afterlife. Even in its "destituted" form, the institution retained sufficient symbolic force to shape practices, expectations, and modes of legitimation across the ecumene. This afterlife, far from being marginal, should therefore not be underestimated. Indeed, it helped sustain a significant nexus between the habitualizing process fostered by the *hadith-adab* amalgam (see Chapter 2) and the edifice of *fiqh*, together with the operative principle of *maslaha*. Through this nexus, the Caliphate continued to underpin the institution and funding of a wide range of social services, most notably via the *waqf* (Yılmaz 2018, 277–278).

In this way, even as its political embodiment waned, the Caliphate remained embedded in the deeper instituting dynamics of the ecumene.

And yet, during the Later Middle Period this process was facilitated by a parallel—if ultimately convergent—exhaustion of the older ideal of the Caliphate modeled on the four Rightly-Guided Caliphs as successors of the Prophet Muhammad. What became increasingly apparent was a marked decline in the tangible prestige of the juridical theory of the Imamate itself. This erosion was registered not only among Turko-Mongol rulers, who had little incentive to revive a constraining caliphal model, but also among their orthodox critics. A paradigmatic expression of this latter position was articulated by Ibn Taymiyya (1263–1328), the leading Hanbali scholar who sought to rethink political authority from within a rigorously orthodox framework. By coining the influential compound *al-siyasa al-shar'iyya*, Ibn Taymiyya deliberately bypassed what he regarded as the increasingly inert ruminations of jurists on an idealized theory of the Imamate centered on the uncontaminated authenticity of the first four Rightly-Guided Caliphs. Rather than opposing the existing political order outright, he carved out a critical position from within the capillary instituting process that had long interlaced the *hadith-shari'a* complex with its *adab-siyasa* counterpart. In doing so, he acknowledged the historical transformations of rulership while insisting on anchoring political practice in normative religious principles. At the opposite end of the spectrum, the Timurid Empire (1370–1507)—the most prominent instance of a Turko-Mongol ruling synthesis—deliberately refrained from any explicit reconstruction of the Caliphate. Instead, it pursued a markedly different path. As will become clearer shortly, Timurid rulership relied on a phantasmagoric assemblage of titles, symbols, and cosmological claims that collectively served to legitimize what had previously been little more than the de facto power of the Sultanate (Melvin-Koushki 2018, 354–361; Yılmaz 2018, 108). In this way, the Later Middle Period witnessed not simply the decline of the old caliphal ideal, but the opening of multiple, competing avenues for rethinking not only legitimacy, but the very grammar of political power in the ecumene.

Unsurprisingly, when the caliphal title began to circulate again in the 14th century, it almost immediately and unequivocally diverged from the "classical" orientation centered on legitimate succession to the Prophet Muhammad. Instead, it was brught back to the Qur'anic trope of the *khalifa* as God's plenipotentiary on earth. This resemanticization was readily folded into Sufi-inspired titles such as *wali*, *qutb*, and even *ayat Allah*, the sign of God. Significantly, the latter designation was attributed by the previously mentioned Davud-i Kayseri (see Chapter 6) to an Ottoman ruler at a time when he still bore the quintessentially Turkic title of *beg* (Yılmaz 2018, 107–109). Taken together, this increasingly dense—if hardly linear or internally consistent—layering of resignifications shifted the caliphal title away from a primarily juridico-theological register toward a saintly-philosophical, and ultimately cosmopolitical, orbit. This shift owed much to the progressive instituting of Sufi life and organization across multiple levels of the ecumene (see Chapter 3). The culmination of the instituting process in reconstructing the legitimacy of governance, eventually crystallizing once again around the Caliphate, was thus decisively aided by Sufi conceptions of *walaya*. Importantly, this was not the outcome of mere conceptual bricolage. It rested on sustained Sufi work "on the ground": the habitualization of intercorporeal connectivity (see Chapter 3) and the upgrading of tribal *asabiyya* into a countercyclical factor of cohesion capable of stabilizing social life across changing contexts (see Chapter 5). In this respect, Ibn Khaldun's recurring examples of the Sufis as retracing the trajectory inaugurated by Muhammad and his Companions—transcending tribal bonds to generate a transtribal connective force capable of instituting and governing urban life—offer a compelling illustration of a kind of super-*asabiyya* powered by prophecy and saintliness.

This process unfolded more or less simultaneously in two broad settings. On one side, we find the successor states of the Mongol Chingizid Empire, where rulers creatively merged Mongol and Islamic traditions of rulership. On the other, we find those polities that resisted the Mongol onslaught, most notably the Mamluks in Egypt and Syria and the emerging Ottoman *dawla*. The Ottomans, in particular, drew on a well-assorted tableau of ideas and practices of rulership, some directly inherited from the ʿAbbasids and others adapted from broader Turko-Mongol conceptions of sovereignty. Owing to their frontier position and their long phase of institutional experimentation, they were especially well placed to retrospectively appropriate lines of continuity with the old Caliphate. This experience shaped Ottoman sociopolitical milieus through a prolonged and relatively open-ended instituting process, sustained by a corresponding political cosmology and fueled by the continuous influx of Sufi masters and adepts from across the ecumene.

As Yılmaz succinctly summarizes (2018, 235), "Ottoman historical narratives portrayed the House of Osman as having earned the Caliphate by merit and inherited it by right as part of a divinely ordained eschatological scheme." The primary background to this development lay in the Sufis' continuous distillation and appropriation of ruling titles pivoting on a foundational concept of *khilafa*. Rather than deriving from the juridical theory of the Imamate and its binding to the paradigm of the four Rightly-Guided

Caliphs, Sufi elaborations of the Caliphate proceeded directly from its articulation in the Qur'an and the *hadith* corpus (ibid., 117). In this sense, they could hardly be dismissed as deviant. At the same time, to situate the Ottoman trajectory of re-instituting the Caliphate within its proper historical frame, the catastrophe of the Battle of Ankara in 1402 must be understood as a moment of "creative destruction." This trauma enabled the still fragile and embryonic Ottoman *dawla* to reconstitute itself in innovative ways attuned to the rapidly shifting socioreligious and political dynamics of Anatolia. From this point onward, drawing on Sufi reworkings of the Caliphate—often in conjunction with messianic designations—became less an elective strategy than a structural necessity for Ottoman dynasts and their court scholars. The ruler who ultimately prevailed in the civil war of succession following Ankara, Mehmed I (r. 1413–1421), was explicitly described by Abdülvasi Çelebi not only as the bearer of a great *dawla* but also as a *wali* (in Ottoman Turkish, *veli*) and as the messianic "God-guided" one, the Mahdi. A closely related line of thought appeared in the work of another Sufi-inclined scholar of the period, Hızır b. Yakub[1] who authored a treatise on the beautiful names of Allah drawing on key ideas of Ghazali and Ibn 'Arabi. There he asserted that insofar as rulers could reflect the divine attributes, they were legitimate Caliphs—that is, deputies of Allah on earth.

The emphasis in caliphal attribution thus shifted toward the primary Qur'anic meaning of the Caliphate as vested in Adam and, by extension, in humankind as a whole. From this perspective, the post-Qur'anic understanding of the Caliphate as succession to the Prophet Muhammad through the Rightly-Guided Caliphs—an understanding that became foundational for the theory of the Imamate—created a partial historical divergence from a more originary scriptural horizon. Retracing this Qur'anic meaning configured the Caliphate as a kind of *Ur*-institution, almost the equivalent of Allah's endowment of humanity with the capacity to institute life forms on earth: the first, indispensable, God-willed spark of *'umran* and of the instituting process underlying it. On the one hand, this Qur'anic seed of the Caliphate was rearticulated through Akbarian[2] ideas such as *al-insan al-kamil* and the *qutb*, centered on the narrative of Adam's crowning by Allah. This narrative closely resembles a Sufi initiation, in which a disciple is invested by a master with authority and responsibility. In this reading, the Caliph appears as God's disciple, entitled to exercise *siyasa*—that is, to govern the earth—on His behalf. On the other hand, as the last Prophet in a chain extending back to Adam, Muhammad was understood as the inheritor of this primordial endowment, the embodiment of this foundational institution, and the most accomplished prototype of human perfection. Several Ottoman authors therefore emphasized that *walaya* was intrinsic to *nubuwwa*, or prophecy, such that rulership infused with the former could be conceived as a spiritual crowning of the prophetic mission itself (Yılmaz 2018, 121–128; 201).[3]

At the same time, in the interval between the Ottoman civil war and the conquest of Constantinople, Sufi authorities and imaginaries occupied an unstable position. They oscillated between legitimating ruling authority through a top-down, court-centered messianism and mobilizing rebellion against rulers by intensifying expectations of redemptive justice. The latter tendency found a powerful expression in the uprising led by Shaykh Bedreddin (1359–1420) in 1416, in the immediate aftermath of the civil war, which mobilized overlapping constituencies against the government (see also Chapter 8). Crushed by Mehmed I, this challenge nevertheless left a lasting imprint. His successor, Murad II (r. 1421–1444; 1446–1451), responded to the persistent risk of Sufi-inspired mobilization by forging a durable alliance with the rising Mevlevi confraternity. Although already flourishing in several parts of Anatolia, the Mevlevis had previously remained relatively distant from the core Ottoman territories and their ruling elites. By consolidating authority through this and other alliances with influential Sufi groups, Murad II's reign also marked a shift toward more consistent claims to universal rulership. These claims were articulated through the progressive appropriation of ruling titles, in what appeared increasingly as a competitive race with contemporary rivals—most notably the heirs of Timur—to secure the aura and authority of what has been aptly described as the figure of the "saint-philosopher-king" (Melvin-Koushki 2018, 356–362). This figure combined Hellenic and Irano-Semitic traditions of rulership and was defined by the capacity to hold together, and actively manage, the bundled forces of knowledge and power. Within this constellation, the title *sahib-qiran*, or Lord of Conjunction, which synthetically united immanent authority and divine predestination, became central to the legitimation of sovereign prerogatives. Among the Ottomans, this type of astro-cosmopolitical charisma had a deep genealogy. It owed less to the refined idiom of courtly *adab-siyasa* than to practitioners of a combined shamanic and Sufi wisdom. The lineage extended back to Osman, the eponymous founder of the dynasty, who was proclaimed Lord of Conjunction by the leading Sufi master known as Kumral Baba, or Abdal. Yet shifting to advanced stage of elaborating sovereign charisma, a decisive transformation occurred only under Mehmed the Conqueror. He postured as a centralizing and universal ruler who sought relative independence from the esoteric authority of the *abdalan*, while at the same time sublimating their knowledge into a new and more complex synthesis of sovereign attributes—a development to which we will return shortly (Yılmaz 2018, 240–242).

It should not be overlooked, however, that the benchmark in the race to appropriate astro-cosmopolitical titulature during the crucial transition from the Later Middle Period to the early-modern era was set by none other than Timur—more precisely, and decisively, by the posthumous work of his court scholars. Having begun his career as a sheep raider and later an *amir* (see Chapter 6), Timur's charismatic consecration as a receptacle of *walaya* came to sharply transcend the forms of ruling legitimacy previously associated with nomadic empires, Mongol ones included. During his lifetime, he was revered within military camps as a savior-warrior. After his death, however, his image was substantially refashioned in ways that anchored his authority in a far more elevated symbolic genealogy. Most notably, Timur was made to descend simultaneously from ʿAli—who by this time was increasingly celebrated in popular lore as a paramount paragon of valor and *walaya*—and Alanqoʾa, the mythical princess-mother of the Mongols. According to this narrative, Timur was conceived when a beam of light, taking the form of ʿAli, invested the chaste Alanqoʾa, who thereby became a bearer of divine luminosity in an unmistakable case of immaculate conception. Unsurprisingly, the inscription on Timur's grave echoed and reworked fragments from the Sura of Maryam in the Qur'an, thus embedding his person within a scriptural and cosmological register that fused prophecy, saintliness, and sovereignty (Moin 2012, 37–39; Melvin-Koushki 2018, 357; Salvatore 2018, 166).

The Culmination of *Walaya* as the Cypher of the New Caliphate

Along this trajectory, the ideal of the saint-philosopher-king emerged as a distinctive cosmopolitical inflection of royal authority, resonating across rival empires. Particular attention must therefore be paid to the ways in which the Ottomans, between the 15th and 16th centuries, proved capable of simultaneously emulating and ultimately eclipsing Timur's legacy, especially as it crystallized under the reign of his grandson Iskandar Sultan (r. 1409–1414). Iskandar famously styled himself as *al-insan al-kamil* (the Perfect Human) theorized by Ibn 'Arabi (see also Chapter 8), as Caliph of God, and as universal ruler. While this was the first post-Mongol appropriation of the Caliphate that fully conformed to the template of saint-philosopher-kingship, the Ottomans pursued the redesign of the Caliphate with far greater persistence and coherence. Beginning with Murad II, in the aftermath of the double trauma of defeat at the hands of Timur and the ensuing civil war, the ruler's anointing as a saint-philosopher-king rested on a consciously refurbished political cosmology of the Caliphate. As reflected most clearly in the *Enisu'l-Celis* of Ankari—whose original version, likely in Arabic, is no longer extant—the spiritual powers and virtues of *khilafa* came to be treated as indispensable for legitimizing *saltana*, understood less as the "office" of the sultan than as an effective prerogative of rulership. Within this framework, the Caliph was fully reimagined as *al-insan al-kamil*, the figure who mediates between macrocosm and microcosm by embodying the creative power of the Divine Word, that is, by manifesting the divine attributes grounded in the Qur'an (Yılmaz 2018, 131–139).

At this juncture, it is worth stressing that several of the key titles reflecting the rising mystical and messianic semantics of knowledge-power—most notably Mahdi, but also *mujaddid*, the "renewer" of Islam expected at the turn of each century—were anchored primarily in the *hadith* corpus. Only *khalifa*, however, was firmly rooted in the Qur'an itself and thus uniquely capable of articulating both the "source" and the apex of the instituting process. Yet, as already suggested, the title that most directly expressed the plenitude of *walaya* ultimately exceeded the scriptural corpus and pointed instead to the rise of a Sufi-inflected political astro-cosmology. The concept and attribute of *al-insan al-kamil* occupied an axial position within the unparalleled legacy of Ibn 'Arabi, a legacy that, as will become clear, played an increasingly central role in the Ottoman early-modern dispensation. The success of this formula lay precisely in its capacity to provide a full mystical specification of the Qur'anic *khalifa*. Recast through the image of the Perfect Human, the renewed caliphal title implied that temporal rulership and its legitimacy were but a preordained emanation of a wider knowledge-power constellation inscribed in cosmic government. In this vision, the Caliph partook in divine sovereignty exercised simultaneously over angelic and earthly realms, the unseen and the seen, eternity and temporality—realms ultimately mediated by the eschatological horizon of the End of Time (*akhir al-zaman*). Ottoman culture, at both elite and popular levels, played a decisive role in articulating this messianic and eschatological legitimation of rulership. Scriptural commentaries informed by this reconstructed vision of the Caliphate spilled over into the perception of *Rum*—the former "Land of the Romans"—as a divinely favored abode destined to host the final denouement of human history. In this context, the inflection of the figure of the Mahdi became integral to the conception of an eschatological *dawla*, that of the Ottomans, whose rulers could claim to derive the quintessential wisdom of power from God's most beautiful names. Within this dispensation, the administration of mercy and generosity was understood as a precondition for the exercise of justice, while accountability emerged as an essential corollary of sovereign authority (Yılmaz 2018, 279–283).

The final shape of the new Caliphate was powerful to the extent that it combined such novel traits with key elements of the old instantiation represented by the trope of the Rightly Guided Caliphs and the theory of the Imamate. This is also why most leading Ottoman jurists played along with the mystical and messianic turn of the Caliphate. Yılmaz reminds us that one thread in the reconstruction of this institution was also a multivocal and creative reclaiming of the legacy of the ʿAbbasid Caliphate. After the Ottoman *dawla* survived the cataclysmic clash with Timur, this reconciliation of the old with the new appeared as the most secure road to tie the claim to universal rulership with more solid, and ultimately better Islamically grounded credentials than the Mongol (Chingizid) articulation of statehood had ever been able to display. This path proved even more necessary as the Ottoman realm gradually emerged as the bulwark against the radical, Shiʿi, apocalyptic messianism of the Safavids and the associated, persistent Turkmen disturbances within the empire's borders, which will be addressed shortly. While this development has been recently read in terms of the consolidation of an Ottoman Sunni orthodoxy, it was the reflection of the much more compelling imperative to renew the caliphal *dawla*—the only one predestined to survive Khaldunian cycles—after the Mongols had discontinued its temporary, rather than final, carrier, namely the ʿAbbasid dynasty. As a response to the previously mentioned inscription on the tomb of Timur, which blended Chingizid mythology and ʿAlid charisma, the grave of Süleyman the Magnificent (r. 1520–1566) enshrined the Ottoman mission, begun by Osman, to reestablish the ʿAbbasid caliphal *dawla* on the blessed and promised land of Rum. This was the *dawla* predestined to seamlessly fold in the Caliphate of the coming Mahdi across the horizon of the End of Time (Yılmaz 2018, 284–285; Krstić and Terzioğlu 2022).

This powerful shift began to become tangible at the onset of the Later Middle Period, even if most of the conceptual tools for what Yılmaz (2018) has called the "mystical turn" of the Caliphate had already been assembled by leading Sufi authors in the final phase of the Earlier Middle Period, beginning with Ibn ʿArabi. Unlike the earlier al-Ghazali, Ibn ʿArabi moved decisively beyond endorsing the enfeebled "classic" Caliphate, which had been irreversibly diminished by the increasingly nominal authority of the ʿAbbasids in Baghdad, first under Buyid and then under Seljuq tutelage. By creatively elaborating Qurʾanic vocabulary and imagery—most notably in the *Fusus al-Hikam* ("Bezels of Wisdom")—Ibn ʿArabi paved the way for a consistent view of the cosmocratic ruler as a likely instantiation of the ideal of *al-insan al-kamil*, simultaneously conceived as *qutb* and as the ultimate embodiment of *walaya*. The impact of this conception in the land of Rum at the beginning of the Later Middle Period can hardly be overstated. At the same time, Ibn ʿArabi's political cosmology is often seen as distinct from, yet complementary to, the approach of the slightly earlier master Yahya Suhrawardi (ca. 1154–1191). An exquisite thinker and, unlike Ibn ʿArabi, deeply enmeshed in the politics of his time, the founder of the *ishraqi* (illuminationist) school exerted a marked influence on Seljuq conceptions of rulership in Rum, where he spent a significant period before settling in Aleppo. As Yılmaz argues, this influence is also visible in Seljuq iconography, which frequently depicts the ruler as infused with divine light—a symbol and concept central to *ishraqi* teachings. It has even been suggested that Suhrawardi's martyrdom in Aleppo marked the epilogue of an attempt to politically implement his vision, possibly through a plan to install an Ayyubid prince who would translate illuminationist principles into a ruling methodology (Arjomand 2025, 64–65).

No conception of the Caliphate envisioned a more seamless synergy between pure knowledge and enlightened power. This vision was impregnated with ideas inherited from the leading philosophers al-Farabi (d. 950) and Ibn Sina (d. 1037), and nourished by original appropriations of Neo-Platonism and Neo-Pythagoreanism—what Suhrawardi famously called "the leaven of the ancients." In combination with the no less powerful, though distinct, Akbarian conceptions, this synthesis ultimately enabled the trope of the "saint-philosopher-king" to serve both the movement toward the revival of the Caliphate, which reached its apex in the Ottoman domains, and alternative, more radical trajectories, such as those pursued by the rival Safavids, who largely circumvented caliphal legitimation. In either case, the outcome was the configuration of a kind of super-*walaya*—a form of authority that aspiring world conquerors were eager to appropriate as a marker of expansive and holistic universality of rule. At the same time, these cosmocratic conceptions remained firmly anchored within confraternal settings and could just as readily fuel challenges to state power, as earlier exemplified by the case of Bedreddin. In this regard, the trajectory of Bidlisi, first mentioned in the previous chapter, is particularly revealing. More than a scholar, Bidlisi had served as chief secretary at the Aq Qoyunlu court of Western Iran before joining the Ottoman court. Like several other Sufi-minded intellectuals of the period, he deftly navigated the divide between Sunni and Shiʿi milieus. Though, as Markiewicz (2019) notes, more an adapter than an architect of Ottoman political theology,[4] Bidlisi ultimately produced a mature synthesis of the approaches of Ibn ʿArabi and Suhrawardi, as already filtered through figures such as Davvani (d. 1502), with whom he studied in Shiraz. Repackaged in the idiom of early-modern Persianate *adab-siyasa*, his work culminated in a sophisticated conception of the Caliphate tailored to the historical trajectory of the Ottoman *dawla*—an outcome that exemplifies the decisive role of scholarly elites in redesigning the legitimating formulas of early-modern emperors (Moin 2012; 2018; Melvin-Koushki 2018, 359; Yılmaz 2018, 42–43; Arjomand 2023, 116–118; 2025, 234–237).

More broadly, and independently of the formal restitution of the Caliphate, this transformation was enabled by a structural shift within the *amir-aʿyan* system discussed in previous chapters. The counterpart to the *aʿyan* was no longer primarily a sultan or an amir, but increasingly a ruler understood as a holder of *walaya*. Such rulers cultivated privileged relationships with the Sufi core of the educational-charitable complex and with scholars acting as astronomers or astrologers, alongside continued reliance on the skills provided by the *adab-siyasa* complex. As Matthew Melvin-Koushki, drawing on Mir-Kasimov (2014), has aptly put it, *walaya* functioned as a "quicksilver category," marked by malleability and polyvalence, and thus well suited to compensating for the long latency of the Caliphate during the Earlier Middle Period. Shaped by Sufi masters and theorists in close interaction with post-Mongol dynasts, *walaya* matured in ways that did not constrain but rather amplified its versatility—qualities that proved particularly congenial to the Persianate zone of the ecumene and the early-modern states emerging there. In this context, Bidlisi stands out as a leading figure in the competition among court scholars to creatively refurbish *walaya* for rulers presiding over what Hodgson famously, if imperfectly, termed military patronage states. Yet even as court scholars refined the concept, its effectiveness often depended on how aspiring saint-philosopher-kings articulated their relationships with the leaders of Sufi confraternities, who continued to be regarded as the primary custodians of the same charismatic attribute (Melvin-Koushki 2018, 354; see also Salvatore 2020, 29–30).

This climactic retooling of *walaya* as a core attribute of the saint-philosopher-king, both within and beyond the reconstituted Caliphate, brings into focus a recurrent semantic issue that we began to address in Chapter 3: the apparent bifurcation of meaning in Arabic—though not in Persian or Ottoman Turkish—between *walaya* and *wilaya*. This distinction derives from a shift in the vocalization of the initial consonant *waw*, with *walaya* most commonly associated with closeness or friendship to Allah, and *wilaya* more directly connoting authority or rule. Yet this oscillation does not amount to a semantic rupture. Rather, it establishes a fundamental twinning between two verbal nouns that belong to the same lexeme. As Elmore has shown, even where lexicographers acknowledged a difference in nuance produced by vocalization, they generally treated *walaya* and *wilaya* as variants of a single root, and not infrequently used them interchangeably. That said, *walaya* more often conveyed meanings of assistance, protection, or alliance, whereas *wilaya* tended to gravitate toward the semantic field of *sulta* or power. This tendency reflects a broader grammatical pattern: verbal nouns with an *i* vowel in the first syllable often denote a function and its exercise, much as *khilafa* designates the function of the *khalifa*, while those with an *a* vowel tend to indicate a state of being—an ontological condition, as it were—sustained by a corresponding political cosmology (cf. Elmore 1999, 114). The twinning of the two terms can therefore be expressed succinctly: the state of being a *wali* (*walaya*) entails the exercise of a corresponding function (*wilaya*). The distinction between ontological state and functional exercise should be understood as a soft one, in sharp contrast to the rigid dichotomy—rooted in medieval European political theology—between "spiritual" and "temporal" power. As Elmore emphasizes, since the two nouns articulate complementary dimensions of a single semantic field, some authors appear to have preferred one form or the other without signaling a substantive conceptual difference. At no point does this bifurcation imply a division between an inherently spiritual capacity and an externally imposed temporal authority.

It is significant in this respect that Ibn ʿArabi consistently preferred the term *wilaya*. Although his usage is predominantly oriented toward the ontology of spiritual realization, it clearly encompasses the functional exercise of the power inherent in that state (Elmore 1999, 121). Indeed, in Ibn ʿArabi's thought even the spiritual condition itself functions as the leaven of a highly operational political cosmology, a point to which we will return shortly. This is also why I have deliberately avoided invoking the European medieval doctrine of the duality of powers—spiritual and temporal—in analyzing the Islamic ecumene, despite its frequent use in the secondary literature, including by authors on whose historical and sociological authority I otherwise rely (e.g., Yılmaz and Arjomand). That European distinction emerged within a specific political theology[5] that generated conceptions of early-modern statehood fundamentally different from those that developed in the ecumene. Here, by contrast, *walaya* was embedded in a monistic political astro-cosmology, in which the only meaningful doubling is between the visible and invisible worlds, rather than between two autonomous spheres of authority. The appropriation of *walaya* by rulers nonetheless required successive adjustments. One may also note how the growing centrality of Middle Persian in the grammar of saint-philosopher-kingship facilitated the fusion of the two dimensions, since Persian offers no lexical bifurcation corresponding to *walaya/wilaya*, relying instead on a single term, *velayat*. Both the emergence of the Arabic distinction and its effective absorption into Persian usage should thus be situated within the broader trajectory of semantic and cosmopolitical interventions pursued by Persianate court scholars of the period, whether or not they were explicitly Sufi-inclined. On this basis, and in line with the argument developed in the previous chapter, we can retain *walaya* as the fundamental attribute of a gifted form of rule—understood, once again, not in a narrowly personal sense, but as an eminently relational and dynamic capacity. At the same time, one should not lose sight of the dense core of *walaya* as expressing closeness not only to Allah but also to the House of the Prophet Muhammad. This is crucial for understanding both the sustained, and often increasing, centrality of the Prophet as a spiritual model in Sufi thought—whether mediated through the virtues of ʿAli or articulated otherwise—and the persistent emphasis on the continuity between *nubuwwa* (prophecy) and *walaya* in the reconfiguration of the Caliphate (Yılmaz 2018, 180–213). It was precisely this continuity that allowed *khilafa* to be released from the juridical armature of succession to the Prophet and reinserted into a more foundational dimension, shared with prophecy itself: the reflection of divine speech, signs, and beautiful names.

To recapitulate, as argued by Melvin-Koushki (2018, 354–362), this process of resignification of *walaya* was crucial to modeling the category of the saint-philosopher-king out of precedents elaborated across both Irano-Semitic and Hellenic traditions since classical antiquity. It exalted a form of gifted, knowledge-based rulership by appropriating Neo-Platonic and Neo-Pythagorean motifs—most notably the trope of the philosopher-king—and fusing them with popular narratives of heroic and saintly warriors, which frequently fed into eschatological longings. In the post-Mongol Islamic ecumene, many rulers could thus plausibly posture as messianic saint-philosopher-kings. This figure also fit seamlessly with the idiom of wise and just rulership articulated by the *adab-siyasa* complex, whose analysis will be resumed in the next chapter. At the same time, one should not lose sight of what may be identified as the main missing link in Khaldunian theory: the indispensable background condition for instituting the saint-philosopher-king, and indeed for the transition to the Later Middle Period and the early modern era, lay in a pervasive sense of divine mission and predestination that accompanied the Mongol conquests and their ambitions to universal rulership—well before Mongol elites embraced Islam as the majority religion of the ecumene. The prestige accruing to the Mongol legacy played a decisive role in cementing the authority of the *yasa*, or analogous forms of dynastic law, within the constellation of elements that shaped the cosmopolitical character of the saint-philosopher-king. After all, the decrees of the *yasa* were issued "by the power of the Eternal Heaven" (Arjomand 2025, 20), a formula that accrued to—rather than conflicted with—the *walaya* of a saint-philosopher-king, whether Timurid or Ottoman.

The Messianic Climax

Indeed, in the prominent case of the Ottomans, the lengthy transition from frontier chieftainship to universal rule and the reconfigured Caliphate went hand in hand with a realistic apprehension of power relations and what we might call the limits of sovereignty. Here the spiritual and the pragmatic dimensions of rulership converged in rendering obsolete the idealistic expectations attached to the old Caliphate. The sense of an inherent expansiveness of the Islamic ecumene—conveyed first by the experience of frontier warfare and later by the continuing identification of empire with conquest—never erased the awareness that rulership remained conditioned by encounters, competitions, and conflicts. No doubt, with Mehmed the Conqueror the Ottoman sovereign surged to the status of a new Alexander or Caesar, earning the title of the Absolute God's Caliph in the Eastern and Western lands of the ecumene. Yet universal rulership also entailed what we might call a geopolitical presence of spirit: an orientation that simultaneously transcended provincial *ghazi* identity and marked a decisive break with the model of the High Caliphate. One immediate casualty of this shift, during Mehmed's reign, was the intense intercourse with—and at times dependence on—the prestige and prowess of the *abdalan*, together with the protection traditionally afforded to *waqf* property. The partial erosion of these safeguards affected both Sufi orders and Turkmen grandees (Yılmaz 2018, 77, 241–243). In this sense, the messianic climax of Ottoman rulership temporarily dented the unprecedented level of social autonomy achieved by the instituting process in the Middle Periods, which had relied on the centrality of what we have termed the instituting matrix and the instituting conduit of the ecumene, namely *tariqa* and *waqf*.

That this policy risked overplaying the rupture with inherited institutional balances became clear under Mehmed's son Bayezid II (r. 1481–1512), who pursued a course of reconciliation. This included both the restitution of confiscated *waqf* properties and the creation of new endowments in favor of Sufi constituencies. Such measures amounted to a tacit recognition that the stability of the *dawla* continued to depend on securing a congruous degree of consensus among key components of the *a'yan*, particularly those who still held, as it were, the keys to *walaya*. This adjustment illustrates how the military patronage state theorized by Hodgson did not dissolve the instituting dynamics and balances inherited from the Earlier Middle Period but rather brought them to a higher level of integration. At the same time, the prototypical collaboration—and at times complicity—between rulers and masters, cemented by a shared *walaya*, could not be eliminated by increasing centralization without risking the depletion of the *dawla*'s ultimate source of legitimacy. By the end of the 15th century, looking back, one could observe how urban *'umran* had been decisively enriched by a continuous influx of Sufi masters and scholars, particularly from the East. Since the Mongol onslaught, they had continued to view Rum as a uniquely fertile terrain for cultivating *walaya*—a vocation that presupposed ongoing collaboration with rulers driven by ambitions of conquest and valor. This perception was symbolically sealed with the composition, in 1503, of the *Qutbname*, which epically celebrated Bayezid II as *qutb al-aqtab*. This attribution effectively completed the cumulative logic of saint-philosopher-kingship, following earlier bestowals of the titles of *wali* (*veli* in Ottoman Turkish) and *sahib-qiran*.

The recalibration of the Sufi and messianic identity of the Ottoman *dawla* at the beginning of the 16th century was further reinforced by the spectacular conquest of the Mamluk realms of Syria and Egypt during the short but fiery reign of Selim I (r. 1512–1520), before reaching its apex under Süleyman I the Magnificent (r. 1520–1566). The unprecedentedly vigorous—and indeed reticular—astro-cosmopolitical titulature that accompanied these developments, corroborated by what appeared to be an unstoppable sequence of conquests, endowed the new Caliphate with what we may paradoxically describe as a form of messianic stability. This consolidation occurred precisely at the moment when the Ottoman polity confronted a formidable challenge that materialized simultaneously as internal sedition and external military threat (Melvin-Koushki 2018, 359–360; Yılmaz 2018, 141, 249). This messianic stabilization—or, in Arjomand's terms, "realization"—has often been explained as a response to the rivalry posed by the rising Safavid *dawla* in Iran, a challenge perceived by the Ottomans as existential both geopolitically and ideologically. In this light, Arjomand (2025, 24) has spoken of an Ottoman messianic counterrevolution as perhaps the most effective, if not the only, means of containing the revolutionary thrust of the radical messianism articulated by the Sufi Safawiyya. Originating in the 12th century as a branch of the Suhrawardiyya founded by Abu al-Najib Suhrawardi (Arjomand 2025, 24; see Chapter 3), this confraternity metamorphosed into the Safavid *dawla* when it seized control of Iran, at the time fragmented among post-Timurid principalities within the collapsing Aq Qoyunlu Empire. Significantly, the name of the *tariqa* turned *dawla* remained unchanged, as if retroactively confirming the enduring convertibility of knowledge-power between confraternal bonds and instituted statehood. More broadly, the success of thw Safavid revolutionary state formation conforms closely to Khaldunian patterns, not least because of the Safawiyya's capacity to pool the tribal power of a nomadic Turkmen coalition. For the Ottomans, this development revived the specter of Sufi-led, radically messianic insurrections that had reached a peak in the 15th century with the rebellion of Badreddin and resurfaced in the civil strife surrounding the succession to Bayezid II in the early 16th century, which in turn partly overlapped with the inception of the Safavid revolution and *dawla* (Arjomand 2023, 86).[6]

Arjomand (2023, 88–109; 2025, 246–264) has provided an articulate interpretation of messianic, Sufi-inflected revolutionary movements, among which the Safavids stand out as uniquely successful, in grounding a long-lasting and powerful *dawla*. He views this type of movement as the most formidable counter-hegemonic force to the Turko-Mongol model of state formation that reached its apex at the transition from the Earlier to the Later Middle Period, particularly in the Timurid realm. At the same time, this configuration proved exceptionally consequential in Anatolia. The leader of the Safavid revolution, Shah Isma'il, was deeply embedded in the messianic expectations associated with, and further intensified by, Mehmed II's conquest of Constantinople half a century earlier. It is also noteworthy that even before that watershed moment, in the early 15th century, the then leader of the Safawiyya, Khwaja 'Ali, recruited followers of Badreddin who had escaped the suppression of his uprising (Arjomand 2023, 87). More broadly, the appropriation by Safawiyya leaders of ruling titles well before Shah Isma'il's sweeping campaigns in Iran reflected a wider pattern unfolding in Anatolia and beyond, involving not only *tariqa* formations but also *futuwwa*. This subterranean political landscape, which Arjomand has aptly described as a network of "underground kingdoms," functioned as a persistent zone of resistance to Timurid authority, especially in Iran (Arjomand 2025, 178–200).

Against this broader backdrop, the case of Shah Isma'il may be understood as a late and particularly successful manifestation of anti-Timurid messianic contestations by Sufi groups. Within this pattern, the movement's leadership mobilized *walaya* as the worldly manifestation of the Mahdi. Recruiting widely not only among nomadic Turkmen but also among urban *akhi*s (Arjomand 2025, 250), the Safawiyya remained closely intertwined with Anatolian developments. This was in part because, after being expelled from Ardabil in Azerbaijan—where the *tariqa* had already formed the nucleus of a *dawla*—Isma'il's grandfather, Shaykh Junayd, became active in Anatolia. There he organized bands of Sufi frontier raiders drawn largely from Turkmen groups. Such patterns were not new to Anatolia. Since at least the 14th century, they had been cultivated by *baba* figures and *abdalan* who retained significant elements of pre-Islamic shamanic practice, often encouraging forms of leader divinization. This dynamic was also evident in the careers of Junayd and his son Haydar. It reached its culmination under Shah Isma'il, to whom accrued the messianic designation of Lord of the Age (*sahib-i zaman* in Persian sources). This title—significantly, one that had already been bestowed upon Mehmed the Conqueror half a century earlier—was further reinforced by the appellation of Caliph of Allah, ultimately culminating in the anointing of Isma'il as the Mahdi, or the Sword of God (Arjomand 2023, 90–93).

The Turkmen supporters he mobilized in Anatolia, known as the Qizilbash after their red headgear, held intense messianic devotion toward Shah Isma'il while also harboring deep grievances against Ottoman rule. Many had been dispossessed of land grants (*timar*s) traditionally allocated to cavalrymen (*sipahi*s) within the Ottoman system, particularly in the wake of the centralizing policies pursued by Mehmed the Conqueror (Arjomand 2023, 96). The Safavid revolution thus drew on multiple and intersecting roots, many of which emerged in direct antagonism to the core trajectory of Ottoman state formation. At the same time, the Khaldunian configuration that underpinned Shah Isma'il's rise—namely, the fusion of Sufi messianic leadership with a nomadic confederation—was structurally analogous to earlier successful movements. These included not only the Safavids' Ottoman rivals in their own formative phase in the 13th century, but also the Almohad movement in the Maghreb in the 11th century, whose leader, Ibn Tumart, was likewise acclaimed as a Mahdi (see Chapter 6).

In 1500 Shah Isma'il began conquering major cities in Northern Iran with the support of the Qizilbash. Their recruitment in Anatolia continued throughout the campaign and relied heavily on the trope of suffering and martyrdom associated with Husayn, the grandson of the Prophet Muhammad and the son of 'Ali. In his Iranian campaigns, Isma'il postured as the "messianic avenger" of Husayn. It should be specified, however, that 'Alid motifs were already widespread among Sufi confraternities in a long progression that stretched across the Later Middle Period and beyond (Rahimi 2018). At the time of its early 16th-century conquests, moreover, the Safawiyya was still placed within the Sunni fold. Even so, the primary oppressors were now unequivocally identified with Ottoman authorities (Arjomand 2023, 97–98). While Bayezid II managed to secure Ottoman territories against Qizilbash uprisings, in 1502 Isma'il proclaimed from Tabriz his new *dawla* and formally committed it to the Imami Shi'a. This move may have been intended to domesticate Qizilbash radicalism by channeling it into an institutionally controllable form of 'Alid commitment. At the same time, it facilitated the suppression of rival Sufi confraternities, which Isma'il suspected of harboring competing potentials for state formation or outright rebellion. Notably, Bayezid II did not initially read this shift as a direct challenge of Ottoman Sunni orthodoxy. He responded with moderation, addressing Isma'il in a paternal tone and acknowledging him less as a revolutionary insurgent than as the sovereign of a new and expanding *dawla* on the Ottoman Eastern frontier.

By 1511, however, at the onset of a new Ottoman succession crisis following Bayezid II's prolonged illness, the prospect of "exporting the revolution" back to Anatolia—where much of its momentum had originated—appeared increasingly plausible. Isma'il nonetheless continued to prioritize the consolidation of power in Iran. In contrast, within Ottoman territories the Qizilbash, now joined by one of Bayezid's sons, destabilized multiple institutions, including Sufi lodges. The decisive turn came under Bayezid's successor, Selim I, who responded with a competitive, and explicitly counterrevolutionary, messianic strategy. He brought the conflict into Safavid territory, framing the Qizilbash sedition as an apocalyptic eruption of Gog and Magog (Arjomand 2023, 119). This trope had circulated for centuries, even prior to the Mongol invasions, to denounce the influx of Turkish nomadic forces into the ecumene (Yılmaz 2018, 246). As Selim I moved decisively against Isma'il, the Safavid ruler completed his transition from Imami Mahdi to Persianate monarch and redirected his efforts toward building the institutions of a durable state. In doing so, he relied heavily on former Sufi masters and Timurid notables who had previously occupied high-ranking administrative and military positions. Simultaneously, he condemned several leaders of the Qizilbash uprisings in Ottoman lands as betrayers of "his father," Bayezid, inaugurating a restorative trend that would later be carried further by Shah 'Abbas I (r. 1587–1629). To anchor the legitimacy of his rule, Isma'il increasingly emphasized *walaya* as the defining attribute of the *khandan al-walaya* (or *velayat*), the House of *walaya*, now decisively modeled on the figure of 'Ali as the exemplary *wali Allah* (Arjomand 2023, 102–105, 110; 2025, 254). Even as Safavid power and legitimacy solidified in Iran, endemic insurrections by Qizilbash-linked Turkmen tribes continued to afflict Ottoman territories well into the early 17th century, if not beyond. These movements posed not only a persistent security threat but also undermined Ottoman legitimacy by sustaining 'Alid narratives and loyalties that remained popular within the empire's borders. Their resonance was amplified by the circulation of vernacular literature—stories, songs, and poems—especially in regions bordering the Safavid realm. Throughout its duration, Qizilbash sedition articulated *walaya* in consistently radical and messianic terms, diverging sharply from the more disciplined and court-centered discourse prevailing in Ottoman scholarly and administrative milieus. In this context, figures who migrated to Ottoman lands from the former Aq Qoyunlu domains conquered by Shah Isma'il assumed particular importance. Among them was the previously mentioned Bidlisi, whose role was central in shaping a "counterrevolutionary" Ottoman version of what Arjomand has described as "realized messianism." This project required anchoring legitimacy in the political cosmology of Ibn 'Arabi. Selim's campaigns against the Safavids followed closely on his war against the Mamluks, including the conquest of Damascus in 1516—a city of special symbolic value for the Ottomans, not least because it was where Ibn 'Arabi spent his final years and was buried (Arjomand 2023, 102–105, 110, 116–117; 2025, 254; see also Melvin-Koushki 2018, 360).[7]

Not by chance, while in Damascus Selim I endowed a shrine and a mosque dedicated to Ibn 'Arabi, an act that sanctioned the Greatest Master's status as an overarching patron *wali* and *qutb* of the Ottoman *dawla*. Bidlisi, who accompanied the Ottoman ruler during the conquest of the city, played a pivotal role in consolidating this political cosmology within the reigning Ottoman knowledge-power equation. A pseudo-epigraphic work, *al-Shajara al-Nu'maniyya fi-l-Dawla al-Uthmaniyya* ("The Crimson Tree in the Ottoman State"), apocryphally attributed to Ibn 'Arabi, crowned the Ottoman dynasty as the final worldly power before the End of Time. Concomitantly, Bidlisi stood out for repeatedly calling Selim I the Caliph of Allah during the Syrian and Egyptian campaigns. Yılmaz does not fully corroborate Arjomand's observation that Bidlisi's construal of the "new" Caliphate lacked support among Ottoman scholars who adhered to juridical expressions of the "old" Caliphate. Instead, Yılmaz argues that the Ottoman reappropriation of caliphal authority was consummated through a durable long-term trend grounded in a carefully calibrated mix of continuity and rupture with the 'Abbasid title. Most notably, Ibn 'Arabi's political cosmology was appropriated and defended even by leading jurists. This process entailed a partial sanitation of Akbarian thought and, more broadly, a stabilization of what Melvin-Koushki has aptly called the "quicksilver category" of *walaya*, enabling it—especially in the face of the Safavid challenge—to operate in a distinctly counterrevolutionary register. As will become clearer in the next chapter, the thought of the Greatest Master proved particularly well suited to the form of triumphant, yet circular and associative, sovereignty that crystallized in the age of Süleyman the Magnificent (Yılmaz 2018, 18, 253–267; Markiewicz 2019, 270–274; Arjomand 2023, 121–123; see also Salvatore 2016, 188).

It is worth recalling that the architrave of Ibn 'Arabi's political cosmology—culminating in the idea of rule by the *awliya'* and the *qutb*—postulated the governance of both the seen and unseen worlds by a saintly body that remained structurally removed from public visibility. This raises a crucial question: what enabled historical rulers, most famously Süleyman the Magnificent, to acquire the titles of Pole and Caliph within what Yılmaz (2018, 205) has defined as "a context of complex and overlapping imageries of the caliphate and poleship"? The question becomes even more acute in light of a tradition, already present in early Ottoman frontier lore, according to which the convergence of caliphal authority and poleship properly belongs to the summit of the invisible hierarchy of *awliya'* assisting the rulers, rather than to the rulers themselves. An authoritative systematization of this problem was articulated in two closely related works by Yiğitbaşı Veli (d. 1505), a scholar affiliated with the Halveti *tariqa*. Titled *Tabakat al-Awliya'* ("Ranks of Saints"), these works ingeniously argued that the old Caliphate itself was an instantiation of poleship primarily accruing to the *awliya'*, a claim reinforced by the fact that all *turuq* traced their lineages back to either Abu Bakr or 'Ali—the first and the last of the Rightly-Guided Caliphs. From this perspective, the *abdalan* could be seen as occupying high, though visible, ranks within the saintly hierarchy, thereby playing a crucial mediating role: assisting Ottoman rulers while maintaining liaison with the invisible ranks of the *awliya'*. Within this framework, the relationship between the *qutb* and the historical ruler who bore the title of Caliph—specifically, the ruler's subordination to the Pole—remained largely implicit rather than formally codified. For this reason, the model did not yield a consistent theory of two distinct powers, spiritual and temporal. Power was always understood as singular and cosmic in nature; the relevant bifurcation was not between spiritual and temporal authority but between the visible and invisible worlds. Consequently, the ruler's authority was not undermined but ultimately reinforced by this political cosmology, precisely because the Pole—at the apex of the hierarchy of *rijal al-ghayb* ("men of the unseen")—could never, by definition, visibly interfere with governance.

Ultimately, for Ibn 'Arabi the powers of the Pole and the Caliph were, in reality, one and the same. His radically monistic—though internally differentiated rather than hierarchically dualistic—political onto-cosmology posited that visible rulership must consistently appear as receiving and manifesting God's beautiful names. It was therefore incumbent upon the ruler to configure authority in a publicly legible way as the dispenser of justice, thereby anchoring sovereignty in a cosmically grounded yet historically articulated legitimacy (Yılmaz 2018, 18, 203–205). Ibn 'Arabi's theory was authoritatively echoed in the age of Süleyman the Magnificent by the work *al-'Adliyya al-Süleymaniyya*, attributed to a Şirvani of otherwise unspecified biography. This work, which elevated justice (*ʿadl*) to a cosmic principle and anchored it to the Süleymanic dispensation, belongs to a panegyric-juridical subgenre produced by scholars operating in the orbit of the court in order to consolidate an exemplary legitimist discourse. As such, it was calibrated to address multiple audiences and proved fully acceptable both to the Ottoman rulers and to the administrative elite (ibid., 202–204). The turn to accomplished justice in the Süleymanic age, that the title of the book clearly indicated, did not contradict what Cornell Fleischer (1992) famously identified as Süleyman's conscious attempt, especially in the first part of his long reign, to posture as a realized Mahdi of wisdom: literally a new Solomon (*Süleyman*) of the world, inheriting and sealing the Caliphate at the zenith of Ottoman power. The dense sequence of messianic and juridical shibboleths of sovereignty, unique as it may appear, should therefore be read as the culmination of more than a century of concerted efforts by court scholars to invest Ottoman power with the highest legitimacy of a Caliphate. At that historical juncture, the caliphal title represented the most resplendent, but also the most resilient, flower in what had become a kaleidoscopic garland of sovereign attributes verging on predestination. This assemblage of titles simultaneously teased, treasured, and domesticated the messianic sensibilities of the age into a vision of universal rule oriented toward the End of Time.

Not by chance, one of the ruling epithets acquired by Süleyman was *akhir al-zaman*, a designation that, already present in the Earlier Middle Period, acquired a renewed and politically charged meaning in the context of early-modern state formation beginning with Timur. Nor was it accidental that the same title was appropriated by Süleyman's contemporary and archrival, the Safavid ruler Shah Tahmasb I (r. 1524–1576). Against this background, it is hardly surprising—as in Yılmaz's pointed formulation—that "[t]he best known of all Mahdis was none other than the one who was most disturbed by popular messianism, Suleyman" (Yılmaz 2018, 267). Even less surprising, then, is the fact that this apogee of "realized" messianism in the Islamic ecumene was seamlessly folded into Süleyman's now indelible status as *Qanuni*, or Lawgiver (Melvin-Koushki 2018, 359–370; Şahin 2023, 228–232). It would therefore be myopic to situate the two appellations of Mahdi and *Qanuni* at opposite ends of a charismatic spectrum, as if the former were purely esoteric and spiritual while the latter were clearly exoteric and mundane. Their mutual coherence lies precisely in the fact that only their combination could warrant a redemption of the Khaldunian sociopolitical cycle. That the legal stabilization of the *dawla* required a messianic mantle should not be surprising. This outcome had already been foreshadowed in the Almohad prototype and was also echoed, *mutatis mutandis*, in early-modern Europe's claims to absolute sovereignty, in the processes that led to the construction of the Leviathan and the sanctioning of the Westphalian state—issues to be addressed in Chapter 9.

It should further be noted that a key segment of the Ottoman bureaucratic and intellectual elite converged on the idea of making the sovereign the supreme warrantor of justice in ways that folded the legacy of post-Mongol states back into the symbolic horizon of the ʿAbbasid Caliphate. While the conflict with the Safavids continued to rage, Lütfi Paşa (d. 1564), one of Süleyman's grand viziers, together with other authors, banked on restoring the primacy of the caliph as dispenser of justice without contradicting the Sufi-inflected discourse of *walaya* and mahdiship. This move, while well suited to the Persianate model of rulership, also refined the renewed Caliphate through the selective appropriation of juridical discourse. It was reinforced by translations of works by Mamluk scholars whose sensibilities remained closer to the post-ʿAbbasid Khaldunian conundrum of the Middle Periods than to the post-Mongol legitimating formulas dominant in the Persianate zone. Within this framework, the Süleymanic dispensation succeeded in co-opting, under the Persianate umbrella of the *adab-siyasa* discourse, a renewed elaboration of the older conception of the Caliphate as succession to Prophet Muhammad. The political *adab* of the Süleymanic era thus favored a partial return to the classical idea of the Caliphate as the institution charged with applying the *shariʿa* as a means of guaranteeing justice on earth. Not unlike his illustrious predecessor Mehmed II, Süleyman sealed his dispensation—at the genealogical climax of a realized messianism whose onset reaches back to the previous century—by endowing a monumental complex in Istanbul whose portal celebrated him simultaneously as Caliph, Conqueror, and Shadow of God. *Pace* all taxonomies distinguishing putatively revolutionary from counterrevolutionary forms of messianism among Safavids and Ottomans, it is possible to recognize that both polities shared a deep investment in a mode of "realized messianism." This investment functioned as a necessary means of countering the disintegration of the nomadic patrimonialism from which their polities had emerged, by instituting forms of statehood no longer at the mercy of a Khaldunian cycle (Şahin 2013, 142–145; Yılmaz 2018, 166–167, 274; Arjomand 2023, 122).

Notes

1. Both authors' lives spanned the late-14th to mid-15th century, but the exact dates are uncertain.
2. This adjective notoriously covers the intellectual legacy of Ibn 'Arabi as *al-shaykh al-akbar* and his followers.
3. Another leading voice that contributed to redesigning the Caliphate after the civil war was Musannifek, whom we already encountered in Chapter 6. Even though he provided a more practical view of the Caliphate, wrapped within standards of Persianate rulership, he specified that the institution is grounded on self-governance and culminates in its highest form, *al-khilafa al-akbariyya*, to be bestowed on the *qutb al-aqtab* (the Supreme Pole). He was very explicit in spelling out this *walaya* as coinciding with the office of *wali al-amr*, representing an exquisitely executive bundle of ruling functions. Yılmaz shows that this less mystically intense, and rather exoteric, conception of the Caliphate was more typical of Sufi lineages claiming a *silsila* going back to Abu Bakr rather than 'Ali. It was inspired more by the Mevlevis and the heritage of Rumi rather than the teachings of Ibn 'Arabi or the ethos of the *abdalan* (Yılmaz 2018, 135–150).
4. According to Christopher Markiewicz (2019), rather than acting as an architect of Ottoman political cosmology, Bidlisi worked primarily as a skilled intermediary who translated and adapted late-medieval Perso-Islamic models of kingship—shaped in Timurid and Aq Qoyunlu milieus—to the Ottoman context. His contribution lay in refracting existing idioms of rulership into forms usable by the Ottoman court, rather than in delivering a distinctively Ottoman conception of the Caliphate.
5. It is too often neglected that the very idea and discipline of "theology" has a specific European genealogy, including—and especially in—its institutionalization. The fundamental divergence between the instituting processes in Europe and in the Islamic ecumene has been preliminarily sketched in Chapter 4 and will be examined in greater depth in Chapter 9, as well as in the Conclusion, where its broader implications for the formation of knowledge-power regimes and statehood will be drawn out more systematically.
6. Historians tend to use a wide range of terms to capture the rich assortment of ideas and titles—above all that of the Mahdi—which I subsume here under the heading of messianism. Millennialism, millenarianism, chiliasm (more or less synonyms), and apocalypticism all figure prominently alongside messianism and even "mahdism." Although these terms point to distinct dimensions of the messianic idea and its historical unfolding—and although most historians (including the historical sociologist Arjomand in his recent trilogy: Arjomand 2022; 2023; 2025) are fully aware of these differences—they are often,

though not always, used rather freely and at times interchangeably. To avoid confusion, I have chosen in this volume to employ only messianism and its adjective messianic. That said, it is useful to specify that the apocalyptic dimension—signaling the imminence of the End of Time—while not absent in revolutionary outbreaks of the Earlier Middle Period, such as the Shiʿi Imami Fatimids in North Africa or even the Almohads (see Chapter 4), became more prominent in oppositional movements that developed throughout the Later Middle Periods, notably with the Safawiyya prior to the foundation of its own *dawla*. One may also add that millenarianism, in its early-modern context, most often refers to the anticipated turn of the Islamic millennium, which fell in 1591–1592 CE (1000 AH). From this limited angle—which does not do full justice to the broader spectrum of meanings encompassed by messianism, including the idea of Rum as a "promised land" for Turkmen nomadic migrants and Persianate Sufi masters—one might characterize the Ottomans, particularly after the Süleymanic zenith of power, as post-millenarian rather than, throughout the conflict with the Safavids, "countermillennial." The latter term is used by Arjomand (2025, 11) in the more general sense of countering the radical messianism of Sufi-inspired rebellions.

7. While primarily corresponding to *walaya*, *velayat* is, as previously noted, semantically invariant. As such, in different—mostly later—administrative contexts it also came to encompass the meaning of *wilaya*, without implying a conceptual rupture between spiritual proximity and the exercise of authority.

References

Arjomand, Said Amir. 2022. *Messianism and Sociopolitical Revolution in Medieval Islam*. Oakland, CA: University of California Press.

Arjomand, Said Amir. 2023. *Revolutions of the End of Time: Apocalypse, Revolution and Reaction in the Persianate World*. Leiden: Brill.

Arjomand, Said Amir. 2025. *Kings and Dervishes: Sufi World Renunciation and the Symbolism of Kingship in the Persianate World*. Oakland, CA: University of California Press.

Elmore, Gerald T. 1999. *Islamic Sainthood in the Fullness of Time: Ibn al-ʿArabī's Book of the Fabulous Gryphon*. Leiden: Brill.

Krstić, Tijana, and Derin Terzioğlu, eds. 2022. *Entangled Confessionalizations? Dialogic Perspectives on the Politics of Piety and Community Building in the Ottoman Empire, 15th–18th Centuries*. Piscataway, NJ: Gorgias Press.

Markiewicz, Christopher. 2019. *The Crisis of Kingship in Late Medieval Islam: Persian Emigres and the Making of Ottoman Sovereignty*. Cambridge: Cambridge University Press.

Melvin-Koushki, Matthew. 2018. "Early Modern Islamicate Empire: New Forms of Religiopolitical Legitimacy." In *The Wiley Blackwell History of Islam*, edited by Armando Salvatore et al., 353–76. Oxford: Wiley Blackwell.

Mir-Kasimov, Orkhan. 2014. "Introduction: Conflicting Synergy of Patterns of Religious Authority in Islam." In *Unity in Diversity: Mysticism, Messianism and the Construction of Religious Authority in Islam*, edited by Orkhan Mir-Kasimov, 1–20. Leiden: Brill.

Moin, A. Azfar. 2012. *The Millennial Sovereign: Sacred Kingship and Sainthood in Islam*. New York: Columbia University Press.

Moin, A. Azfar. 2018. "The *'Ulama'* as Ritual Specialists: Cosmic Knowledge and Political Rituals." In *The Wiley Blackwell History of Islam*, edited by Armando Salvatore et al., 377–96. Oxford: Wiley Blackwell.

Rahimi, Babak. 2018. "The Consolidation of Sunni and Shi'i Legitimacies." In *The Wiley Blackwell History of Islam*, edited by Armando Salvatore et al., 311–28. Oxford: Wiley Blackwell.

Şahin, Kaya. 2013. *Empire and Power in the Reign of Süleyman: Narrating the Sixteenth-Century Ottoman World*. Cambridge: Cambridge University Press.

Şahin, Kaya. 2023. *Peerless among Princes: The Life and Times of Sultan Süleyman*. Oxford: Oxford University Press.

Salvatore, Armando. 2016. *The Sociology of Islam: Knowledge, Power and Civility*. Oxford: Wiley Blackwell.

Salvatore, Armando. 2018. "Sufi Articulations of Civility, Globality, and Sovereignty." *Journal of Religious and Political Practice* 4 (2): 156–74.

Salvatore, Armando. 2020. "East of Westphalia: Shaping the Body-Politic Via Institutional Charisma." In *Political Theologies and Development in Asia: Transcendence, Sacrifice and Aspiration*, edited by Giuseppe Bolotta et al., 18–39. Manchester: Manchester University Press.

Yılmaz, Hüseyin. 2018. *Caliphate Redefined: The Mystical Turn in Ottoman Political Thought*. Princeton, NJ: Princeton University Press.

8

THE *TADBIR* OF *WALAYA*

Explaining the Associative Rationale of Statehood in the Ecumene

Vicious Cycle vs. Virtuous Circle? A Critical Reappraisal by the Carriers of Statecraft

By the early 16th century, the charisma of rulership embodied in the saint-philosopher-king had been fitted into patterns of reflexive stabilization of the *dawla* within the increasingly self-preserving shell of a more integrated instituting process. Significantly, this was also the period in which, within the Ottoman Empire, discussions of legitimate rulership—supported by a growing number of original works and translations spanning a wide range of genres—began to circulate far beyond restricted circles of elite scholars. These debates were increasingly sustained by a burgeoning body of documents produced not only by high-ranking bureaucrats-literati, but also by middle-level and provincial administrators, together with their interlocutors in what was gradually taking shape as a broader reading public. The expansion of bureaucratic, educational, and judicial institutions, along with the growing number of personnel trained to staff them, provided the material infrastructure for this shift. Paradoxically, despite the doubling of the empire's territory in the first half of the 16th century, the supply of trained personnel came to exceed the number of available positions. At the same time, increasing numbers of learned and skilled individuals clustered around high dignitaries and bureaucrats. This conjuncture generated both unrest and curiosity. It fostered a shared interest in the instituting process itself—its internal logic, its promises, and its constraints—as well as in its relevance to individual ambitions and collective aspirations. In this climate, questions of legitimate and effective rulership moved to the foreground. Reflecting this trend, during the Süleymanic age the traditionally expansive *adab-siyasa* complex began to coalesce around a more identifiable core, owing to the rise of a type of book that manuscript copyists increasingly labeled *Siyasetname*, that is, quite simply, "book on government/governance/ politics."

A leading author of the age, Taşköprizade (d. 1561), explicitly argued that *ʿilm al-siyasa* should not remain the monopoly of the ruling elite but ought to be open to the cultivation of subjects more broadly, since it was the science that determined welfare and civility—an argument he framed through the classical philosophical trope of the "virtuous city." This development is all the more significant given that *siyasa*, as a field within the broader complex, continued to resist crystallization into a sharply delimited subgenre. Yet, symptomatically, the shared labeling of this body of writings—and the widespread assumption that it originated with the work of the celebrated Seljuq vizier Nizam al-Mulk (d. 1092)—signaled the emergence of a reading public that expected to be instructed on, and to debate, matters of *siyasa*. The very perception of *siyasa* as a distinct field reflected a desire for works conceived as internally coherent handbooks of what we might call administrative "best practices" (Yılmaz 2018, 12, 40–46).

At the same time, a continuity was often posited between this literature and the Persianate advice literature addressed to rulers, conventionally labeled by Orientalists—by analogy with medieval and early modern European works—as "mirrors for princes" (*specula principum*), despite clear shifts in literary style and textual architecture. In other words, while the anchoring of *siyasa* in *adab* was further reinforced, the *adab-siyasa* discursive complex was also becoming more internally articulated and differentiated. Crucially, this process unfolded in tandem with the growing emphasis on the functional autonomy of the state. Far from displacing a Sufi-inspired political cosmology, this emphasis rendered it ever more indispensable, to the point of being taken largely for granted. Indeed, the enduring—and in some respects deepening—Sufi inflection of *adab-siyasa* discourse was evident even at the level of book titles, signaling a need to address the sensibilities of an expanding and increasingly composite reading public attuned to a Sufi vocabulary. Where this inflection did not appear through an explicit classification under *tasawwuf*, it nonetheless operated as the most effective means of reaching multiple, often overlapping—and not infrequently conflicting—constituencies. The benchmark for refining, and even reforming, governance thus remained the pursuit of the exemplar of *al-insan al-kamil*, a figure no longer (if ever) reducible to a narrowly "spiritual" model. Rather than being eroded by the growing stress on state autonomy, this paradigm became even more necessary as its cosmopolitical foundation, however further complexified. The holdings of the palace library of Bayezid II offer striking evidence of how the early-modern period ultimately sealed—indeed, canonized—the mainstreaming of a Sufi political cosmology that had been in the making throughout the Middle Periods. What emerged was not a retreat from cosmological foundations of power, but their stabilization and routinization within the apparatus of governance itself (Yılmaz 2018, 64–69).

On the other hand, it should be noted that throughout the 16th century the ruling apparatus found itself in a condition of continuous adaptation. This was in part necessitated by the challenge of integrating the highly diverse administrative structures and regulatory regimes of newly conquered territories, stretching from Iraq to Hungary—a process that decisively affected the Ottoman state and altered its modes of governance. Such developments encouraged a growing emphasis on the effectiveness of the institutional network, accompanied by an increasing awareness of the relative autonomy of the *dawla*. And yet, even as this institutional self-consciousness deepened, the symbolic and charismatic dimensions of sovereignty were not eclipsed. Thus, while Süleyman's vizier Lütfi Paşa and the head of the chancery Celalzade (ca. 1490–1567)—both staunch statesmen—did not hesitate to refer to the emperor as the Mahdi of the End Time. Despite continuing conquests and fierce contests for universal rulership, now also involving rising Western European powers, Süleyman's reign was ultimately remembered above all through his epithet of *Qanuni*, as introduced at the end of the previous chapter. This designation consecrated him as a legislating sovereign who oriented his rule toward building a stable and prosperous *dawla* as the durable shell of *'umran* and its instituting process. The caliphal dimension of Süleyman's rule became itself associated with his role in attempting to contain the early colonial aggressions of the Portuguese, who sought to impose trade monopolies along key commercial routes of the Indian Ocean. Regardless of the multiple motives that underlay Süleyman's interventions to shield the flourishing maritime trade networks of the Islamic ecumene from European encroachments, this strategy accrued to his reputation as a righteous Sunni universal ruler—indeed, as a Caliph of rectitude. According to this narrative, Süleyman appeared as a sovereign committed to the welfare of the ecumene even in oceanic regions far removed from the empire's conflict-ridden frontiers, and where the pragmatics of everyday life prevailed over the clash of crystallizing confessional identities, such as those affecting the Ottoman–Safavid conflict (Casale 2011, 129–150; Lambourn 2011; Yılmaz 2018, 267).

Nevertheless, to grasp the full significance of Süleyman's paramount attribute of *Qanuni* at this crucial stage in the consolidation and stabilization of the Ottoman *dawla*, it is necessary to revisit the meaning of *qanun*. If translated as dynastic or sultanic law, its meaning is drastically impoverished. While *qanun* was sometimes associated with *yasa(q)*—the Mongol concept briefly examined in Chapter 7—it was in fact derived from the Greek *kanon*, with its Latin equivalent *canon*, inherited through the East Roman (Byzantine) administrative, fiscal, and legal tradition. Yet, not unlike the Mongol *yasa*, Ottoman *qanun* was also rooted in a pre-Islamic, tribally and even shamanically inflected will of the commander. In this two-layered synthesis of Mongol and Roman legacies, the former might appear to function merely as a symbolic marker of sovereignty. This impression, however, dissolves once we consider the structural continuity of *qanun* with a form of law affirming collective rights acquired through *ghaza*, prior to its transformation into an administrative rationale associated with ruling prerogatives. In this sense, *qanun* articulated a principle of distributive justice among the grandees of a *dawla*, grounded in accrued merits and recognized rights. Not by chance, some of the criticism directed against the institutional and legal innovations of imperial centralization invoked precisely this time-honored dimension of *qanun* (Yılmaz 2018, 244). At the same time, and hardly paradoxically, Süleyman's title of *Qanuni* also reflected the sustained effort of leading jurists and administrators to harmonize *qanun* with *shari'a* through the continuous production of decrees and regulations characteristic of the new era. This labor of synthesis was legitimated by the very evolution of the *dawla*, whose Islamic and caliphal credentials had to meet Khaldunian conditions of effectiveness. The underlying question at this juncture was whether—and to what extent—this sovereign synthesis could secure a long-term neutralization of the cyclicality and instability diagnosed by Ibn Khaldun.

After the apparent peak of Ottoman power under Süleyman, the imperial *dawla* continued to flourish and even expand well into the following century, seemingly contradicting Ibn Khaldun's prognosis. Yet, already in the late 16th century, a number of Ottoman scholars began to mobilize direct or indirect Khaldunian tropes to reflect on whether the empire's trajectory carried within it the risk—or even the inevitability—of decline. Clearly, the spectacular rise of Ottoman power at the threshold of the modern era did not relegate the work of the Maghrebi scholar to a brilliant yet ultimately forgettable chapter of intellectual history, relevant only to a premodern age—the Middle Periods—marked by recurrent sociopolitical upheaval and institutional instability. Quite the opposite, interest in the *Muqaddima* arguably reached its historical zenith within the Islamic ecumene as the Ottoman 17th century unfolded. Even when articulated through a retrospective grammar of lost glory, this was the moment when a distinctly critical intellectual discourse emerged among multiple categories of scholars, both those embedded in courtly and central administrative milieus and those operating at some distance from them. This discourse adopted a diagnostic stance toward the fragility of the sociopolitical bond and, more explicitly, toward its reflection in the vulnerability of state administration—a thematic core that resonated powerfully with the legacy of Ibn Khaldun's thought.

This critical sensibility found expression in pamphlets and treatises denouncing the rise of centrifugal forces whose material causes were readily identifiable, including rampant inflation, chronic fiscal crisis, and military overstretch.[1] Khaldunian motifs surfaced in this literature of "decline and reform" well before the renewed engagement with Ibn Khaldun culminated in the Ottoman Turkish translation of the first five chapters of the *Muqaddima* by Pirizade[2] (1674–1749). What this indicates is not a sudden rediscovery, but a prolonged process of appropriation and reinterpretation. Scholars of successive generations who took part in these debates discussed Ibn Khaldun's views in diverse ways: sometimes by completing themes he had left undeveloped, sometimes by integrating them with the historical transformations that had occurred between his time and theirs, and often by privileging the specific trajectory of the Ottoman Empire. Over time, the debate came to mirror a broader reconfiguration of how history, society, and politics were conceptualized—not only among leading segments of the Ottoman intellectual and bureaucratic elite, but also among rank-and-file officials. In this sense, the Khaldunian framework functioned as a foil through which a reality check on the ideal of universal rulership within the Islamic ecumene was conducted (Salzmann 2004, 76; see also Salvatore 2016, 185).

At the core of this reflection lay the question of how the *dawla* might affirm its autonomy from dynastic contingency and sultanic caprice by acknowledging its reliance on a rational, reform-oriented, and increasingly self-conscious bureaucracy. This bureaucratic core comprised both the bureaucrats-literati, commonly identified as the *kalemiyye* (the men of the pen, or secretarial class), and the religio-juridical scholars, designated as the *ilmiyye* (the men of learning, especially in *fiqh*). The emerging consensus was that the endurance of the *dawla* depended less on charismatic sovereignty than on the institutional coherence and ethical responsibility of these knowledge-bearing strata. As argued in a now classic study by Cornell Fleischer (1986), the first major figure to articulate this reflexive engagement with Ibn Khaldun was the historian and chancery official Mustafa ʿAli (d. 1600). Writing shortly before the onset of the 17th century—at what was at least retrospectively perceived as the apogee of Ottoman power—this "bureaucrat and intellectual" subjected Süleymanic claims to universal sovereignty to a sober historical assessment and found them dangerously fragile. Closely connected to leading court bureaucrats and scholars, Mustafa ʿAli addressed mounting anxieties about institutional decay in a wide range of writings spanning multiple genres. These interventions articulated fears that the empire, having reached its zenith under Süleyman the Magnificent, now faced the risk of systemic unraveling. This conjuncture may thus be described as a distinctly "Khaldunian moment" in the growing self-awareness of the Ottoman elite. It marked the point at which they began to apprehend themselves as the primary site of production of the knowledge–power equation upon which the fate of the *dawla* ultimately depended.

Among Mustafa ʿAli's various arguments and tropes, two stand out with particular clarity. The first reflects an emerging awareness that the post-Süleymanic Ottoman Empire had become one regional power formation among others, rather than a polity still moving toward an uncontested horizon of world dominion. Süleyman himself, Mustafa ʿAli acknowledged, was neither a new Alexander nor a second Chingiz (Fleischer 1984, 54; Melvin-Koushki 2018, 371). This assessment amounted to an early recognition of the potential vulnerability of the Ottoman *dawla* to a Khaldunian cycle of rise and decline. The second, and more consequential, line of argument followed directly from this recognition and took shape in Mustafa ʿAli's sustained engagement with the long-term logic of the Circle of Justice or Equity, *Daʾirat al-ʿAdl* (Ott. *Daʾiretüʾl-ʿAdalet*; Fleischer 1986). This formulation designated a motif or aphorism that had circulated—albeit intermittently—across multiple genres of the *adab–siyasa* complex and had significantly contributed to its internal coherence. Kınalızade (d. 1572), a senior contemporary of Mustafa ʿAli, gave the Circle its canonical Ottoman name. Apocryphally, the aphorism was traced back to a letter allegedly written by Aristotle to his pupil Alexander, advising him on how to establish and preserve a flourishing polity. Historically, however, the motif can be followed back to the High Caliphate, when it was often attributed to the

Sasanian ruler Ardashir, in line with conventions typical of the *adab* strand that later generated the so-called mirrors for princes. Its first extant, unabridged, and systematic articulation appeared in a work known as *Sirr al-Asrar*. Through a series of reformulations—including a version titled *Kitab al-Siyasa*, itself reworking an even earlier Umayyad court text—the aphorism reached a relatively stable form in the 10th century. It subsequently entered European circulation under the title *Secretum Secretorum* (Yavari 2014, 9–16). The aphorism consisted of eight interlinked propositions, each highlighting a crucial relation among ruler, subjects, and army, mediated by key instruments of governance such as law and taxation, with justice or equity functioning as the binding—and animating—principle of the Circle (Darling 2009; 2013a; 2013b). Significantly, Ibn Khaldun himself approvingly reformulated the aphorism at the opening of the *Muqaddima*. He did so as if to suggest that his own project aimed to clarify the conditions under which a *dawla* might achieve the harmony envisioned by the Circle, while also insisting that the inherited teachings of the *adab-siyasa* tradition required supplementation by a new science capable of explaining how virtuous government actually comes into being (Ibn Khaldun 2005 [1967], 41).

In his *Akhlaq-i 'Ala'i* of 1565, Kınalızade—following, directly or indirectly, Ibn Khaldun's reflections—translated the aphorism into a visual schema, rendering it as a circle with eight radiating spokes and naming it emphatically the Circle of Justice or Equity. Fully consistent with the logic of the aphorism, this gesture foregrounded justice as the organizing principle of Süleyman's *Qanuni* dispensation—a golden age of the Ottoman realm and of the Islamic ecumene that, by the later 16th century, was nonetheless increasingly perceived as vulnerably exposed to strain (Darling 2013a, 1, 140). Shortly thereafter, the Circle assumed its definitive Ottoman form through a heavily edited translation of *Sirr al-Asrar* produced in 1571. This version, prefaced and furnished with an extensive introduction by Navali (d. after 1572), was dedicated to Sokollu Mehmed Paşa, the powerful grand vizier of Selim II (r. 1566–1574). Sokollu's tenure has often been identified as marking an epochal shift of effective governmental authority from the person of the ruler to the upper echelons of the bureaucracy. It is precisely this transition that helps explain the intensification of anxiety about the future of the *dawla*, which in turn fueled critical, neo-Khaldunian reflections on the Circle, on political longevity, and on the prosperity of the ecumene. Unsurprisingly, Navali's translation was carefully adapted to the conceptual and technical idiom of contemporary administration. It was further enriched by citations from the Qur'an and the *hadith*, a common feature of the broader *adab* multigenre tradition and especially of the mirrors for princes. Particularly telling is the way Aristotle appears in this text as the grand vizier of the Caliph Alexander, a move that effectively collapsed historical distance and re-inscribed classical authority within an Ottoman political imaginary (Yılmaz 2018, 63, 197–204). As Yılmaz succinctly observes, Navali "eliminated historical distance and made the text a fresh product of Ottoman culture and relevant to current expectations in political thought and government practice" (ibid., 204).

Mustafa 'Ali's reflections matter here not despite, but precisely because he did not directly reference Ibn Khaldun, and it remains uncertain whether he was in fact familiar with his work. Either way, his intervention reveals an internalized Khaldunian affinity in the way he sought explanations for the functioning—or malfunctioning—of the dynamics of the Circle. In this sense, his contribution marked a first high point of a neo-Khaldunian orientation within the Ottoman *adab–siyasa* complex, whose significance was arguably enhanced by its initial, and later recurrent, lack of explicit references to Ibn Khaldun himself (Fleischer 1984). The most prominent scholar to engage Ibn Khaldun directly in the 17th century was Katib Çelebi (1609–1657), whose work contains early traces of a rationalizing agency aimed at rethinking and redressing the sociopolitical institutions of the empire (Zemmin 2019). Katib Çelebi focused in particular on the critical nexus between the charisma of rulership and a conception of justice circulating through relatively autonomous, yet complementary, organs and limbs of the sociopolitical body. He summarized his views in a distinctly "reformist–constitutional" idiom in *Dustur al-'Amal li-Islah al-Khalal* ("Work Blueprint for the Reform of Shortcomings"), a treatise that prioritized confronting the acute fiscal crisis gripping the empire in the 17th century. In this work, Katib Çelebi reactivated the long-standing metaphor of society as an organic body, explicitly situating it within a consideration of the Khaldunian cycle. Like several of his contemporaries, he continued to frame his analysis in terms of restoring the lost glory and institutional solidity of the Süleymanic age. Yet he went further than most in opening the way toward a more rigorous search for neo-Khaldunian sociohistorical explanations than those advanced, for instance, by Mustafa Na'ima (1655–1716). This shift was catalyzed by a succession of unprecedented military setbacks, which led many observers to question the very foundations of a *ghazi* empire whose vitality appeared to rest primarily on continued conquest (Hagen and Menchinger 2014; Sariyannis 2019, 285–322).

The Institutional Texture of the *Dawla*: The Role of *Tadbir*

Seen from a longer-term perspective, the trajectory that marked an increasingly critical self-understanding among the bureaucrats-literati—and of the ruling tradition they inherited—was nourished by an appreciation of the *dawla* as an autonomous institution and, as such, the peak institution of the ecumene. On the one hand, the political astro-cosmology underpinning ruling prerogatives continued to provide a necessary condition for conceiving a "turn of fortune" (*dawla*) projected toward universal rule—however idealized—at the service of justice and prosperity in the unfolding of *ʿumran* across the ecumene. On the other hand, the concrete challenges and vicissitudes of governing territories and populations were precisely what fostered an awareness of the critical hinge between intellectual labor and administrative practice. The outcome was a delicate institutional balance in which the *dawla* appeared as a "state" defined by a distinctive tension between dynamism and steadiness. Suh an insight rested on recognizing that the state's autonomy was primarily embodied in institutional carriers rather than in personal authority alone. The neo-Khaldunian momentum in the Ottoman Empire thus amounted to a simultaneously humbling and energizing recognition: the state is by definition post-messianic, cannot be frozen into a blissful dispensation like the Süleymanic one, and is subject to perpetual becoming. It therefore demands continuous refinement in the day-to-day navigation of tasks and problems, supported by the conceptual and meta-institutional apparatus of *adab-siyasa*.

A full examination of how Ibn Khaldun's style, epistemology, and method shaped the vocabulary and imaginary of Ottoman bureaucrats-literati—including leading religious scholars—between the late 16th and the 18th centuries cannot be undertaken here. Nonetheless, the Khaldunian problematic serves as an indispensable foil for understanding the nuanced and adaptive processes through which early-modern patterns of rulership were produced and legitimated. These patterns were characterized by rationalizing and reflexive bureaucratic steering, oriented toward both the power of the state and the well-being of its subjects. This orientation represented, in effect, the reverse side of Ibn Khaldun's theory of the cyclical character of the *dawla* (Menchinger 2018, 459–460). Once the cycle of the *dawla* could be so inverted, the Circle of Justice/Equity often emerged as the preferred diagnostic and reformist schema. It encapsulated the idea that the charisma of rulership can be sustained only through the circularity of mutual commitments, guaranteed by a sufficient degree of relational justice. The failure of even a single linkage or transmission among the spokes of the Circle threatened the onset of sociopolitical disorder. Yet, to grasp the full implications of the Ottoman Circle, it is necessary to rewind the narrative slightly, as was done in the previous chapter on the trajectory of the Caliphate's idea and institution. This step guards against the assumption that the post-Mongol order amounted to a comprehensive reset of the parameters of "sovereignty." We should therefore briefly revisit elements inherited from *Sirr al-Asrar*, often known under its alternate—and more articulate and authoritative—title, *Kitab al-Siyasa fi-Tadbir al-Riyasa*, which may be rendered, imperfectly, as "The Book of Governance in the Management of Rulership." In this work, *siyasa* appears as the central concern and, in many renderings of the Circle, as the label of one of its principal stations or spokes. Equally significant, however, is the second key term in the title, specifying the locus and mode of governance: *tadbir*. Fully apprehending its meaning is essential for understanding the fine grain of the process through which the autonomization of the state came to be conceived as the telos of an instituting process sustained by an expanding culture of governance.

Against this background, it is useful to return to the formative moment of the *adab-siyasa* discursive apparatus itself. In *Disenchanting the Caliphate*, Hayrettin Yücesoy (2023) reminds us that this apparatus was first articulated during the high point of the High Caliphate. As we saw in the previous chapters, the initial surge of this alternative approach—one that re-signified the Caliphate—did at first represent a challenge to the theory of the Imamate, which was primarily supported by jurists. At the same time, and for the reasons laid out in Chapter 2, we also acknowledged that the *adab-siyasa* complex enabled the instituting process alongside, though not necessarily against, the formation of mainstream conceptions of legitimate rulership. This was all the more evident during the most unstable phases of the Middle Periods, in Khaldunian terms. Over time, *siyasa*—regardless of explicit attempts at delegitimating it, such as those advanced by Maqrizi (see Chapter 5)—became a far less contentious notion than it may have been at the outset of the process. It even underwent a full, if provocative, cooptation into assertions of the primacy of *shari'a*, most famously in the arguments advanced by Ibn Taymiyya. Yet at this early stage it was not *siyasa* in the abstract, but rather its articulation and practical implementation through *tadbir*, that came to the fore as the operative core of the *adab-siyasa* complex (see Al-Daghistani 2022, 61–62; Coulon 2023, 597).

It is precisely in order to illuminate these beginnings, at a crucial juncture of the High Caliphate, that Yücesoy (2023, 142) carefully guides the reader through the meaning and significance of *tadbir*:

> According to lexicographers, the root verb *dabbara* (from the root *d-b-r*, *dubur*, "the hindmost," "the end") and the verbal noun *tadbīr* connote cleaning up after something or someone; to do, to manage, direct, administer, govern, take care of something or someone; to act prudently with consideration of the issues or results of affairs and exercising, forecasting, or forethinking by anticipating the outcome; to consider or forecast the matter or results of the affair or event; to look into something, consider it, examine it, or study it repeatedly to understand it. It evokes a sense of devising, planning, or strategizing a thing against another because doing so requires consideration of the issues or results of the affair. One says someone manages, conducts, orders, or regulates the affairs of the provinces or country in this sense. It may have been derived from Aramaic, as in Syriac *dabbar*, "to run, govern, administer something." In the qur'anic text, too, as a corresponding contemporaneous dialogic text, it refers to the power and will to govern (direct, regulate, arrange, manage) the affairs (*yudabbiru al-amr*) and the deliberate and careful reflection, mediating and thinking upon something (*yatadabbar*).

As we previously saw, the *Kitab al-Siyasa fi-Tadbir al-Riyasa*, also known as *Sirr al-Asrar*, appeared during the final stretch of the High Caliphate. This was also the period in which, thanks to philosophers such as al-Kindi (d. ca. 866) and al-Balkhi (d. ca. 934), active in the 'Abbasid capital Baghdad, key Aristotelian works—notably the *Nicomachean Ethics* and, more obliquely, the *Politics* (which, significantly, was never translated or paraphrased into Arabic)—were mobilized to articulate an approach to *siyasa* in its nexus with *adab*. This nexus was inflected through the register of Aristotelian practical wisdom or rationality (*phronesis*; see Salvatore 2007). Most notably, al-Balkhi revised Aristotle's notion of politics as a science and instead construed *siyasa* as a craft oriented toward securing the *'imara* of the ecumene—a term sharing both root and meaning with Ibn Khaldun's *'umran*—and the *maslaha* of the people (Arjomand 2025, 93–94). Articulating a comparable vision, yet proving far more influential across the centuries than the philosophers' post-Aristotelian systematizations, the apocryphal *Kitab al-Siyasa fi-Tadbir al-Riyasa* elaborated the connections that would later crystallize into what became the Ottoman Circle. The figure of its purported author, Aristotle, was recast as the embodiment of royal wisdom: a mentor and advisor—indeed, a kind of "grand vizier"—to the prototypical universal monarch, Alexander. This wisdom was enhanced by the capacity to transmit *sirr*, "arcane lore," through methods conventionally labeled magical or talismanic, which can be understood as integral to the reigning political astro-cosmology. At the same time, *tadbir* classically denotes the ordering of the household (*tadbir al-manzil*), a notion that closely matches, in Aristotelian parlance, *oikonomia*. The household thus appears as the most basic cell of human society, requiring thoughtful and reflexive management.

Beyond the household, this conception of rationalized and reflexive management was extended to the Aristotelian *polis*, which in the ecumene could be identified either with the city proper or with a broader sociopolitical realm—both adequately rendered by *madina*, especially in political philosophy and adjacent genres. To these two levels one must add the *tadbir* of the self and the body, a dimension that played a decisive role in the emerging conceptions of the Caliphate explored in previous chapters. This level was ultimately both individual and connective, cosmologically and qur'anically, insofar as it concerned all members of the progeny of Adam and Eve. While the coexistence of what may appear, from a eurocentrically Aristotelian perspective, as "magical" and "rational" components might seem odd, *tadbir* is precisely the point at which practical reason and political astro-cosmology converge. The result is a highly original sociopolitical anthropology that resists assimilation to any neatly bounded "Western" or "Eastern" model. Within this creatively remolded post-Aristotelian horizon, *tadbir* invites further specification. It may be understood as the operative logic—the "operating system," as it were—of the instituting process culminating in *siyasa*, a dynamic sense already conveyed by its verbal form. As such, *tadbir* stands in sharp contrast to the relatively static idea of "institution," which projects a misleading image of consecrated stability and corporate fixity—much as the modern notion of "state" does. Both "institution" and "state" derive from a Latin semantic field of standing or setting, a genealogy that is foreign to the conceptual universe under discussion here (see Chapter 9). The eurocentric projection of this institutional imaginary back onto an alleged Aristotelian authenticity supposedly enshrined in the *Politics* is historically untenable regarding the Islamic ecumene, not least in light of the absence of Roman law and its medieval and early-modern Latin reappropriations of institution, corporation, and statehood (see Chapters 4 and 9).

At the same time, one should avoid the opposite fallacy of reducing the "management" implied by *tadbir* to mere reordering. In a context where institutions are not theopolitically modeled on a charismatic collective person or body, management and its *phronesis*—in a broadly Aristotelian sense—are central not only to *praxis* but also to *poiesis*, to making. In this respect, *tadbir* names a process that creates while it orders and thus provides a more precise term for what we have provisionally—and still eurocentrically—described as the "instituting process." What is at stake here is a mode of making whose processual character, rather than an instituting sovereign fiat, is foregrounded. It is the making of an artisan or engineer—or, for that matter, of an alchemist or magician—rather than creation by a "supernatural" entity. Finally, *tadbir* also functions as a reflective and strategic interface between the habitualizing prism of *adab* and the executing functions of *siyasa*. All three are intelligible only when grasped as integral moments within an unceasing process.[3] This configuration marks not only a divergence from early-modern European trajectories but also a legitimate reworking of Aristotelian categories into what can retrospectively be understood, following Shahab Ahmed (see Introduction and Chapter 1), as "the importance to be Islamic" in generating and managing a distinctive instituting process. By cutting across the private–public dichotomy inherited in Europe from Roman law (see Chapter 4), *tadbir* delineates a continuum that runs through the individual body, crossing the household, and extending to the connective fabric of the ecumene, culminating in the "sovereign." Even if one retains this eurocentric label, sovereignty appears in a fundamentally different light: not resting on a collective body set over and against society, but circularly and associatively embedded within a web of continuously instituted relations (see Chapter 9).

One should also recall that, unlike *siyasa*, the concept of *tadbir* appears in the Qur'an itself, where it carries a clear onto-cosmological sense of infusing things with their proper—indeed, even beautiful—order, not unlike the Greek sense of *kosmos*. This is why, although *tadbir* retained something of this elevated meaning as it evolved from the High Caliphate to the Ottoman era of institutional critique and reflection, it never acquired the theopolitical valence associated with a Pauline economy of salvation (cf. Agamben [2007] 2011). On the one hand, as we have seen, *tadbir* was articulated through an original inflection of the Aristotelian tradition; on the other, it entered into a productive tension with *walaya*, understood as a relational—if differential—configuration of knowledge-power (see Chapters 3 and 7). The art of managing and assembling, in other words, presupposes more than technical know-how: relationality must be known, inhabited, and practiced for one to acquire the capacity to "govern" it. The risk, of course, is to dilute the combined force of *walaya* and *tadbir* into merely "spiritual" or "moral" counsel offered to rulers[4]—or, conversely, into a narrowly "secular" pragmatism of administration[5]—rather than recognizing them as a formidable double engine of the *dawla*, simultaneously legitimizing and operationalizing the instituting of life.

Nasir al-Din al-Tusi (1201–1274) is often identified in the scholarly literature as the thinker who laid the cornerstone for a systematic theorization of *tadbir* within an Aristotelian framework, in which the management of the city is modeled on that of the household (see, e.g., Al-Daghistani 2022, 61–62; see also below in this chapter). Arjomand (2025, 99–100), however, has drawn attention to other contemporaneous figures, such as Siraj al-Din Urmavi (1198–1283), who privileged *siyasa* and reversed the Aristotelian and Tusi-inspired sequence by treating the governance of the polity or city as the model for managing the household—and ultimately the self. In this inversion, Urmavi also likened the ruler's function to that of the heart in the human body. If one recalls the comprehensive understanding of the heart in Sufi thought (see Chapter 3), this move—especially striking in a juristically oriented scholar like Urmavi—can be read as implying that sound *siyasa* and effective *tadbir* ultimately originate in a form of *walaya* inspired by the heart as the primary organ of apprehension. In a pointed yet critical vein, Arjomand (ibid., 173, 206, 212) further situates discussions of *siyasa* and *tadbir*—at times explicitly, at other times through poetic and symbolic idioms—within the ongoing becoming of resilient, if often antagonistic, sub-state formations such as the confraternities, and in particular the *futuwwa*. This institution survived the Mongol onslaught and emerged as a locus of resistance in which a diffuse and "grassroots" form of *tadbir* could be cultivated and transmitted.

As discussed in Chapter 3, al-Nasir's attempted revival of the old Caliphate can be interpreted as an effort to absorb the *walaya* of the *futuwwa* into an institutional armature imposed from above. By contrast, one may suggest that the new Caliphate effectively absorbed a form of *tadbir* that had already been unfolding for centuries within the life-instituting dynamics of the confraternities, through the convergence of the *adab* of spiritual training and the civic codes of the urban professions. At the same time, a process of differentiation and partial emancipation between *tariqa* and *futuwwa* should be noted. In this differentiation, *futuwwa* displayed a greater predisposition toward bottom-up articulations of civic politics and the legitimation of rulership, and thus of the entire *adab–siyasa–tadbir* complex—particularly in contexts of resistance to Mongol and Timurid policies of state centralization from above (Arjomand 2025, 101–104). From Ibn al-Muqaffaʿ at the height of the High Caliphate to the threshold of early modernity, it was this ongoing dialectic between top-down and bottom-up articulations of the *adab-siyasa-tadbir* complex that lent continuity and resilience to the instituting process—arguably far more so than the discontinuous trajectory of the Caliphate itself.

As a reflective awareness of the centrality of the *adab-siyasa-tadbir* complex in the instituting process deepened among the bureaucrats-literati of the early-modern Ottoman Empire, the *Muqaddima* came to function less as a direct source than as a symbol of how a new science capable of grasping the regularities of social and political life could be folded into a practice of governance nourished by *tadbir*. Significantly, while sharing in the apocryphal attribution of the Circle to Aristotle, Ibn Khaldun himself surmised that it had been expounded in Aristotle's *Politics* (Ibn Khaldun 2005 [1967], 41). As already noted, however, this work was never translated into Arabic and, even where it was known in the Islamic ecumene, circulated only through fragmentary and highly mediated receptions—a point repeatedly emphasized by Arjomand (2025, 95). This attribution error is revealing. *Pace* Arjomand, the absence of a translation, paraphrase, or faithful reception of the *Politics* should not be read as a wilful ignorance that caused the Islamic ecumene to "miss the train" of a Western-style political pedagogy supposedly leading to sound institutional understandings of civility and participation—a claim whose problematic legacy will be addressed in Chapter 9. It is more plausible that the *Politics* was neglected because of its limited utility. Any straightforward transposition of the political setting of the Greek *polis* into the notion of *madina* in the ecumene—whether in concrete or idealized form, as in al-Farabi's philosophical constructions—would have required substantial and ultimately unsociological allowances. Most importantly, unlike Aristotle, the dominant analogy between polity and human body in the ecumene could only be articulated through the Neo-Platonic-inflected binary of microcosm and macrocosm inherent in the notion of *walaya*, that is, through what has been described here as a political onto-cosmology. More generally, as Arjomand himself repeatedly stresses, any influence of putatively Aristotelian ideas—including the idea of the Circle, whether authentic or apocryphal—was mediated through Persianate conceptions of rulership and ethical governance, as exemplified even by al-Tusi's *Akhlaq-i Naseri*, itself a rearticulation of Aristotle's *Nicomachean Ethics* (ibid., 98).

As an integral component of *adab*, the aphorism embedded in *Sirr al-Asrar* thus strategically combined a Hellenistic—already post-Aristotelian—and a Persianate wisdom of power. In the making since the high point of the High Caliphate, it is essential for understanding the instituting process in the Islamic ecumene. That process cultivated a sense of continuity with prestigious pre-Islamic formations while generating, within the ecumene, a distinctly cosmopolitical *tadbir*. Yet it was only in the early-modern era that the Circle was transformed from an aspirational ideal into the foil for a consistent methodology of rule, even as it retained a significant symbolic and legitimizing charge. The effective "squaring of the Circle"—that is, moving beyond metaphor to trace the perimeter of a viable form of statehood in the ecumene that could still fully count as "Islamic"—required a series of innovations. These included the systematic valorization of the dynamism of composite, often multi-communal urban economies once the worst effects of the Mongol devastations had receded; the development of new administrative patterns that overlaid earlier networks and flexible institutions with more legitimate and effective mechanisms of territorial and population control, particularly in support of fiscal and military policy; and, ultimately, the appropriation—most fully realized in the Ottoman Empire, heir also to Byzantine imperial traditions—of a conscious capacity and determination to deploy centralized power in order to allocate resources across space to diverse constituencies (Salzmann 2004, 14). Taken together, these developments radiated a diffuse yet powerful sense of legitimacy toward something approaching an idea of the state as an entity distinct from the titles, merits, fortunes—and not least the households and patrimonies—of individual rulers or even of the Ottoman dynasty as a whole, despite its unparalleled longevity. In other words, quite apart from the undoubtedly interesting semantic vicissitudes surrounding elite understandings of the Ottoman version of *dawla* (see Zemmin 2019), what emerges here is a breakthrough in what may be called an institutional culture: an increasingly reflexive grasp of the instituting process itself and of the rules governing its management. Its consolidation marked the onset of what Baki Tezcan has aptly described as a "second Ottoman state," in which "the *devlet* [Ottoman Turkish for *dawla*] of a sultan . . . was now a much more impersonal affair" (Tezcan 2010, 187). This achievement, in turn, underwrote the growing self-awareness among senior bureaucrats that they constituted the enduring spine of the state, regardless of its military, dynastic, and ostensibly "patrimonial" origins.

No *Tadbir* Without *Walaya*?

Yet it would be a grave reductionism—more than a mere anachronism—to interpret the *tadbir* of *siyasa* as a plainly "secular" art of governance, let alone as a Foucauldian *dispositif* of governmentality (Yücesoy 2023, 4, 256). In its full sophistication, the justification of *tadbir* required a further inflection of the idea of circularity. *Tadbir* was not conceived as a self-identical praxis of statecraft, complete in and of itself. Rather, it was understood as a shadowing of divine *tadbir* as envisaged in the Qur'an, and legitimized through cosmopolitical analogies with the work—at once *praxis* and *poiesis*—of rulers and administrators. Unlike the Aristotelian model, however, neither the *madina* nor the *dawla* could function simply as the *telos* of a politics of expert and wise arrangements. Statehood instead took shape within a field of tension generated by the mutual mirroring of macrocosm and microcosm. This mirroring, a continuous and circular back-and-forth, could only be secured by *walaya*—or, more precisely, the mirroring itself is *walaya*. At this stage, *walaya* saturates the instituting and managing process as such, rather than merely shaping the wise and saintly figure of the ruler, who appears instead as the reflection of a cosmopolitical process of mirroring implemented through *tadbir*.

The attribute of sovereignty that most directly registers this cosmopolitical circularity is that of the Caliph as the "shadow of God" (*dhill Allah*) on earth. This title was repeatedly attributed to rulers by court scholars of the age. Supported by a dense repertoire of learned narrations and popular lore, the expression designated the ultimate quality of the *wali* or *qutb* as a paradigmatic form of human perfection—a typology that necessarily includes the ideal ruler of the ecumene. Closely related is the concept and title of *say'a-i Haqq*, used by Bidlisi to convey the same trope of shadowing through a ruler's striving in the service of the Divine Real/Truth/Right. Here Allah is designated through His ultimate esoteric name, gesturing beyond all names, namely the Real (*Haqq*). The notion of *say'a-i Haqq* thus dovetails with the Qur'anic and cosmopolitical sense of *tadbir* as the shadowing of divine governance. To grasp the force of this constellation of metaphors and titles—and their capacity to capture the instituting impetus of *tadbir*—one must attend to a deeper stratum often obscured by the proliferation of titulature itself: the notion of fortune (*kut*) as a sign of divine selection characteristic of Turko-Mongol steppe rulership. This selection was confirmed, quasi-tautologically, by the very fact of effective power. As *kut* was transposed into the Persianate notion of *farr*, often rendered as "charisma," this logic of legitimation—typically validated through victory over rivals—functioned simultaneously as a shorthand for a Khaldunian climax of nomadic power and as an index of perfected leadership sustained by the self-perpetuating momentum of a *dawla*. As Yılmaz has astutely remarked, even as *dawla* came to signify something approaching a "state" in the early-modern period, it never shed its foundational meaning as a "turn of good fortune," precisely because rulership remained cosmopolitically justified. Circling back, then, from *walaya* as divine election to *tadbir*, the latter marks the ultimate impersonality of rulership as practiced through *siyasa*. The affairs of the realm are conducted by reflecting—or shadowing—the self-ordering of *Haqq*. The divine light condensed in *farr* is transmitted through its elected shadow. This logic was already explicit in Suhrawardi's definition of rulership as the intuitive capacity to receive and reflect royal light (*farr-i izadi*) as the vehicle of divine governance, thereby becoming Caliph of God and *qutb* (Yılmaz 2018, 110–111, 156–158, 183–188; cf. also Moin 2018; Arjomand 2025).

The lexical and conceptual intertwining of *tadbir*, as the engine of the *adab–siyasa* complex, and *walaya* was powerfully enacted in one of Ibn 'Arabi's early works, *Kitab al-Tadbirat al-Ilahiyya fi-Islah al-Mamlaka al-Insaniyya*, later revised by the author. Ibn 'Arabi himself emphasized the importance of this book at the beginning of his more famous *Anqa'*, where he sought to elevate and complete his cosmopolitical vision. In *Kitab al-Tadbirat*, the Greatest Shaykh intersected and complemented the teaching of *Sirr al-Asrar* with a conception of the Caliphate, making the relation between *khilafa* and the self-governance of the human being as microcosm the privileged site for articulating a consistent model of rulership. The work elaborates analogies between the mutual dependence of bodily organs and those of the sociopolitical, connective body—an embodied reworking of the image of the Circle that, as we discussed in Chapter 7, would later be reprised, in explicitly reformist terms, by Katib Çelebi in the 17th century. Hüseyin Yılmaz has stressed that, alongside—and in some respects even more directly than—*Fusus al-Hikam* and *al-Futuhat al-Makkiyya*, *Kitab al-Tadbirat* played a strategic role in infusing Ottoman reflections on rulership with Sufi tropes of wayfaring. In the mutual mirroring of the *tadbir* of the self and that of the ecumene, rulership unfolds through the power and beauty of the divine names and attributes. The work's importance for the Ottoman elite is further confirmed by the presence of multiple copies in the early 17th-century palace library. It is also worth recalling that Ibn 'Arabi came from a noble, well-connected family and that his father held a major post in Almohad service. As a young man, prior to his spiritual transformation, Ibn ʿArabi was even promised a position as scribe to the governor of Seville, the Almohads' administrative capital in al-Andalus (Addas 1993 [1989], 18–31). This experience might have acquainted him firsthand with the *tadbir* of *siyasa*, while his spiritual path articulated its optimal alignment with *walaya*. For sure, the outcome of Ibn ʿArabi's approach is a political onto-cosmology that grounds a reflective and associative—rather than monopolistic—conception of sovereignty, in which the administrative know-how of *tadbir* is inseparable from, and animated by, the higher intellection of *walaya* (Elmore 1999, 237; Yılmaz 2019, 511–512; Patrizi 2021, 297–301; Arjomand 2025, 115).

This approach is clearly echoed in the Ottoman context by the previously mentioned Şirvani, for whom the ideal ruler—as *al-insan al-kamil* and *qutb*—is also, by necessity, the *mudabbir* of the affairs of the world. There is no Weberian split between "office" and "personality." The *mudabbir* appears as the "squarer" of the Circle, or more precisely as the one who ensures that the Circle squares itself. As such, this role is markedly transpersonal and unconsecrated, unlike sovereignty in early European statehood, where distinct—if intensely theopolitical—notions of person and office are constitutive (see Chapter 9). Of course, actual rulers may fall short of these requirements. Even so, their power is understood as derivative of the supreme *qutb* (*qutb al-aqtab*), who alone holds the veritable *khilafat al-Haqq*, that is, the deputyship of the Ultimate Truth or the Real, whether or not this figure is visible and whether or not it coincides with the apparent ruler (Yılmaz 2018, 185–186, 200–201, 211–214). The blending of *tadbir* with an Aristotelianly inflected imagery of wisdom and advice—rather than with a formal "political theory," as also evidenced by the lukewarm reception of Aristotle's *Politics*—was mediated through a Sufi cosmology and refracted by the sociopolitical culture of the ecumene, especially within court milieus. Accordingly, *tadbir* also found a place in the mirrors for princes that proliferated during the Middle Periods as condensations of *adab*. As will be discussed in the next chapter, this trajectory highlights how parochial Weber's postulation was that charisma, as a factor in the instituting process, cannot be rationally accounted for. The paradox lies less in the historical material than in the culture of the Western interpreter, which dichotomizes religious and civil orders and struggles to grasp a differential—rather than dichotomous—*barzakh*-oriented logic. One must therefore recognize that both *siyasa* and its operational engine, *tadbir*, as articulated within *adab* discourse, were intended to be simultaneously "charismatic" and "rational," that is, sovereignly effective. To connect higher *tadbir*, legitimized by *walaya*, with the idea of the ecumene not merely as continuously unfolding but as materially and institutionally "built" prosperity, another leading author of the early Süleymanic era, Ibn Kemal (d. 1534), explicitly deployed the terminology examined in Chapter 1 to delineate the instituting process. He described as *ma'mur* the effect—accruing to the sovereign's titulature—of properly exercised rulership as reflected in the Circle. One may observe how the process of building and instituting a prosperous ecumene as *ma'mura* was thereby elevated from a primarily social dynamic to a distinctly political achievement. In this sense, it marked the culmination of the long trajectory of the *adab-siyasa* complex, powered by *tadbir* and legitimized by *walaya* (ibid., 224–226).

It is also noteworthy that during the reign of Süleyman the *şeyhülislam* and eminent jurist Ebussu'ud (1490–1574) confirmed the ruler's prerogatives in a comparable Sufi-inflected idiom, even while arguing in rigorously juridical Hanafi terms (Yılmaz 2018, 214). The post of *şeyhülislam*, which had gradually emerged during the 15th century, particularly through the centralizing interventions of Mehmed the Conqueror, was definitively institutionalized during the reign of Selim II. Notably, Ebussu'ud, as the chief jurist of the *dawla*, played a crucial role in bridging the old and the new Caliphate by identifying the prerogatives of the Ottoman ruler as a functional replacement for earlier models of the Caliphate/Imamate supported by the juridical tradition. He did so while also making a decisive contribution to suturing *qanun* with *shari'a*. It was at the cusp of this reconstructed idea of the Caliphate that the Ottomans were able, to a large extent, to mend the hiatus between the two primary forms of legitimation discussed in this and earlier chapters: legitimation "from above," through the everyday exercise of sovereignty by the Caliph and his central court and government, and legitimation "from below," through spokesmen for the ecumene's autonomy or *a'yan*, among whom religious scholars and jurists played a role alongside *tariqa* and *futuwwa* masters. In light of what was argued in Chapter 2 regarding the simultaneous distinction and amalgamation of the *adab* and *hadith* corpuses, this trajectory should not appear surprising. If there is anything distinctly "Islamic" in this development, it lies very much in the spirit of Shahab Ahmed's interpretation (see Chapter 1), that is, in its navigation of contingencies, ambivalences, and contradictions. The process rested on a *barzakh*-inspired logic, as delineated by Bruce Lawrence, which does not dichotomize spiritual and temporal powers but simultaneously distinguishes and amalgamates them, making each the condition of the other depending on the contingent positioning of observers or stakeholders. In this sense, one could even speak of a "higher" *tadbir* consisting precisely in managing the contingencies of multiple interests and values that may conflict yet also calling for reconciliation—far removed from the worn-out, largely orientalist narrative that pits a juristic against a Sufi conception of political legitimacy in general, and of the Caliphate in particular.

The relationship between *walaya* and *tadbir* should ultimately be read against the background of the culmination, in the early-modern Ottoman Empire, of the formation of administrative cadres and leadership groups. This outcome also owed much to a strategy of recruitment and training designed to sever officials from dependence on family or clan ties. The origins of this model lie in the constitution of elite "slave" military corps, first in the ʿAbbasid Caliphate and later, during the Middle Periods, in a variety of principalities, as preliminarily discussed in Chapter 6. The model acquired remarkable institutional solidity in the Later Middle Period among the Mamluks, whom Ibn Khaldun served toward the end of his life and career. In the Ottoman Empire, the institution known as *devşirme* enabled the recruitment of young men of Christian background (mainly from the Caucasus and the Balkans) through a levy imposed on their communities of origin. They were raised as Muslims and placed in direct service to the ruler, whether militarily—as in the case of the formidable and long-influential Janissary corps—or administratively. These two branches were conceived as complementary sides of the same *askeri* (literally, military) ruling elite, both of which played a crucial role in the functioning of the Circle of Justice (Yacioglu 2018, 443).

In this sense, the emergent conception of rulership and statehood aimed to domesticate the tribal energy of *ʿasabiyya* by relocating it within a class-based habitus of rulership and high administration (see Chapter 5). The trajectory that matters most here involved the systematic training of high-ranking administrators in palace schools, feeding into the estate known as the *kalemiyye* and extending all the way to the increasingly influential office of grand vizier. Over time, the Ottoman *kalemiyye* assumed the contours of an autonomous bureaucratic corps in tandem with the unfolding of a reflective and critical reassessment of the strengths and limits of the post-Süleymanic *dawla*. It was Mehmed the Conqueror who, as part of his transformation of the *dawla* into a universal empire, took decisive steps to replace Ottoman Turkish grandees with administrators trained through the *devşirme* system. The frequent classification of the Ottoman polity within the family of Persianate states tends to obscure the innovative character of these measures, which were fundamentally extraneous to the more traditional—if continuously updated—mechanisms of elite reproduction typical of Persianate rulership. Significantly, when in the 17th century the *devşirme* system of elite slavery gave way to the recruitment of local Muslims into palace schools, the underlying model remained intact: it continued to privilege expert knowledge and bureaucratic competence, reinforcing the growing self-understanding of the *kalemiyye* as the backbone of the *dawla*, rather than reverting to older patterns of negotiated aristocratic cooptation at court (Yılmaz 2018, 38).

This institutional turn also found explicit articulation among leading members of the administrative elite. An unequivocal plea for making the *kalemiyye* the centerpiece of government came from the previously mentioned Celalzade, the chief of chancery whose career spanned the reigns of Süleyman and Selim II. While also a poet and historian, Celalzade displayed a striking awareness of the power and mission of his estate in preserving the *dawla* and fostering the prosperity of the ecumene. This awareness is all the more notable given that he hailed from a family associated with the *ilmiyye*. After initial training in the *madrasa* system, he consciously opted for an administrative career, rapidly ascending the ranks of the *kalemiyye*. Most remarkable was his ambition to draw on his own experience as a senior bureaucrat to produce a comprehensive account of government, institutions, and procedures. Although this project remained unfinished, his sustained engagement with the autonomy of legal frameworks and institutional life marked a clear departure from the long-standing model that treated the governance of the self as the primary template for governing the polity (Şahin 2013, 214–252; Yılmaz 2018, 53, 71–72).

From a markedly different social trajectory, the celebrated grand vizier Lütfi Paşa—already encountered in the previous chapter—pushed this shift further by doubling up, very unusually for someone in that office, as a theorist of rulership and administration. His reflections brought to full fruition the sensibility of a genuine product of the *devşirme*, trained from childhood within the palace's elite educational system. Unsurprisingly, his approach mirrored the experiential world of his formation and career as a paradigmatic embodiment of the institutional autonomy of the *dawla*. The centerpiece of his theory was Ottoman *qanun*. Originating in the quasi-shamanic charisma of early Ottoman chieftainship, *qanun* had evolved into a self-perpetuating instrument for managing the affairs of rule. At this level, it functioned simultaneously as the expression and the instrument of *tadbir*, which no longer required explicit conceptual elaboration to be operative (Yılmaz 2018, 76–77). What emerges here is a decisive move away from the trope of a "wisdom of power" embedded in the life forms idealized by the classical *adab-siyasa* complex, still visible in authors such as Kınalızade and Celalzade. Lütfi Paşa's intervention instead heralded a new wave of writings—among them an anonymous treatise likely authored by another experienced administrator—significantly titled *Masalihu'l-Muslimin*. Centered on the goods and interests of the members of the ecumene, these works assumed that only the solidity of the *dawla* and its *qanun* could secure collective welfare. Their perspective was grounded directly in the practical challenges of administration and articulated through its own operative concepts (ibid., 12–15, 78–79).

Far from rendering earlier frameworks obsolete, this transformation reconfigured the very meaning of the Caliphate. Understood as the institutionalization of the political onto-cosmology of *walaya*, it enabled a decisive shift in emphasis from the persona of the ruler to the relative autonomy of government, administration, and procedures, together with their continuous remodeling in response to the changing circumstances of the ecumene—all while remaining guided by the cosmopolitical rationale of *tadbir*. If there had ever been a form of "patrimonialism" in which the *dawla* was identified with the ruler's household, this nexus was now effectively severed. The precedent for this break lay precisely in the literature of *tadbir*, where the city or polity provided the model for governing the household and even the self and the body, rather than the other way around. In this sense, the culmination of the *adab-siyasa-tadbir* complex did not signal the exhaustion of Islamic political imagination, but its institutional maturation, setting the stage for a post-messianic, intensely reflexive governance.

Notes

1. One should also take into account that some of the transformations which Ottoman scholars tended to attribute primarily to the internal trajectory of their *dawla* were in fact shaped by broader shifts in global markets linked to the increasingly aggressive policies of European powers. Most prominently, these shifts included the opening of Atlantic trade routes following the genocidal colonization and exploitation of the Americas. The massive influx of precious metals from the New World dramatically intensified the strategic importance of monetary circulation and, in turn, the need for its centralized regulation and control by ruling elites and courts.

2. Symptomatically, perhaps, this translation appeared before Pirizade's appointment as *şeyhülislam*, the head of the religio-juridical hierarchy—an office that had been established in the 15th century and that played a crucial role in securing the stability of statehood by validating the authority of the emperor.
3. While the foregoing has largely been missed both by the anthropology of Islam associated with Asad's school—which tends to posit an Aristotelian convergence between premodern Europe and the Islamic ecumene—and by the sociology of Islam represented by Arjomand, who more orthodoxly assumes an Aristotelian divergence between them (thereby effectively granting the West a monopoly on Aristotelian authenticity), Setrag Manoukian suggested several years ago that *tadbir* be understood as a kind of "constituting process" or practice. As our exchanges took place in our shared native language, Italian, the expression used in the discussion was *processo costituente*. Not by chance, the dialogue unfolded on the margins of an academic "institution" such as McGill, at the same time as I was reading—and endorsing—Hayrettin Yücesoy's book (2023), which I have frequently cited, and conversing with him on several occasions. Taken together, these conversations helped crystallize the understanding of *tadbir* developed in this chapter. At the same time, I came to see *processo costituente*, which is the concept preferred by other authors belonging to *New Italian Theory*, as a competing notion to Roberto Esposito's *processo istituente*, which I have chosen to adopt in this volume when speaking of an "instituting process." Productive exchanges and mutual clarifications with Manoukian on this issue—where we appear to share a convergent critique of strands of contemporary anthropology and sociology of Islam still prevalent in anglophone academia—are ongoing. In Chapter 9, I will advance further arguments to clarify what I call the "Islamic difference" by way of understanding the *tadbir* as the engine of the instituting process, while also explaining why the above described point of discussion is more than terminological: the notion of a "constituting process" risks straining and teleologically fixing—by, for example, projecting it toward some form of "constitution"—the fundamentally open-ended character of *tadbir* and its intimate connection to life, as captured by Esposito's paradigm of "instituting life" (see Chapter 1).
4. This is a conceptual reduction that is still quite frequent in the literature on state and governance in the Islamic ecumene—even in the otherwise seminal study of Yılmaz (2018), on which we have so crucially relied.
5. This is the main interpretative line offered by Yücesoy (2023).

References

Addas, Claude. 1993 [1989]. *Quest for the Red Sulphur. The Life of Ibn ʿArabī*. Translated by Peter Kingsley. Cambridge: Islamic Texts Society.

Agamben, Giorgio. 2011 [2007]. *The Kingdom and the Glory: For a Theological Genealogy of Economy and Government*. Translated by Lorenzo Chiesa and Matteo Mandarini. Stanford, CA: Stanford University Press.

Al-Daghistani, Sami. 2022. "Beyond *Maṣlaḥah*: *Adab* and Islamic Economic Thought." *American Journal of Islam and Society* 39 (3–4): 57–86.

Arjomand, Said Amir. 2025. *Kings and Dervishes: Sufi World Renunciation and the Symbolism of Kingship in the Persianate World*. Oakland, CA: University of California Press.

Casale, Giancarlo. 2011. *The Ottoman Age of Exploration*. Oxford: Oxford University Press.

Coulon, Jean-Charles. 2023. "*Adab* et magie dans l'Islam médiéval: Une lecture de traités arabes de magie à travers le prisme de l'*adab*." In *L'*Adab*, Toujours Recommencé. "Origins", Transmissions, Metamorphoses of* Adab *Literature*, edited by Francesca Bellino et al., 577–615. Leiden: Brill.

Darling, Linda T. 2009. "The Circle and the Tree: A Vision of Justice in the Middle East." In *Historical Dimensions of Islam: Essays in Honor of R. Stephen Humphreys*, edited by James E. Lindsay and Jon Armajani, 151–82. Princeton: Darwin.

Darling, Linda T. 2013a. *A History of Social Justice and Political Power in the Middle East: The Circle of Justice from Mesopotamia to Globalization*. London: Routledge.

Darling, Linda T. 2013b. "Circle of Justice." In *Encyclopaedia of Islam Three Online*, edited by Kate Fleet et al., 3rd edition. Leiden: Brill. https://referenceworks.brill.com/display/entries/EI3O/COM-24405.xml

Fleischer, Cornell. 1984. "Royal Authority, Dynastic Cyclism and 'Ibn Khaldunism' in Sixteenth Century Ottoman Letters." In *Ibn Khaldun and Islamic Ideology*, edited by Bruce Lawrence, 46–68. Leiden: Brill.

Fleischer, Cornell. 1986. *Bureaucrat and Intellectual in the Ottoman Empire: The Historian Mustafa Ali (1541-1600)*. Princeton: Princeton University Press.

Hagen, Gottfried, and Ethan L. Menchinger. 2014. "Ottoman Historical Thought." In *A Companion to Global Historical Thought*, edited by Prasenjit Duara et al., 92–106. Oxford: Wiley Blackwell.

Ibn Khaldun. 2005 [1967]. *Ibn Khaldūn. The Muqaddimah: An Introduction to History*. Translated by Franz Rosenthal, edited and abridged by N. J. Dawood. Princeton, NJ: Princeton University Press.

Lambourn, Elizabeth. 2011. "Khutba and Muslim Networks in the Indian Ocean (Part II)—Timurid and Ottoman Engagements." In *The Growth of Non-Western Cities: Primary and Secondary Urban Networking, c. 900–1900*, edited by Kenneth R. Hall, 131–58. London: Lexington.

Melvin-Koushki, Matthew. 2018. " Early Modern Islamicate Empire: New Forms of Religiopolitical Legitimacy." In *The Wiley Blackwell History of Islam*, edited by Armando Salvatore et al., 353–76. Oxford: Wiley Blackwell.

Menchinger, Ethan L. 2018. "Intellectual Creativity in a Time of Turmoil and Transition." In *The Wiley Blackwell History of Islam*, edited by Armando Salvatore et al., 459–78. Oxford: Wiley Blackwell.

Moin, A. Azfar. 2018. "The *'Ulama'* as Ritual Specialists: Cosmic Knowledge and Political Rituals." In *The Wiley Blackwell History of Islam*, edited by Armando Salvatore et al., 377–96. Oxford: Wiley Blackwell.

Patrizi, Luca. 2021. "Ṣūfī Terminology of Power." In *Sufi Institutions*, edited by Alexandre Papas, 292–302. Leiden: Brill.

Şahin, Kaya. 2013. *Empire and Power in the Reign of Süleyman: Narrating the Sixteenth-Century Ottoman World*. Cambridge: Cambridge University Press.

Salvatore, Armando. 2007. *The Public Sphere: Liberal Modernity, Catholicism, and Islam*. New York: Palgrave Macmillan.

Salvatore, Armando. 2016. *The Sociology of Islam: Knowledge, Power and Civility*. Oxford: Wiley Blackwell.

Salzmann, Ariel. 2004. *Tocqueville in the Ottoman Empire: Rival Paths to the Modern State*. Leiden: Brill.

Sariyannis, Marinos. 2019. *A History of Ottoman Political Thought up to the Early Nineteenth Century*. Leiden: Brill.

Tezcan, Baki. 2010. *The Second Ottoman Empire: Political and Social Transformation in the Early Modern World*. Cambridge: Cambridge University Press.

Yaycıoglu, Ali. 2018. "Global Transformations in the 'Muslim World': Connections, Crises, and Reforms." In *The Wiley Blackwell History of Islam*, edited by Armando Salvatore et al., 435–58. Oxford: Wiley Blackwell.

Yavari, Neguin. 2014. *Advice for the Sultan: Prophetic Voices and Secular Politics in Medieval Islam*. London: Hurst.

Yılmaz, Hüseyin. 2018. *Caliphate Redefined: The Mystical Turn in Ottoman Political Thought*. Princeton, NJ: Princeton University Press.

Yılmaz, Hüseyin. 2019. "Books on Ethics and Politics: The Art of Governing the Self and Others at the Ottoman Court." In *Treasures of Knowledge: An Inventory of the Ottoman Palace Library (1502/3–1503/4)*. Vol. 1: *Essays*, edited by Gülru Necipoğlu et al., 509–26. Leiden: Brill.

Yücesoy, Hayrettin. 2023. *Disenchanting the Caliphate: The Secular Discipline of Power in Abbasid Political Thought*. New York: Columbia University Press.

Zemmin, Florian. 2019. "The Janus Face of Kātib Çelebi: Reflecting on the Ottoman Saddle Period." *Turcica* 50: 327–54.

9

Wither the "Body Politic"?

The Political Theology of Leviathan

In this chapter, we will deepen the analysis of the process of instituting statehood to explain how, despite apparent differences in how rulership was instituted in the early-modern empires of the Islamic ecumene, they were similarly oriented to preserve, at least ideally, the circular and associative character of the process. By opposing this model to the European Leviathan, we will appreciate the caution needed in flatly applying the notion of "sovereignty" to statehood in the Islamic ecumene. This is because whenever we evoke this concept in Western languages, it is inevitably mediated by the historical experience of the Westphalian state formations that followed the Leviathan model of the "body politic," which we will discuss here to contrastively highlight the originality of Islamic patterns of instituting statehood.

To further enhance the contrastive effect, for the scope of this last chapter, it is also suitable to turn our attention for a moment to the third major (indeed, the most populous and wealthiest) early-modern *dawla* of the Islamic ecumene that flourished alongside its Ottoman and Safavid counterparts. I am referring to the Mughal Empire in India that was ruled by a branch of the Timurid dynasty and whose splendor peaked under Emperor Akbar (r. 1542–1605). His reign reflected a dispensation of power and prosperity comparable to, if not exceeding, the one experienced in the Ottoman Empire during the Süleymanic era. Akbar's reign stands out for its political cosmology, which contributed to revealing the original traits of the combined trajectory of centralized rulership, autonomy of administrative steering, and the instituting process in the ecumene. What sets the Mughal case apart from the Ottoman model was that its trajectory unfolded without the support of a "slave" elite, thus altering the way the knowledge–power equation affected and inflected statehood.

A significant nexus between the rise of the Mughal Empire and the Safavid revolution lay in the fact that its founder, Babur (r. 1526–1530), was one of the last Timurid princes still in charge before the Safavid conquests and, for a while, a vassal of Shah Isma'il. Not less significantly, the new Mughal state hosted Iranian exiles who, according to Arjomand (2025, 11), contributed to carrying into the Mughal domain the model of "realized messianism" that the Safavids ended up sharing with the Ottomans after the consolidation of their *dawla*. More generally, and given that the dynasty that founded and ruled the Mughal state was of Timurid provenance, we should recall the central role that Timurid court scholars had played in assembling the ruling prerogatives that legitimized early-modern state formation and centralization in the Islamic ecumene overall (see Chapter 6). It is in this context that one should understand Akbar's claim to the title of Mahdi. While also supported by the role played at court by a descendant of Shah Isma'il, this messianic attribute owed to a highly imaginative, Sufi-inflected, political astro-cosmology and attending institutional arrangements. Crucial in the process was the institution of a court-centered confraternity whose master was Akbar himself, and that Arjomand considers a blatant and somewhat artificial—if effective—imitation of the Safavid model, which Akbar's son Jahangir (r. 1605–1627) further refined (Moin 2012, 136; Arjomand 2023, 111–112; 2025, 255).

The Sufi-styled confraternity that buoyed Akbar's ruling charisma was significant also because it reflected the role played at court by Abul Fazl (1551–1602), a religious scholar by training rather than a professional bureaucrat. He was the author of the *A'in-i Akbari* ("Institutes of Akbar"), part of the broader *Akbarnama* ("Book of Akbar"), and midway between a manual and a gazetteer. It was designed to institute the specific rulership of Akbar as nothing less than the most perfect incarnation of *al-insan al-kamil* and as the supreme *qutb* of the age. The *Akbarnama* overall retraced for Akbar the myth of origins that had been produced by Timur's court scholars in the early 16th century (see Chapter 6). It told the story of how a ray of sun impregnated a Mongol princess and engendered a line of rulers that was perfected in successive manifestations, culminating in the figure of Akbar. However, this was not just a myth of the production of rulership and statehood. It delineated the very condition for Earth's blossoming into *'umran* and yielding a *ma'mura* or ecumene, rather than being doomed to perpetual barrenness. Only Akbar, as the Supreme Pole, could wed Earth to Heaven. We have here the most consistent construction of a political cosmology, or "cosmocracy," among the states that flourished in the early-modern ecumene. The dispensation of a comprehensive peace (*sulh-i-kull*) that Akbar claimed to have delivered should be probably considered the most consistent articulation of the "realized messianism" prevailing in the ecumene during the early-modern epoch (Moin 2012, 137; Melvin-Koushki 2018, 367; Yılmaz 2018, 155).

This culmination of the political cosmology of rulership in the early-modern Islamic ecumene provides the most vivid contrast with the roughly contemporary genealogy of a political theology of sovereignty among the rising European states at the end of a long, if tortuous, process that yielded in the 17th century the Westphalian regime of statehood and sovereignty. To understand this process and its institutional outcome, we need to tie up our discussion here to what we wrote in Chapter 4. In that analysis, we argued that a sociopolitical theology of incorporation provided the conceptual and legal grammar to the instituting process and the very notion of an institution as a collective body or corporation. We outlined a process of what we called a magico-sacramental absorption of the positions and identities of individual subjects into the cohesive body of a corporate institution whose pristine model was the Church, conceived as the body of Christ.

Let us take stock here by elaborating on the work of Roberto Esposito, whose oeuvre I have elected as a conceptual guide in this study of the instituting process of the Islamic ecumene, for the ways it aligns with the specific trajectory of repositioning I underwent in developing an "Islamic frame" (see Introduction and Chapter 1). He reminds us how medieval jurists (glossators and canonists), mainly from the Italian peninsula and variably related to the Church, intervened on the pre-Christian conception of institution found in Roman law by imposing a distinctive Christian theology on it. They did so, however, without erasing the fundamental meaning of "institution" intrinsic to the word itself. The Latin *institutio* derives from the verb *instituere*, which we, following Esposito, referenced in Chapter 1 in the locution *vitam instituere* (or "instituting life"). It signifies something akin to setting in a place (and so infusing a stability or state into) something that would otherwise be in an unstable flux, with the result of ultimately establishing, indeed instituting, it. However, as explained by Esposito, in its original pre-Christian, Roman understanding, for the instituting process to unfold one needed a somewhat artificial intervention on a magmatic substratum assumed to be as other than "natural"—and therefore in need of manipulation by some external, indeed instituting, agency. The innovation of the European Christian lawyers on the pre-Christian Roman law tradition consisted in placing, by contrast, "nature" itself (conceived as a divine creation) at the source of the instituting process. Nonetheless, they did so without cancelling out the sense of "artfully making" intrinsic in the process. The artful operator here is none other than *Deus institutor*. Instituting appears here as a subcategory of creating and therefore fundamentally compatible with "natural law" (Esposito [2021] 2022, 25).

We are alerted, nonetheless, to how this theological intervention in the making of the European legal tradition needed to rely on the notion of persona, which we also preliminarily addressed in Chapter 4. Esposito reminds us that it was Sinibaldo de' Fischi—a canonist who later became Pope Innocent IV—to provide key theoretical work to mold the concept of persona inherited from Roman law into the construal of a *persona ficta* as the legal foundation of a collective body (Esposito [2021] 2022, 109).[1] The concept of *persona ficta* served the goal to institutionally and juridically buttress the existence of the Church itself, while sharing the same institutional model with other derivative institutions, such as a monastery or a university (ibid., 27–31). Esposito insists in stressing how this operation was facilitated by the pre-existent theological conception of the Church (Gr. *ekklesia*) as it originated in Paul's letter to the Romans, where it was founded as an order to last on earth. Most notably the *ekklesia*, consisting in the gathering of its members, was affirmed as being "one body in Christ" (Esposito [2002] 2011, 61).

Medieval canon law jurists and glossators folded this idea of the Church as a body (Lat. *corpus*) into the framework provided by the idea of institution inherited from Roman law. The operation resulted in the notion of a corporation that, indeed, filled and sealed the space that the theological idea of Christ's divine incarnation had left partly open. The flesh was now fully embodied into an organic frame, namely the collective body of the Church as the "bride" of Christ. Alongside other thinkers belonging to *New Italian Theory* discussed in Chapter 1, like Massimo Cacciari (2013) and Giorgio Agamben ([2007] 2012), Esposito reminds us of a key nexus between Pauline ideas and medieval European theopolitical elaborations. The nexus resided in how the idea that the *ekklesia* as an organic body (and, as will be seen shortly, a corporation, and as such the model and source of all instituted collective personas) was prefigured in the enigmatic figure of the *katechon* (Gr.) present in Paul's letter to the Thessalonians. Several subsequent Christian authors, ancient and modern, up until Carl Schmitt, have identified the *katechon* with the force that "holds down" evil and disorder, thus indefinitely procrastinating the arrival of the Antichrist that ushers in the end of the world. As such, it was identified with the power that allowed the Church to subsist and endure: the power to be, indeed, an institution (Esposito [2002] 2011, 62–63; see also Salvatore 2013).

The *katechon* is usually understood by its interpreters as the Christian empire, or, more analytically, what turned out to be the "peak" institution of the *societas* or *res publica christiana* (Salvatore 2007, 107), namely the premodern approximation of statehood. More than the Church itself, it was its "secular" arm. In this sense, it was already a post-eschatological stabilization of sacred rulership, a curious inversion of what in the previous chapters we have dubbed, following Arjomand, as the "realized messianism" of early-modern statehood in the Islamic ecumene, which inaugurates, rather than procrastinates, "the time of end" (Yücesoy 2025; Salvatore 2025, 242–243). As such, the *katechon* should be considered an intense and quite immediate theopolitical antecedent to what will become Westphalian "sovereignty." The European overarching state of medieval times, the Sacred Roman Empire, considered itself the source of all legitimacy of mundane power, while being entangled in a complicated condominium with the Church. One can interpret such a political formation grunded on the *katechon* as a state of waiting for Christ's second coming, in the knowledge that this coming is delayed, and de facto destined to be postponed to post-historical times. In other words, the state's mandate is to govern profane time before the second coming. Through the figure of the *katechon* messianism indirectly, or negatively, legitimizes the realm where power is exercised over the *saeculum*, which is what the state is understood to be in this context. There is here a first clear tautology of such a secular power *ante litteram*: it is secular to the extent it creates the conditions for its perpetuation, that is, pausing the fulfilment of the eschatological promise of Christianity, and therefore the exit from human history (Salvatore 2013). By perpetuating human history the force of the *katechon* buttressed rather than contradicted the medieval idea of a *res publica christiana* that fed into the renewal of Roman law that we just described. It also helped break through the institutional dualism between the Pope and the Emperor and justify the formation of the first kernels of the autonomous centripetal forces that took the first contours of what would become national states, like England and France.

Esposito ([2002] 2011, 67) convincingly argues that the reading of the proto-theopolitical institution of the *katechon* through the lens of the body of Christ, or what will become the *corpus mysticum*, traverses the Latin Christian political theology until early-modern times. This is when, in an unsurprising twist, it morphed into the "body politic." This is more than a time-honored metaphor of the polity as a human body, of the type that can be detected in both European and Islamic premodern sociopolitical thought. In Europe, the concept of the body politic was by contrast one key outcome of the work of late-medieval canon law on the previously mentioned idea of *persona ficta*. Forged out of the latter's theopolitical and juridical matrix, the body politic was conceived as a dynamic entity that can uphold rights and responsibilities, adapting seamlessly to changes in leadership while maintaining its continuity over time. The construct was further elaborated by early-modern English court lawyers such as Edmund Plowden (Kantorowicz 1957). According to Esposito, the intervention of Latin Christian, European (both medieval and early modern) jurists completed a process of "excarnation" of the Christian goods of salvation into the incorporated personality of the modern state, protecting the body politic (with which it ultimately identified) from implosion and fragmentation. In this sense, the process was a reversal of the Christian myth of incarnation, and one that inverted the salvific message of the Church. What the early Christian teachings configured as relatively open soteriological horizons allowing for nonhierarchical forms of organization and subversion of established authorities via the errant, exposed, and sacrificial flesh (Esposito [2002] 2011, 72–73) were now sealed off by incorporating this flesh into the sovereign body of the modern European Westphalian state (Salvatore 2013, 96).

Ultimately the construct of the body politic took the iconic form of a densely corporate Leviathan. This was depicted in the shape of a majestic body-like form in the famous cover of Thomas Hobbes's book by the same name, which the author commissioned from a French professional engraver and frontispiece-maker (Bredekamp 2007, 44–47). On the cover, the Leviathan is iconized via the mutual incorporation of the sovereign and his subjects through the king's acquisition of a second body and a second person, not unlike the Christ. Both the language and the iconography of Hobbes's *Leviathan*, almost exactly contemporary to the Westphalian sanctioning of modern state sovereignty in 1648, were intended to provide stability to the body politic through a monstrous bodily entailment—that is, incorporation—of its subjects into the corporeous icon of the sovereign (see Esposito ([2002] 2011, 69). Here the ruler is both the comprehensive mega-body and every cell of it. The result is a "plated armor," whereby the mortality of every individual cell allows, via incorporation, for the self-perpetuation of the mega-body (ibid., 71). "What we have here is a double incorporation, between the body of each individual and the collective body, derived from the incorporation of each individual body into a common body" (ibid., 116). Without the incorporation of the subjects (later, citizens) in the body politic, there would be no such powerful, potentially omnipotent state. They were integrated in the latter's apparatus finalized to guarantee certainty (of contract compliance) and security (of the individual bodies of the subjects/citizens), that is, the modern surrogate of salvation. Robert Yelle provides more details on the combination of cultural inheritance and political innovation in Hobbes's concoction of vision and theory (Yelle 2018, 34):

> While insisting on the indivisibility of sovereignty, Hobbes acknowledged this tension explicitly by depicting the Leviathan as a composite figure, formed by the concatenation of the masses of individual bodies from which the sovereign derives his power, indeed his very substance. This image drew upon the older idea of the king's incorruptible body as composite and corporate, and upon Hobbes's identification of the polity as a congregation, facing the Leviathan—their mortal God—in prayerful reverence and obedience.

To recapitulate, the concept of the modern state emerged through a modern turn in the political theology of Latin Christendom that configured it as an abstract body, distinct from all individual bodies, including the mortal one of the monarch. The state was conceived as a polity-centered reconfiguration of the body of Christ: as a projection of the *corpus mysticum* of the Church on the screen of mundane humanity (Arnason 2003, 253). If we consider the state's existence as dependent on the juridical figure of the corporation of medieval origins, then the incorporation of the Leviathan marks the final stage of a long process that is indissolubly political and religious.[2] If the modern Westphalian state in Europe was able to concentrate in its hands an unprecedented amount of coercive force and administrative capacity, it was not only thanks to a process of "rationalization" of rule via the monopolization of violence. It was also, if not mainly, through the support of the political theology of the Leviathan and the juridical apparatus that articulated its prerogatives. The outcome was the idea of the corporation as the basis of legitimation of institution-building overall. It would be reductive, however, to interpret this process of production of European modern statehood as a sheer funneling of a premodern Christology and ecclesiology—however altered—into a modern political theology. As clarified by Esposito (2020, ix), we are dealing here with a specific theopolitical twist that construes and consecrates the Leviathan through an ontological negation. This negation was initially articulated in the *katechon*'s figure of what we might call a "suppressed/compressed messianism," contrasting with the "realized messianism" of statehood in the

Islamic ecumene. The European theopolitical twist provided legitimacy to an institution, here the state, for its capacity not to express social demands and provide for social needs, but to filter them via repurposing the *katechon*. The state now appears in all its glory as the theopolitical machine that succeded in instituting secular time by procrastinating messianic redemption, severing the human flesh from its bodily connectedness, and incorporating it into the plated armor of the body politic (Esposito 2020, 163).

That continuities overlay discontinuities in the breakthrough to modern statehood (and, in parallel, to capitalism) is also shown by how, until the 18th century, there was a fundamental indistinction between the organic and the mechanical dimensions of the Leviathan, like in Hobbes's dubbing it an "artificial animal" (Esposito [2002] 2011, 114–115). The metaphor of the state as a *machina machinarum* ("machine of machines") does not replace but supplements the idea of the body, like a "metal skeleton" protecting the otherwise mortal body. As put by Esposito (ibid., 115–116), "the body-machine, the machine-body, is a body that can no longer be undone because it is already undone and rebuilt, as if embalmed, in its bodily armor. As a body that is permanently such as it is—because it has no gaps, no openings, no wounds—it is entirely coincident with itself and therefore everlasting: all body, one body, forever body." This mechanistic dimension of the body politic introduces a sharp discontinuity with earlier metaphors of the polity as a body, whose health depended on the harmony and balance between various organs and humors. The machinic body consists of rather undifferentiated cells, representing the bodies of the individual subjects. As such, it is a rather monstrous body with only one visible organ, the crowned head of the state, that is, the monarch, towering over the body politic in *Leviathan*'s frontispiece. There is to date no better image of the modern state as a sovereign body.

The Modal Articulation of the *Adab–Siyasa–Tadbir* Complex

One can start appreciating the magnitude of the contrast between the European theopolitical construal of statehood and sovereignty and the cosmocratic articulations of *walaya* in the Islamic ecumene. In the latter case, the needs and demands produced by the life of connected bodies were mediated at differential (potentially infinite, though humanly finite) stages and levels of interaction/intercorporeality (see Chapter 3), rather than by imposing an artificial body on the life of bodies collectively incorporated into a "state" that cannot be challenged and is, therefore, "sovereign" by definition. The Islamic political onto-cosmology appears more attuned to the trope of perpetual creation, which gained increasing prestige within the Islamic ecumene, particularly under Seljuq and, later, Ottoman patronage. Talk of an "Islamic difference" alludes not only, or not even primarily, to its distance from a purported (European, Western) model but to how an unceasing, process-like onto-cosmological articulation of "difference" in the creaturely sphere preempts any magico-sacramental procedure of *reductio omnium ad unum* via incorporation—one where unity is folded from an Aristotelian or Neo-Platonic ontological matrix into a juridical procedure, culminating in techniques of incorporation that squeeze multiplicity into a single, if artificially omnipotent, body and will.

Nonetheless, to be able to appreciate the Islamic distinctiveness more comprehensively—particularly in contradistinction to the negation of life entailed by incorporation within the European trajectory—one should take further steps in understanding the peculiar concept of the persona, which we alluded to in Chapter 4, when we first discussed incorporation, and reprised earlier in this chapter. As we saw, the idea of *persona ficta* culminated in the formation of the totalizing juridical personality of the state. The corporate mega-body of Leviathan, facilitated by the political theology of incorporation, postures as an overarching artificial persona that can magico-sacramentally reshape all forms of horizontal, including confraternal, bonds. In other words, the state is the culmination of the instituting process centered on the artful machinic making of collective, literally nonliving persons in the form of corporations. To fully understand the working of this process, Esposito ([2007] 2012, 8–9) deftly unpacks the theological density of the concept of person. He reminds us that, derived from Roman law, the Christian tradition appropriated and inscribed this notion into the Trinity. From there it evolved into a veritable *dispositif* built within the gulf between persona as an artificial (theopolitical and juridical) entity and the living human being who is expected to fit this shell or, indeed—as this was persona's original meaning in Latin—mask. This fitting, or lack thereof, ultimately discriminates among persons as subjects of rights within a sovereign domain. The late-modern notion of human rights as personal rights, far from offsetting discrimination, aggravates it based on how well a subject can appropriate the shell/mask of the person (Esposito [2007] 2012, 69–70).

Now, it is well-known how Weberian sociopolitical theory, recognizing such features of the European instituting process as unique, has tended to construe the institutions and the state, in the Islamic ecumene, as a bundle of deficits, if measured against such singular (since theopolitically determined) European standards (Salvatore 2016, 90; see also Chapter 4). However, the only dimension that the instituting process in the Islamic ecumene lacked—given that it was not needed—was precisely the magico-sacramental procedure of turning the living human being into a fully juridified persona plumbed in the multitude of subjects as cells of the one Leviathan-state. By contrast, "unity" in the Islamic ecumene and its institutions is produced through incremental difference and circular connectedness. As also reflected by the working of the *adab–siyasa–tadbir* complex, if in the ecumene cultural carriers were often prone to utilize astrological, numerological, and lettrist strategies to manage difference and connectedness, opportunities and dangers, it was precisely because their culture was utterly alien to any magico-sacramental logic of unification. If one insists on dubbing the Islamic approach as magic as well, one should specify that it is magico-differential rather than magico-sacramental. No *corpus mysticum* apportioning sacramental power is available, not to say necessary.

That our contrastive comparison is more than a concluding detour is also shown by how Hodgson himself criticized the approach of reading statehood in the ecumene as chronically lacking legitimacy. This approach was particularly well represented in the work of leading orientalists like Gustave von Grunebaum and Hamilton Gibb, who directly or indirectly followed in the footsteps of Weber (Salvatore 1997, 118–127). Surprisingly, perhaps, Hodgson singled out Bernard Lewis—who has often been considered the foremost incarnation of Islam-hostile anglophone Orientalism—for being, allegedly against the mainstream, ready to acknowledge the specific factors of strength emanating from the early-modern Ottoman model of court-centered administration of the empire (Hodgson 1974, II, 112). No doubt Lewis recognized in the Ottoman Empire the most transparent case in Islamic history of a political-administrative, territorial, state-like entity entailing an institutionalization and hierarchization of ruling functions. However, he derived from this view what we could call a hyper-orientalist prejudice, viewing it as a specific Ottoman exception within the broader Islamic difference. Lewis viewed the early-modern Ottoman state as something akin to the utmost limit of rational adjustment of governance allowed from within what he, not unlike many of his fellow orientalists, saw as a historical, religious, and cultural environment inherently hostile to providing a consistent legitimacy to any form of government and articulation of statehood. This putative mother of all deficits was usually extended back—not rarely through a chain of no less dubious inferences on an alleged general Islamic political culture, or lack thereof—to the entire instituting process in the ecumene, seen as verging on haphazard informality and hostile to a "proper" institutionalization benchmarked on Western patterns of incorporation. Such chains of inferences operated without even problematizing—let alone being aware of—the negativity-bound exceptionalism of Western institutionalization as well as incorporation and their underlying political theology.

One should hold against such complacent orientalist views—often nourished by blanket bias and relatively thin on intellectual nerve—that *tadbir* as the engine of the *adab-siyasa* complex and ultimately the "operating system" of the entire instituting process was the very opposite of so misperceived informality. It is a mode of instituting that invests precisely in what we may call a differentially inflected "open-ended modality" rather than the sacramentally sanctioned "routinized formality" of Western patterns. As such, it dispensed with the absolutistic constraints of the political theology of incorporation. Not by chance, *tadbir* thrived through successive reformulations of the trope of the Circle that functioned without submerging connectedness and circulation into the organic corporeality of a Leviathan trapping each and every subject as a cell of its mega-body. Significantly, metaphors of the polity as a body did abound in discussions related to the problematization of the Circle, but mostly by assuming a mutual permeability between the polity and the body. There was no one-way reduction of the body politic to a machinic and functional corporeality, to a corporation, but an open-ended differential, while mutual, patterning, via circulation, among complementary organs and limbs of the sociopolitical body. Like in the seminal *al-Tadbirat al-Ilahiyya* by Ibn 'Arabi, it was often, and quite deliberately, left undecided whether the primary "body" is the human one or the polity itself. No threshold or boundary between the "natural" and the "artificial" was instituted in determining what is a body—and, most crucially, how intercorporeality operates.

Most fundamentally, this modal, rather than theopolitical operation of connecting by difference shunned the homogenization by fiat of the Leviathan. Indeed, the Circle of Justice/Equity was not only, and perhaps not even primarily, geared toward legitimizing ruling and administrative "bodies." It was mainly understood as the source of a type of reflexive thought on the nature and delicacy of the social bond, which required a careful modulation of the mutual roles of the subjects, the administrative class, and the ruler, ideally endowed with *walaya*. The seminal role of the *waqf* itself in the instituting process in the ecumene, examined in Chapter 4, and which further thrived in the Ottoman Empire, could be seen as arranged via the modal nexus of *tadbir*, as were also several articulations of the *tariqa-futuwwa* institutional matrix (see Chapter 3).[3] Seen this way, even Arjomand's emphasis on the existence of a "civil law of *waqf*" appears as perplexing—as a rather defensive formula for claiming that "the Islamic ecumene too" relied on a rational nexus between civility and institution. Even if not intended so, at least in the readers' perception, Arjomand's suggestion may anachronistically evoke the European trope of "civil law" as an alleged shibboleth of democratic civility, as if put forward to allay orientalist bias on the heteronomy of *waqf* vis-à-vis the agency of socioeconomic actors. What such a move omits to clarify is how what is originally called civil law, in its European shape, could only germinate as part of the work on canon law grounded on incorporation. Against this view, we observed that the *waqf* shunned incorporation and any matching, rigidly formal institutionalization. The avoidance of entrenching its authority in the corporate sacralization of juridical personalities often allowed individuals of several social classes (the ruling elites, the scholars/administrators, and a wide array of *waqf*'s beneficiaries) to modulate their participation in decisions on its use (Gerber 1994; 2002). Of course, one can also intend the "civil" of civil law in a different sense, much better aligned with our discussion on civility in Volume I (Salvatore 2016). Nevertheless, one should specify that the *tadbir* of *waqf* did not rely on "law" as such, but on a mild modulation of *fiqh* permeable to a variety of overlapping (if often conflicting) interests among various sociopolitical actors, with key agents of the *adab–siyasa* complex also playing a role.

In fact, what could appear as the continuing reluctance within the Islamic ecumene to sacralize corporate identities—from the *waqf* to the *dawla*—in a theopolitical fashion comparable to the European case is in fact the product of a specific type of civilizing and instituting process rather than a cultural deficit betraying a lukewarm will to power or a deficient rationalizing capacity. Once more, one should examine the process through the lens of the knowledge–power equation rather than via a self-conceited neo-orientalist conception. *Tadbir* would then be seen not as the simple technical management of an already crystallied institution but as a complex relational articulation of the balance of knowledge and power prevailing in each constellation of administrators and stakeholders. *Tadbir* could then be interpreted as the signature of a "modal" (rather than sacramental) instituting process, wherein a sense of appreciation of power relations prevails over principled assertions of institutional autonomy and sovereignty. This interpretation applies to potentially revolutionary situations framed in messianic terms as much to the "realized messianism" of major empires—as also manifest in the management of the dangerous triangle between the old Ottoman state, the new Safavid state, and the Qizilbash insurgency in Ottoman territories in the 16th century. The violence unleashed through this conflict, though undoubtedly considerable, was way inferior to the one that plagued the Wars of Religion between multiple Protestant and Catholic principalities in the same early-modern era and brought Europe to its knees. This prolonged warfare, not surprisingly, contributed by reaction to unleashing the beast, namely the overarching power of the Leviathan designated to disarm everybody but itself and monopolize the control of legitimate violence. Its sovereign making by fiat was viewed as the sole remedy to the risk of self-destruction, so ushering in the Westphalian dispensation grounded on the primacy of the confession of the sovereign (*cuius regio eius religio*). This outcome was as much juridically as it was theopolitically significant, as it still conditions the parameters of legitimization of sovereign violence in the world we inhabit.

The idea of the *katechon* that entered the Westphalian regime as a theopolitical wager should be contrasted with how in the Islamic ecumene messianic expectations were folded in the general prerogative of *walaya*. This inflection of messianism can be interpreted without the need to surreptitiously borrow Weber's notion of institutionalization as the routinization of charisma, given how defective the concept of charisma is, as argued in Chapter 4 and elsewhere in this volume, if imposed wholesale on the institutional dynamics of the Islamic ecumene. Even Arjomand's notion of "realized messianism," which we prima facie espoused, cannot entirely disguise the fundamental difference in the instituting process in the ecumene. Here messianism is always "managed" to some degree—and only in this sense "realized"—while also, and quite inevitably, missed and mystified, to some extent, in its institutional outcomes. Most notably the management of messianism does not produce, and even less legitimize, any irreversible fiat. Its "realization" is never complete and always contextual, precisely to the extent it is always managed to the effect messianic language is reabsorbed within a broader ecology of ruling legitimacy, whereby *walaya*, supported by a multilayered *'asabiyya*, feeds into the longue durée of the instituting process (cf. Salvatore 2025, 424–428).

To recapitulate, the construal of the saint–philosopher–king in the protective shadow of *walaya* and across the metamorphosing instituted prerogative (rather than the Weberian "office") of being a caliph reflects a symbolic suppleness matched by a cosmological opening. They sharply diverge from the theopolitical crudeness of the iconic, simultaneously machinic, organicist, and corporate character of European patterns of consecration of state sovereignty. The complex, yet elegant patterns of instituting rulership in the Islamic ecumene were characterized by interdependence and even interpenetration. This dynamism contrasts with the heavy and rather static symbolism suitable to the European notion of the "state," the corporate monster enveloping the individual bodies of all subjects. In the Ottoman case, by contrast, we observe a reflexive and even sociologically sensible articulation of connectedness that does not erode the relative autonomy of the entities and groups incessantly interacting within the Circle.

And yet, in suggesting this contrast, we should care to position ourselves at a safe distance from the merely conceptual exegesis of the putative divergence between the European idea of the state and the Islamic, including Ottoman, concept of *dawla/devlet*, (in)famously linked to the work of Bernard Lewis (1961, 3–6, 18–22). As previously alluded to, this type of operation has served to orientalistically construct the Ottoman difference as a set of deficits, primarily located in a type of imaginary that—so the argument—is trapped in the idea of the turns of fortune signified by the *dawla*, instead of seeking the corporate and organic stabilization of the "state." With all due respect for more recent iterations of a strategy calling for a rigorous historicization of concepts (Zemmin 2019), including *dawla*, I opted for a sociopolitical analysis of broader imbrications of the instituting process. Of course, concepts matter here too, but not outside the prism refracting the inevitable hermeneutic tension between the location of their historical carriers and the position of the present interpreters (see Chapter 1).[4] Given my repositioning, and as will be further explored in Volume III, the growing global awareness of the exploitative, extractive, and suppressive dimension of Westphalian state forms in the colonial and postcolonial eras provides, by contrast, the best possible background for reappraising the potentials (clearly floating between ideals and realities) of early-modern forms of statehood in the ecumene. In particular, to be reevaluated is the underlying, cumulative instituting process that attributed a fair amount of—if impermanent—power to demands and aspirations proceeding from the bottom up, like in the case of the wayfaring of *tariqa/futuwwa* and the circulating gifts of *waqf*—without the filter of the corporate cage that in Europe ended up disseminating across society itself the "negative" logic of the *katechon*.

While the 14th-century Maghrebi scholar Ibn Khaldun highlighted the unstable cyclical character of state formation and found its causes in socio-political dynamics through which tribal solidarity overwhelms urban civility, the Ottomans assembled in their trajectory the necessary know-how to stabilize the cycle. They did so by upgrading their initial, quasi-shamanic charisma as tribal warrior chiefs into the role of mediators of a cosmologically justified, yet sociologically grounded, circulatory justice. The key to the upgrade lay precisely in the process of simultaneously reenacting and transcending the pristine formulas of Islam's inception—Muhammad's revolution, so to speak—into a blend of civility and charisma facilitating successive, if diverse, replications of the pristine "state of grace" of the rise of Islam, while spiraling into the cosmopolitan horizons of the ecumene in the making (Lawrence 2010). About this development, Melvin-Koushki (2018, 371) has daringly spoken of the early-modern advent of a "supra-Islamic," if not "post-Islamic," dispensation. The only problem with this diagnosis is the identification of Islam with a rather given set of norms and values (a biased understanding even Hodgson succumbed to) that could be superseded by a new vision rather than, much in the spirit of Shahab Ahmed (2016), seeing in it as a sociohistorical force with a self-transcending potential (see here Bamyeh 2019, 205–220). This is why I would prefer to tag this early-modern dispensation as "super-Islamic," since it is not the case of an immutable Islam that was transcended, but of a dynamic Islam that transcended itself into more powerful versions of itself that still, or ever more, deserved to be called "Islamic."

In this undertaking, it was worthwhile to elaborate on Ibn Khaldun's fundamental intuitions rather than viewing his work as a prepackaged transhistorical theory ready for use in various contexts, including late-modern ones, as claimed by many authors seeking an alternative, non-Western sociology. In this context, we have seen *'asabiyya* at work also, if not most effectively, in non-tribal contexts as an engine of a broader (or perhaps we should say deeper) instituting process, like the one we explored and conceptualized in the previous chapters. The process did not delineate a one-way road leading to the ultimate formation on which the power of military dynasties rested, namely the *dawla*. Indeed, the component that the Khaldunian model tended to underestimate was precisely the potential autonomy of a bottom-up urban civility to be explained differently from the myopic and Western-centered Weberian formulas of glorification of the allegedly unmatched uniqueness of European municipalities. As we saw, their fundamental "exception," far from translating into a monopoly of sociopolitical autonomy, was ultimately a peculiarly sacramental form of incorporation. In contrast to this model, regarding urban civility in the Islamic ecumene Arjomand has had the merit of stressing the pristine unity and strength of the *tariqa-futuwwa* confraternal aggregations, before they first differentiated and underwent a partial reaggregation in the form of the *akhi* associations (see Chapter 3). Following Arjomand, we suggested that the logic and ethos of *tadbir*, far from being a monopolistic product of a top-down *adab–siyasa* apparatus, might have also flourished in those milieus of city-based self-organization and solidarity. We find here an autonomous urban locus of a simultaneously practical and enchanted *ʿasabiyya* (see Chapter 5; Rahimi and Salvatore 2018).

Significantly, we see here *ʿasabiyya* upgraded from sheer connective power into refinement of industriousness, instruction (most notably via *adab* manuals), and collective self-management enlivening the world of trade and crafts, which were the lifeline of *ʿumran*. Furthermore, one sees with better clarity how both solidarity and management were pursued via an intense intercorporeality. This was at its highest in the life of such urban "clubs" that constituted the *futuwwa*, where body cultivation closely intersected community rituals and practices of self-defence. In this context, *tadbir* cannot be sanitized into a quasi (if *avant la lettre*) biopolitical technique of governance or governmentality. Here we need to pair the necessary inoculation against Weberianism with one against Foucauldianism (Salvatore and Obuse 2022, 20) and maintain the focus on *walaya* as the gravitational force of this seminal intercorporeality (see Chapter 3). For sure, we can find intercorporeality also in the mutual companionship undergirding the life forms of the bureaucrats-literati—the class conventionally in charge of the *adab–siyasa* complex—expressing their own dimension of *ʿasabiyya* (see Chapter 8). This was clear since the time of Ibn al-Muqaffaʿ at the transition between the Umayyad and the ʿAbbasid caliphates (Arjomand 2022, 89). Here too, however, the stratum of professional administrators didn't hold a monopoly on *adab–siyasa* but shared it with urban popular milieus far removed from court culture and at times revolting against it. This was particularly clear at the crucial juncture when the alliance of the Persianate secretarial class with the Mongol rulers triggered a response by groups acting in defense of the (largely, though not exclusively, Persianate) articulation of urban civility and its sociopolitical autonomy (Arjomand 2025, 177–200). We have here to do with a non-incorporated dramatization of bodies and their connectivities that propelled a continuous instituting (and, at times, destituting) process.

In this light, it is helpful to look at *walaya* and *tadbir* through a *barzakh*-oriented type of lens, that is, not as opposite extremes (the one "transcendent," the other "immanent") but as two sides of the same coin. Here *walaya* grants a "polished mirror" reflecting the Real, and, therefore, appreciating the realized and realistic game of how life forms, strategies, and the *dawla* itself are assembled, arranged, and managed—the very opposite of the "sovereign decision" consecrated by a Leviathan-like statehood. The Islamic model configures an original form of political modernity, intended as reflecting the autonomy and self-consciousness of ruling and administrative elites in the rational management of the state on behalf of the ecumene and its underlying *'umran*. While this model deflates the shaky Weberian idea of charisma (as allegedly first fluid and then instituted/routinized), it requires the concomitant construal of the saint–philosopher–king as the hub of a circular and associative type of sovereignty. This character was not available, or still in the making, in the High Caliphate (with its dual and competitive structure between the Caliph and the religious scholars) or within the ensuing *amir–a'yan* system (where a de facto legitimacy of rulership in the form of the Sultanate depended on patterns of exchange between patronage and blessing). This alternate sovereignty of the saint–philosopher–king, "hubbing" the Circle and supporting the increasing autonomy of the *dawla*, in turn rested on the trope of the wise, self-conscious, well-advised ruler that had been long in the making, before being perfected in the Süleymanic age.

The decisive period of formation for this type of statehood extended from the mid-13th to the early 17th centuries and was marked by structural transformations at both the level of instituting the social bond and the organization of rulership. This trajectory seems to blur the Hodgsonian chronology that banked on the rise of the "gunpowder empires" (by which he meant mainly the Ottomans, Safavids, and Mughals). Nevertheless, it also recalibrates the weight of what we still lazily tag as "Sufism" to designate a distinctive inflection of Islamic forms of instituting life, depending on specific patterns of intellectual and power lineages, and grounded on the key institutional matrix of the confraternity. We have by contrast emphasized the parallel development of *walaya* and *tadbir* as crucial components in the rise of an original form of statehood and its matching political modernity, both of which were decisively determined within the *tariqa-futuwwa* conglomerate. Blurring the chronology of the early-modern gunpowder empires and relativizing the impact of "Sufism" per se are interventions deconstructing one of the main corollaries of the postulate of methodological modernism (a collateral construal of Weberianism), and which we may call "methodological institutionalism." Within Islamic Studies this corollary is indirectly supported by the still prevalent singling out of organized "Sufism," which occurs even when—or even more so when—propelled by the antiquarian acumen of highly specialized Sufi historical studies. This approach too often ended up reproducing, whether consciously or not, a Weberian binary logic distinguishing between formal and informal organizations, "*tariqa* Sufism" and "authentic mysticism," as if between routinized and fluid charisma. It ignores the much more subtle, *barzakh*-inspired logic at play in the incessant process of instituting the ecumene.

What is common to early-modern forms of statehood in the Islamic ecumene is that a concern with general prosperity and the common good (with a shifting emphasis on *maslaha* and *'umran* as two articulations of flourishing) operates by fading into an inevitably "unrealized" messianic horizon of harmony and justice. It does not solidify into a theopolitical charisma that warrants absolute cohesion and stability. A continuously evolving jurisprudential discourse supports an ongoing pragmatic accommodation of a variety of legitimate interests amenable to the instituting logic of *tadbir* and a corresponding deferral of any pretension to solidify an ultimate mundane order sacramentally. Our findings diverge sympathetically from Hallaq (2014), who argued that it is impossible to legitimize a modern state in an Islamic setting, supposed to rest on the autonomy of a *shari'a*-inspired order entailing the impossibility to legitimize statehood in Islamic terms. This interpretation risks mirroring the above-mentioned orientalist argument that fails to recognize that early-modern state formations in the ecumene did enjoy a high degree of Islamic legitimacy and achieved a fair amount of centralization and effectiveness of political rule. I have argued in this book that any alleged impossibility of building an Islamically legitimate state only applies to a sacralized, if artificial, collective body akin to the *machina machinarum* of Hobbes. In later developments from the 19th century onward, this European model happened to feed into organic forms of secular solidarity within the rising European nation-states. This being a token of European exceptionalism and of the only absent possibility—indeed, absent necessity—in the precolonial Islamic ecumene, the interpretive and practical possibility has been ever since open to developing different (if "early") types of political modernity rooted in the vitality of a precolonial instituting process. This process culminated in original, and for long flourishing, forms of statehood, which were not only possible but regarded as necessary from a variety of Islamic viewpoints—before succumbing to the overwhelming violence and exploitation of European colonialism and imperialism supported by Westphalian state forms.

While Hallaq's argument could only stand by accepting the historically ill-founded assumption of a monopolistic holding of modern statehood by the colonial West, Arjomand raised a more historically situated question concerning the notion of politics that emerges from the study of instituting the ecumene. It is the question of how the inflection of the *adab–siyasa* complex via *tadbir* was aided by original elaborations on Aristotle's *Nicomachean Ethics* grounded on the instituting power of the habitus, rather than his *Politics*, given the dissonance of the latter from the question of rulership as inherited from the Persianate tradition. We addressed this question in Chapter 8 to show how the orientation toward the one main work of Aristotle rather than the other occurred precisely due to the specific nature of the instituting process in the ecumene, rather than because of any cultural distance from an allegedly "correct" understanding of politics intended as manifesting autonomy and participation, supposedly inherited by the West from the Greek *polis*. Leading Ottoman historians, including scholars on whose work I gratefully relied in the previous chapters (e.g. Kefadar, Tezcan, and Yılmaz), may have been eager to demonstrate that "Ottomans too" developed a broader basis of legitimation of their rule that compares with the idea of constitutional guarantees and rights typically considered a trademark of the Western (or "Atlantic") political tradition. In contrast to this trend, the interstitial and liminal positioning of Southern Italy within that tradition allowed me to look in a more disenchanted way at such a "constituting" dimension and appreciate the much more seminal (and sociologically plausible) "instituting" process that characterized the Islamic ecumene, including or especially at the historic height reached with the early-modern Ottoman dispensation. The reason I insisted on viewing an "instituting" rather than "constituting" process derives from the approach I adopted in this book, informed by my own trajectory of repositioning, as illustrated in particular in Chapter 1.

To further clarify my approach, I should summarize how Roberto Esposito (2020) has masterfully explored the currents of sociopolitical thought that conceptualize either "constituting" or, inversely, "destituting" processes, to finally explain his preference for the third, "instituting" option championed by Vico (with illustrious predecessors of the stature of Machiavelli and Spinoza). This is the approach that steers a middle way by neither sacralizing nor demonizing the idea of an institution but by problematizing it. It does so by articulating the relation between life and institution as of a process of instituting life (Esposito 2023), by relying on an original type of "instituting thought." While Esposito is largely silent on the Islamic ecumene, he delineates what may be called a "minor tradition" within Europe which plays a major role within *New Italian Theory* (see Chapter 1) that we saw as resonating with what we have identified—through a Khaldunian lens or otherwise—as the process of instituting the Islamic ecumene. I am here deepening my own interpretation and appropriation of Esposito's thought, filtered through the research question I have addressed in this volume. The option for an instituting rather than constituting process derives from how the latter still reflects a Weberian polarization between personal charisma and instituted office. In parallel, the mutually opposing foci on destituting vs. constituting processes in different strands of Western thought could be said to conceal an oscillation between the opposite figures of the messiah (as covering the destituting option and its making tabula rasa of existing institutions) and the *katechon* (for providing the bedrock of the constituting option, premised on neutralizing the destituting and messianic impulse by octroying personal and collective rights to the "subjects" of the Leviathan, so overcoming its political absolutism).

There are significant threads in the history of sociopolitical thought that justify and encourage a move to see a European minor tradition (which is not so minor from a Southern/Italian perspective) as latent or oppositional within Western political history, while potentially matching a majoritarian trend (approximating Shahab Ahmed's "Sufi-philosophical amalgam") in the Islamic ecumene. This is precisely the thread innervating the instituting process that culminated in early-modern forms of statehood in the Islamic ecumene. In my last two books (Salvatore 2007; 2016), I have laid the groundwork for exploring this interface, and the present volume has provided an opportunity to articulate it in more explicit and better situated ways, also by clarifying my own trajectory of repositioning.

Instituting Life in the Ecumene

Ultimately, the conceptual axis around which this interfacing revolves has been exemplified by Roberto Esposito (2023) by reference to the ancient Roman paradigm of *vitam instituere*, according to which human life is seen as instituted from its beginning (see Chapter 1). Apparently, this formula was invisibilized by medieval and modern developments of European sociopolitical thought. Yet, through the lens of instituting life, we were able to look at Islam not simply as a "living tradition," but as a habitualizing prism facilitating an ongoing practical molding of life into appropriate forms—however diverse these forms may be—as ways to institute it. As the instituting process peaked at the level of rulership and governance via an emphasis on the life politics of the *adab-siyasa* complex, we were allowed to examine statehood from outside the hard prism of sovereignty that dominated early-modern European thought and the Westphalian dispensation inaugurated in the mid-17th century that determined the national and international armature of instituted power. As an alternative to this restrictive prism, the paradigm of instituting life helped deflate—and reconstruct on a different, i.e. associative, circular, and noncorporate basis—the meaning of sovereignty.

It is significant that in *Vitam Instituere* Esposito (2023, viii–xi)[5] starts by considering what we call human life beyond its sheer biological foundation—that is, as a life form—in its being intrinsically, and simultaneously, instituting and instituted. This approach seems to be a quintessential articulation of what we have called several times a *barzakh*-inspired logic, which is quite extraneous to mainstream Western sociopolitical theory. Nevertheless, Esposito sees the paradigm of instituting life as reflected—on a level that connects seamlessly life forms and politics—in the work of Machiavelli, which most scholars view quite uncritically as foundational of the Western mainstream. Yet, Esposito's study delivers an original interpretation of Machiavelli's legacy where politics is not merely a level or field of human life torn by conflict, but, precisely in its conflicted dimension, unfolds as a collective plot fed by the vicissitudes and complexities of existence. This approach is far from stereotyped views of the work of Machiavelli as a proptotypical modern coverage of "politics" as such, which do not make justice to its embeddedness in the specific sociopolitical environment of the early-modern Italian peninsula. This setting was indeed, as discussed in Chapter 1, quite at variance with the European trends that were soon to lead to the establishment of the Leviathan. This reinterpretation of the work of Machiavelli bears several analogies with how we defined the unfolding of the ecumene as *maʿmura*, a self-perpetuating flow of bustling life.[6] Esposito agrees with Machiavelli on seeing in the flow, or the plot, a certain primacy of the instituting over the instituted dimensions of sociopolitical live. However, he hurries to remind us how this predicament is even more clearly expounded by Spinoza,[7] who conceived of an irresistible, continuing *potentia*, which we could explain as a living potency or potentiality.[8] This looks like another *barzakh*-inspired concept, which can be compared to the way we reconstructed *'asabiyya* in Chapter 5. *Potentia* matters not only when teleologically captured into the rise of a *dawla*, but also—and even more so—when it creases the very waves through which *'umran* unfolds. Likewise, Spinoza conceived of the rights of human subjects possessing *potentia* as irreducible to the civil rights granted to them by the artificial, incorporated state. This is precisely because everybody's right coincides with their potency, and the instituting process is identical with the unfolding of people's potencies. This is also why the only thing that can be instituted is ultimately people's lives. Far from producing a Leviathan through the magico-sacramental tautology of a sovereign fiat, the instituting process in the Islamic ecumene did not negate the life force of *'umran* but built on it, therefore making an artificial, machinic body politic neither admissible, nor even possible.[9]

Neither Spinoza's nor Esposito's approach can be downgraded to a utopian political philosophy. Spinoza was fully aware that ontology and politics cannot be fully aligned, as much as the unceasingly unfolding process of instituting life cannot be seamlessly folded into the finite dimension of institutional politics. To mediate between the finite and the infinite in the instituting process intervenes the social imaginary, not unlike the role played by the infinite signs of the "imaginal world," the *'alam al-mithal* famously theorized by Suhrawardi and Ibn 'Arabi. This imaginary plays a quintessentially *barzakh*-oriented function between the infinite and the finite. It is channeled via habitus and fuels an instituting process adequate to its sociopolitical conditions, that is, to the given potencies of the social actors in each situation, where patterns of conflict and cooperation inevitably overlap. Through such interventions, the formal categories of Roman law—whether in their original format or through the alterations undertaken by medieval canonists and modern political philosophers—make little sense if they are not matched with understanding life, along with the needs and desires that spring from it, as the vital energy of the instituting process, and politics itself. Politics so conceived relies on a civility that Machiavelli rescued from its more neutral and sterile classical sense (that is, of pertaining to urban life) by becoming the foil for the inflection of the "common good." In this approach to the civilizing and instituting process, unlike in Hobbes (and, we may add, Weber), statehood remains a potential, if often inevitable, outcome rather than the theopolitically determined telos of the process. In a remarkable syntony with a *barzakh*-inspired logic, for Spinoza life and institution, immediacy and mediation are not opposed but complementary parts of the same instituting process. One could even say that if institutions are to be invigorated by life, this, to be human, is always instituted (Esposito 2023, xii–xviii, 31–33, 63).

That every instantiation of life is a "life form" articulating life's indissolubly instituting and instituted dimensions is illustrated by Spinoza's famous notion of *conatus*. This concept names the immanent power by which every living perseveres in—and thereby expands—its being. *Conatus* is not a latent potentiality but the very actuality of power as *potentia*. This is a "natural right" only insofar as right is identical with power, that is, expressing itself as a fundamental, immanent instituting force. Nevertheless, Esposito continues, *conatus* is never self-contained within the self, as it is always mediated via relations with others. It is inherently relational, given that human affects cannot indefinitely turn upon themselves. Mediation, however, is not an informal remedy to the formal rigidities of an institution; it is identical with it. The modal and mediating character of *adab–siyasa* is therefore indispensable to institute what we call "law" (including "Islamic law"). Therefore, contra Hobbes, institutions are not artificially imposed on humans due to a theopolitical imperative but are "second nature" to them. Nevertheless, for a political realist like Spinoza, command by the sovereign and the matching obedience owed by the subjects are understandably, and quite inevitably, the forms through which humans represent the instituting process in legal parlance. Rulership (*imperium*) is not the antithesis of the power of the multitudes but only its necessary, if distorting, mirror that contributes to the indispensable mediation between the reality of being (the ontological potencies) and the nature of politics, which requires articulation via conflict and the imagination (Esposito 2023, 64–68).

Unlike Hobbes, but in a singular analogy with Ibn 'Arabi's *al-Tadbirat al-Ilahiyya*, Spinoza, while fully cognizant of sovereignty, did not grant it primacy, directing his attention instead to the polity. This appears as a living body that owes obedience to the sovereign without thereby relinquishing its own instituting vitality. Sovereignty, in turn, is anything but autonomous, as it depends upon that living, connective body. In Spinoza's account, therefore, sovereignty operates both as a filter and as an attractor of the component of the process driven by a particular excitement of the human imagination as manifested in the connective body that is the polity. In the formation of the *dawla* within the Islamic ecumene, we observed this imaginative faculty culminating in the work of court scholars who established the prerogatives and titulature of the ruler. It is this power of the imagination that mediates, if often in a polarizing way, between the potency of the multitudes and the prerogatives of rulership. This work of coordination and filtering, which is integral to governance, was performed in the ecumene mainly via the functioning of the *adab–siyasa–tadbir* complex. Precisely given the functionality of what one might call the (ontologically deceiving and delusive, but politically inevitable) imagination of *imperium*, the horizontality of potencies will never replace seamlessly the verticality of sovereignty (or the *potestas* inherent in *imperium*).

And yet, not only are *potentia* and *potestas* never in a mutual contradiction, but they strengthen each other, given that it is the latter that creates the conditions for the former. This occurs in particular by securing the thriving of the life of multitudes, or *'umran* itself, an imperative that was pretty much at the core of the functioning Circle of Justice/Equity. On the one hand, the grammar of *imperium* and the underlying sovereignty can be ultimately delusive, as when (like in the political theology of Leviathan) they rest on a type of imagination unable to express the real concatenation of affects and the mutuality and circularity of the potencies at work. On the other hand, this circularity cannot be equated with a folding of the political into the social and the erasure of sovereignty. Precisely since they can never coincide, an instituting process is necessary (Esposito 2023, 69, 78–84). We can add the observation that Hallaq's theory of the impossible state risked conveying the wrong impression that the Islamic *shari'a* can exist as a purely social expression of people's determinations and as intrinsically alien to any imagination and legitimation of statehood.

Rather than trying to qualify and rebalance the observation on the consequences of a putatively defective Aristotelian notion of instituted politics due to the absence of Arabic translations of *Politics*, we have had the chance to appreciate, while studying the sociopolitical life of the ecumene, the three principles outlined by Bamyeh and discussed in Chapter 1, including the frequently highlighted heteroglossia. The creative reinterpretation of the Aristotelian principle of *oikonomia* as *tadbir* should be viewed as tapping into heteroglossia as a resource, thus shunning the monological understanding of institution as corporation that paved the way to the absolutist Leviathan. *Tadbir* provided a creative and adaptive rationale for building institutions and governance, particularly in the absence of a linguistic, cultural, and religious homogenization of the ecumene. Here, too, discussions unfolding within Southern/Italian thought can support the analysis (Amendola et al. 2017, 175–206). The instituting process in the ecumene and the modal dimension of *tadbir* can be read through the lens of a politics of interacting bodies and of congruous means (Stimilli 2023), arranged via mutual—or, as we saw, circular or spiral—correlation rather than by responding to an overarching telos. This is where the Aristotelian notion of *phronesis* as practical rationality comes into play. *Tadbir* rests accordingly on a wise, prudential, and experiential method, not unlike the one that inspires jurisprudence. In this regard, *fiqh* manifests a good match to *phronesis* as prudence, before it acquires an outright legal connotation as jurisprudence (Salvatore 2007, 166–171). We can see how, through the lens of *tadbir*, *fiqh* itself and the entire dimension of "law" in the Islamic ecumene do not appear as sui generis. Questions of obedience and coercion, though not absent, operate quite in the background. In this light, the idea that legal adjudication is immanent to the civilizing and instituting process rather than imposed on it as if from the outside gains plausibility.

Here again, Weber's confinement of premodern rationality to a realm of "values" appears shallow and quite instrumental to delineating what he, by contrast, construed as a distinctive type of modern rationality, purposive and achievement-oriented. Against this alleged benchmark of modern rationality, the rationality of *tadbir* may appear as consisting of an eclectic assemblages of means, rather than as a unilinear value rationality (which for Weber was the "traditional" type of rationality) or goal rationality, that is, strictly purposive (Weber's "modern" type of rationality). Of course, goals are pursued in the process, and the *walaya* supporting *tadbir* docks its relational immanence onto a spiritual level of authorization, which in a Weberian interpretive grid would be inescapably tagged as transcendent and therefore heteronomous, that is, other than modern and secular. What matters, however, is how the means rationality at play in *tadbir* excludes a Kantian or Foucaultian delineation of the subjects as, respectivey, preexisting to, or, coexisting with, the process: an assumption on which Western sociology still decisively relies (see also Esposito [2021] 2022, 50).

Against this subject-centered view of agency, a politics of bodies and means privileges intercorporeality and relationality over subjectivity. Nor should one anachronistically see in *tadbir* as *oikonomia* the unfolding of a type of Foucauldian governmentality, as adumbrated by the otherwise path-breaking analysis of Yücesoy (2023, 4, 256). Indeed, Southern/Italian theory often insisted on seeing governmentality as a new instantiation, under advanced modern regimes of governance over composite populations, of the same type of corporate sovereignty associated with the Leviathan, and therefore as still, ultimately, theopolitical. *Tadbir*, by contrast, is neither governmental nor salvific, as it would be through the lens of a Pauline economy of salvation,[10] which is quite extraneous to it. Its rationality does not quite fit into any of the binaries of either Western political theology or social theory. And yet, it looks differently if read through the lens of Southern/Italian thought. Indeed, what seems to be shared by all those Southern/Italian thinkers who argue against the primacy of the law and obedience in the process of instituting life and even statehood is that they express a subterranean trend, or a "minor tradition" within the West. While to the extent they address the power–knowledge and governance structures of the Westphalian state their ideas may be downgraded to wishful thinking, whether they are aware of that or not—and with rare exceptions, they seem not to be—they happen to catch key traits of the unfolding of the process of instituting life, law, and the state, in the Islamic ecumene. Quite notably, one occasionally detects scattered admissions—even if detached from sustained historical-comparative arguments—that the conception of instituting life articulated by Southern/Italian thought, and particularly by Esposito, can find tangible realization only "outside of the Western juridical tradition" (Amendola et al. 2017, 190). Being interstitial and yet infuential, the thought expressing this "Italian difference" seems to offer the only effective hermeneutic bridge to capture the "Islamic difference" without completely abandoning the lexical and conceptual instruments of Western thought. This creates a favorable tailwind in navigating the rough epistemic waters of the post-orientalist condition.

Notes

1. The university emerged as a new institution in the High Middle Ages as a *universitas*: a corporate operator forged within the theopolitically oriented, emergent juridical culture of Latin Christendom. Predominantly staffed by clerical scholars and built around the "higher disciplines" of theology and law (in varying proportions across sites such as Paris and Bologna), the *universitas* helped define, stabilize, and disseminate incorporation as a winning instituting pattern in Europe: the production, by juridical fiat, of a collective persona that can endure and act as a unit precisely by abstracting from—often disciplining, if not suppressing—the connective life of human relations that compose it. In this sense, the medieval *universitas* provided decisive intelligence for the very idea of incorporation and for the broader European protocols of institution-building that would travel far beyond the university into the surrounding sociopolitical order.

Yet the corporate form of the anglophone university today is frequently obscured by the rather self-validating rhetoric of a besieged *City of Intellect* (Dirks 2023) and by the related myth of the "secular humanities" as theology's displacement—both of which conceal the enduring theopolitical legacy of the European *universitas* in shaping and legitimizing the corporate structure that modern academic institutions tacitly share with the broader sociopolitical order, including—or especially—the contemporary versions of Leviathan: see also https://www.mcgill.ca/arts/article/look-back-2025-maxwell-cummings-lecture-professor-nicholas-b-dirks (accessed 12 November 2025). For a rare critical diagnosis of how the *universitas* was constituted by theopolitically trapping knowledge that was largely produced within the Islamic ecumene, see Masuzawa 2022 and https://www.mcgill.ca/religiousstudies/channels/event/birks-lecture-series-professor-tomoko-masuzawa-341594 (accessed 12 November 2025).

2. Strictly speaking, while the concept of *persona ficta* directly produced the notion of *institutio*, the category of *corporatio* developed in parallel, probably based on the notion of *collegium* rather than on the model of the *universitas*. While it would be incorrect to postulate a linear teleology producing the occidental notion of the institution as a corporation, the gist of Esposito's argument that I espouse is that the identification of institution with corporation increased in parallel to the rise and consolidation of the modern state, iconized by Hobbes' Leviathan and consecrated by the Westphalian dispensation in the 17th century (Esposito 2020, 162). Here, like elsewhere in the chapter, I quote from Esposito's original work in Italian, rather than from its English translation (Esposito [2020] 2021).
3. The leading scholar al-Tusi, who as we saw played a major role in codifying *tadbir*, was appointed by the Mongol conqueror of Baghdad Hülegü as first head of the post-'Abbasid *waqf* administration (Arjomand 1998, 120).
4. A long key chapter (Dumolyn and Van Steenbergen 2020) of an interesting volume produced in connection to the project "The Mamlukisation of the Mamluk Sultanate," and comparatively extending its focus to the Timurid and Ottoman realms, invokes categories of pre-eminently Western historical comparative sociology, starting with Weber and Elias, to downsize the relevance of the *dawla* to just one conceptual building block of political narratives crafted by secretaries and chroniclers. Also covering some of the—especially older—historiographic literature that the present book could not reference, the piece treats Khaldunian questions as if they were purely theoretical constructs comparable with the Western ones rather than embedding them in what the authors view as rhetorical and context-specific legitimation strategies of the carriers of the *adab–siyasa* discursive complex—as if these strategies were detached from any proactive work on building consistent institutional constellations out of the underlying instituting process. While I acknowledged the way the notion of *dawla* was embedded in dynastic discourse and its deployment in legitimating narratives, I

also argued that precisely due to the inherent open-endedness of *dawla*, the concept operated as much more than a sheer discursive marker of power contentions and determinations. Therefore, the *dawla* should be situated at the point of culmination of an instituting process that we can interpret, indeed, through a much broader conceptual network. Situated within the *adab–siyasa* complex and a Sufi-inflected political onto-cosmology, like at the intersection of *'asabiyya* and *walaya*, these concepts bridged the cyclical logic of dynastic succession with emerging structures of rulership or, as it were, sovereignty. From this perspective, the *dawla* becomes a dynamic category that allows us to understand the shift from fragile cycles of rise and decline toward more durable and "ecumenic" forms of statehood in the post-Mongol period: a category that became part and parcel of a broader grammar of knowledge-power that underwrote the Ottoman, Safavid, and Mughal syntheses. And this is precisely why I still agree with the authors of the chapter that the process should be located within patronage networks and ritualized practices, rather than being reduced to a reified, once-and-for-all institutionalized "state."

5. Its English translation is Esposito [2023] 2025, but I was only able to quote from its original Italian version.
6. This convergence on the paradigm of instituting life may reflect a longer-term interfacing between this minor tradition within the West, which may go back to the Pre-Socratics of Southern Italy, like Pythagoras and Parmenides, whose contributions we should value on their own terms, and not only through the filter of the later Plato. This minor tradition also finds a crucial early modern milestone in the thought of Giordano Bruno from Nola, one of the oldest continuously inhabited cities in Italy, predating Roman rule, and located very close to Naples. He was burned at the stake as a heretic in Rome in 1600 for rejecting core doctrines of the Catholic Church, including the Trinity, and embracing an infinite universe (Esposito [2013] 2015, 151–162), whose cosmology echoed significant elements from the thought of Ibn 'Arabi and Suhrawardi. An even more direct interfacing could be seen in how Neo-Pythagorean influences affected the early modern paradigm of the saint–philosopher–king in the Islamic ecumene (Melvin-Koushki 2018, 258; Moin 2018, 381; Rizvi 2018, 394–400), or even earlier, in how Dante Alighieri's vision of imperial authority—as a rational, unifying force presiding over the temporal and spiritual realms—recombined Aristotelian and Neo-Platonic traditions in such a way that may have been indirectly influenced (e.g. through Andalusian, Sicilian, or even Latin Averroist intermediaries) by intellectual currents of the Islamic ecumene, not least through the political cosmology of Ibn 'Arabi.
7. The Spinozian legacy, occupying a space where ontology and politics intersect, is particularly significant as a token of the largely invisible interfacing between the European minor tradition and the Sufi-philosophical amalgam of the Islamic ecumene. A thinker of the caliber of Eric Voegelin (1999, 126) lucidly saw Spinoza as introducing into European thought currents and motives originating

from the Southern Mediterranean. He was then influential also on Vico and many other Neapolitan thinkers of the age (Salvatore 2007, 180–184). A Sephardic Jew, Spinoza inflected a Judeo-Islamic mode of thought that had found fertile terrain in al-Andalus throughout the Middle Periods. This is where, right at the beginning of Europe's modern era, the genocidal, simultaneously Judeophobic and Islamophobic policies of *los Reyes Católicos* Ferdinand II of Aragon and Isabella I of Castile, led to the persecution and expulsion Jews and Muslims from Christianized Spain. Spinoza's family took refuge first in Portugal and, after the country joined Spain's oppressive policies, in Amsterdam in the early 17th century. Thus Spinoza was, to all intents and purposes, a second-generation refugee. This background, even if well known (see e.g. Nadler 1999, 1–23), has been largely neglected by the plethora of contemporary European enthusiasts of Spinoza's thought (see, however, Albiac 1987).

8. Potency has a stronger ontological valence, while potentiality fits better within a sociopolitical view. Like in Ibn Khaldun, I tend to conjoin the two planes. After all, Spinoza uses *potentia* also when his argument shifts to a sociopolitical plane. The claim that politics ultimately cannot align with ontology is an interpretative commentary by Esposito, stemming from his situatedness within Southern/Italian thought, which he emphatically understands as a "living thought" (*Pensiero Vivente*; Esposito [2010] 2012) capable of generating fresh, if often eccentric, interpretations of past thinkers, whether Italian or not.
9. Another author who occupies a rather eccentric and refreshingly critical position within *New Italian Theory*, Rocco Ronchi (2025, 13), has formulated the primacy of potency as the marker of a "minor tradition" within Western thought that clearly defies the Western "orthodox" Aristotelianism grounded on the metaphysical dualism of potency and act: "The order of the cosmos is sustained by the impossibility of potency not exercising itself."
10. This is another inflection of *oikonomia*, one that plays a decisive role in the Western theological genealogy of government (Agamben [2007] 2011).

References

Agamben, Giorgio [2007] 2011. *The Kingdom and the Glory: For a Theological Genealogy of Economy and Government*. Translated by Lorenzo Chiesa and Matteo Mandarini. Stanford, CA: Stanford University Press.

Agamben, Giorgio [2007] 2012. *The Church and the Kingdom*. Translated by Leland de la Durantaye. London: Seagull Books.

Ahmed, Shahab. 2016. *What Is Islam? The Importance of Being Islamic*. Princeton, NJ: Princeton University Press.

Albiac, Gabriel. 1987. *La sinagoga vacia. Un estudo de las fuentes marranas del espinosismo*. Madrid: Hiperion.

Amendola, Adalgiso, et al. 2017. "Filosofia e diritto tra *French Theory* e *Italian Thought*." In *Effetto* Italian Thought, edited by Enrico Lisciani-Petrini and Gianluca Sturniello, 175–206. Macerata: Quodlibet.

Arjomand, Said Amir. 1998. "Philanthropy, the Law, and Public Policy in the Islamic World before the Modern Era." In *Philanthropy in the World's Traditions*, edited by Warren F. Ilchman et al., 109–32. Bloomington, IN: Indiana University Press.

Arjomand, Said Amir. 2022. *Messianism and Sociopolitical Revolution in Medieval Islam*. Oakland, CA: University of California Press.

Arjomand, Said Amir. 2023. *Revolutions of the End of Time: Apocalypse, Revolution and Reaction in the Persianate World*. Leiden: Brill.

Arjomand, Said Amir. 2025. *Kings and Dervishes: Sufi World Renunciation and the Symbolism of Kingship in the Persianate World*. Oakland, CA: University of California Press.

Arnason, Johann P. 2003. *Civilisations in Dispute: Historical Questions and Theoretical Traditions*. Leiden: Brill.

Bamyeh, Mohammed A. 2019. *Lifeworlds of Islam. The Pragmatics of a Religion*. New York: Oxford University Press.

Bredekamp, Horst. 2007. *Thomas Hobbes visuelle Strategien: Der Leviathan—Urbild des modernen Staates*. Berlin: Akademie Verlag.

Cacciari, Massimo. 2013. *Il potere che frena*. Milano: Adelphi.

Dirks, Nicholas B. 2023. *City of Intellect: The Uses and Abuses of the University*. Cambridge: Cambridge University Press.

Dumolyn, Jan, and Jo Van Steenbergen. 2020. "Studying Rulers and States across Fifteenth-Century Western Eurasia." In *Trajectories of State Formation across Fifteenth-Century Islamic West-Asia*, edited by Jo Van Steenbergen, 88–156. Leiden: Brill.

Esposito, Roberto [2002] 2011. *Immunitas: The Protection and Negation of Life*. Translated by Zakiya Hanafi. Cambridge: Polity Press.

Esposito, Roberto [2007] 2012. *Third Person: Politics of Life and Philosophy of the Impersonal*. Translated by Zakiya Hanafi. Cambridge: Polity Press.

Esposito, Roberto. [2013] 2015. *Two: The Machine of Political Theology and the Place of Thought*. Translated by Zakiya Hanafi. New York: Fordham University Press.

Esposito, Roberto. 2020. *Pensiero istituente: Tre paradigmi di ontologia politica*. Roma–Bari: Laterza.

Esposito, Roberto [2020] 2021. *Instituting Thought: Three Paradigms of Political Ontology*. Translated by Zakiya Hanafi. Cambridge: Polity Press.

Esposito, Roberto [2021] 2022. *Institution*. Translated by Zakiya Hanafi. Cambridge: Polity Press.

Esposito, Roberto. [2023] 2025. *Vitam Instituere: A Genealogy of the Institution*. Translated by Zakiya Hanafi. Cambridge, UK: Polity Press.

Esposito, Roberto. 2023. *Vitam instituere: Genealogia dell'istituzione*. Torino: Einaudi.

Gerber, Haim. 1994. *State, Society and Law in Islam: Ottoman Law in Comparative Perspective*. Albany, NY: SUNY Press.

Gerber, Haim. 2002. "The Public Sphere and Civil Society in the Ottoman Empire." In *The Public Sphere in Muslim Societies*, edited by Miriam Hoexter, Shmuel N. Eisenstadt, and Nehemia Levtzion, 65–82. Albany, NY: SUNY Press.

Hallaq, Wael B. 2014. *The Impossible State: Islam, Politics, and Modernity's Moral Predicament*. New York: Columbia University Press.

Hodgson, Marshall G. S. 1974. *The Venture of Islam: Conscience and History in a World Civilization*, Vol. 1–3. Chicago: University of Chicago Press.

Kantorowicz, Ernst H. 1957. *The King's Two Bodies: A Study in Mediaeval Political Theology*. Princeton, NJ: Princeton University Press.

Lawrence, Bruce B. 2010. "Islam in Afro-Eurasia: A Bridge Civilization." In *Civilizations in World Politics: Plural and Pluralist Perspectives*, edited by Peter J. Katzenstein, 157–75. London: Routledge.

Lewis, Bernard. 1961. *The Emergence of Modern Turkey*. London: Oxford University Press.

Masuzawa, Tomoko. 2022. "Queen in the Attic: Theology and the University." Montreal: McGill University, Birks Lecture Series, 11 and 12 October.

Melvin-Koushki, Matthew. 2018. "Early Modern Islamicate Empires: New Forms of Religiopolitical Legitimacy." In *The Wiley Blackwell History of Islam*, edited by Armando Salvatore et al., 353–76. Oxford: Wiley Blackwell.

Moin, A. Azfar. 2012. *The Millennial Sovereign: Sacred Kingship and Sainthood in Islam*. New York: Columbia University Press.

Moin, A. Azfar. 2018. "The *'Ulama'* as Ritual Specialists: Cosmic Knowledge and Political Rituals." In *The Wiley Blackwell History of Islam*, edited by Armando Salvatore et al., 377–96. Oxford: Wiley Blackwell.

Nadler, Steven. 1999. *Spinoza: A Life*. Cambridge: Cambridge University Press.

Rahimi, Babak, and Armando Salvatore. 2018. "The Crystallization and Expansiveness of Sufi Networks within the Urban-Rural-Nomadic Nexus of the Islamic Ecumene." In *The Wiley Blackwell History of Islam*, edited by Armando Salvatore et al., 253–72. Oxford: Wiley Blackwell.

Rizvi, Sajjad. 2018. "New Sociopolitical Formations and the 'Renaissance' of Philosophy." In *The Wiley Blackwell History of Islam*, edited by Armando Salvatore et al., 393–412. Oxford: Wiley Blackwell.

Ronchi, Rocco. 2025. *La rana e lo scorpione. Il canone della potenza*. Roma: Castelvecchi.

Salvatore, Armando. 1997. *Islam and the Political Discourse of Modernity*. Reading: Ithaca Press.

Salvatore, Armando. 2007. *The Public Sphere: Liberal Modernity, Catholicism, and Islam*. New York: Palgrave Macmillan.

Salvatore, Armando. 2013. "Beyond the Political Mythology of the Westphalian Order? Religion, Communicative Action, and the Transnationalization of the Public Sphere." In *Rethinking the Public Sphere Through Transnationalizing Processes: Europe and Beyond*, edited by Armando Salvatore et al., 91–106. New York: Palgrave Macmillan.

Salvatore, Armando. 2016. *The Sociology of Islam: Knowledge, Power and Civility*. Oxford: Wiley Blackwell.

Salvatore, Armando. 2025. "Religion, Revolution, and Statehood in the Islamic Ecumene: A Review Essay." *European Journal of Sociology* 66 (3): 420–434.

Salvatore, Armando, and Kieko Obuse. 2022. "What Went Wrong? Western Sociology and the Fiction of the Middle East." In *The Oxford Handbook of the Sociology of the Middle East*, edited by Armando Salvatore, Sari Hanafi, and Kieko Obuse, 3–25. Oxford: Oxford University Press.

Stimilli, Elettra. 2023. *Filosofia dei mezzi: Per una nuova politica dei corpi*. Vicenza: Neri Pozza.

Voegelin, Eric. 1999. *The History of Political Ideas*, Vol. 7: *The New Order and Last Orientation*." In *The Collected Works of Eric Voegelin*, Vol. 25, and with an introduction by Jürgen Gebhardt and Thomas A. Hollweck. Columbia, MO: University of Missouri Press.

Yelle, Robert A. 2018. *Sovereignty and the Sacred: Secularism and the Political Economy of Religion*. Chicago: University of Chicago Press.

Yılmaz, Hüseyin. 2018. *Caliphate Redefined: The Mystical Turn in Ottoman Political Thought*. Princeton, NJ: Princeton University Press.

Yücesoy, Hayrettin. 2023. *Disenchanting the Caliphate: The Secular Discipline of Power in Abbasid Political Thought*. New York: Columbia University Press.

Yücesoy, Hayrettin. 2025. "Review of *Messianism and Sociopolitical Revolution in Medieval Islam*, by Said Amir Arjomand, Oakland, CA: California University Press, 2022." *Journal of the American Oriental Society* 145 (1): 202–6.

Zemmin, Florian. 2019. "The Janus Face of Kātib Çelebi: Reflecting on the Ottoman Saddle Period." *Turcica* 50: 327–54.

Conclusion

Before Succumbing to Colonial Sovereignty: An Original Political Modernity in the Ecumene?

A Civilizing-*Cum*-Instituting Process (Writ Islamic)

In his perceptive commentary on Volume I,[1] my friend and McGill colleague Setrag Manoukian suggested that my positioning within Southern/Italian thought—epitomized by my reliance on Giambattista Vico (see Chapter 1), with its emphasis on the close interaction between life and politics—had at times been overshadowed by a somber German discourse centered on capillary, top-down disciplining and the "civilizing process." His amicable yet pungent criticism has been among the factors prompting me, in this volume, to scrutinize and lay out more explicitly the trajectory and steps of my own repositioning. Manoukian also remarked on the extent to which Volume I was reflected—or perhaps insufficiently so—by the image chosen for its book cover. That image, selected without my full awareness of its broader meanings and implications, is now reproduced—this time more deliberately and fittingly—on the cover of the present volume. It depicts a nocturnal view of the Khaju Bridge in Isfahan, a city designated as the Safavid capital at the end of the 16th century by Shah Abbas I. The bridge may be read as an emblem of early political modernity in the Islamic ecumene, within which the Safavid state occupied a central position: geopolitically, situated between its Ottoman and Mughal counterparts, and typologically, in terms of the specific process by which statehood was instituted and stabilized. This process was articulated less through an abstract logic of sovereignty than through a cosmocratic grammar grounded in *walaya* and *tadbir*, in which authority emerged from the mediation and circulation of forces across the living body of the ecumene. In this sense, the Safavid case reflects an early-modern reconfiguration of Khaldunian factors (see Chapter 7), where the management of connected bodies and their affects took precedence over their subsumption into a singular, artificial unity. At the cusp of its power, materially in-built (*ma'mur*, indeed) in the lavish architecture of its new capital, the Safavid state condensed both the strengths and the limits of early-modern statehood. Its institutions functioned as sites of filtration and coordination, channeling the instituting energies of the ecumene through practices of *tadbir* that sought to stabilize, rather than arrest, the ongoing articulation of *walaya*. In doing so, the Safavid polity appeared as the culmination of a long yet effective process of instituting the ecumene, one that held together civilizational continuity and political innovation without recourse to a reductive logic of incorporation.

The bridge was built by Shah Abbas II around the middle of the 17th century. As noted by Manoukian, the photograph on the book cover features diffuse illumination and foregrounds the rhythmic, entangled design of the bridge as an architectural artifact that is at once useful, edifying, and entertaining. The shah and his court stood at the center of various celebrations held on the bridge, events marked by varying degrees of publicity and complexly related to the specific Islamic character of Safavid rule. The elegant construction was adorned with tiles and painted patterns, inner galleries, and calligraphy, where moral admonitions intersected with relatively liberal depictions of mundane scenes. The inner octagonal pavilion also functioned as a teahouse. At the same time, as Manoukian reminded us, the bridge did more than connect: it also operated as a dam. In this sense, he continued, it may be read as symbolizing the need to govern the human mosaic of desire, aggression, and excess through mastery, rationalization, and beauty, thereby blending self-expression with self-composure. In a few strokes, Manoukian's intervention compellingly accounted for how the details of the image cohere into a powerful whole. Here civilizing patterns and the making of the ecumene as *ma'mura*, through an intense articulation of the knowledge–power equation, coincide with a moment in which the flow of *'umran* peaked into a process of instituting life in a markedly holistic manner. This was a conjuncture in which powerful states, even while pursuing confessional homogeneity, took hold of the ecumene without erasing its complexity and diversity. The ecumene continued to unfold through its key factors of development, as identified by Bamyeh (2019): partial control by the state—which, in the Safavid case, retained a Khaldunian tribal–nomadic dimension even amid processes of centralization—the free movement of people, ideas, and goods, and heteroglossia.

The patterns of statehood woven in the Islamic ecumene during the Later Middle Period, and culminating in the early-modern dispensation, combined a marked centralization of power with what may be described as a non-absolutist and distinctly associative conception of rulership. I harbor doubts as to whether the notion of "sovereignty" should be retained intact for this model (Moin 2012), given how closely the term is tied to the Westphalian dispensation in Europe and to its appropriation of the Church's code of incorporation. One might therefore prefer to envisage a circular—or, more aptly, spiral-like—form of sovereignty. Yet this formulation verges on oxymoron if sovereignty is understood as depending on a theopolitical fiat in its Western, corporate sense (see Chapter 9). And yet, as the foregoing chapters have shown, messianism played a significant role in both the European and the Islamic trajectories toward early-modern statehood. Whereas the European *katechon* represented a case of curbed or tamed messianism, one may prima facie accept Arjomand's definition of "realized messianism" for the Islamic case. Ultimately, following Arjomand, both the Ottoman and the Safavid—and arguably the Mughal—patterns of sovereignty may be described as "countermillennial." They appropriated and neutralized the messianic contestation of Turko-Mongol power that had often been cultivated within the *tariqa-futuwwa* compound. This contestation had proven particularly threatening during the transition from the Earlier to the Middle Periods, and even more so after the disintegration of the Mongol polity in the region, the Il-Khanid Empire. Insurrectional peaks were registered through the activities of the Babais and the Abdalan in Anatolia, the Sarbedaran in Iran, and later the Hurufis, the Nurbakhsis, and the great revolt of Badreddin—before culminating in the Qizilbash movement, which continued to incite uprisings in Ottoman territories until the early to mid-17th century (Arjomand 2025, 247).

The Qizilbash insurrection was the paramount factor in generating deep enmity between the Ottoman and Safavid states, which became confessionally polarized as the Sunni and Shiʿi bulwarks of the ecumene. Considerable research has examined the confessionalization of statehood, notably in support of the Ottoman Sunni case (Krstić and Terzioğlu 2022), while the Safavid instance has often appeared self-evident from its inception with the *dawla* of Shah Ismaʿil (r. 1501–1524). Although the Ottoman–Safavid conflict cannot be equated with the pervasive and existential threat to the sociopolitical fabric posed by the Wars of Religion in early-modern Europe following the Protestant Reformation—given the comparatively lower levels of violence it entailed—one may nonetheless discern elements warranting a parallel examination, provided we avoid the uncritical assimilation of concepts drawn from the European historical experience, an approach that can only impair analysis and, with it, the appreciation of "the importance of being Islamic." We will seek to deepen this line of inquiry, and to refine its requisite methodological tools, as we move toward the preparation of Volume III. Yet if we were to offer a rough generalization of the difference between the Westphalian type of statehood and the form that developed in the Islamic ecumene, we might say that whereas the former rested on a radically tamed actualization of a one-sided, sacrificial understanding of messianic charisma—deployed through the body of Christ, now recast as the body politic, and reinforced by Westphalian confessionalization—the latter worked toward deferring messianic redemption, thereby sustaining ongoing and, to a degree, open-ended heteroglossic dynamics.

In this light, it is useful, in this Conclusion, to revisit the conceptual device of the "knowledge–power equation," first developed in Volume I to explain how the patterning dynamics of civility provide flesh, bone, and nerve to the social bond underpinning the Islamic ecumene. This conceptual operation required a constructive critique of prevailing treatments of the relationship between knowledge and power, particularly those shaped by leading Western social theorists. The knowledge–power equation emerged from an unpacking of the civilizing process as conceived most influentially by Norbert Elias ([1939; 1968] 2000): a process through which a culture generated within an early-modern court society—modeled by Elias primarily on France—"trickles down" to the bourgeoisie and lower social strata, civilizing them into membership in a national society (Salvatore 2016, 176–178). Volume I sought to emancipate the concept of the civilizing process from the theopoliticaly heavy—indeed, Westphalian—presuppositions that, while often implicit, remain deeply embedded in Elias's work. This was achieved by examining the articulation of the knowledge–power equation during the Middle Periods of the Islamic ecumene, revealing an exceptionally high degree of mutual permutability between knowledge and power. Early-modern centralizing states subsequently relied on this permeability rather than neutralizing it. They worked through the Khaldunian cycle instead of suppressing it, as would have occurred through a theopolitical fiat imposed by a newly consecrated state machine modeled on the Leviathan. The Islamic case thus proves not only impermeable to unilateral and biased Weberian comparisons but also distant from Elias's eurocentric conceptualizations of the civilizing process as binding knowledge to power through the cultured habitus of elites in ways that dovetail with the corporate centralization of governance. Our refinement of the concept proceeded by integrating Islam's historical—and highly variable—unfolding of the knowledge-power equation in grass-roots dynamics such as the intercorporeality of wayfaring (Chapter 3 of the present volume), the circulation of the gift (Chapter 4), the cohesive dynamics of mixed sociopolitical formations (Chapter 5), and, most notably, a radically different deployment of the cultured habitus of court elites (Chapters 2, 6, 7, and 8), in conjunction with original forms of charisma—if the term may still be retained—and governance.

The result has been to reframe the concept of civility in ways that clarify the dynamic and open-ended unfolding of *'umran*, comparable to the model proposed by Ikegami (2005; see Chapters 2 and 3), rather than relying on one anchored in Elias's view of a largely monodirectional and "trickle-down" process. For precisely these reasons, civility does not emerge as the outcome of a process that unilaterally reflects and nurtures state formation and its underlying patterns of sovereignty. It depends instead on a capillary—if hardly homogeneous—process of habitualization. The ongoing and overlapping patterning of civility in the Islamic ecumene was, to a considerable extent, inscribed within the field of tension and reconciliation between two major domains of knowledge production and their associated life forms, namely *adab* and *hadith* (the latter also operating as a key source of *fiqh* and *shari'a* law more generally), which we have defined as the *hadith-adab* amalgam. In precolonial times, across the vast and diversified realms of the ecumene, the lines of distinction between these two domains remained largely open-ended, enabling a fluid process of continuous mutual demarcation and re-amalgamation. It is often difficult—if not moot—to separate a "religious" from a "civil" (or even "secular") component, or to draw a sharp boundary between top-down and bottom-up directionalities.

The historical difficulty in conceptualizing such processes—given a tacit complicity between the overexposure to Western sociological paradigms and the resilience of orientalist categories—has also led to an overestimation of "normativity" as impacting society in its own right. Normativity is what many observers and participants have inferred as the vector of the instituting process, thereby focusing on it as a given outcome to the detriment of the process itself. In other words, normativity is often apprehended through its instituted, rather than instituting, side—namely, through an emphasis on the conceptual foundations of experts' (jurists') law (*usul al-fiqh*) and on the standards of jurisprudential practice that emerged following processes of consolidation among legal schools. As a result, the role of habitus and narrative in the instituting process is systematically undervalued. To counter this reductive view, we have foregrounded *adab* as a "bio-epistemic"—rather than merely "worldly"—engine of habitualization generated by a narrative complex. This complex mobilized branches of knowledge capable of animating a plurality of forms of life, which necessarily also impinged upon the fields regulated by the *shari'a*. It is the concatenation of narration, habitus, and norm that instantiates the only plausible notion of "tradition," of which "pious practice" constitutes merely a possible—rather than necessary—aspect or lateral manifestation. Sociologically speaking, its mainstream expression lies in the instituting process itself, holistically conceived. Such a process could never operate on the basis of the sheer "authority" of instruction or injunction alone; it must be activated by the prophetic imaginary, which in turn enacts narratives articulating "the abiding presence of the divine which extends to and touches upon the most insignificant manifestations of daily life" (Sperl 2007, 482).

One may conclude that, by strategically suturing narrativity and normativity, it is habitus that provides the not-so-hidden engine of the instituting process explored in Volume II. Going one step further, the habitualization set in motion by the discourse of *adab*, situated at the intersection of religion and civility, may be regarded as the core Islamic meta-institution, the primary avenue of the instituting process writ Islamic. Following Bruce Lawrence (2021), the instituting power of *adab* can be understood as the hallmark of the "spirit" of Islamic cosmopolitanism. This spirit, in turn, reflects a *barzakh*-inspired logic that simultaneously demarcates and amalgamates—without ever confusing or conflating—the "religious" and the "civil" dimensions of the process. From this perspective, such an instituting process ought to be sociologically prioritized over normativity as such, or even over "law." Law should instead be viewed as one—albeit crucial—outcome of the sociologically seminal nature of the instituting process.

Beyond "Contractualism": Between Partnership and Companionship

The reconstruction of the instituting process, nurtured by narrative and habitualization, also required a critical revision of how— as discussed in Volume I—Hodgson weighed what he took to be the advantages and drawbacks of the Islamic approach to regulating social life. In contrasting this approach with a European formal-corporatist model, he characterized it as moral-contractualist (Salvatore 2016, 279–282). Hodgson thus developed the well-known—if by now near-canonical—idea that Islam was a trade-friendly religion from its inception, grounding this claim in Muhammad's biography and in the context of Mecca as a peninsular trade hub. This orientation, he argued, profoundly altered Sasanian aristocratic prejudices against commercial activity. Within this line of argument, emphasis is often placed on the centrality accorded by Islamic jurisprudence to commercial regulation. Hodgson accordingly stressed the importance of the mercantile class, itself closely linked to, or overlapping with, the group that administered the colleges and played a key role in managing the *waqf*—the so-called *'ulama'*, or, more broadly, the notables (*a'yan*). This configuration facilitated the development of a commercial model of partnership whose longevity, innovativeness, and malleability were acknowledged even by Kuran (2011, 45–77), notwithstanding his insistence on the alleged inability of partnership to evolve into a corporate form. Kuran's argument relies on the longstanding claim that Islam feared tribal fragmentation and therefore shunned the attribution of juridical personality to autonomous associations—an aversion that, in his view, explains a failed transition to the corporative model. Perhaps more surprisingly, and not entirely unlike Kuran, Hodgson also famously emphasized Islam's theological stress on the individual's "face-to-face" posture toward Allah, which privileges individual accountability at the expense of intermediary bodies, whether tribal, associational, or institutional (Hodgson 1974, II, 63). It is at this juncture that Said Arjomand offered a succinct yet incisive critique of what he termed Hodgson's insistence on an Islamic "invariant contractualism" (Arjomand 2004, 215)—a critique that warrants further elaboration.

The phrasing employed by Hodgson, which identifies contract with a theologically supported form of individual initiative and accountability, risks deflecting attention from what actually enabled the success of a distinctive instituting process within the ecumene. That success rested instead on a reflexive relationality capable of weaving together a pliable yet resilient fabric of associational and institutional life. Here, the emphasis falls on life no less than on the institution itself (see Chapter 1). Indeed, the theological pattern invoked by Hodgson is very much that of a lived religion, one that is such precisely because it is intrinsically entangled with the making and maintenance of multiple civic ties. The contrast, in this respect, is with the theological model of the *ekklesia* as the body of Christ, which was abstracted to the point of providing a corporate model of limited liability (see Chapters 4 and 9). This model helped propel the profit-oriented instincts that became central to capitalist accumulation. Such a trajectory was accompanied by the elaboration of a specific "contract law" at the juridical level and by the rise of "contractualism" as a sociopolitical theory. Together, these developments proved crucial to the emergence and institutionalization of capitalism and modern centralized regulatory frameworks under the aegis of emerging European state formations, which benefited from capitalism in multiple ways and whose Leviathan-like corporate identity would have been dysfunctional without it.

For this reason, as a corrective to Hodgson's stark opposition between Islamic "contractualism" and European "corporatism", one should recognize how the very idea of contract—conceived as binding the wills of individuals—became increasingly abstracted, yet ever more powerful and central, within the European model. In this sense, it is hardly surprising that contractualism came to play such a pivotal role in European political and legal theory. By contrast, it would be more appropriate to suggest that what prevailed in the Islamic ecumene was not "contractualism" but rather a focus on partnership. Partnership embodied a far more plastic and holistic mode of collaboration, grounded in the negotiation of mutual interests, than "contract," understood as an abstract legal instrument, could in itself facilitate. The idea of partnership better captures the connectivity and relationality expressed in both the *tariqa* and the *waqf*, within a process that eschews the systematic and abstract formalism characteristic of the many shades of Western contractualism. The concept of *ʿaqd* (literally "binding" or "tie") in *fiqh*—which undoubtedly underpins a sophisticated regulation of what is conventionally translated as "contract"—should thus be understood as a specific and legally technical instantiation of a broader notion of partnership. In this sense, it comes closer to what Hodgson sought to single out as a model contrasting with European "corporatism." While the European system supplied abstract legal tools designed to buffer and protect individuals from risk and error, the Islamic ecumene neither left individuals entirely alone before Allah, as Hodgson suggested, nor confined them within a communitarian web hostile to autonomy and innovation, as implied by Kuran's argument. The instituting modes that prevailed in the Islamic ecumene were instead grounded in an intense and living relationality, far removed from both radical individualism and suffocating communitarianism. It was the habitualization—prior to formal regulation—of this living relationality that both oriented and protected the individual entering into an *ʿaqd*.

An illustrative instance of the operation of such instituting patterns, grounded in an intensely reflexive relationality and crucial to the formation of partnerships, was reputation. While attached to individuals, reputation emerged from processes of habitualized relationality, recording how a given person related to fellows and partners over time. Here again, no sharp boundary was typically drawn between personal and professional life, or between the "private" and the "public." Moreover, reputation was both continuously in the making and perpetually subject to revision, insofar as it rested on mutuality. Everyone was potentially a maker of another's reputation, on the basis of relational experiences and the reflections generated by them. In such settings, an unlimited limitation of liability was inconceivable, whether for a discredited commercial partner or for a teacher who failed to verify sources or attend to students. At the same time, a "benefit of the doubt" was intrinsic to these relational arrangements, since the health of the social fabric could not withstand an excess of individual failures produced by an overly destructive and intrusive, "communitarian" mode of reputational scrutiny. Forbearance and the capacity to "agree to disagree," and ultimately what Bamyeh has termed heteroglossia—that is, the legitimate coexistence of different voices and idioms (Bamyeh 2019, 179–191)—were key features of this fabric of partnerships. They fostered mediation and negotiation in both informal interactions and more formal judicial settings. To be sure, arbitrary and self-serving evasions of individual accountability by members of the ruling strata were far from rare, but they were usually contained within the counterbalancing mechanisms of the *amir–a'yan* system.

By contrast, corporatism furnishes a pitiless mechanism for shielding influential individuals who belong to powerful corporations from reputationally grounded accountability, to the detriment of non-members, non-citizens, and strangers—and it is by no means the only device devised to buffer individuals from excessive liability. Quite the opposite. Contrary to Hodgson's characterization of the Islamic ecumene vis-à-vis what Weber famously termed the Occident, it was the distillation of the "spirit of capitalism" out of the "Protestant ethic," unfolding in tandem with the trajectory of incorporation, that exacerbated a possessive dimension of individualism. This distinctly occidental configuration ultimately insulated individuals from legal accountability by shifting responsibility onto corporate liability. Such an arrangement protected entrepreneurs from the legal consequences of ethically dubious pursuits of profit, yet not before subjecting them to an intense and often consuming "face-to-face" with the Creator. In Calvinist theology, this exposure could culminate—as Weber famously argued—in nothing less than a decree of damnation in the event of entrepreneurial failure, interpreted as a sign of withheld divine grace. Within the Islamic ecumene, instead, reputational dynamics prevailed over theological refinements or doctrinal twists. Reputation complemented, rather than constrained, the dynamism of social and geographical mobility. As Bamyeh has emphasized, in the corporate world of European capitalism and Westphalian centralizing states, the borders regulating the movement of people—and often ideas—were rigidly policed, even as "free trade" came to enjoy increasing institutional support. This stands in sharp contrast to the Islamic ecumene, where the principle of free movement thrived precisely through the porosity of borders to travel and mobility, extending well beyond the circulation of goods or their carriers, the traders. Travel was not only essential to the cultivation of a scholar's reputation, which depended on covering long distances to locate sources, teach new students, and debate with reputable peers (Bamyeh 2019, 174–179). Among members of the *a'yan* endowed with good reputation, the motives for travel far exceeded the demands of success in any single profession. Mobility was sustained by an awareness of belonging to a shared "ethical cosmos" of the ecumene. Indeed, "the traveler could in the same voyage act sometimes as a merchant, at another time as a pilgrim, or an adventurer, or a paramour" (ibid., 175).

The concomitant principle of "partial control"—namely, the fact that rulers could not impose rigid boundaries—was not a sign of state weakness but depended decisively on the combined workings of reputation and networking, both local and translocal. This combination ultimately accrued to *'umran* and, through it, to the instituting process culminating in a *dawla*. The social power of the *a'yan*, which constrained the arbitrary authority of the ruling military class, especially during the Middle Periods, rested on a reputation sustained by the mild instituting force of reflexive relationality. It was precisely this relationality that the *waqf*, rather than the sacramental magic of incorporation, was able to support both financially and administratively. The *waqf* enacted a mutuality of responsibility and enabled a significant degree of civil monitoring of its administrators, who were drawn primarily from the class of scholars–jurists and, secondarily, from the secretarial class. This arrangement rested on a general imperative to care for both reputation and effectiveness, while subjecting them to scrutiny in a non-corporate manner. At times, a higher level of oversight could be provided by the *qadi*, whose judicial functions were themselves at least partially embedded in the *amir–a'yan* system and in the workings of reputation.

At the same time, access to judicial recourse for violations of *waqf* provisions was often open even to commoners able to claim a stake as potential beneficiaries. This meant that a relatively tight formal control of the *waqf*, grounded in the presumption of legal accountability, could coexist with and be tempered by the quotidian operations of reputational relationality. Legal rationality itself relied on taking into account the mutual knowledge and lived experience of multiple stakeholders. Here again, Ibn Battuta's travels are paradigmatic of the interpenetration between the instituting channel of the *waqf* and the life of a traveler ardently in search of new knowledge, valuable experience, and employment opportunities—including the post of *qadi* he was able to secure while in India.

To be sure, the approach developed in this volume was not intended to convey a falsely irenic—or worse, Islamically conformist—view of social relations in the ecumene, as if these were free from exploitation, injustice, or corruption. Ambivalence, attrition, and conflict were no doubt the rule rather than the exception, and associative patterns of sovereignty can only be understood in relation to how the unceasing instituting process responded to such endemic fissures in the fabric of the ecumene. Moreover, because this instituting process was premised on the narrative constitution of semantic registers that inspired codes of action, the resulting horizons of meaning and practice were intrinsically open to contestation. Contention among diverse positions (*istikhlaf*) was not shunned within either the *shari'a* or the *adab* domains. Antagonisms and challenges were instead regarded as integral to an ontology—and a style of politics—that accepted difference and conflict and thrived on the tensions and imbalances of relationality.

Sociopolitical actors with divergent outlooks, interests, and goals—most typically the ruling class, the scribal class, and the holders of religious knowledge known as the *'ulama*—could therefore articulate either code in multiple, often conflicting, competing, or dialogic ways, depending on context and circumstances. The manner in which boundaries were drawn between fields of activity and genres of writing allowed for shifts and mediations, as we saw in the case of the *hadith* and *adab* corpora. While this may appear to resonate with the notion of an Islamic "culture of ambiguity" (Bauer [2011] 2021), it should not be misconstrued as evidence of an "Islamic exception" to modern norms of differentiation. The instituting process of the ecumene reflected an agency capable of distinguishing spaces and concepts and of acknowledging the repercussions of a world of differences on forms of life and lifeworlds, yet it rarely crystallized these distinctions into irreversible institutional dichotomies, such as that between "religion" and "secularity."

One might even say that differentiation was recognized as intrinsic to *'umran* and, as such, did not occupy center stage in the instituting process. Ultimately, the impression of pervasive "ambivalence" arises only when Western standards are imposed from without; sociologically speaking, it is more accurate to say that conflict, contention, and mediation constituted the very lifeline of the ecumene. Far from denoting a sterile or conflictless social order, a civility writ Islamic thus emerged as an open-ended and multifunctional modality of the social bond, capable of feeding—variably and contingently—into legal regulation and bureaucratic steering. It also functioned as the engine of diverse trust-based networks in which companionship and intercorporeality played a decisive role, albeit in ways markedly different from the production of *homo clausus* (Elias [1987] 2001, 116), or of the self-absorbed or "buffered" self (Taylor 2007, 135–143). The residual utility of Elias's approach for the study of the Islamic ecumene is therefore not fundamentally different from that of Weber's. It should be understood as a reasonably faithful sociological rendering—within the evident conceptual limits of sociology—of the Western path of theopolitical incorporation, and, by reflex, as a means of highlighting how distinct this model is from the instituting process operative in the Islamic ecumene. Elias's framework contributed to clarifying the form of bodily subjectivity imposed upon individuals in order to fit them into the body politic of the Westphalian dispensation, up to the point at which the civilizing process itself became dependent on state authority. At that juncture, the internalization of external constraints described by Elias could no longer be distinguished from the machinic incorporation of subjects into Leviathan, and from the ensuing theopolitical acquisition of sovereignty by its own fiat.

Singling out this Western model as the only possible form of political modernity has become increasingly questionable—quite apart from the appeal of the paradigm of multiple modernities (Salvatore 2016, 23–24). One option is to treat early modernity merely as a temporal marker, circumscribing an epoch during which the most powerful states of the Islamic ecumene were variably entangled and competing with their European and Asian counterparts. Alternatively, if more consequentially for our analysis, we may posit the existence of an original form of Islamic political protomodernity that flourished in particular between the 16th and the 17th centuries. We may speak of modernity here precisely because of the mutual imbrication of state and society that followed their—however balanced—displacement during the Middle Periods. In this regard, it is worth recalling Hodgson's oft-cited remark that "[i]n the sixteenth century of our era, a visitor from Mars might well have supposed that the human world was on the verge of becoming Muslim" (Hodgson 1993, 97; see also Salvatore 2016, 34–35). This Islamic early modernity was, of course, not insulated from the growing impact and eventual disarticulation brought about by the colonial advances of several European powers—initially through their direct interventions in the Indian Ocean, and subsequently, more indirectly, through the impact of the increasing dominance of Atlantic circuits. It is for this reason that we have adopted the qualifier "precolonial" to designate this form of modernity, in order to underscore its originality and its autonomy from any direct influence of the Westphalian model of statehood, even in its adapted, weakened, or dependent variants. Such a model would only be imposed upon the ecumene through direct colonial and imperial encroachment on Muslim lands, a process that began to disintegrate Islamic—or, as we have also suggested, "super-Islamic"—patterns of modernity over the course of the 18th century.

Regardless of the foregoing, I trust that this volume has offered a fair assessment of whether—and to what extent—despite asymmetries and imbalances between European and Islamic forms of statehood, the trajectories of the Ottoman and other early-modern Muslim empires may be regarded as modern state formations in their own right. My reliance on Southern/Italian thought, enabled by the trajectory of repositioning outlined in Chapter 1, has intervened in reshaping and updating an interpretive model that may be called Spinozian, and that displays constitutive affinities with the sociopolitical thought accompanying the paths to statehood in the Islamic ecumene. Spinoza himself was an early-modern thinker, a second-generation migrant to Amsterdam from regions that aggressive, theopolitically-driven Iberian state-building—at the hands of colonial powers such as Spain and Portugal—had genocidally emptied of Muslims and Jews, along with their leading schools of thought. Even if Western scholarship on Spinoza has rarely acknowledged this genealogy, he inherited multiple traditions of Iberian Judeo-Islamic sociopolitical thought and carried them to what was then the pulsating heart of modern, colonial Europe: Amsterdam. Roberto Esposito has shown how the instituting process, when conceived along Spinozian rather than Hobbesian lines, expresses the creative resilience of bodies and their affects. At the same time, imagination—through the narrations that shape habitus—resonates with affects and sustains the instituting process (see Chapter 9). In a Spinozian modality, instituting is a continuous process that combines affects and imagination into articulated ideas that nourish *'umran*. Islam came to function as the leading idea of the ecumene, whose flourishing affirmed "the importance of being Islamic." On this view, institutions may be said to "give a body" to the idea of Islam. More precisely, it is the force of imagination—supporting affects within mutually connecting bodies—that institutes the ecumene as Islamic.

There is here no Hegelian, or idealist, operation of an idea independent of bodies and their affects. Yet the power of imagination introduces an element of dissonance—or a modicum of transcendence—into the otherwise immanent ontology of what we termed, in Chapter 3, the dynamics of intercorporeality. *Walaya*, as a quintessentially Islamic concept grounded in proximity and intimacy, defined a key mode within this process. Immanent bodies never yield to a sharply transcendent metaphor of incorporation; they connect mutually and are thus contingently instituted as multitudes. Ultimately, the idea of Islam entails a form of knowledge–power capable of aligning bodies and minds and, in this sense, manifests a "bio-epistemic" force that embeds them in the real, inhabited, and built environment of the social world we call *'umran*. In this spirit, Esposito has convincingly argued that the institution is ultimately a life form, in which life is indissolubly both subject and object of the instituting process. While this process is continuous, the institution introduces a distinctive modulation within it, generating the waves through which *'umran* unfolds. The institution thus configures a promise of discontinuity—a blessed interruption in the otherwise relentless flow of impermanence—condensed, as it were, in a fold, a pause, or a moment of compassion. This is best understood as a form of "messianic realization," rather than as a fully instituted and routinized, or "realized," messianism in Arjomand's sense, which still operates within a fundamentally Weberian conceptual lexicon. Crucially, this blessed and mildly messianic interruption of the flow of *'umran* never hardens into the theopolitical fiat that constitutes the Leviathan.

This approach allows us to sidestep the dilemma outlined in the Introduction: whether Islam should be analyzed as a concept derived from "objective" historical knowledge or dismissed as a retrojection produced via postcolonial processes of reconstruction and redescription, whether by Western orientalists or by Muslim reformers. The need to avoid dwelling within this epistemic impasse emerged as a point of broad consensus during the IIUM debate of July 2023, briefly discussed in Chapter 1. It is my hope that our grasp of the importance of being Islamic will continue to be refined as we further reposition ourselves within the methodological dialogue on how to discern an Islamic frame. In this volume, as laid out in Chapter 1, I sought to bring to fruition epistemic resources associated with the "Italian difference," deploying them to capture—under our shared post-orientalist condition—the "Islamic difference" in instituting the ecumene and shaping early-modern forms of statehood. Volume III, *ReOrienting Islam*, will hopefully take this effort a step further. It will reengage the resistant trade-off between difference and centrality in the study of Islam by tracking a bundle of "cosmopolitan refractions": shifting, intersecting frames through which Islam appears not as a bounded essence or a peripheral variation, but as a generative site for bringing "home" (i.e. to the fields where academic "institutions" and networks operate) the global study of the knowledge–power equation within the murky epistemic swamplands of post-Orientalism.

Note

1. Setrag Manoukian's commentary was given at in the framework of a book roundtable that took place at McGill in April 2016, right after the publication of the book https://www.youtube.com/watch?v=OOaPD_Fnn6Y (accessed 12 November 2025).

References

Arjomand, Said Amir. 2004. "Transformation of the Islamicate Civilization: A Turning Point in the Thirteenth Century? In *Eurasian Transformations, 10th to 13th Centuries: Crystallizations, Divergences, Renaissances*, edited by Johann P. Arnason and Björn Wittrock, 213–45. Leiden: Brill.

Arjomand, Said Amir. 2025. *Kings and Dervishes: Sufi World Renunciation and the Symbolism of Kingship in the Persianate World.* Oakland, CA: University of California Press.

Bamyeh, Mohammed A. 2019. *Lifeworlds of Islam. The Pragmatics of a Religion.* New York: Oxford University Press.

Bauer, Thomas [2011] 2021. *A Culture of Ambiguity: An Alternative History of Islam.* Translated by Hinrich Biesterfeldt and Tricia Tunstall. New York: Columbia University Press.

Elias, Norbert [1939; 1968] 2000. *The Civilizing Process.* Oxford: Blackwell.

Elias, Norbert [1987] 2001. *The Society of Individuals.* Translated by Edmund Jephcott. London: Continuum.

Hodgson, Marshall G. S. 1974. *The Venture of Islam. Conscience and History in a World Civilization*, Vol. 1–3. Chicago: University of Chicago Press.
Hodgson, Marshall G. S. 1993. *Rethinking World History: Essays on Europe, Islam and World History,* edited, with Introduction and Conclusion, by Edmund Burke III. Cambridge: Cambridge University Press.
Ikegami, Eiko. 2005. *Bonds of Civility. Aesthetic Networks and the Political Origins of Japanese Culture*. Cambridge: Cambridge University Press.
Krstić, Tijana, and Derin Terzioğlu, eds. 2022. *Entangled Confessionalizations? Dialogic Perspectives on the Politics of Piety and Community Building in the Ottoman Empire, 15th–18th Centuries*. Piscataway, NJ: Gorgias Press.
Kuran, Timur. 2011. *The Long Divergence: How Islamic Law Held Back the Middle East*. Princeton, NJ: Princeton University Press.
Lawrence, Bruce B.2021. *Islamicate Cosmopolitan Spirit*. Oxford: Wiley Blackwell.
Moin, A. Azfar. 2012. *The Millennial Sovereign: Sacred Kingship and Sainthood in Islam*. New York: Columbia University Press.
Salvatore, Armando. 2016. *The Sociology of Islam: Knowledge, Power and Civility*. Oxford: Wiley Blackwell.
Sperl, Stefan. 2007. "Man's 'Hollow Core': Ethics and Aesthetics in Ḥadīth Literature and Classical Arabic *Adab*." *Bulletin of the School of Oriental and African Studies* 70 (3): 459–86.
Taylor, Charles. 2007. *A Secular Age*. Cambridge, MA: Harvard University Press.

INDEX